The Totorore Voyage

There's a land where the mountains are nameless,
And the rivers all run God knows where;
There are lives that are erring and aimless,
And deaths that just hang by a hair;
There are hardships that nobody reckons;
There are valleys unpeopled and still;
There's a land – oh, it beckons and beckons,
And I want to go back – and I will!

Robert Service

The Totorore Voyage

AN ANTARCTIC ADVENTURE

Gerry Clark

CENTURY

London Melbourne Auckland Johannesburg

To my wife Marjorie, and all my family, who still love me in spite of my having seriously neglected them throughout the long years of the preparation for, and execution of, this expedition.

First published in 1988 by Century Hutchinson New Zealand.
This edition published in 1988 by Century Hutchinson Ltd,
Brookmount House, 62-65 Chandos Place, Covent Garden,
London WC2N 4NW.

Century Hutchinson Australia Pty Ltd, PO Box 496,
16-22 Church Street, Hawthorn, Victoria 3122,
Australia.

Century Hutchinson New Zealand Limited, P.O. Box 40-086,
Glenfield, Auckland 10, New Zealand.

Century Hutchinson South Africa (Pty) Ltd, PO Box 337,
Bergvlei, 2012 South Africa.

Set in Plantin.
Printed and bound in Singapore by Singapore National Printers Ltd.

British Library Cataloguing in Publication Data.

Clark, Gerry, 1927 –
  The Totorore voyage.
  1. Antarctic Ocean. Voyages, 1983-1986 by
  yachts. Totorore (Ship). Biographies
  I. Title
  910'.09167

ISBN 0-7126-2438-4

Contents

List of Maps

Note: Many of the places where we anchored were not named on our charts, so for our convenience and reference we gave them our own names, such as 'Caleta (Cove) Marjorie,' or 'Ivon and Barbara Cove'. Some of these names have been mentioned in this book, but they have not been registered and are in no way official. All maps have been drawn by Elizabeth Rippey from various British and Chilean charts. The end papers show the overall route of the *Totorore* voyage.

Introduction

I love the sea, I love birds, I love adventure. In what better way could I indulge myself, in these later years of my life, than to undertake an expedition in the great Southern Ocean?

The Southern Ocean extends continuously right around Antarctica. Because of melting ice, much of the water in the southern parts is less saline than elsewhere, and it is also colder. Differences in salinity, in temperature, and in surface turbulence caused by the strong westerly winds over most of the ocean cause considerable movement in the water in the form of surface currents, deep layer currents, and vertical upwellings and sinkings. This water is extraordinarily rich in mineral salts and nutrients brought to the surface from the sea floor by these upwellings, and fed upon by minute plant organisms called phytoplankton, which convert them to growth in themselves through a photosynthetic process using energy from the sun. The phytoplankton is in turn fed upon by zooplankton, the rather larger animal plankton, including various forms of crustacea, among them being the prolific and well known krill. Higher animal forms, fish, birds and mammals, feed on the zooplankton, and many of them feed on one another. The basis of all this life in the ocean, starting with the single-cell diatoms of the phytoplankton, is the mineral salts and nutrients, and these are provided by the decay of the corpses and excreta of all the forms of life I have mentioned, thus completing the cycle.

Birds play an important part in keeping this cycle moving. As a result of surface currents and submarine movements there is a great interchange of water between the oceans of the world, so it can be seen that the health of the abundant life in the Southern Ocean can affect life in the sea everywhere, and that in turn can affect ourselves. The ecology of the Antarctic and sub-Antarctic is held in a delicate balance which needs to be protected from our unwise actions, which could easily destroy it.

My wife Marjorie has long believed in the need for balance in all things, and very clearly demonstrated this to me in our citrus and sub-tropical fruit orchard in the north of New Zealand. When we first started our orchard in 1958 I did everything which the Department of Agriculture told me I should do. I spread chemical fertilisers all over the land, and sprayed poisonous chemicals on our trees to try to control fungal diseases and insect pests. In so doing, I killed the healthy organisms in the soil and the beneficial insects in the trees. As fast as I killed off one pest, another took its place. More sprays. There was no end to it. 'Where are the worms?' Majorie asked. 'And where are the ladybirds, the praying mantises, the wasps?' I began to listen to her. She was right. I had destroyed the balance of nature in our orchard. With her help we set about putting it right. It was not easy to undo the harm we had done, and it took a long time. By making tons of compost and using animal manure we now have a living soil, and our bird and insect friends control our pests for us, relieving us of the work, expense, and danger of using sprays.

The Southern Ocean is the ocean so far least affected by our actions, yet there is already plenty of evidence to show that the balance of nature even there has been upset. The wholesale slaughter of seals, then penguins and whales, have had dramatic effects the final outcome of which has yet to be assessed. The seal and penguin species which were persecuted are recovering at an incredible rate, and this may be linked to the massacre of the krill-eating whales. Sea birds are seriously affected too. The Wandering albatross, the most majestic of all birds, has declined significantly in numbers. This could possibly be partly due to overfishing of squid in the favourite albatross feeding areas, such as south of Australia. There has been a phenomenal increase in the size and numbers of fishing vessels now harvesting the riches from the Southern Ocean, following the considerable depletion in fish reserves almost everywhere else in the world. But one of the gravest dangers to the sea birds is the loss of their breeding habitat. Their feeding range over the Southern Ocean is vast, and the majority of them come to shore only to breed. Most of the continent of Antarctica is covered with ice, to which very few species have adapted themselves for breeding. That leaves only the offshore islands, mostly in the sub-Antarctic, where the birds have bred for thousands of years. The total area of these islands is very small, and now the area available for use by the birds, especially the smaller petrels, has been more than halved by human activities. Introduced predators such as rats and cats have been the worst problem, but in some instances the destruction of the natural vegetation has had a similar effect. On previous voyages in a small boat to our own New Zealand outlying islands, in the sub-tropical zone as well as in the sub-Antarctic, I had seen for myself how birds had been forced away from their habitual breeding places and were densely overcrowded on other small islets.

Discussing all these things with my family and with friends of like mind was like 'putting the world to rights'. It was so easy to see the faults and point them out, but not so easy to find a solution, and even more difficult to think of something which one could do, personally, to help the situation. I spoke to ornithologists in New Zealand, and I wrote to eminent ornithologists all over the world, including the International Council for Bird Preservation. The overall consensus was that as far as the Southern Ocean was concerned, the most important thing to do first of all was to assess the position as it stands at present. If it is going to be possible to control exploitation in the area, the situation will need to be monitored, and the operation of any scheme to do this will depend on facts. There is still a great deal that is not yet known about the distribution and habits of the vast populations of sea birds in the Southern Ocean. That, then, was something we could do. Go forth into the Southern Ocean and observe the birds and seek out new information about them to fill in some of the gaps in present knowledge. Any new data would be a worthwhile contribution.

The seeds of the *Totorore* expedition were sown.

Chapter One

Early Trials

There were several important requirements before I could undertake an expedition in the Southern Ocean. First of all I needed the approval and support of my wife Marjorie and her mother and our family of four daughters. These were given unstintingly, and in that regard I am very fortunate indeed. The next requirement was a good strong boat which could stand the rigours of the most tempestuous areas in the world, and could safely complete a circumnavigation of Antarctica. As we did not have much money, it was soon obvious that to obtain the craft we wanted I would have to build her myself. How little did we know then what a strain the building of the boat was to put on all of us! A further need was to raise the money. We sold a part of our orchard, and during the course of the building I had to spend several periods of up to two months away at sea, much of this time in fishing boats, to earn more to keep the project moving.

Meanwhile we had chosen the name for our boat, which was taking shape painfully slowly in what used to be the packing shed for our orchard. *Totorore* is, according to Butler's Maori Dictionary, the name for the Antarctic prion, a typical bird of Antarctic and sub-Antarctic seas. The proposed expedition came to be known as the *Totorore* Expedition.

Totorore is built of wood, because I like wood. It is a natural substance which is pleasant to work with, and which up to a point I can understand. I can like a boat of steel, of aluminium, of fibreglass, or even of ferro-cement, but I do not like working with those materials which, to my mind, have no soul. Wood is different; I can love a good boat built of wood.

The wood I used was New Zealand kauri, recognised as one of the finest boatbuilding timbers ever since Captain Cook first came to New Zealand shores. It was hard to obtain because it was becoming rare, and the felling of kauri trees was restricted. I too love the mighty giants of the forest, and it was only after the Forestry Department had declared that the standard practice of thinning young stands of kauri and culling dead or dying trees could keep the country's boatbuilders supplied indefinitely at the present level that I felt I could, and was able, to purchase what I needed. Because I could not obtain heart kauri I took medium and sapwood, and had it all tanalised, which is a chemical treatment to preserve it. For decks, coach roof and coamings I used laminations of Australian coachwood marine ply.

I wanted a very strong, medium displacement boat about ten metres long, with twin keels so that she could sit unsupported on a beach or shelf of rock in parts of the world where I would not find facilities for hauling her out of the water. Alan

1

Wright, a well known New Zealand designer with a reputation for extremely strong twin-keeled boats sold me a plan for a Nova 28, which was the nearest I could find to what I wanted. It was smaller and lighter than I needed, but I used the frame sections to give me a good hull shape, and followed the same general form of construction; I also lengthened her, changed the bow and the stern, added a large and heavy skeg, put the rudder right aft and outboard, and altered the deck and interior layouts considerably. She became very much a one-off design.

Throughout the seven years of building *Totorore* I never lost sight of the fact that above all she must be strong. I had no illusions about the tests to which she would be put. We would be working in some of the least known, and least charted, parts of the world, in the worst possible weathers, with the world's highest and most dangerous seas. If we should be unfortunate enough to hit rocks, she had to be able to take it; likewise if we were to hit ice. She also had to be able to withstand storm waves 30 metres in height. Failure under any of these circumstances meant those on board would not survive. Some of the many good friends who helped me with the building of *Totorore* thought that I had too vivid an imagination, and went too far in my determination to make her strong. In the event, during the years that followed she did encounter all of those things, not once but several times, and somehow, miraculously, she survived – as did her crew. Her mast did not, and she lost it twice. In hindsight I wished I had used a stronger mast, but I never had any such misgivings about *Totorore* herself and there is nothing I would have changed, apart from the fact that I never did fit the intended stainless steel guard over the stem on the forefoot, a place which was superficially damaged rather often in collisions with ice and rocks.

Although I like wood, I am not a real traditionalist and used the best of modern materials to bond my wood together, mostly epoxy glue with additional bronze screws and nails, or in some cases copper rivets, or monel bolts. All outside surfaces were coated with Dynel, a synthetic cloth, and epoxy resin. The hull construction is double diagonal planking over closely spaced stringers, seventeen on each side, on laminated frames and heavy floors. The foredeck is made of four layers of 6 mm plywood over laminated beams, and the coachroof is plywood and polyurethene foam-sandwich construction. The interior is much compartmented by bulkheads, to add considerable strength, and this also enabled all space to be fully utilised. A neighbour once jokingly likened her to an egg carton. Somebody else said that she was built like a battleship, which was perhaps close to the truth, because in a sense that is what she had to be.

For the programme of work for the expedition I wrote to ornithologists in many countries seeking advice, and ideas grew to such an extent that the whole concept became much bigger than had been originally envisaged with the result that we had to appeal for sponsors to assist with the expenses. Apart from the Ornithological Society of New Zealand, our major sponsors were private individuals who believed in what we were doing. Although our expenses were considerable, in comparison with other expeditions to the Southern Ocean they were minimal, and our original claim of a high results-against-cost ratio still stands.

Our attention was drawn to the outer islands of the southern Chilean Archipelago right down to Cape Horn itself. There was less literature on the birds of these islands than anywhere else, and many of them had never been visited by an ornithologist. The examination of these islands was to become one of the biggest and most fruitful tasks which the expedition set itself to accomplish. All the islands of the sub-

2

Antarctic which we had in mind are difficult of access due to their inhospitable shores and the harsh sea and weather conditions which prevail around them. To tackle them we needed good camping gear, and at least three of us on board so that with two to make the landings there would always be somebody to look after the boat.

It was difficult to arrange a crew for an extended voyage and we had to organise a relay of people who could come for varying periods of time, and had to ensure that *Totorore* was in certain places at predetermined times for crew changeovers. Ideally, we wanted a combination of ornithologists and sailors, but that was not always easy to arrange. In the event it turned out that the ornithologists became sailors, the sailors became ornithologists, and it all worked out very well. The most important requirement for crew members was that they should have enthusiasm for the project, and altogether I was extraordinarily lucky that all twenty-six of the people who came to join me were of sterling character and were excellent and courageous companions under all circumstances.

Marjorie stayed home and valiantly kept our orchard going as well as supplying the very necessary base support for the expedition. A committee of supporters was formed to deal with some of the logistical problems which arose from time to time, and the Friends of the *Totorore* Expedition did a great deal of work behind the scenes to keep the expedition in the field.

Kerikeri gave me a heart-warming send-off. Most of my family and hundreds of friends and supporters gathered for luncheon in the lovely garden of the Stone Store Tea Rooms, overlooking the landing steps where *Totorore* was lying alongside, patiently waiting. When we had all eaten and made our personal goodbyes our vicar, the Reverend Bill Law, came to the landing steps to lead a prayer for our safety and to ask for God's blessing on *Totorore* and her crew.

I said a few words to the gathering, emphasising that this was to be *their* expedition, that my crew and I were merely the operators, and promised to carry it out to the best of our ability. Bill then led the singing of the hymn 'For those in peril on the sea' as we cast off from the steps and motored slowly away. Before *Totorore* turned the bend in the river they all sang 'For he's a jolly good fellow'. It was a very emotional moment. Followed by a flotilla of boats in all shapes and sizes we moved out of the river and down the Kerikeri Inlet.

We had to go first to Auckland, about 120 miles south of Kerikeri, to conclude some final arrangements. For the sail down the coast I had with me Ken Back, my first crew, and Squirrel Wright, a keen helper who would leave us in Auckland. From there Ken and I would take *Totorore* to Valparaiso in Chile, stopping on the way at the Chatham Islands, which are part of New Zealand and lie about 400 miles off the coast in latitude 44 °S. My main reason for wanting to go there was to rectify any teething troubles which might show up on the 650-mile run from Auckland, as we had not had time for a shake-down cruise before the expedition started.

By the time we left the Bay of Islands both Ken and Squirrel were seasick, which gave me some practice at handling *Totorore* on my own. All the way to Auckland I cooked and ate my meals alone, but Squirrel, sick though he was, kept a lookout occasionally to allow me to get some sleep. In Auckland Squirrel was a tremendous help, and with some other good friends we soon had all the last-minute jobs under way. Future expedition team members Jim Watt and Anthea Goodwin brought us more gear and equipment, and also joined in the work. It was very encouraging.

3

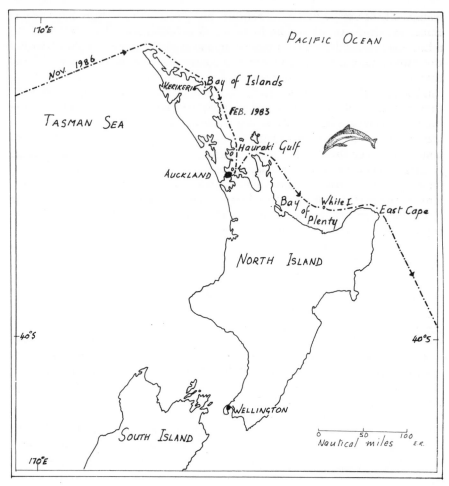

Map 1

By the day of our departure, 26 February 1983, we were ready. Squirrel collected our 50 loaves of Vogel's bread, specially vacuum-packed for us and donated by Klissers Bakeries, and stowed it away below. We were scheduled to sail from Admiralty Steps at 1400 hours. Marjorie and all four of our daughters had gathered with friends to see us off, and while I was saying tearful goodbyes – it would be the last time I would see my family for several years – Squirrel stepped aboard and hoisted the sails. He jumped ashore to cast us off, and joined the wellwishers who waved us out of sight.

At last we were on our way! I felt churned up inside and quite exhausted. Ken was a good companion, quiet and understanding, and he gave me space to relax as we motored across the windless Auckland Harbour. Once past the lovely sun-drenched islands and into the Hauraki Gulf, a light wind enabled us to spread all the sail we had and stop the engine. The great adventure had begun.

All the next day the winds were light and the sailing gentle; this gave us a chance to settle in gradually while enjoying the scenery of the coast and islands. There

4

were plenty of birds to keep us company, and we saw Flesh-footed shearwaters, Buller's shearwaters, Fluttering shearwaters, and some gannets. There was even a Little blue penguin or two. I started to record what we saw – a practice I was to continue until my return to New Zealand, 44½ months later. At first I was dismayed by Ken's lack of knowledge of sea birds. He asked me, 'What strange kind of gull is that?' while indicating a gannet! But he was beginning to take a real interest and I could see that with experience he would make a good and a reliable observer. Having been a meteorologist in South Georgia and other Antarctic stations, Ken was able to give me much valuable and interesting information about conditions down there.

Large schools of Common dolphins played around *Totorore*, gladdening our hearts by day and also by night when they left brilliant trails of phosphorescence. Crossing the Bay of Plenty we started to see albatrosses, the magnificent birds which never fail to excite the imagination and conjure up pictures of the vast and mysterious Southern Ocean to which we were bound.

Monday 28 February
It was both a surprise and a pleasure when we saw a flying fish this morning, a huge one too, far bigger than those one normally sees in the tropics...he flew for about 100 metres. We also saw a Giant petrel, which makes me think that we are coming back among the sub-Antarctic birds that I love so much. I have had some quite lively exercise with the twin headsail poles up on the bow and it is good for me to have this practice. I am beginning to learn how to handle them better, and work out a proper technique...it really is a nice breaking-in.

There is a fair swell now which makes *Totorore* quite agile, and so different from when sailing in the Bay, or even in the Hauraki Gulf. Probably as it is now quite a.long time since I was deep-sea in a yacht, I have become unused to it, but even simple jobs seem to be so difficult when she is leaping about like this. It is not really violent yet, but I can't help wondering how I will manage when it is!

We passed White Island this afternoon, only a quarter of a mile off, and it looked magnificent! It is an active volcano, 328 metres high, sticking straight up out of the sea about 28 miles off the coast. The crater rim is broken down on the southern side, so that we could see right into it. It was putting on a really awe-inspiring display with dense clouds of steam and smoke billowing upwards.

While we were photographing this, a sudden wind change blew the vaporous gases in our direction, drastically reducing visibility and nauseating us with the stench of sulphurous fumes. We had seen the remains of the buildings of the old sulphur works on the edge of the crater, and thought about the unfortunates who were killed there when the volcano erupted in 1914. Ken had never been close to a live volcano before and was most impressed.

Soon after we had left White Island astern the wind freshened and the sea became moderately rough, which ended Ken's enjoyment of the trip. He was sick, took to his bunk, and stayed there until after we had anchored at the Chatham Islands!

5

At about 0200 hours on 1 March we rounded East Cape, the easternmost part of the main islands of New Zealand, and headed out into the Pacific Ocean towards the Chathams. This is a notoriously rough stretch of water with which I was familiar, having piloted many fishing boats across it in the past. Some teething troubles began to show up; and I found that there must have been a bad leak in the electrical system and that the batteries were not being properly charged. I had been assured that the solar panel and the wind charger alone would be sufficient to run the Satellite Navigator, but this was not the case. Electrical problems were to cause us much anxiety and delay for several months before we finally had them under control.

We were taking rather a lot of water in the rough weather and I could not find where it was coming in. Every now and again when *Totorore* was heeled well over, I would see bilge water spilling over the cabin sole and would have to pump and swab it out. With her twin keels, *Totorore* has no natural sump to which water will always drain for the pump. This means that where the bilge water is lying is usually not where the suctions are, and a sponge and bucket, or a portable hand pump, are required to remove it.

Thursday 3 March

It's blowing a gale today and I am a bit frightened. I gradually reduced the mainsail, until now I have it off altogether, and we are tearing along under just two small twin jibs poled out, the wind dead astern. The whole system works very well, but for some reason I can't stop her from rounding up now and again and broaching. It is usually when a big sea breaks under the quarter, and throws her off course. Then the sails, the poles and the whole boat flog and shake in a horrifying manner. How can the rigging and gear stand such abuse? 'Ivon', the self-steering gear [named after my very good friend who helped make it] cannot bring her back on course after she has broached, so I have to go out to do it myself. Apart from that, she is going well. I did wonder about towing warps, but I am scared that they may tend to hold the stern down and let more of the big seas come onboard. I think we are probably overloaded, but what to do? We need all the extra gear we have if we are to go camping on the islands down south, so I'll just have to learn how to handle these conditions. But when the seas are much worse – oh dear, it hardly bears thinking about!

...At about 2000 hours conditions became impossible, so I took the poles off with great difficulty and hove her to, under just a slightly backed staysail, with the helm lashed down. She is lying comparatively comfortably most of the time, but when the seas hit her it is terrifying! We will get used to it, I expect. There is a great roar, a crash, and *Totorore* is thrown on her side and the sea breaks over her. Not very nice.

Friday 4 March

The swinging stove is working very well and I can cook as usual even in this awful weather. On the port tack only, the stove reaches the end of its travel at an angle of heel of 63°, when it stops suddenly, and anything loose on it comes flying off. I normally put the milk jug on the tray at the back of the stove, so the milk was spilt the first time it happened. Luckily I was not actually cooking at the time, but the pressure cooker and the kettle came hurtling across the cabin. There could have been a nasty accident. Now I am better prepared, and tie the pots onto the stove – there is really nowhere else to keep them – and keep the empty milk jug in the sink.

When I go outside I have to take out the heavy washboard and sometimes I get caught by a sea while I am climbing out. One came through the hatchway and went all over Ken, lying dead to the world in the port quarter-berth. I looked at him rather anxiously, but he just opened his eyes briefly and said, 'That was a big one!' Later when I came back in I saw him propping himself up on one elbow and scraping water out from underneath him with the edge of his other hand. Poor chap! I am a bit worried about him as he has not had anything to eat, and even the weak sweet tea which I gave him came straight back up...I try not to run the engine for too long when charging the batteries, as it is not pleasant for him with his head right next to it.

Bird-watching is certainly difficult because the heavy drifting spray makes it hard to use binoculars. Of course, even to go outside means putting on full heavy-weather gear and that's quite a hassle in itself. Trying to get the trousers on when she is flying around is the worst part. It's like using the head...even though it is fore-and-aft, it is quite difficult to stay sitting on it, and to undress and dress yourself you need to be a contortionist...Once outside, it is really worthwhile as there are many albatrosses now, and lots of prions but I can't tell which ones. Probably they are Broad-billed prions from the Chathams. There are some interesting petrels, too; Black-winged and White-necked, both of which I am surprised to see as far south as this, and some Grey-faced petrels.

We are now in very good radio contact with the Chathams.

Saturday 5 March

The gale is still blowing but beginning to moderate. I am feeling very tired as I have not had a good sleep for several days. However, I am more confident now. The seas really have been enormous and *Totorore* has handled them very well. It is thrilling to see the way she lifts and comes through each breaker, laughing! She is a great little ship, and I am proud of her! If anything goes wrong, it will be my fault not hers.

One trouble I had was when a sea broke aboard and washed the jib sheet off the winch, and the staysail sheet out of its jam cleat. The result was that both sails flogged fearfully, and by the time I got to them the sheets had tangled together in an enormous knot which had pulled tight and took me an hour and a half to undo...I could neither sit nor stand comfortably to work at it, and as the deck was wet and heaving wildly, it was a difficult job...I must always re-knot the end of the staysail sheets, so that they cannot come out of the jam cleats, and I must turn up the jib sheets on another cleat as well as that on top of the winch.

I am still having trouble with the electrical system, so am using kerosene lamps.

Sunday 6 March

I actually saw a Taiko petrel today. What a thrill! It is the first I have ever seen. It was so distinctive with its dark head that I had no difficulty in recognising it, and luckily I had a very good view...

Monday 7 March

I had a bad fright in the early hours. Not wanting to use the radar because of the electrical problems I was keeping a lookout for Somes Point, our Chatham Islands landfall. Suddenly the rain cleared and I saw rocks close ahead and also to starboard. Wowee!

The sea was still quite wild so I wore her around and started the engine to get us out of trouble. Too close to be funny – although I did laugh afterwards...

I found the correct channel without further difficulty, and at 0800 hours in cold showers we arrived at Waitangi, the capital, and anchored just off the pub. I was very tired, having been awake and alert all night.

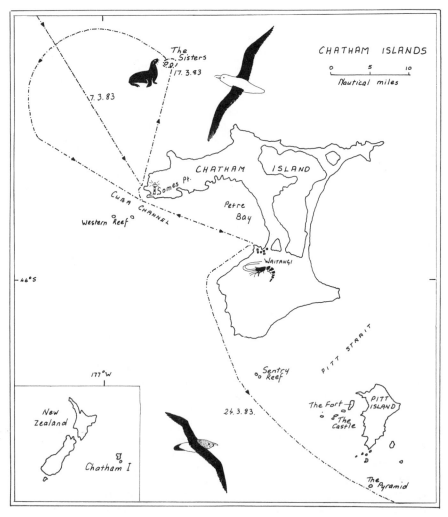

Map 2

Frank Saxton, the Fisheries Officer, rowed out to us and kindly offered us beds at his house, taking Ken back with him. Shortly afterwards dear old Jack Tuanui, with whom I had worked in fishing boats, came out with a friend to assist me in moving *Totorore* to a mooring in the lee of the wharf, opposite the Chatham Islands Company fish packing shed.

Chatham Islands are a group which including outlying islets and reefs extend over an area with a radius of about 30 miles. The two largest islands, Chatham and Pitt, are inhabited mainly by Maoris and have a population of about 500. The chief occupations are fishing for crayfish and blue cod, and sheep farming. The climate is damp and windy, as the islands lie in the 'Roaring Forties'. They are interesting bird islands with many unique species, and are the principal breeding place of the northern species of the Royal albatross. Several of the land birds are on the endangered species list, and many different kinds of petrel breed in large numbers on the smaller islands.

Ken was happy to be on dry land and remained with Frank and Suzie Saxton. He never came on board *Totorore* again. I too enjoyed the hospitality of their home but I always slept on board to be ready for any emergency in bad weather.

I phoned Marjorie to ask her to find me a new crew while I tried to sort out our electrical problems. Eventually the Chatham Islands Company engineer David Holmes came to the rescue and gave me many hours of his own time to put things right.

Mike Hurst arrived by plane to replace Ken. Aged 32, he had given up a good job at the National Museum to come across to Chile with me. While still waiting for Mike's papers to arrive by plane, and to give him a short familiarisation trip, I decided to go out to the Sisters, a pair of islets and some big rocks about eleven miles north of Chatham Island and 35 miles from Waitangi. Frank Saxton had said that he wanted to count the Fur seals and I was interested in seeing the Royal albatrosses which nest there.

Thursday 17 March
We arrived off the Sisters after midnight and crept close in the lee, looking for water shallow enough to anchor...a foretaste of what we will be doing often in sub-Antarctic islands. In the dark we cannot even see the islands except for the whiteness of the huge breakers on the rocks. The radar and the echo sounder tell us that we are safe, at a distance of three-quarters of a cable – about 140 metres – but if we did not have the radar, our eyes would tell us that we are much too close! The breaking sea looks frightful! As it was deep, and the weather calm apart from a heavy swell, we hove to under main and staysail and did not anchor. We are keeping watches to check our position and now I can see that we are drifting slowly farther away, which is good. There is a strong smell of seals, and I can hear their barks and yelps. Both Mike and Frank were seasick on the way across, but they are sleeping well now. They will not like being woken, but I must have some sleep myself...

When daylight came it was raining, with poor visibility. We sailed over close to the reef where most of the seals are, then motored around the whole group of islands and rocks. Seals are not easy to count, but it was fun. They are often among rocks the same colour as themselves, and some groups are densely packed. As they keep moving about it can be very confusing. Between the three of us we counted about 350. On the two Sisters, which are about 30 metres high and have fascinating holes and cavelets in their lava rock, we could see numbers of Royal albatrosses on their nests, and also Buller's mollymawks. There were some cormorants, too, and plenty of Red-billed gulls. There was too much swell and the sea was too choppy for us to attempt a landing, much as I would have liked to. I feel that I must not take any risks so early in the expedition...

We put a couple of fishing lines over, and caught some fine blue cod very easily.

When we started to sail away from the islands, passing through a rather scary passage between the rocks, the wind suddenly freshened and within an hour it was blowing a gale from the south-south-west, the direction of our return. Beating into the head sea made Mike and Frank sick again. The wind reached about 50 knots during the afternoon and the sea was very rough indeed. I hove *Totorore* to, under a backed staysail. I fear that we are being blown a very long way from Chatham Island. When it became dark, the wind eased to about 30 knots and I resumed sailing, after which I had a good dinner of fresh fish all by myself.

The next day the weather was kind to us and my crew recovered. Frank put out a trolling line and caught a barracuda, so we had fish for breakfast and lunch, and arrived back at Waitangi in the evening in time to have dinner cooked by Suzie of wild bacon shot and cured by Frank.

Frank drove us out to 'Taiko Town', the very efficient-looking camp set up in the bush in Tuku Valley by David Crockett and his assistants in their continuing search for the Taiko petrel. They have caught and banded a good number of these birds, thought previously to be extinct, and are now trying to find the nesting area. It was interesting to see the extent of the work they had put into this exciting project.

On 23 March Mike's papers arrived on the plane so we made ready for sea, and the next morning at 0730 hours dropped the mooring and motored out of the thick kelp into the fog-shrouded bay. Very quickly we lost sight of Chatham Island, and never saw it again even though we sailed close down the coast, and across Pitt Strait.

The enforced delay at the Chathams had not pleased me, and I worried about the wisdom of following my intention to sail down to the Antarctic Convergence so late in the year. Apart from being close to the Great Circle (the shortest distance between two points on the earth's surface), the Convergence is an area of great upwelling from the ocean depths and an important feeding zone for sea birds. The risk of meeting icebergs was slight, but the danger of encountering abnormal storm waves was very real. *Totorore* had been well tested in some pretty violent weather on the way down to the Chathams, but my new crew was an unknown factor. It seemed a pity to start reneguing on our declared observations programme this early in the expedition, so I decided to carry on as planned. My excitement on getting away at last was thus not without some apprehension.

This was the start of what would be the longest ocean voyage of the whole expedition – about 4600 nautical miles, as there are no islands in the Southern Ocean between New Zealand and Chile.

Chapter Two

Southern Ocean

Storms — Antarctic Convergence — Juan Fernandez Islands

Thursday 24 March
Sailing along in the thick fog is quite eerie, but having the radar takes the
worry out of it in these reef-infested waters. We did not see many birds but
in the afternoon, when we were south of Pitt Island, we were lucky: the fog
lifted and the sun came out. What a wonderful spectacle these islands are,
with a blue sea, blue sky and the rugged crags of Fort and Castle Islands
looking so wild. We passed the islands with full sail set, making over six
knots.

I wanted especially to go close to Pyramid Rock, the southernmost islet
in the whole group. It is sheer-sided, rises to 173 metres, and is the only
known nesting place of the Chatham Island mollymawk. It looked
magnificent, but although I could see large numbers of mollymawks high
up on top, and in a cave on the side, I could not really identify them and
was disappointed that around the Rock there were only Buller's
mollymawks flying about and sitting on the water...A few squalls,
accentuated by the rock, shot us past at great speed. Soon afterwards the
fog closed in and we were again in our own tight little world with few birds
visible...

Our first radio report to the Chathams was not very encouraging as there
was so much traffic on the air, mostly French and Japanese, but we did
hear a gale warning.

Thursday 24 March (again!)
...and we have crossed the date line. We had a good breeze in the morning
and are averaging about five knots. Mike is still off-colour and spent all day
in his bunk, but there is not much for him to do so that is all right...

I am kept busy with sailing and my bird watches...I saw a Black-browed
mollymawk today — the first I have seen since just off East Cape, which is
surprising as I expected them to be the commonest of all. Another surprise
is that I have not seen a single Cape pigeon.

During the day we had both headsails poled out, full main and the
staysail set. A very good rig, but as the wind increased I gradually reduced

11

it all, and now in the evening the wind has freshened considerably and backed from north-west to south-west so we are reaching under staysail and small jib only.

Friday 25 March
A full gale gave us a noisy, uncomfortable night. Heavy slamming and banging, with violent movement and big seas breaking right over the boat...this afternoon the wind has eased to about 25 knots, and now the sun is shining cheerfully. However there is another gale warning for tonight. I suppose we can expect a regular succession of them down here.

A Light-mantled sooty albatross accompanied us today. They are my favourite birds, I think. They are so graceful in flight, and having seen them close up on their nests I know how beautiful the tones of brown in their plumage are. We also have 20 to 30 prions with us all the time, wheeling around constantly and often pattering on the water. The splashing of the boat seems to bring to the surface the plankton on which the prions feed. It gives me much pleasure to watch them, but I am not yet good enough to be able to identify the species – they twist and turn so fast and are never still for a moment...There are other birds about which there is no doubt, like the White-headed petrel, the Grey-faced petrel and some dear little Grey-backed storm petrels. Of particular interest to me was a Soft-plumaged petrel – my first.

I am worried by the electrics still, even after all the work at the Chathams. The batteries don't seem to be charging up properly, and keep going flat. There must be a bad leak somewhere, and I can't find it. The engine itself is giving trouble too. Something to do with the alignment, because it vibrates terribly and keeps loosening the holding-down bolts. It is quite a job to work on the engine in wild weather, taking the casing to pieces and finding somewhere to put it all where it cannot fly around. Tools keep disappearing into out-of-reach places. Very frustrating, but it is all part of my initiation...I will gradually work out a system to have everything properly under control, regardless of the weather. It is like cooking really. To start with, it seemed impossible; but on principle I want three cooked meals a day and intend to have them, however difficult it may be.

Sunday 27 March
We had a very good radio contact last night with Chathams and they gave us a forecast of north-west winds at 30 knots, probably for the next three days. In fact last night it blew 40 knots, and we had a pretty violent sort of a time, and it has been blowing 40 knots all today. I have wedged myself into the chart table seat and every now and again I hear a great hiss and a roar as a huge breaking sea comes along; there is an almighty crash and the big square port right by my side is soon quite blue as it goes right under the water. I am used to it now and it does not bother me at all.

Earlier, I really enjoyed being outside watching the sea. I sit up in the little conning tower of a hatch above the main hatch – in fact I sit on the main hatch, closed with the storm washboard in to stop any water from going down below – and I wedge myself into that little hole with my nice waterproof binoculars and watch for the birds. I do get a really marvellous

12

view. It is a great privilege to be here, I feel...The sea is wild but majestic...I see these great big breakers rearing up, they come higher and higher, tumbling and turning as they approach the boat, and just before they hit I turn my head away, close my eyes, hold my breath, hang on tight, and there is a terrific crash as she heels right over and water comes all across the boat and across me. I turn away because my hood deflects the water and I get very little down my neck...I am really getting a terrific kick out of it.

At the same time I am able to watch my little ship making her way bravely through it. When one of these big breakers comes over her she shudders a bit, of course, and she goes away over on her ear; but she comes up full of life, throws the water off, and away she goes again. She is still sailing, and I am really pleased with her.

I think, too, that sitting up there gives me a better view than I have ever had before of the birds...when the main is up, I do not see quite so much. I just have two little jibs up forward to get in the way, but I have been able to keep a really good lookout. I have spent many hours out there today. A bit cold in the wind but I am well wrapped up with only my face exposed...I must admit that in this sort of bad weather, I do not know where the birds go, because there are never quite as many in the gales as there are at other times...I saw a great big white albatross today, but could not determine whether it was a Royal or an adult Wanderer. The trouble is, I keep getting spray all over my binoculars, and that makes it very difficult to see properly.

Anyway, really not a bad sort of a day at all. A bit thumpy, a bit bumpy inside...I really have not got enough to hold on to in the galley area. One can sort of hold on to the fiddle but it is at the wrong angle and it tends to be slippery down on the sole. We could have done with another hand-hold, but there really should be a strap around the galley to hold us in...

Mike has not enjoyed any of it, I am afraid. He is still very much under the weather and he eats and drinks very little and spends most of his time in bed. I think he is so very sleepy because he is taking a lot of seasickness pills.

We did 142 miles today which is really jolly good. That is 5.9 knots, the best we have done yet. If we can keep up over five knots we are going pretty well. I did not expect to in the bad weather, because although she is tearing along with a very small sail set she does yaw off course pretty wildly (although Ivon is out there at the helm and doing very well) when the sea hits the stern. She swings around and broaches, and that's when we get the big thump. There is not very much we can do about that.

I made myself a big stew tonight with fresh vegetables from the Chathams and corned beef, and I added the herb-and-onion stock. My golly, that is good stuff...Finished up with an apple and a piece of chocolate, and a nice cup of coffee.

Tuesday 29 March
There was another gale during the night and I was really disappointed in the morning to find that our Windex wind indicator had blown off the top of the mast. I had thought it was pretty tough and would stand up to

anything, but it has gone completely with the little side vanes for on-the-wind sailing...I tied some ribbons (which I found in the 'house-wife') on to the shrouds for tell-tales but they are not nearly as good as that little arrow up at the top. It was like a friend...

While I was out on the foredeck this morning (I had to do some work up there on the sails) I noticed the sound from our 'organ pipes' – our two poling-out poles which have slits in them which catch the wind. I was amazed, because it actually was playing 'Come to the cookhouse door, boys, come to the cookhouse door'!...it was so real that I just had to come down and get myself some lunch...

It is still blowing quite hard this afternoon but during the nice fair periods in between squalls along came a Black-browed mollymawk. I have been surprised that I am not seeing very many of them this time, so I was pleased to spot this one. He was only young and seemed incredibly friendly. I had a little talk to him and he landed in the water close to the boat. He started preening himself, and I was very interested in the way he seemed to avoid the breaking seas; as each big rolling breaker came up, somehow or other he managed to miss it. I expected to see him fly up out of the way before it hit him, but he always found a quiet patch in between and rode buoyantly over the top and down the other side...After a while I would lose sight of him, and then suddenly he would be up near the boat again, flying right around and then landing once more quite close in the lee...

Something else that gave me a lot of amusement and pleasure was looking out of the hatch and watching the end of our tiller. It looks just like some kind of a long-necked monster, peering over the stern and sniffing the air. It goes from side to side as if sounding out what is on board. Not an unfriendly monster, only a very amiable one...I feel I ought to paint a little mouth on it, with teeth and possibly some eyes farther back, just where it bends...

My poor unhappy crew is perking up a little bit. I managed to get him up for a short spell, but he always bolts back into his bunk...He told me today that he is not really seasick, but when he stands up he feels nauseous so that he can really only tolerate it when he is lying down.

Wednesday 30 March

We have just had one heck of a night! It blew a gale fairly early in the evening and under very much reduced jib we were tearing along making not too bad a course. I went to bed for an uneasy sort of a sleep but at 0200 hours I just had to get up and take the sail off because it was blowing furiously. It was a good 50 knots. When I got out there I saw that the wind generator was whipping around at terrific speed, making a clickety-clack noise, and the wind was ripping the vanes off it. They were bending back so far that they were touching the stem and were flipping off at an alarming rate.

Fortunately there was a moon. I got my harness attached to the U-bolt in the cockpit and climbed up and held on to the 'Eiffel Tower' that holds up the radar, trying to reach over to stop the thing. I managed to turn it sideways with my hand and then I saw there were only three blades left!

It was very difficult hanging on, it was so wild, and it was freezing cold. The wind had obviously gone right around to the south-south-west. I was wishing I had put my gloves on because in less than no time my hands were becoming almost useless. But I did not dare let go of the wind generator to release my harness...I had a terrible struggle trying to undo a length of cord to lash the thing.

When I finally succeeded, I thought I might as well try to save what was left. I had some spare blades, but after this I will have only two left...obviously it just is not made for such strong winds.

It was certainly a night to remember, with a very big sea which kept breaking over us. I noted a lot of water coming out on to the chart table...I thought, 'Crumbs, is she opening up or something?' but it was coming out of a little locker just above the table, where I was keeping flags. How the heck could it get in there? Might it be coming down the chain plate? But I could not see anything coming down there, so I was really worried...

It is daytime, but there is too much water going over the deck and I am unable to have a look to see if there are any cracks in it. I cannot imagine that there could be...I will have to have a look as soon as I get a chance.

Mike was beginning to come right. He had got over his seasickness but admitted to being frightened, which upset his stomach. I could sympathise with him because it really was a pretty violent first trip deep-sea. He gradually took over all the cooking, and also the daily mopping out of the bilges, giving me more time for my bird observations and other on-deck work. The leak in the locker did turn out to be from the chain plate U-bolt, to which the starboard lower shroud is attached, and it was a relief to know that it was nothing worse.

Almost constant heavy weather accompanied us as we ran ever farther south. On deck I received many soakings. Each of the twin jibs has its single sheet, and its own furling gear, so that we use only the jib on the lee side, unless we are running before the wind when we use both together. The gear on the lee side often goes under water, and when I was working it I frequently had a sea right over my head. No wet-weather gear is proof against that much water and I started to run out of dry clothes. Even on the foredeck I often had one or both of my seaboots filled with water, and that alone meant two pairs of woollen socks wet, plus my long-johns and trousers. In order to save at least one complete outfit of dry clothing, I began putting wet clothes on to go outside. It was not very pleasant, and the changing was such a chore that it took great self-discipline to make the effort to go out six times a day to do my bird counts. Putting wet-weather gear on in those conditions is quite a battle, and a complete change was worse: what an exhausting struggle it was to pull sticky wet socks over cold feet! However I think I benefited from having dry clothes on most of the time inside. To avoid too many changes I stayed outside for longer periods, but it was bitterly cold.

The appearance of Little shearwaters added new interest to my bird-watching. I was surprised to encounter them in these cold waters, and it was a while before I could plainly see that the line of demarcation on the face between the almost-black above and the white below was much lower than on those I was used to seeing farther north. The chance of having noted something unusual or new is always exciting, and adds a necessary stimulus to one's observations.

Saturday 2 April

I am feeling very annoyed with myself today because when I was working up on the foredeck, changing sail, the staysail knocked my nice green woolly hat over the side. I was very fond of that little hat...It is a shame to be starting to lose things so early in the trip.

We are about 1200 miles from the Chatham Islands now and are still making radio contact. It is not easy because there is always too much traffic on the air. We try different frequencies to see which is best: today Chathams told us to stand by on 4419.4 kHz, but there were some yachts off the coast of New Zealand chatting to each other...I wanted to give our position, pass on weather information and receive a forecast, but could not get through because those chaps were talking about horse-racing and other irrelevancies. However we did make contact, which is good at this distance.

Sunday 3 April

...As it was Easter Day, Mike produced some little chocolate Easter eggs somebody had given to him just before he left home and we enjoyed them with our morning tea. After dinner he made a sweet of seameal custard with candied peel as a special treat...

Thursday 7 April

I think we crossed the Antarctic Convergence last night. Nothing dramatic, and it is not very easy to tell, but the sea temperature has suddenly dropped about two degrees to 6 °C. At this time of the year it is as far north as it ever gets in mid Pacific. It is still blowing a gale, and the thumping *Totorore* takes is sometimes violent and frightening. I am certainly glad I made her strong, but I cannot help wondering if she is strong enough. It is amazing just how much punishment a boat can take...

The pretty little Blue petrels, with their conspicuous black caps and white tails, are around now, flying with the prions. They are a good indication of the Convergence area. I find it difficult to count how many are prions and how many Blue petrels when they are all mixed up and flying around us so fast. There are more Grey petrels now, as many as the White-headed petrels, and they seem to enjoy having *Totorore* to look at. They bank and wheel around us and are very entertaining. I am looking forward to having Bill Bourne on board, after Valparaiso, another bird enthusiast to talk to about what we see.

Sunday 10 April

We are still about 56½ ° South and trying to avoid being pushed farther down in a strong north-north-easterly gale. To try to hold the course we have a tiny triangle of mainsail, the staysail and a very small jib, but it is on-the-wind sailing and extremely uncomfortable, with a very steep angle of heel and cruel pounding. I want to make as much distance as possible because the barometer has dropped alarmingly to 967 millibars and I am scared stiff of what is going to happen.

Even with all the insulation around the inside of *Totorore* she is now very damp in the cabin, and up in the head everything is dripping. The humidity is always over 90%. The two bronze ports in the forward coaming are a nuisance. The glass itself is all right, with its double glazing, but the bronze frames around them run green water down onto the bunks.

In spite of the low barometer nothing untoward happened and I thought that the barometer might be broken and giving a false reading. For a week I did not even bother to look at it. Then it gradually came up again and I realised that it had been functioning normally!

Sunday 11 April
A glorious sunny morning. Flashing whitecaps on the waves, but the sea is a deep, beautiful blue. There is a nip in the air at 6 °C, but it is absolutely delightful. It is the first time I have been able to see the horizon for days. Regardless of some of the hassles and discomforts we have had, I really am enjoying sailing this boat. I spend most of the day outside, in all weathers; I feel that I am getting to know *Totorore* better and I think she is getting to know me, too. She's a little beaut...she has her faults, of course, but haven't we all?

Apart from the sailing it is good to be out among the birds. Sometimes I stand up in the pulpit, jammed between the twin forestays, and sometimes, if the main is furled, I sit astride the boom with my back to the mast. That is a wonderful place, but I have to hang on tightly to the lower shrouds. This morning I greeted our first Cape pigeon so far...disappointingly, he stayed with us for only about an hour. There are always many more birds around in fine weather, so I hope we will have more of it for a change.

Tuesday 12 April
Heavy overcast with rain makes it gloomy on board. The sea is rough and Mike had a couple of tumbles. Not his fault – it is very difficult working at the galley on the port tack. The best one can do is brace one's feet against the chart table and lie, it seems, almost horizontal, with one's head level with the galley bench. Like that it is difficult to see into the pot. Once Mike upset the jar of coffee powder and that made a terrible mess, sticking to all the damp surfaces...

We found that the stern gland had come loose, which accounted for much of the water coming into the bilge. We also worked on various fuel filters, all of which had water in them and a lot of silt too. The valve from the forward tank was blocked up with muck. It seems that the diesel from the Chathams, collected in an old drum, was very dirty. We had great difficulty starting the engine, even after bleeding the fuel lines, and almost gave up. Mike has taken to hand starting it now because of our electrical problems, and I think it does him good and gives him a sense of accomplishment when it finally goes.

Wednesday 13 April
Mike has not so much as stuck his head out of the hatch for two weeks, so today, as it was sunny and not too rough...I managed to get him out on deck. I want to teach him about sailing, and the rig, and about some birds too.

17

We saw some Sooty shearwaters migrating to the north, and also some Arctic terns at the beginning of their incredibly long journey back up to the Arctic...blown about like snowflakes, we wonder how they can do it...We think that our records of them, with positions and dates, could be significant.

Mike is managing to turn out jolly good meals now, considering the limitations of our stores and the cooking facilities...he pores over the stores book for hours. Today, to celebrate being half way to Chile, we had a nice tin of self-saucing steamed pudding...

Gradually we were able to work north out of the stormiest latitudes; we had fewer gales and more fine days when we could do maintenance jobs on deck. Mike started to take a real interest in the birds. He was particularly useful in making sail repairs, which he liked. After we had crossed the 50th parallel on 20 April I decided that we should head direct for Robinson Crusoe Island. It was a bit of a gamble: the distance was only an extra 100 miles, but we did not know how long the formalities of entering Chile might take us, and we were already running late to meet Dr. W.R.P. Bourne in Valparaiso in early May. We were going to be honoured by having Bill, a recognised world authority on seabirds from the University of Aberdeen, work with us at Juan Fernandez. It was the thought of adding Bill and John Atkinson and their gear to a presently very full *Totorore* that made up my mind. I decided somehow to offload all our camping gear, with Mike to look after it, and then carry on to Valparaiso on my own to pick up the others.

Between gales there were periods of calm, and our average speed for the voyage dropped steadily. We moved out of the area in which icebergs might be encountered; even though we had not seen any, it was good to know that there was no longer a possibility of hitting one in the dark. As the air and sea temperatures rose, the humidity became less, and it was possible to get clothes almost dry. The salt-water sores that had developed on my wrists, chafed by salt-stiffened cuffs, and on my feet from constantly wet socks, began to heal, and life became more pleasant. There were many more albatrosses and mollymawks to look at, and soon we started to see Stejneger's petrels and Juan Fernandez petrels, both from the islands we were going to visit, but unexpectedly far south.

Thursday 28 April

I had a small accident in the cockpit today when I broke my best sea-water thermometer. I was annoyed with myself, because I had always taken so much care in rough weather. I have to pull up a bucketful of water, put the thermometer into it, and then somehow hold the bucket, the thermometer and myself while waiting for a minute before taking the reading. Today it was so nice outside that I did not even have my wet-weather gear on and a sudden slop of water ran off the cockpit seat straight into my boot. I turned quickly, and bang! The damage was done.

This evening, Ivon stopped working. A pin holding a sheave which leads one of the cords from the wind-vane mechanism down to the tab on the rudder had somehow fallen out. I started to repair it and asked Mike to assist me, as it is too easy to drop tools or parts into the sea. Darkness beat us, so we will have to finish the job tomorrow. Meanwhile I have put the Autohelm on, and it is working very well. [The Autohelm is an electronic apparatus which moves the tiller with a motor-driven arm to keep the boat on course as directed by its own compass.]

Friday 29 April

Some more bad luck today. Mike and I went forward to pole out the jib, and the double pole-end fitting on the mast track fell to pieces. The pole came down and hit me on the shoulder. Fortunately I escaped with no more than a bruise but I was disappointed in the gear, which was very expensive. I will be able to repair it in Valparaiso if I can buy some more stainless steel rod. Anyway, I was jolly thankful that it happened today while the weather is good, and not when we were down south when it was rough and I was struggling with it alone in the dark.

As it was a sunny day I had a good bath in the cockpit, but I am not tough and I still like to heat up a saucepan full of salt water on the stove. I use cold salt water to wash my clothes, and the ordinary detergent is reasonably effective.

A big oil tanker, the *Western Lion*, passed us going south. Mike was quite excited about it and came out with his camera. Certainly it is the only ship we have seen, but personally I felt it rather an intrusion and was glad when the ugly thing was lost from sight.

The temperature rose to 15 °C and suddenly, no birds! One of the worst bird days we have had. Perhaps it was the Sub-tropical Convergence.

Sunday 1 May

Last night during a south-westerly blow the main topping lift carried away. It had chafed through at the masthead. It did not matter while we were under way, but it is needed when we furl the sail. After splicing it I had the job of replacing it. From the end of the boom it runs up and over a sheave in the masthead, then down inside the mast to an exit box at the bottom, where it comes out to a cleat. Getting it back into the mast proved to be much more difficult than I had anticipated. Although there are steps up the mast, it was still very strenuous holding on up at the top. The rolling of the boat is much accentuated up there, and the jerk at the end of each roll, trying to throw me off, put a great strain on my arms and legs. The masthead fitting was small, and the space above the sheave was too tight, so I could not get the rope through for a long time. When I did manage it, after about an hour, the rope jammed up inside the mast...

Next I tried lowering a light cord down, to pull the topping lift through. Mike went up to give me a spell. It seemed ridiculous, but that small job took us all day, and even then we left a long cord with a shackle pin on the end stuck up inside!

During the night we had more strong winds and a big sea, and the Autohelm was swamped and is now out of action too. So many things seem to be giving trouble. It's as though they are all tired from the rough and rugged trip, like me.

Tuesday 3 May

Fine calm weather today gave me a good chance to prepare a spare anchor, chain and warp for possible use at Robinson Crusoe Island. I have heard stories of vessels being blown out of the anchorage there, so we can expect

19

violent squalls off the mountains. I had several splices and whippings to make while Mike was busy cleaning down below. We still have about 100 miles to go...

Thursday 5 May

...We can see Robinson Crusoe Island ahead and it is a wonderful, inspiring sight with high mountains and magnificent steep cliffs. After all these years of thinking and planning, I can hardly believe that it is me, right here now!

...our sails are furled, the mainsail cover is on, and we are all tidied up and looking respectable. Our ensign is flying proudly at the stern, and the fine-looking red, blue and white Chilean flag is flying from the starboard spreader, with the yellow quarantine flag below...

Rubbernecking our way along, close to the towering rock walls, we marvelled at their grandeur. One open wooden boat, brightly painted and with two men in it, ducked out of sight around a point of land, and up in a valley there were some grassy patches, a few horses, sheep and cattle, and a small hut. Most of the lower slopes of the mountains looked barren, but higher up were well wooded.

Rounding Punta Pescadores (Fishermen's Point) we entered picturesque Cumberland Bay, dominated by the 915 metre mountain, El Yunque, the Anvil, shaped as the name suggests. The small village of San Juan Bautista nestles at the foot of the mountains, and we could see a pier with a small crane at its end. Out on the water bobbed many more of the open boats like the one which we had seen.

I had been warned not to try to go alongside the pier because of the dangerous surge, so we dropped the anchor well off the end, watched by a small crowd of curious residents. A man and a boy rowed out to us in a heavy wooden dinghy to take our stern line. 'Buenos dias,' they said. 'Buenos dias,' I replied. My first words in Spanish. We had arrived in Chile. It was 5 May, so we had taken 43 days to sail 4571 miles from the Chatham Islands at an average speed of 4.4 knots.

Wandering Albatross

20

Chapter Three

Fabled Islands

Isla Robinson Crusoe — Valparaiso — Isla Robinson Crusoe — Isla Más Afuera — Isla Santa Clara — Valparaiso

The Juan Fernandez Archipelago, in the eastern Pacific Ocean, lies in roughly the same latitude as Valparaiso. Robinson Crusoe Island is about 360 miles from the coast, and Más Afuera is about another 85 miles farther west. The Archipelago resembles the Chatham Islands in that it supports a population of around 500 whose main occupations are crayfishing, fishing and a little agriculture.

Mike and I went ashore in the dinghy, landing on the steps of the pier, where we were greeted by many friendly and interested fishermen. We were led past a row of their heavy, double-ended wooden fishing boats on which craftsmen were working, making repairs in the traditional way. A low, white building with a green corrugated iron roof and the Chilean flag flying from its corner, was the office of the Port Captain to whom we had to report and who no doubt represented the Customs, Health and Immigration Departments. I was a little worried about arriving in Chile at a place which is definitely not an official port of entry, but I thought that at the worst el Capitan would tell us to carry on to Valparaiso.

El Capitan was not in, and with my limited knowledge of Spanish I gathered that he had gone to the other side of the island in a fishing boat, where there had been an accident. While shooting goats up in the mountains, two men had fallen to their deaths. He should be back in the evening; I kept asking if anybody on the island could speak English, but it seemed there was nobody who could.

Wanting to send a telegram home, I went to the tiny post office but it was closed. Just opposite, across the dirt road which is the main street of the village, was the rather smarter Government Office, also with a Chilean flag flying from a white flagpole. In its little garden was a small round gun turret, salvaged from the wreck of the German warship *Dresden* which had been scuttled in Cumberland Bay during the First World War. Nearby was the only store, and a row of mostly unpainted houses. The foreshore was tree-lined, which gave a pleasing effect, and muddy tracks led steeply up the hillside to other rather shabby houses among groves of introduced eucalypt trees, and wattle trees brilliant with yellow blossom around which hovered and darted tiny hummingbirds. The ruins of an old fort lay above the village, its cannons pointing out across the bay.

As we wandered, people kept coming up to us to shake us by the hand and ask us questions. Where had we come from, and how long had it taken us? How many were we on board, and did we have enough water to drink? And did we like Isla Robinson Crusoe? One old fisherman told me that if I see the 'botes' (pronounced 'bortez'), the fishing boats, being pulled out of the water, it means that a north wind is coming and it would be dangerous for us to stay in the bay.

When he finally returned after dark in a boat carrying the two bodies, el Capitan del Puerto met me in his office. Tired though he was, he was courteous and charming. The language difficulty made the formalities and form-filling a formidable task, and eventually he produced a letter which I had written to him several months before, from New Zealand, explaining that we would be coming, and about the purpose of our visit. He had not even opened it!

The next morning he allowed us to bring a large quantity of gear and equipment, plus surplus food supplies, and stack them in the corner of his own office. (He said that there was really nowhere else where it would be safe.) He also made arrangements for Mike to stay in a 'pension', a boarding house across the road, while I was away. This was going to cost US$14 per day, which I thought was very steep, but a room at the small hotel across the bay, obviously designed to cater for rich tourists, would cost US$96 a day! Apparently all foreigners are thought to be wealthy.

The house was less shack-like than most of the others, but rather dilapidated. Doors, even outside doors, have no handles or locks. To open them, one pulls a string which leads through a hole and lifts a latch on the other side. We knocked, and a voice called 'Adelante!' The senora, dumpy but attractive, showed us the rooms. These were very Victorian, like a scene in an opera, but quite pleasant. We each had a shower, but although the senora had said the water would be hot, the primitive system with its pipe hanging from a bent nail managed to produce barely tepid water. Some of the wiring for the electric light was quite bare of insulation, and when I went to turn it off I received a shock from the switch. The next night we went to the 'casa' for a meal, hoping to have something fresh. The senora gave us fish soup, followed by fish with white rice. There were no vegetables. Afterwards we had black coffee; there was no milk.

On Sunday 8 May, having established Mike at the casa, I made preparations to leave. The Capitan gave me a 'zarpe', an important clearance paper which I found later that I had to obtain from a similar representative of the Chilean Navy (the Armada) for every departure from a Chilean port. This usually entailed the making of a chart to illustrate our intended route. We were told to report to the Armada by radio, twice a day.

Two young fishermen asked if they could come with me to Valparaiso. At this time of the year no ship calls to collect crayfish, and the planes are infrequent and expensive. I had wanted a few days to myself to have space to collect my thoughts and do some maintenance jobs on board, but they seemed nice lads so I said yes. They kept me waiting for about an hour while they fetched their baggage and a sackful of crayfish, but then willingly helped me to stow away the dinghy after casting off the stern line. 'Valparaiso, here we come!'

Monday 9 May

My two passengers have settled in well. They do not know their way around a sailing vessel, but they always want to be helpful and of course are used to being in a boat. Liter has taken over the galley and produces meals enriched with cayenne pepper. Today he gave us crayfish for lunch. They

22

like to have the radio on loud, with awful American pop music...I said that I would like to hear Chilean music, but they told me that there never is any on the radio because nobody wants to listen to it! The songs are in English, and they listen to them even though they cannot understand a word...At night I called them out to see some dolphins, which put on a beautiful display of phosphorescence.

It is my birthday, so I opened a letter which Belinda (my second daughter) had left on board for me before we sailed, with instructions not to open it until today...

Tuesday 10 May

It was a bit rough and bumpy in the night, so none of us had much sleep. In the morning I asked my two amigos to sing their national anthem...I was impressed that they both knew it right through, as it has many verses...

Wednesday 11 May

Italo and Liter gave me a good long spell in the night and now they are both asleep it is very peaceful. The wind is light, and ahead it is so hazy that I cannot see Valparaiso or even any mountains, but all around the boat it is a bird-watcher's paradise! We are in the cold Peruvian Current (formerly called the Humboldt Current) and there are Pelicans, Peruvian boobies, Sooty shearwaters, Royal albatrosses, Shy mollymawks, Grey gulls, and the truly beautiful Inca terns with facial plumes looking like curled moustaches! There are even Black-backed gulls like we have at home, and White-chinned petrels and Wilson's storm petrels. What a fantastic place!

Long before land was in sight we were ploughing through thick oil on the surface, carrying a disgusting amount of city rubbish. We were no more than a mile away from Valparaiso by the time we could see it through the smog. This was disappointing, because with the white buildings spreading high up the hillsides, and some fine buildings in the city, it would have been a beautiful sight in clear weather.

On the VHF we were directed to the yacht club; luckily my friends knew where it was, a few miles north of the port. There, an old man in a boat assisted us on to one of the empty moorings in front of the clubhouse, where a short breakwater gave some protection from the ocean swell. Many yachts were up on the hard, but there were none in the water.

The clubhouse and grounds were attractive and well appointed, but almost deserted; we met only two distinguished-looking gentlemen who invited me to lunch after my passengers had left me to go home. They said that if the wind came from the north or north-west I would have to take *Totorore* away as quickly as possible because it would be dangerous where she was, and it would soon become impossible to leave.

I was joined by John Atkinson, a young and experienced mountaineer who had given me considerable help in the pre-voyage preparations back home. He had flown over from New Zealand and had been waiting for me at Valparaiso for several days. Luckily we had been given an introduction to the shipping agency A.J.

Broom, y Cía., a firm with branches in all the ports of Chile. 'Brooms', as we later affectionately called them, were the best thing that could have happened to us. The manager, who had the most unlikely name for a Chilean of Peter Smith, had spent some years in a similar capacity in New Zealand and his English was faultless. I was worried that I could not really afford to pay agency fees, but he said that as our work was not commercial, and provided that we did not ask for too much he and his staff would be pleased to help us without charge. 'For New Zealand,' he said with a warm smile. And help us they certainly did! Peter and his assistant Rodney McIntosh (also a Chilean!) were very busy people, but always found time to sort out our many problems.

On the night of 13 May we were given warning of bad weather from the north, so John and I slipped our mooring at the Club Yates de Recreo at about 2300 hours and motored to the port, the only alternative. Inside the long protecting mole, lined by warships large and small, were the wharves for commercial shipping; we were directed to a berth near some landing steps right in the corner. Two large and efficient-looking lifeboats were moored off the steps next to us, and at the top was a guardhouse with two armed Armada sailors. This gave us a sense of security as far as unwanted visitors were concerned, having been warned about thieves in the port. (As it turned out, we never needed to lock the hatch all the time we were there.) We dropped our anchor ahead and laid out a stern line to the dock wall. It was then that we noticed the main city sewage outlet was right next to us – a two-metre-square hole in the dock wall from which a revolting flow of raw sewage constantly flowed. From that moment our new birth lost its appeal!

Our stay in Valparaiso proved to be a nightmare of frustration. I was trying to get our electrical problems put right, but the technicians who worked on it did not seem to know what they were doing and made it worse. Bill Bourne arrived from Aberdeen in the middle of all this, which worried me considerably as his time was short and he had come to study the birds at Juan Fernandez Islands, not to hang around this filthy dock. Luckily big and jovial Bill was very understanding, indicating that he had never known an expedition to be ready on time!

John Atkinson was a tremendous help; having been in South America before and able to speak some Spanish, he soon found his way around. He and Bill went to Santiago for the tedious business of making contacts and requesting permits, and ferreting out further information which could be of use to us in our work. Meanwhile I had to go to the Armada headquarters to be interviewed, since we were asking for permission to go wherever we wanted as a registered research vessel. I was interested to see that they had a thick file on the *Totorore* expedition which even held an article from the local newspaper, so it seemed that they were really keeping tabs. I was received with dignity and courtesy by senior officers and felt glad that I was wearing my jacket and tie, as befitted the occasion! It was impressed on me that we must at all times keep the Armada informed of our movements, and that we were on no account to enter certain areas which Capitan Figueroa, the director of the Hydrographic Department, pointed out to me on the charts. No reason was given for this prohibition, but I was told that if we were caught in one of these areas we would be told to leave Chile immediately, and never allowed to return!

Bill took long walks to look at birds, and John attended to most of the shore work for me while I was obliged to stay on board because of the electricians, and to shift *Totorore* frequently as a dredger moved around the dock, dragging up bucketsful of ordure to load into a lighter for dumping farther out to sea. Often

I saw a big bull Sea-lion or lobo ('lobo marino', sea wolf), poke his head out of the foul water near the dredger, to be met by a barrage of stones flung at him by the crew.

On 25 May, two weeks after my arrival at Valparaiso, all appeared to be ready, and at about 2130 hours we cast off from the dock and headed out to sea, hopefully to rejoin Mike who was patiently waiting for us at Robinson Crusoe. There was no wind so we had to motor. After about an hour it was obvious that something was still very wrong with the electrical system, with both the alternator and the starter/generator overheating badly. I stopped the engine and we drifted. Both Bill and John began to feel ill and retired to their bunks. I kept watch myself all night, sailing when the very light winds made it possible.

Early in the morning I decided that we must return to Valparaiso, disappointing though it was for all of us. I disconnected the alternator and the starter/generator, and to appease Bill Bourne, whose well-controlled impatience was beginning to surface, we sailed down to Pta. Curaumilla, about ten miles southward from Valparaiso, to watch the dawn dispersal of birds from some small islands. It was an exciting spectacle, with thousands of boobies and Pelicans taking off and flying out to sea.

I telephoned the Volvo agents and they said that their men would come aboard at 1500 hours. Eventually the white-overalled foreman and his electrician turned up at 1615 hours. An argument, which soon became as hot as the alternator, ensued. The foreman said there was nothing wrong with the alternator or the starter/generator; I complained that there was much wrong somewhere, in spite of the big bill which I had paid them to put it right. I felt that my Spanish was very inadequte to handle the situation, but eventually the foreman with very bad grace took the equipment away again, saying that he would bring it back at noon the next day.

To cheer ourselves up we went ashore to a Chinese restaurant for dinner and a bottle of wine.

I had seen very little of the city and was interested to have a look around. There are some ornate and elaborate shopping centres, such as one might expect to see in the United States, but elsewhere it looked as though the city had known better times. The streets were dirty, and the once beautiful tiled pavements had many tiles missing, leaving ankle-twisting holes. Traffic was fast, and although there were very few traffic lights, all vehicles stopped abruptly when a pedestrian stepped confidently out on to one of the poorly marked crossings. The people generally were smartly dressed in the city, and those with whom we came in contact were very pleasant and friendly, with a charming old-fashioned courtesy.

The next day, 27 May, the electricians brought our equipment back on board and worked on it for a few more hours before pronouncing it to be all right. I was not at all satisfied, but decided that we could wait no longer and must sail with or without electric power. At 1630 we cleared port and were soon sailing westwards in a good southerly breeze, Bill keenly bird-watching and in renewed good spirits.

I navigated by sextant to save taxing the electrical system by using the 'Sat-Nav', and we had a good sail all the way to Robinson Crusoe – even though Bill and John were seasick most of the way!

Bill was the first to see the mountains of Robinson Crusoe, dead ahead I am glad to say. There were many Cook's petrels flying around, which would be nesting there soon, and he spotted a Pink-footed shearwater. He also saw a Giant petrel feeding on a seal carcase, and some Juan Fernandez petrels and Cape pigeons browsing on the oil slick around it. Mike came aboard, glad to see us back. Not speaking Spanish, he had found his time with non-English speaking people quite a strain: when we addressed him, he would reply 'Si, si'! He had done some useful reconnaissance work on the island and had talked to the Forest Rangers, who said that they wanted one of their men to come with us to Más Afuera. With four of us on board, a fifth was going to make it very crowded, but we were hardly in a position to refuse. Mike had an itchy rash over much of his body, which he suspected, and Bill confirmed, was from flea-bites sustained in bed at the senora's house. Bill and I went for a short walk to look at the hummingbirds in the wattle trees, and were rewarded with some good views of both the Green-backed firecrown and the less common and larger Juan Fernandez firecrown.

The next day we went to the headquarters, on the island, of CONAF (Corporación Nacional Forestal) who look after the National Park. The Chief Ranger, Gaston Gonzales, was a keen and well informed young man who was pleased to show us his nursery of trees to be planted out, hoping to re-establish the native and natural forest with which the island was once covered. He explained their problems with goats and the even more unwisely introduced Coati, which the locals call 'oso' (bear). Coatis are highly destructive, omnivorous animals, and destroy birds' eggs and young as well as seedlings of trees and other vegetation. There are also many cats and rats.

In the afternoon, Bill and Mike took our small tent up into the mountains to camp for the night, while John and I prepared *Totorore* for sea, and camping and other gear for the assault on Más Afuera. Because there were fishing boats at the steps, unloading their catch of bacalau, or groper, we landed on the shore next to the pier, where they haul up the big fishing boats. This proved to be unwise because of the surf, which swamped the dinghy. We carried the dinghy back along the pier, where many willing hands helped us to load our gear across the fishing boats.

Throughout the afternoon we had seen squalls and williwaws lifting spray from the middle of the bay, and by evening it was becoming violent at the pier. At about 2100 hours we cast off and motored across to Pangal Cove, site of the tourist hotel. It was very dark and not a single light showed at the hotel, which must have been closed for the off season.

Next day the weather appeared to be settled and I thought we could sail to Más Afuera as soon as everybody was on board. Bill and Mike came back in the after-noon, having seen quite a lot of Red-backed buzzards, a kestrel, and many feral pigeons, as well as a Coati, looking much like a big anteater. There were Cachuditos, small grey birds with curly tufts on their heads, in the bushes. Bill brought back some bird bones and a Coati skull to study. My heart sank when he said, 'If I never come back to this island, I have seen enough!' I was not sure what he meant, but hoped that we might find something more interesting for him on Más Afuera.

By the time we were aboard, together with Bernardo Lopez, the young ranger who was to accompany us to shoot goats, we were definitely overloaded and could hardly move for gear. We had to work a system of watches and 'hotbunks', so that a man coming off watch took the bunk of the one who had just relieved him. Luckily it was less than a day's sail across to Más Afuera. On the way we examined the impressive cliffs of the north and west coasts of Robinson Crusoe without seeing many birds, but observed Cook's petrels flying around the small rock stack of

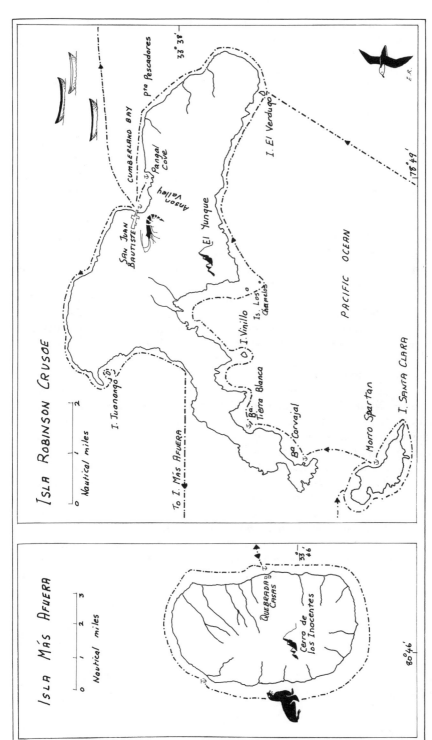

ISLA MÁS AFUERA

Nautical miles
0   1   2   3

Quebrada de Casas

Cerro de los Inocentes

33° 46'

80° 46'

ISLA ROBINSON CRUSOE

Nautical miles
0   1   2

To I. Más Afuera

I. Juanango

San Juan Bautiste

Cumberland Bay

Pangal Cove

Pta Pescadores

Anson Valley

El Yunque

I. Vinillo

Is. Los Chamelos

Bª Tierra Blanca

Bª Carvajal

Morro Spartan

I. Santa Clara

I. El Verdugo

PACIFIC OCEAN

33° 38'

178° 49'

E.R.

Map 3

Juanango. Bill would have liked to land, but it looked difficult with the big swell surging around it, and I wanted to press on while the weather remained favourable. Arriving at Quebrada Casas we could see an untidy collection of huts, used by crayfishermen in the season but now deserted, and some ruins of an old penal colony. One of the huts belonged to CONAF, and that was where our party was to make its base.

There was a big swell breaking at the landing place so we moored to a small buoy and John and Bernardo took the dinghy ashore without any gear. They got rather wet, but John soon came back alone to take the end of a 100-metre floating line ashore so that he and Mike could haul the dinghy to and fro. All the camping gear, food and extra clothing had to be packed in watertight bags. John took Bill ashore, and by the time nearly everything else was on the beach and John and Mike had come back for the last load, the surf was worse and further landings were out of the question. That left Bill and Bernardo ashore together without a common language and John and Mike on board, but without their sleeping bags and other gear. We were able to find enough extra bedding to make them comfortable, and since I was not happy to stay at the buoy overnight with an onshore wind we cast off and motored away clear of the island to heave to for the night.

The next day the wind was still from the east, blowing straight into the landing place. We sailed around the island to see if we could find a lee and a possible landing place on the west coast, but there was none: the wind and sea followed the coast right around. Watching through the porthole in the bottom of *Totorore* we could see that nowhere was there good holding ground – it was smooth grey rock with white streaks and large boulders lying scattered around. At a slight indentation on the north-west coast there were smaller rocks and the anchor could possibly get a grip. We tried our 16 kilogram CQR anchor in three fathoms and it held. After lunch, and an hour of unsuccessful fishing, we started to wind up the chain on the windlass. The anchor was jammed in a crack in the rock and we had great difficulty in getting it out. With *Totorore* motoring hard over it, it came up, but clear of the water we saw the shank had bent right back on itself – something I never expected to see on our main working anchor! I had imagined the 8 mm chain would have broken before that could happen. In the meantime I did not like to risk using our storm anchor, the 20 kilogram Bruce, in case we lost it, so I shackled on the 11 kilogram CQR kedge anchor, held for emergency use. I decided then that we would not try to anchor again at Más Afuera. In hindsight, I think we could have safely used the Bruce which we later employed on all such occasions with excellent results and which never once gave us serious difficulty in retrieving it.

Coati

Friday 3 June

...Sailing down the west coast we gazed with awe at the enormous cliffs, up to 1000 metres...knife-edged ridges separated deep chasms, and we could see that it must be a very difficult place to explore on foot. There were many goats traversing impossible vertical rock faces in single file, and we saw a Red-backed buzzard. Offshore were flocks of Juan Fernandez petrels, and close to the cliffs we saw some fledglings which had fallen to the sea and could not take off again, doomed to perish on the rocks...

On the chart were marked some beaches, but they were merely boulder banks with small grassy slopes above them...the water was shallow, with submerged rocks not shown on the chart at all, so we gave them a good berth...

Saturday 4 June

...passed through a school of very large tuna which were leaping out of the water and were attended by about 200 Juan Fernandez petrels. This was the most we had seen at once of these handsome birds...we saw a few catch fish about 20 cm long and fly off with them. We usually saw them land farther off, but not how they dealt with the fish. Passing the south coast we were surprised to see sixteen cattle on a grassy ledge near the shore, probably survivors from a small farm when the penal colony was here.

As we approached Quebrada Casas we saw Bill and Bernardo, who waved to us. The swell was quite bad and it was difficult for us to pick up the buoy holding the mooring rope because of a lot of other smaller fishing floats all around, each with a long line attached. I was scared of tangling one of those lines in the propeller if I put the engine astern, and with the wind catching the bow and swinging it off, I did not like it at all...The first attempt was a failure, as we did not manage to catch hold of the buoy and had to motor around again at full power to have another go...

Our floating line from the buoy to the shore had chafed through in the bad weather and come adrift, so John and Mike had to row the dinghy with the last of their gear to the landing place. The swell was still running high, and as they went I kept losing sight of them completely in the troughs...I saw the dinghy rear up until I could see only the bottom, and then fall down over its occupants, upside down...Fortunately most of the gear was well lashed into the boat, and they afterwards told me on the VHF that nothing was lost. A good exercise in reasonably warm water, but how to avoid a similar happening farther south? With my crew safely ashore, I cast off from the buoy and motored carefully out clear of all the other buoys and ropes before setting sail.

It is a relief to be on my own again with *Totorore* and it gives me a chance to tidy up and do some maintenance jobs, which are impossible when there is a crowd on board. But the main thing is that we are here, and we have put a team on the island. Now I just hope that they find something really exciting! I told them to stay for at least five more days so that they can get right up to the top among the Juan Fernandez petrels, which we know are nesting, and see if they can find any burrows of Stejnegers petrels too. Nobody yet knows exactly when they do nest, and as we saw some offshore, it could be now. And nobody has seen the little Más Afuera Rayodito (Thorn-tailed creeper) since 1928, so they will be keeping a good lookout for him...It is a bit disappointing for me not to be able to scale the mountains with them, but this is all part of it, and to get the results is the main thing.

Our small hand-held VHF has been giving some trouble, with the transmit button sticking, so in case it does not work we have arranged a system of signals at the landing place. A red rag displayed will tell me that they cannot, or do not wish to, come off, or that landing is dangerous. A white rag means that it is safe and that I should bring *Totorore* in to the buoy. If they scrawl a big M on the side of their hut they need medical assistance, and I should go back to Robinson Crusoe to fetch a doctor. I will pass by the landing place everyday to check it out.

I drifted in *Totorore* for several days, always away from the island, and sailed back close every morning. I cleaned her up nicely and felt pleased with myself. Twice every day I reported to el Capitan del Puerto at Robinson Crusoe on the radio, but never heard from our team ashore on the VHF. On the third day as I was approaching Quebrada Casas to see if there was a signal, I started the engine and was horrified to find that it rattled and shook violently, a bolt in one of the bed brackets having sheared off.

Wednesday 8 June

I was up at 0530 hours to make a start on the big job, and found that we had drifted a long way from the island. The wind was blowing about 30 knots from the east and it was very rough...I sailed up to find a lee under the island. As before there was none, but at least I knew that with the wind straight onshore they would not expect me at the landing place today.

Strong williwaws came off the mountains and knocked *Totorore* almost flat on her beam ends. I had prepared an anchor buoy on a long line, as I thought I would try anchoring again and the line would help us to retrieve the anchor later if we lost it. But it was too rough to contemplate, and I felt that I would rather work in the bigger sea outside than put up with these rather frightening williwaws...

I have spent a very uncomfortable day working on the engine. The bolt which had sheared off could not have been in a worse place. It was right underneath the engine and almost impossible to get at. Before I could reach it I had to take so many other parts off, and in this weather it was a rotten job...It is now 1900 hours; we are hove to under just the staysail, and have probably drifted about ten miles from the island. I am not going to do anything else except cook my dinner and go to bed. The weather is so awful, with strong wind and heavy rain, that I expect my team will have had to come off the mountain. I hope they are OK.

The next day the bad weather continued. We had blown about 30 miles away, and I could not see the island. Because of the electrical troubles I did not use the radar and sailed straight for the island until I could see it only about a quarter of a mile away.

...Around the south-west corner the sea built up viciously, and I had to use the engine to make any way at all. It took several hours to pass the south coast, but I was pleased that the engine continued to run smoothly, assisted by the sails when the wind and course allowed...This is the stuff that expeditions are made of! I saw this great mass looming out of the rain, the tops of the cliffs covered by dense cloud, and from every crack-like gorge and every little gully shot a great spectacular waterfall, thundering down to meet the huge breakers below. The awesome forces of Mother Nature at work!...I would like to go in closer, but I do not dare...I saw our first Southern fulmar today. I knew that they would come up for the winter. Bill will be interested – he has not seen one yet.

It was after 1600 hours by the time we passed the camp, where it was obviously much too rough to think of stopping. I could see all four of the team there, but the VHF was dead and I saw no signal. A pity that none of them knows semaphore or morse. They were watching us through binoculars. As it was a nasty lee shore I kept sailing on past, out to sea, so that I could lash the helm and come inside to keep my sched. with Robinson Crusoe at 1615 hours...

The following morning I sailed close to the camp again, but the breakers at the landing place were still bad. Somebody waved a red flag and I waved a pair of red underpants back to show that I understood. I could not see the others, and hoped that they were back up the mountain doing good work. Meanwhile, I continued with my offshore bird observations.

On 12 June, after knocking around by myself in *Totorore* for over a week, I was able to go back in to the buoy at Quebrada Casas. The sea condition was much improved. John and Mike came off in the dinghy and set up the shore-line to the buoy again; after that the reloading of the gear went smoothly. Bill came out first and sat in the cockpit fishing, which provided our evening meal. I took the opportunity to have my first and only look ashore on Más Afuera, wandering around for several hours.

A good stream, with a crude wooden bridge, runs through the tiny shanty town of rusty corrugated iron huts. Some of the huts were made of old petrol drums, cut and flattened out into sheets. There were more substantial old stone buildings from the penal colony, and in the cliff faces some small shrines in niches carved into the rock and holding the remains of flowers and candles. Most of the plastic figurines of the Virgin Mother in them were broken and looked rather pathetic. Farther along, a few hundred metres from the huts, was a cemetery with a few crude wooden crosses. The only birds I saw were lovely white Cattle egrets which have never been reported on Juan Fernandez before, some handsome Más Afuera buzzards, and a fat Austral thrush.

My crew were in good spirits. Bernardo, who came aboard with two goats he had shot to take back to Robinson Crusoe, had been a great help in knowing which ridge to follow to lead them up to the plateau of Los Inocentes, the peak of which is usually in cloud at 1650 metres. They had camped on the way up, as it was a difficult and arduous climb, and I admired Bill who is almost my own age and of heavy build, for having been able to keep up with the three young men. In dense fern they found plenty of burrows of both the Juan Fernandez petrels and the Stejnegers petrels, but the latter were all unoccupied. They had seen four of the

Más Afuera rayoditos, confirming that the species was thriving, and made a list of all other birds they had seen. After the weather had forced them off the mountain they went round to the west coast and checked the colony of Juan Fernandez Fur seals, a unique species now making a healthy recovery after having been almost exterminated last century.

Bill was pleased with the results of their expedition, and as he was our senior ornithologist, that pleased me. He noted a different species of hummingbird on the island from that which had been previously recorded, and brought back a collection of bones and egg shells which were to give him hours of pleasure, sorting and packing them on the cabin table.

Overnight we motored across a windless sea to Isla Santa Clara, south of Robinson Crusoe. By the time we had anchored in a little bay on the north coast near a spur of land named Morro Spartan, the weather had changed to strong squalls with rain. The seabed was rocky, as at Más Afuera, and our small anchor would not hold. After several attempts to reset it we gave up, but stayed in the area long enough to see plenty of Cook's petrels flying around the cliff faces, and diving into small holes and caves, getting ready for the nesting season.

We went back over to Robinson Crusoe and explored the bays on the sheltered side before going to the small islet named Vinillo. A Kestrel flew overhead, and several Cook's petrels emerged from a hole near the top of the islet. Although we could see strong squalls lifting the water up like smoke, the general sea condition did not seem too bad, and I thought we could make a safe landing without actually anchoring.

Monday 13 June

John rowed Bill over to the island in the dinghy. It was not an easy landing, with a big surge on the rocks, and the rest of us stood by in *Totorore* in case we had to rescue somebody from the water, or save the dinghy from being blown out to sea in a squall. . . The islet is rocky all around the base, but there was grass and other low vegetation over the flattish top. . . we heard Bill shout a joyous 'oi, oi, oi!' as he released a Cook's petrel which he had taken from a burrow under a small bush. . . What was more exciting was a fledgling White-bellied storm petrel in a burrow, always extremely difficult to find, being so small. It was very late in the year for a fledgling to still be there. The presence of rabbits on the island was unexpected. . .

I did not like the idea of going back to Cumberland Bay in this weather, but Bernardo was anxious to get back as soon as possible because the goats, which he had shot three days before, were beginning to smell a bit high. Luckily a fishing boat – wonderful sea-boats, those, with a big outboard motor in a well in the after end – came along, and took him back with them. That left us free to anchor in a well sheltered cove in Bahía Carvajal. . . a very picturesque place, with high cliffs on three sides and the water flat calm. Weird human-sounding cries echoed out of the caves from seals, but we saw no birds. John caught us some good fish for supper.

Tuesday 14 June

It was so calm that I felt that I could go ashore, so went with Bill and John. The young seals were incredibly tame and very playful, really showing off to us. They surrounded us when we landed on some rocks, and were jumping in and out of the water, only a few metres away...they liked to stay motionless upside down in the water with their rear flippers sticking up into the air. After a while they would poke their whiskery faces up to make sure that we were watching!

We scaled the rocks and spent some time trying to reach the top of the cliffs, but it was too steep and too difficult so we gave up and returned aboard...There were no birds to be seen along the huge cliffs of the main island. It is our opinion that the Kermadec petrels, the Pink-footed shearwaters, and even the Cook's petrels have been driven away by the ravages of rats, and more so by the terrible Coati...this makes the small islands more important...

Wednesday 15 June

I went for a walk with Bill up the Anson Valley in low cloud and drizzle, looking out for the large endemic hummingbird, Juan Fernandez firecrown, which is a very handsome bird indeed. The male is of brick-red colour, and the smaller female is vivid green above with white below. Bill was very adept at spotting them, flitting about restlessly as they fed from the flowers of the trees. Above the eucalyptus groves we came into the scrub which covers most of the island and consists largely of maqui, a small tree with vigorous shoots, from which the fishermen make their cray pots, and the wretched bramble, 'zarza', a curse here just as it is at home. There we found only thrushes, and some of their old nests, and also the little Cachuditos which we could attract to us by the noise of kissing the backs of our hands.

...I enjoyed walking with Bill. He is so knowledgeable about birds that I could learn a lot from him. He is very game too. We walked back down a stream bed, thick with bramble, but it did not deter him. I was glad to walk behind as he bulldozed a way through. When we came to a big clump of bramble, and a step down, he would just put a grim expression on his face and sit on it to flatten it. Not having his waterproof trousers on must have made it a prickly business...

It rained all the next day, and strong squalls made me consider shifting to the other side of the island, but before we left I was hoping to buy some diesel fuel from the power station where there was a big tank. However, my powers of persuasion were not strong enough, and even another visit to the Governor's representative did not yield a single litre. I had previously been told that diesel was definitely available on the island, and we had used a lot by having to motor all the way to and from Más Afuera. Luckily our Danforth anchor held well, and we stayed for another night. After dark the overhead lights on the pier kept going on and off, with blue sparks flashing from the tops of the power poles. Nobody seemed at all concerned, so perhaps it was quite normal when it rained.

The news on the radio from Chile was disquieting. There had been unrest and riots in Santiago, a threatened strike in the copper mines, and a union leader arrested. There was talk of a general strike looming, and we wondered how much our expedition might be affected.

Friday 17 June

By the afternoon the weather improved, so we hauled up our anchor to go back to try to land on Santa Clara and found that this anchor too was bent. Not too badly, and we can still use it, but I must have it strengthened in Valparaiso. On the way south we saw another Tropic bird, this time a Red-billed one, whereas the other one we saw before was a White-tailed. We have also seen a Sabine's gull not far away, and a Guanay cormorant – all birds far south of their normal range. It might be something to do with El Niño current up north – a very occasional warm current which upsets the nutrient-rich Peruvian current, and consequently the whole ecosystem of the area, and can have a disastrous effect on sea birds...

Saturday 18 June

I am feeling a bit sad because here we are at Santa Clara where I had wanted to go ashore myself, but it is still squally and our anchor not too reliable, so I felt I must stay to look after *Totorore*...Landing was not easy, but John and Mike are getting pretty good at it and took a grapnel on a long line to heave ashore...It took several trips to get everybody there, and all the camping gear in case I have to clear out and leave them marooned. While offloading gear, John could row away from the rocks when a big wave came in, and then quickly haul back when it had passed, to hand something up to Mike who hastily clambered back out of harm's way. Once I saw Mike caught; the water was up to his waist, but luckily he kept his footing.

Bill went climbing up a gully to disappear over a ridge at the top, while John and Mike investigated Cook's petrel burrows in a scree slope. Some of them were occupied, so they took measurements of a few birds and weighed them. They also endeavoured unsuccessfully to collect some lice, but did bring back some old eggs, including those of White-bellied storm petrels, as specimens for Bill. Bill himself saw a Kermadec petrel, but also counted 76 sheep, which did not please him as much. If this is supposed to be a National Park, it should also be a Nature Reserve and there should be neither sheep nor goats on the island. Not having the Coati, it could be excellent sea bird habitat...

The next day we circumnavigated Santa Clara, but the sea was rough and we could not go too close. We went back to the more sheltered water to the north of Santa Clara and anchored in Bahía Tierra Blanca.

Sunday 19 June

...My crew are away in the dinghy, all wearing lifejackets, and *Totorore* is rolling like one thing! It is sunny and the place is beautiful. The wind is high above us over the hills, about 150 metres up, but we are sheltered by the brown lava cliffs all around the bay...

John is standing off now, keeping the dinghy well clear of the rocks, waiting for an opportunity to go quickly in and land Mike with the grapnel and line. The swell is about two metres; when it hits the rocks it goes up in a terrific fountain up to about ten metres and then comes back off the rocks in a great cascade. Between the rollers there are some quite good intervals when the rock ledge looks reasonably attainable...Yes, now there's a chance! I can see John rowing in fast, and Mike is getting ready to scramble ashore...Mike is climbing upwards with the grapnel, and John is backing off as another wave comes in. The water is around Mike's legs, but he has wedged the grapnel into a safe place and John awaits another opportunity to go in to get Bill ashore.

Eventually and to my relief, my crew, all the gear and the dinghy were safely ashore. But their problems were not over. I had seen Bill having difficulty in climbing the cliff. From on board it looked impossible; there was one particularly nasty vertical knob of rock jutting out which had to be negotiated. John, an experienced mountaineer, managed it slowly and cautiously. Mike climbed as far as he could then threw up a rope to John, who set it up properly to assist the other two.

I can see Bill hesitating. He has the line around his waist, and John up above has belayed it around a rock and around himself, with his feet braced against another rock to take the strain should Bill fall. John is very good at this sort of thing and knows just what to do, but I bet Bill is sweating at the moment. He has not been feeling too good in the last few days because the bites and cuts on his fingers from the Cook's petrels on Isla Vinillo have gone septic...It does not look as though there is a foothold anywhere, and not much to hang onto with his hands either...Good old Bill, he is very game, he will get there somehow I am sure. His leg is around that corner groping for somewhere to put his foot in a place he cannot see. It looks as though he is hanging on by the skin of his teeth, and now he has found something to take his weight and is wriggling, trying to get his other leg across, managing to scrape past that difficult rock face...

Bill got to the top and took off up the slope while John hauled up the gear on the line and helped Mike in his climb. Bill was hoping to find some bones, possibly of birds now extinct, in the loose soil around the airstrip up on the ridge; time was becoming short before we had to head back to Valparaiso. He had booked a seat in a plane to take him to an important conference in Iceland, so we could not be late.

In the evening my crew came aboard safely with a good collection of bones and we returned to Cumberland Bay where we anchored for the night. The wind was strong, and the movement of *Totorore* in the williwaws violent, so it was a disturbed night. I wanted to go to the pier so that we could load the rest of our gear still in the office of el Capitan del Puerto, and finalise our sailing arrangements. When we came to pull up the anchor in the morning we found that there was a tremendous strain on the chain and had great difficulty in raising it at all. Up came an enormous waterlogged log, about five metres long and 0.5m in diameter. Somehow our chain had wrapped around it three times, and then even more incredibly, had tied itself in a half hitch! No wonder we had not dragged our anchor in the night! It took us over an hour to clear it, and then the rest of the day to get ourselves organised for sailing. The *Totorore* Expedition to Juan Fernandez was over. We sailed out into a rough sea, but with a following wind, at 2330 hours on 20 June.

Chapter Four

Rivers and Fjords

Valparaiso − Valdivia − Puerto Montt − Estero Relconcaví −
Estero Quintupeu − Estero Pillán − Puerto Montt

Our voyage back to Valparaiso was uneventful; the sea was moderate to rough all the way, and for three days my crew stayed in their bunks most of the time. In the early hours of 24 June I hove to so that we could cross the bird-rich Peruvian current in daylight, and resumed sailing at daybreak, when I called Bill out to watch. There were Fulmars and Humboldt penguins, but perhaps the most exciting bird we saw was a Red-necked phalarope in her northern summer plumage. What she was doing there at that time of year we could not imagine. She was the first phalarope I had ever seen.

The sea temperature was 13 °C. After happily meandering about among the birds for several hours we made our way back to our smelly berth in the port of Valparaiso, wondering if the general strike would stop Bill from catching his plane.

Our friends at Brooms welcomed us warmly as willing as ever to be helpful. They told us that in Valparaiso at least it was business as usual, in spite of the general strike. I knew I would miss Bill's enthusiasm and his dry humour, but he said that although he had greatly enjoyed the expedition and thought that it had been well worthwhile, it had been rigorous and quite long enough. He would, however, like to join us again if there were another opportunity. With the electrical problems still to put right I was kept very busy. Foolishly, in that dirty place, I had been working on board with bare feet and a cut underneath my foot turned badly septic. When I hobbled into Brooms' office one day our good friends showed much concern and said that I must go to a doctor. I told them I could not afford to. Peter talked to a friend on the telephone and then said to me, 'It will cost you nothing!'. Before I knew it, Rodney McIntosh whisked me off to the German Hospital in his car, and Dr Jorgen Rosenstock took me straight to the operating theatre, saying that it was a very dangerous wound. I was given a total anaesthetic and he cut my foot open, cleaned it out and stitched it up. The whole affair happened so quickly that I was taken completely by surprise. Afterwards it was very painful, and I could hardly walk, but by taking the prescribed doses of antibiotics I soon recovered.

I became very friendly with both the doctor and the anaesthetist, Gonzalo Cordero, and Mike and I took them for a sail with Rodney McIntosh. We left the port at the same time as the beautiful Armada sail training ship *Esmeralda*, on the start of her six month's voyage around the Pacific. The bands ashore and on board struck up with British naval songs such as 'Hearts of oak are our men', which the crew sang lustily in Spanish. As soon as she had set sail, she left us far astern.

Everybody enjoyed it, even though both Jorgen and Gonzalo were seasick. It was the day of the festival of San Pedro, the patron saint of fishermen. There were some crowded and beautifully decorated fishing boats outside a small harbour called Concon, where we stopped to watch the parade on shore. Each of about twelve companies or societies of fishermen entered its own competitive troupe of performers, with a band, acrobats, and a solemn group carrying elaborate, flower-adorned effigies of San Pedro or the Virgin. The costumes were varied, colourful, and outrageous; the noise of the different bands playing together cacophonic. But it was fun. Underneath the clowning one could sense a deep religious sentiment, which I liked. The fishermen look to St Peter or to God for protection on the seas, and I could appreciate that. Every fishing village, or fishing station to which they bring the fish, has a figure of St Peter, and sometimes of Christ or the Virgin Mary. Always looking out to sea to protect the fishermen, they usually have fresh flowers around them, and candles too.

One day Gonzalo took John, Mike and myself out to a long beach north of Valparaiso to see some birds and the big Sea-lions out on the rocks. There were Grey gulls, which nest on the hot desert sands in the north of Chile, Whimbrels, Sanderlings, Turnstones and other waders. Hundreds of Guanay cormorants were starving as a result of the Niño current up north having driven away the small fish on which they feed. Here there were plenty of fish, and we could see the boobies diving, but by the time the Guanays had come this far south most were too far gone on the road to starvation and could no longer digest food. On the way home we called in to see Gonzalo's brother, Sergio, who is an electrician; he said he would be interested to have a look at our problems on board! That gave me some hope after the Volvo agent's costly efforts had been unsuccessful again.

I had the good fortune to meet one of the foremost ornithologists in Chile, Braulio Araya, author of the *Checklist of Chilean Birds*, which I was to find most useful. He took me to his office in the Oceanographic Institute at Reñaca – a beautiful modern building on huge piles right over the beach, and looking out onto wave-swept rocks, with scores of Pelicans and boobies. Braulio is a big man, very genial and hospitable, and he showed me everything he could – specimens, books, papers and photographs. We had a long and pleasant discussion on birds and I knew that I had made a good friend.

Sergio Cordero came aboard to work on our electrical problems. To my dismay he started to undo what the others had done before him. Each time this had cost a lot of money, and then the next 'expert' would come along and start pulling out wires all over the place and putting in new ones. At one time I had more or less understood the system and sincerely wished that I still did, but it had become such a maze of wires that I was completely lost.

Sergio came at night, which was a nuisance, and stayed until 0100 hours each morning. With three of us and himself on board, and sometimes Gonzalo as well, there was not much comfort for any of us. The engine case was open and tools and parts were scattered about, so that we could not move. However we all sincerely hoped that it would be worth it, as we had no option but to trust him. He eventually got it right and we had no more real trouble with it for the rest of the expedition, until it was all swamped when we were capsized on the way home.

Mike and John spent some time sorting and packing stores and gear to send on to Puerto Montt. I was feeling particularly sorry for John, because about half of the time he had available was spent here in Valparaiso while we did repair work. I was equally unhappy to be stuck there, with so many problems so early in the expedition taking up valuable time when we should have been working with birds.

Even in the sheltered port, the weather could be very bad. Once we came back to find that our stern line had parted and the anchor had dragged, and it was only the kind action of the lifeboat crew which had saved *Totorore* from being smashed against the dock wall; they had secured her with heavy warps to the dock and their own mooring buoy.

The Armada had been upset about my not keeping scheds. with Valparaiso. I had been told at Headquarters that they keep a large map on which they stick a pin marked *Totorore*, and they wished the pin to be an accurate record of where we are all the time. I had to report to Captain Vasquez, the senior officer in charge of radio communications. It took me a long time to locate him because I was pronouncing his name as it is spelt. Afterwards I learned that it sounds more like 'Bucky'! He was a friendly chap, and knowing him was to stand me in good stead later, when he was el Capitan del Puerto in Punta Arenas. He sent a senior technician aboard *Totorore* to check our radio installation, which was a good idea in principle but was to nearly drive me to distraction during the three days he was on board demanding my full attention.

Mike had no sense of smell, and this affected his sense of taste. His food had to be very strongly flavoured, and he was keen on tomato sauce. While he was in Santiago I had bought a bottle of 'Aji', which is a hot chilli sauce. On his first night back he saw the red bottle and plastered his dinner liberally with the stuff, which amazed John and me, as we found that a few drops of it were sufficient. Afterwards all he said was 'My gosh, that tomato sauce is strong stuff!'

I had originally expected to sail about 4 July, and had advised Jim Watt, our next crew, to meet us in Valdivia on the 14th. What with one frustrating delay after another, it became obvious that we would still be in Valparaiso on the assigned day. I failed to contact Jim at home, so was forced to go to Santiago to meet his plane coming through at 1100 hours on the 13th. I arrived at the airport half an hour late and some passengers had already come through from the Customs hall, which understandably had me worried. It was an hour before they were all gone, but still no Jim!

I went to the information desk, and they paged him over the public address system, without result. It was not possible for me to see the passenger list, so I tried the International Police, who were very helpful. Yes, Senor Watt *had* arrived on the plane!

Thinking that he must have gone straight to the bus station to catch a bus for Valdivia, I went there myself. The girls at the desk thought that it was a great joke when I asked if I could put a call over the public address system. 'Mr Jim Watt, Mr Jim Watt. If you are here, please come to the information desk.' At this, the girls were doubled up with laugher, but Jim did not appear.

Back at Brooms' office I met Sr McLean (Brooms seem to have many Chileans with un-Chilean names!) who immediately understood my predicament, telephoning both the New Zealand Embassy and Brooms in Valparaiso. I left a note for Jim and slipped out to buy a new alternator for *Totorore*. When I came back I found that Sr McLean had been doing some detective work. Somebody had

38

heard a junior clerk speak to a Mr Watt on the telephone at lunch time. Unfortunately the clerk had gone out but had not arrived home, and nobody could find him. I was in a hurry to get back to the bus station to catch Jim before he left for Valdivia, but Sr McLean insisted on questioning the lunch-time eavesdropper more carefully. The clerk thought he might have heard the word 'Conquistador'. Aha! Yes, Sr Watt had booked into the Conquistador Hotel, and I skipped for joy.

Jim was wearing a 'Roaring Forties' jacket the same as mine, and was very surprised to see me; he had taken a room and had a shower, but since then he had booked a seat in the train for Valdivia that evening and seeing he was able to get to the station before the curfew, he had just come back to cancel his room. It had been a very close thing. Because of the curfew I stayed with Jim in the hotel and the next morning we went to see our Ambassador, who gave us a good run-down on the situation in Chile and told us much that we did not know.

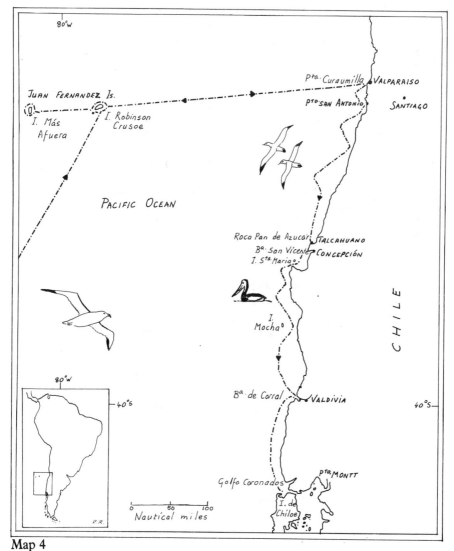

Map 4

Parts I wanted were more readily available and cheaper in Santiago than in Valparaiso, so I went shopping. While we were hurrying along a street a smart-looking woman holding her gloves in her hand bumped into Jim and said something. He stopped to talk to her, and I said, 'No, gracias. Come on, Jim!'

'I thought she said, "Do you want to buy some Chilean ladies' gloves?" Jim told me later, 'and I was considering buying some for Enid.' I was able to tell him that what she'd actually said was, 'Do you want a Chilean lady to make love?' It was going to take a long time for Jim to live that one down!

As we were still delayed in Valparaiso, John and Mike decided to see something of the country by travelling overland to Puerto Montt, where they hoped to meet us in *Totorore*. Meanwhile it was great for me to have Jim on board, and his enthusiasm and practical help were invaluable to me in this unhappy, delayed situation, which he could well understand.

One evening when we were out shopping, a woman behind a counter warned us that we were being watched, and probably followed, by two pickpockets. She pointed out a couple of shifty-looking characters across the street. Sure enough, they followed us, and when we tried to give them the slip they came around the other side of the block. Whatever we did, they seemed to turn up again. It was not at all pleasant. As far as possible we kept to the streets with the best lights and they finally gave up when we came into the port area where the guards were. On another occasion there were three of them and they all looked real thugs; we had to run down a side street to shake them off. We had often been warned about pickpockets, but our general impression of the people in the streets was good.

On Tuesday 19 July we were finally able to collect our 'zarpe' from the Armada, say our goodbyes, and sail for Valdivia, where I hoped to meet Dr Roberto Schlatter at the Universidad Austral de Chile. He is a knowledgeable and experienced ornithologist – one of very few in Chile – and we had arranged that he should join us later on in the expedition. After weighing anchor and casting off from the dock at 1615 hours, we moved out of the port so that we could wash our dinghy in cleaner water outside before stowing it away, and also to wash the decks clean of Valparaiso's filth. The lifeboat came past and the crew all waved to us and called out 'Buen viaje', which I think they really meant.

...I had to stay up to look out for ships, but I managed to take naps of up to half an hour, using my cookery alarm, and then look around and adjust sails. All night I could see the glow of Valparaiso, but if I do not see that place again for a long time it will suit me well. I kept my radio sched. but the operator at Valparaiso sounded like Donald Duck on an old gramophone record and I could not understand him, in spite of having had their man working on our radio for three days. While I was listening I could clearly hear somebody in Townsville, Australia.

Wednesday 20 July

...Jim is still very seasick, but otherwise in good spirits. In the evening we were passing San Antonio, so I called up on the VHF. The operator spoke in English and asked when we had left Valparaiso. When I told him it was at 1615 hours yesterday there was a pause and then he asked, 'Surely, you mean today?' I said, 'No, *yesterday*.' 'But Captain, it is only 45 miles!' I had to explain that we are a small sailing vessel with a strong wind and current

40

against us, but no wonder he was surprised. Progress is *very* slow, and we gain little on each tack. To get a good transect of the birds, I am making long tacks out to sea at night and then coming back across the cold current in the morning. That also makes it safer for me to get a little sleep.

Friday 22 July

I am worried about Jim. He is really sick with bad pains in his stomach, and has lost the use of his left leg. We are both surprised, as he is not usually sick in his own boat. I am afraid that I still have my usual appetite and I am eating far too much. We bought some sausages and as I do not know how long they will last without refrigeration I am eating them up fast. . . I get great pleasure out of watching the long lines of Pelicans, which are real characters. They look so dignified in flight, with slow easy wingbeats, and they have benevolent-looking faces with wise expressions. There are more fishing boats now, and they are larger than those sailing out of Valparaiso. Quite large trawlers, so I have to keep a better lookout. Jim managed to keep a few short watches to give me a spell. . .

Saturday 23 July

The weather is much improved so Jim was able to spend some time in the cockpit with his camera. As we have been motor sailing a lot to get to windward, and as we did not have time to fill up before we left, we are getting a bit short of fuel. One tank ran out just as we were approaching a gap between the rocks outside Talcahuano Harbour. There was no wind, and a big swell was breaking on both sides. To make it worse, several open fishing boats were right in the middle of the gap. . . I managed to bleed the engine in a hurry to get it going again, but the smell of the spilt diesel in the cabin won't help Jim!

Jim got photos of thousands of Peruvian boobies and Pelicans roosting on a big rock called Pan de Azúcar (Sugarloaf), and then we decided to go into Port San Vicente to buy some more fuel. Outside we saw two Magellan diving petrels, recognisable from white patches on the sides of their faces. . . this is pretty far north for them. In the harbour we saw our first big Black vultures planing overhead, and then sitting on fishing boats. It is an attractive natural harbour made hideous by a huge steel mill and industrialisation, but at the far end the big fishing port is picturesque, crowded with fishing boats of all shapes and sizes, including some large Japanese trawlers. We weaved our way in and out and ended up alongside a boat near a diesel pump.

Within a moment *Totorore* was covered with boys, from very young to teenagers. Some kept saying, 'You give me ten pesos!' but mostly they were just interested in us and the boat. . . they made *Totorore* list quite heavily. I did not like to be unfriendly and chase them away, so Jim kept an eye on them while I went to report to el Capitan del Puerto and arrange to buy the diesel. On the wharf, one old lady shook my hand and said 'Bienvenido!' and I think she was expecting us to stay. They were all very friendly, but there were too many people altogether so we were glad finally to get away. . . Outside the bay there was a beautiful sunset, and we had the unforgettable sight of long lines of Pelicans flying against a vivid red sky.

41

We struggled slowly southwards against a rough sea past Isla Mocha, making only about two knots even when we were motor sailing. Trying to get into Bahía Corral against a strong outgoing current we made only one knot, and passed the sleeping town of Corral opposite the mouth of the Río Valdivia at midnight, anchoring a few minutes later in the calm wide inlet Ensenada San Juan. It was so still, and so quiet, we could hardly believe it. We did not even hear the little crab noises under the boat, which usually distinguish shallow anchorages.

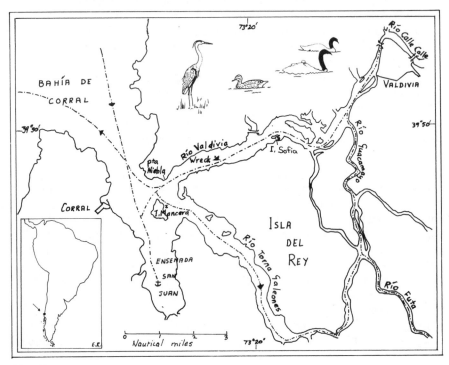

Map 5

Tuesday 26 July

We awoke to a beautiful, crisp, frosty morning. The hills around were dusted white, and across the frost misted water swam many Great grebes with reddish necks, and small crests on their heads. A big Sea-lion surfaced, munching a large fish; he went straight away down for another, and then a third. It was so quiet that we could hear him crunching the bones...The rocks and strata, and the vegetation, reminded us of New Zealand, and we could even see patches of gorse, which made us feel quite at home.

We called up the Armada at Valdivia...and started towards the river. A fog bank hid Corral, and also the river mouth. Feeling our way by radar we passed Punta Niebla (Foggy Point) and followed the buoys and beacons up to a large wreck. We learned later it had been washed out of Corral, three miles away, by a tidal wave at the time of the big earthquake of 1960 which had left much of the low-lying farmland flooded. An Armada patrol boat

42

suddenly appeared out of the fog, turned abruptly, and signalled us to follow – a nice gesture, because if we had not been equipped with radar it would have been difficult for us to find our way through the fog without guidance.

The fog thinned and we could see wooded hills and vast areas of flooded land with rushes, small islands, and occasional dilapidated little abandoned houses. There were some more desirable dwellings, too...one was surrounded by lovely trees, with two stories and a high-pitched roof, and of course wildfowl swimming around the little island on which it stood...

We moored alongside a wooden breakwater at the Yacht Club and various members came out to make us welcome. The commodore, a big German, drove us to the very posh Naguilan Hotel, which he owns, right on the river front...he said we could use the facilities any time we wished. John arrived at the yacht club, having come by bus from Pucon where he had left Mike in a German hospital run by nuns. They had gone to Villarica near the mountains, and Mike had fallen sick with a strange illness rather like altitude sickness, although they were not very high. They were worried lest it be heart trouble.

In about 1850 there had been a large influx of German missionary people into Valdivia and their influence is still very apparent. I visited Roberto Schlatter at the University and was relieved to find that he spoke good English. I liked him immediately, and could see that his extensive knowledge of the birds of Chile would be a great help to us. He was pleased with the dead prion which we had picked up off the coast, saying it was the best specimen of that species he had had. We arranged that he should join us on 15 October, farther south.

Friday 29 July

Jim was away in the dinghy early to try to photograph the beautiful little Seven-coloured tyrant flitting about in the rushes on the other side of the river. I watched a rowing race, apparently an annual event, between two very heavy workboats each with a crew of five strong men, which caused much cheering, urging and hilarity among the spectators ashore.

We wanted to move a few miles down river to dry *Totorore* out with the tide on the small island of Sofía, and then to scrub the bottom. Even for that small journey I had to obtain a 'zarpe' from the Armada...

About half an hour before high water we beached *Totorore* on sand on the southern side of the island, away from the main channel, with a kedge anchor astern and a bow-line to a tree. It is a pretty island, well wooded with conifers and other trees...As the tide ebbed, the sand scoured out from beneath the keels and *Totorore* settled over to starboard at a worrying angle. The wind and water were cold, So Jim donned his wet suit and started to scrub. I worked mainly from the dinghy, using wet-suit gloves to keep my hands warm. The bottom was very dirty, with many goose-barnacles, which accounted for our slow speeds.

Saturday 30 July

At high tide we tried to refloat *Totorore*, but she was so settled into the sand which had banked up around her that she would not come off. We made great efforts to lighten her by removing all the gear we could and piling it on the beach, but it was no good, so we had to wait for the afternoon tide...We carried out a heavy anchor to the main channel on the end of a 100-metre line, after which we dug away as much sand as we could. Our efforts were successful, and *Totorore* swung to the anchor in the fast-running tide, which made difficult the recovery of all our stores and equipment from the beach.

John and Mike were waiting for us when we arrived back at the Yacht Club. Mike had recovered but was still on drugs and had to take it easy. He does not know what his trouble was, but apparently it could be to do with his arterial system.

Sunday 31 July

Oscar Prochelle, a keen member of the Valdivia Yacht Club who has his own boat and is said to know the waterways around here better than anybody else, joined us for a day's exploration and bird-watching. We were rather crowded with five on board, but it was fun, and the weather was out of the box; a bit crisp, with beautiful sunshine all day.

We stopped at Isla Mancera, outside the river mouth, where there are the ruins of a Spanish fort about 300 years old and built to protect the bay against the raids of the pirates and buccaneers of those times...We sailed into the Río Torna-Galeones, where as the name implies, the old galleons used to turn. From half a mile wide, the river narrowed to a few hundred metres as we passed through lovely New Zealand-like countryside, with farmlands, beech forest, hills, some plantations of pine trees and even of eucalypts. Birds were plentiful, with grebes and ducks, and even an Osprey for us to look at, as well as the strident Southern lapwing, and the ever-present Chimango caracara, a medium-sized carrion hawk. An occasional Cocoi heron stood motionless on the riverbank as we motored along, twisting and turning as we followed the bends. After about ten miles we entered the smaller Río Futa...Oscar produced a lunch of red wine, new bread, and German sausage, and we felt as though we were on holiday.

For two more hours we pressed on up the Río Futa, which narrowed to about 50 metres. There were several houses, mean-looking dwellings some of which were still, surprisingly, inhabited, even though they were partly flooded and sticking up out of the wetlands. One two-storey house standing alone, with the water up to its downstair windowsills, attracted our attention...a white figure appeared at an upstair window, above the front door, and as quickly disappeared again. We laughed, a little uncomfortably, wondering if we had seen a ghost.

...When night fell we had difficulty in finding our way between the mudbanks which were all underwater after the winter rains. Stopping and starting, watching the sounder, searching for marks with the spotlight, we finally gained the Río Valdivia, having completely circumnavigated Isla del Rey...

Valdivia itself is a fascinating and intriguing city with the old-world atmosphere of a country town, in spite of some fine modern buildings in the centre near to the river. There were many examples of old German architecture – big, high-pitched

44

roofs – but all in need of repair. There were cobbled streets, and many of the pavements were buckled and warped after the 1960 earthquake. Horses and carts, and pannier-laden donkeys, mingled with motor traffic on puddle-pocked roads, while burly men and blowsy women hefting baskets of 'mariscos' (shellfish of various sorts) harangued the passers-by. The better houses were surrounded by high barred fences, inside of which big dogs like black wolves let it be plainly known what would happen to anybody who stepped within. Jim and I stood and watched with admiration as a man on a long tumbril-like cart skilfully backed it with his horse through a very narrow gateway and up an equally narrow lane.

John and Mike continued on to Puerto Montt by bus while Jim and I worked on board. We had hoped for a journey up the scenic Río Calle Calle to see allegedly enormous numbers of Black-necked swans, but the weather was rainy and unpleasant so we did not go. Jim was a great asset when it came to mechanical repairs, and I handed that side of our work entirely over to him; nor did he like my one-pot cooking, which he called unimaginative, so he took over the cooking as well.

We sailed from Valdivia at midday on 5 August, having stayed in that very pleasant place rather longer than we had intended. We had a hard beat southward, which made Jim really ill again. It was something far worse than seasickness, even if that was what started it, and it completely incapacitated him. By the time we arrived off Isla Chiloé the next evening I was very tired indeed. Once again I was very thankful for the radar as we made our way in the dark and in heavy rain, around Punta Corona at the northern end of that very big island.

Isla Chiloé is separated from the mainland by the Canal de Chacao; 'canal' also means channel, or waterway, and we were to enter a vast system of thousands of miles of 'canals' stretching all the way to Cape Horn. In the Canal de Chacao the tidal streams can attain rates of up to nine knots, and it is necessary to wait for a tide in the right direction before negotiating it.

On Punta Corona there is a manned lighthouse, so I called the keeper on the VHF and asked him to report us to Valdivia and Puerto Montt. To catch the tide in Canal de Chacao we weighed anchor at 0600 hours and went tearing through at a good speed. The drizzle cleared, and we had a wonderful day: the air was crisp and fresh and sweet, the scenery superb. Diving petrels, Fulmars, our first Blue-eyed cormorants, and to our surprise so far south, Pelicans, all added to our enjoyment.

After the 15-mile Chacao, we threaded our way through the maze of colourful islands at the entrance to the gulf named Seno Reloncaví, at the head of which lay Puerto Montt, our destination. The islands were wooded, with settlements with tidy patches of cultivation and pasture, and each had a church. In the background were magnificent snowy mountains with impressive volcanic cones. Jim recovered in the calm of the canals and kept his camera busy on the various birds we passed. Small cargo-laden sailing vessels plied between the fertile and productive island of Chiloé and Puerto Montt.

On arrival at Puerto Montt, we followed the marked channel into the port behind Isla Tenglo and anchored opposite the long and empty main wharf. Hardly was the anchor down when we were visited by a young French couple, Patrick and Pierette Gary, in an inflatable dinghy. They were from the yacht *Negofol* and had come all the way up through the canals from the south without an engine! Shortly afterwards a sailor from the Armada came to see us in a heavy wooden boat, rowed by a boy. He was friendly, and completed the paper formalities, but said that we could not stay where we were and should move tomorrow morning to where the *Negofol* was, alongside at Angelmó. Puerto Montt is a large country town, only slightly smaller than Valdivia, with a population of about 100,000. It is a coastal port for a dairy-farming area, and is the southern end of the national road and rail system. A new road now under construction will push farther south.

Monday 8 August
We weighed anchor very early because we saw a dead Olivaceous cormorant floating by and we wanted to collect its lice. It had obviously been killed by a stone: the fishermen here do not like birds that eat fish or get tangled in their nets. When we neared the *Negofol*, we saw some interesting birds in Canal Tenglo, which separates Isla Tenglo from Puerto Montt...The canal is about 2.5 miles long and is full of activity: small ships and launches, and 'lanchas de vela' (the sailing boats), as well as numerous rowing boats with their oarsmen standing and facing forward, pushing their oars instead of pulling them. Little shipyards and boatyards, and houses on stilts, lined the water's edge...

We spent the whole morning following birds in the canal...Olivaceous cormorants and Blue-eyed cormorants, while large Turkey vultures and Black vultures hovered around overhead. There were Inca terns, South American terns, and Pelicans, but what really interested us was a Silvery grebe, which we mistakenly thought to be rare...There was a big raft of Magellanic penguins, large and handsome with a distinctive black band across their upper breasts, rather like the Humboldt penguins; about 200 together, and they all dived at the same time, and then surfaced at the same time a considerable distance off. They did lead us a merry dance...

It was midday when we tied up to the wharf near *Negofol*. She was alongside an Armada tug, and had an Armada launch outside of her. It was high tide, so we were able to step straight off onto the wharf. But our mooring lines needed constant attention because the tide fell seven metres, which looks a terrible lot when you are not used to it! We soon learned, and we too moved alongside an Armada vessel so that their crew could give the lines the attention they needed. Close by, below the markets of Angelmó where vendors display fish and mariscos, fruit, vegetables and tasty cheeses, the 'lanchas de vela' and some motor launches gathered at high tide. At low tide they rested on the firm mud, and their cargoes of live sheep, pigs, sheepskins, wood, empty bottles, vegetables and anything else one could think of, were unloaded directly into horse-drawn carts which came alongside them. Gentlemen wearing sombreros and ponchos looked over the proceedings, examining items, discussing volubly, gesticulating wildly. They were probably buying and selling even as the wares were taken ashore. There was shouting and laughter, and good-natured jostling among the sailors and the drivers of the carts...

We had been given an introduction from Brooms in Valparaiso to their agents here, Agencias Maritimas Unidas, who again were extremely helpful and friendly, handling both our mail and our problems. They took charge of the stores which we had sent down from Valparaiso and looked after them for us. We were just too

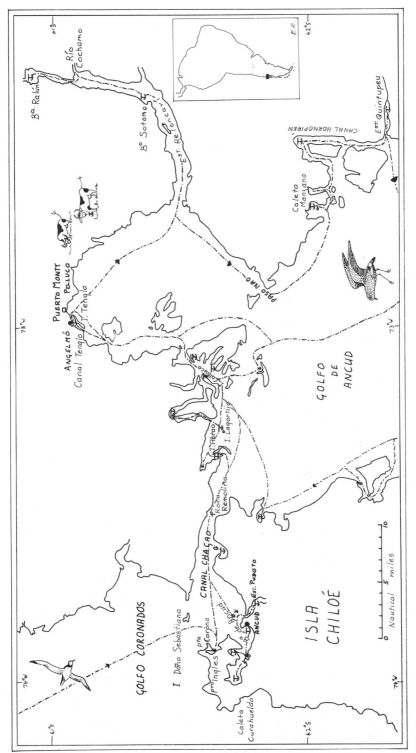

Map 6

late to meet John and Mike, who had had to leave by bus for Santiago to catch their plane back to New Zealand.

We were visited by a pretty girl reporter from the newspaper *Llanquihue*, who brought another lady as interpreter, and also a photographer. They came down into the cabin and interviewed me at length, but Jim would not join us. He stayed on deck with the photographer because he was too embarrassed by a bad smell which had been troubling us, coming from our galley sink waste pipe. The ladies were too polite to mention it, but I did catch them looking sideways at me!

Wednesday 10 August
After lunch we set off for a quick voyage around some of the northern fjords...Yesterday I wrote out a detailed itinerary for the Armada, but it is difficult to know just where we will be on any day, as it all depends on the weather. This morning it still took me over an hour of paper work to get the zarpe to allow us to sail.

We sailed across Seno Reloncaví to the entrance to the fjord Estero Reloncaví, which penetrates the snow capped mountains on the edge of the great Andes range for about 30 miles. The wind was funnelling down the fjord in fierce blasts, with heavy rain and a nasty sea, so that under sail we could make no progress and had to motor using the radar. Soon Jim found that holding the tiller chilled him to the marrow, so we fetched out the Autohelm and put it on the tiller instead...We laughed at the sheer luxury of it as we ate our dinner in the cosy warmth of the cabin, keeping an eye on the radar and giving the knob on the Autohelm control, just outside the hatch, an occasional twiddle to adjust the course...we knew that we could not do it often, as we must save our 'limited life' Autohelm for more serious situations!

We did not want to go too far in the dark, as we could see no birds, so we crept inside a small island close to the shore at the north end of Bahía Sotomó, itself only a slight dent in the wall of the fjord. With Jim at the helm, and me giving him instructions as I watched the radar and echo sounder, we went into the narrow channel very cautiously. Our radar has a minimum radius of half a mile, instead of the quarter-mile which the bigger sets can come down to, so at very close range we lose sight of objects on the screen. When I lost the walls of the gorge-like gut we were entering we just maintained the course while I watched the soundings. Suddenly the depth came up to only a metre under our keels! Full astern! I shone the spotlight and saw a rock wall no more than a boat length ahead! Wow! It gave us quite a start. There were rock walls close on both sides as well, but no harm done, so we eased *Totorore* gently back into deeper water and dropped the anchor.

We thought that we had anchored in a wild and uninhabited placed, but with daylight saw a fishing boat at the head of our cove, and in the dense beech forest above the rocks there were small patches of pasture with a few goats and an occasional hut. There were Brown pelicans on the rocks, and we watched a brilliantly coloured Kingfisher diving down from a branch hanging out over the water. He caught a fish about 15 cm long and was knocking it on the branch for a long time before it was subdued enough for him to turn it around and swallow it.

Two young men in an open fishing boat rowed into the cove and came alongside us. In the centre of their boat was a big pile of 'choritos', small mussels, for which they had been diving. They had an old-fashioned brass diving helmet, supplied with air by a hose from a primitive hand pump in the boat. I said to them in Spanish, 'It's pretty cold here. How deep do you dive, and how long can you stay down?' They told me that they go to eight metres depth and can stay down for an hour. As they had no wet suit, but only flippers, and the water was below 10 °C, we thought they were pretty tough! We exchanged a packet of cigarettes, brought specially for this purpose, for a bucketful of choritos.

Sailing up the fjord, gazing spellbound at the scenery, we passed through dense rafts of Sooty shearwaters stretching ahead and astern as far as we could see. These were birds which are supposed to migrate to the north in the winter, and yet we had seen countless numbers from Valparaiso southwards.

Well up the fjord on the starboard side we saw the estuary of Río Cochamó, and as it was high tide we were able to feel our way into it, almost brushing the rushes on either side. There was a big Heron watching us, and our first Steamer ducks. Steamer ducks always feature in travel stories about this part of the world, so we had been eagerly expecting to see some. They are big, good-looking ducks, mostly gray but with some darker markings and white underneath, and really massive bills. We could not help laughing on seeing them 'steam' away from us at about ten knots, using their feet and beating the water with their wings in a fast, alternate, circular movement which created quite a splashy wake.

We anchored for the night in a fast-running channel between mudflats at Ralún, the basin at the very head of the fjord. There were some interesting birds out on the mud, but houses and a hotel spoilt the look of the place.

Friday 12 August

...We sailed down Estero Reloncaví with both headsails poled out in a stiff following breeze, reaching eight knots at times. Yippeee!...At the mouth, the wind headed us for a while, but outside we were able to go tearing off southwards with just a small jib, going like a train in a wild, breaking sea, brilliant with phosphorescence...

Nearing Paso Nao, the narrow eastern passage out of Seno Reloncaví and into Golfo Ancud, the wind reached gale force and the sea in the passage itself was confused and turbulent, making *Totorore* almost unmanageable. At about 2300 hours I called Jim to look in the radar, sick though he was, as I could not leave the tiller and was very worried. I was already soaked from the seas breaking into the cockpit and hoped for a lee after we turned south-east, through the passage. I was disappointed. *Totorore* heeled over so far that the angle was too great for the radar and only occasionally could we see a picture on the screen. Having more experience with the radar, I changed places with Jim and he too got soaked. We were heading for Caleta Manzano (caleta means cove)...entered through a very narrow gap between an island and the mainland. I hoped the gap, which is about 1 mm across on the chart, with no soundings, would be safe.

Saturday 13 August

As we approached the caleta I furled the sail and we motored into the wind, barely keeping steerage, with spray coming over the bow drenching both of us...we made it inside, and motored as far as possible until soundings showed five fathoms, which as it was high water, allowed for about seven metres of tide. At 0300 hours we dropped the anchor and paid out all 40 fathoms of our chain, with a nylon spring. She yawed a lot, and heeled over as each blast hit her, but I knew it would be good holding in mud so we turned in. Jim was sick, wet and cold...I told him that there would be good birds here, so I hope I am right!

In the morning the wind was still strong, but it had gone south. It was raining. This was a beautiful spot with rocks, trees and a long beach. There were some houses, and on the far side on the already-drying mud launches and a 'lancha de vela' were discharging their cargo into a truck. Jim was watching through binoculars and let out a 'Whoop!' Black-necked swans – about 60 of them – and Oystercatchers and Whimbrels.

A passenger launch came out and the skipper tooted on his horn and signalled to us to follow him. He led us to a tiny cover just inside the entrance we had come through in the night; as there was no swinging room, we secured alongside the launch and Jim rowed ashore to walk along the beach to the birds. By the time he came back several hours later the dinghy although tied to a rock was well and truly afloat, and well offshore! A friendly pair of residents launched a rowing boat and brought him and the dinghy back to *Totorore*.

Jim was pleased with the photos he had taken of the birds, and was eager to find more. The next day we left Caleta Manzano and sailed to the head of Canal Hornopirén, only twelve miles away, which also had a good drying-out mud area. There had been fresh snow on the heavily forested mountain sides and it was fantastically beautiful. There were both flying and non-flying Steamer ducks, Collared plovers, coots, egrets, and most exciting of all, fifteen gorgeous Flamingos! They are waxy pink, with red rear ends, and underwings black with red linings. There were also playful Sea-lions, and many of the most beautiful of all cormorants, the Red-legged, which kept Jim 'shooting'.

That night we anchored in Estero Quintupeu, surely the most picturesque, landlocked anchorage we had yet been in. It is about 4.5 miles long, and half a mile wide, between towering mountains, and the narrow entrance is little more than a concealed crack in the cliffs. Inside was like a lost world. The water was mirror calm, and the only sound was that of numerous spectacular waterfalls. For over a week we pottered about, exploring bays, fjords and islands, and each night anchored in another different and exciting place. Bird watching was rewarding and Jim was building up an impressive list of species photographed.

Tuesday 16 August

...We sailed across to Bahía Pumalín, sheltered by Isla Llahuén, and found the entrance a little bit tricky because it bears little resemblance to what is shown on the chart. It is narrow, shallow, and has many rocks, and a final hairpin bend leading into the bay which is really a big lagoon a couple of miles across. Once inside we could see what an amazing place it is, full of birds. 'Hualas' or Great grebes dived around us, and over 150 Black-necked swans floated majestically past, looking stunningly beautiful with their snow-white bodies, black necks and heads, and bright red caruncles on their beaks. Flamingos on an alluvial bank at the far end of the lagoon caught our eye, and a handsome Buff-necked ibis honked at us as he flew past to land on the beach nearby...we could hear parakeets in the bush, but did not see any.

Wednesday 17 August

...We often see a pair of the small Chilean dolphins, which seem to be resident here, and a big Sea-lion comes close to the boat and pokes his face high out of the water to look at us. In a narrow channel among mud and cockle banks we landed, and walked overland to look at the swans. There were lots of waders, too. Pretty little Winter plovers, with their smart chestnut breasts, Whimbrels, and both kinds of Oystercatcher. Over a low ridge we came across a huge flock of the richly coloured Ashy-headed geese browsing over a swamp, seen against a background of dark forest with the mighty, icy, volcanic cone of Corcovado behind. What privileged people we are to be here!

In Estero Reñihué, one of the fjords, we were surprised to see large numbers of Black-browed mollymawks, White-chinned petrels and Southern fulmars, all of which are birds of the open oceans and far from their breeding places. It is about 80 miles to the open sea, if they come through Chacao, or 120 miles if they come south of I. Chiloé, which is more likely. Fishermen in small open boats were bringing up fine big 'congrios' (conger eels) on hand lines from the bottom, over 100 fathoms deep. At the head of the fjord we found our way through a narrow shallow entrance to a hidden inlet named Estero Pillán, snuggled in among the forested mountains and with a small house and some farmland next to a river at the far end. After a peaceful night at anchor, we rowed ashore to walk up the riverbank to see if we could find some of the Torrent-ducks in the rapids.

Saturday 20 August

We landed our dinghy on the riverbank and pulled it up onto the frosty grass. It had been a hard row to the shore against the current which we thought was the outgoing tide, so we did not tie up and left the dinghy upside down with the oars underneath and Jim's camera bag with his spare lenses sitting on top. The bush was quite dense, but we were able to follow cattle tracks, Jim going one way, and I another. I watched a Fire-eyed diucon, a grey tyrant-bird about 20 cm long and with a bright red eye, but saw few other birds...By the time I was back at the river mouth, I had been away about an hour, and – oh golly, the dinghy had floated away! I had been wrong about the tide. It was still coming in, but the melt-water from the snow in the mountains, rushing down the river, had washed our dinghy far out into the inlet...I felt very ashamed.

I made my way as quickly as I could to a small farmhouse and the farmer came out, wearing a big sombrero...He said, 'Right down at the end of the inlet is a house, where there is a boat. You can walk there – there is a track, but some of it will be under water now as it is high tide'. I thanked him and set off across the paddocks...I had to deviate to avoid getting water over the top of my gumboots. I came across a group of nine Ibises. They have buff-coloured necks, grey on the back, and black under the wings, and their bills are long and curved...I rushed on along the track,

51

which followed the edge of the rocks between the sea and the bush; it was rough going, stumbling over small boulders. Where it was flooded I had to take to the bush. Sitting on a branch right over the track was one of the beautiful big Kingfishers, some white, some grey, and a deep reddish colour underneath. What a sight! As with the Ibises, and without my camera, I got closer than I had ever been before...

In the morning it had been cold and I had put on warm clothes. Now with the exertion I was much too hot, and sweating. When I reached the end of the inlet I found a man building a boat under a lean-to shed...I could not help having a quick look at what he was doing. He was using the age-old method of bending planks in a smoking steambox, and securing them with roves and copper nails, riveted. I would have liked to watch him at work, but I was in a hurry, so I explained the position to him, tapping my head to say I was 'loco'. (This is the name of a shellfish, which if eaten in excess, or with whisky, is said to make one go mad.)...He was very sympathetic and said I could borrow his boat...

We launched his heavy boat from a small rocky beach and he rowed me in pursuit of our dinghy, standing up and pushing tirelessly on the oars. I enjoyed my little ride across the beautiful, calm inlet, and when we came up to the boat, there was Jim's camera case still sitting on top, not even wet! Even more amazing, the two oars were still jammed underneath. We were luckier than we deserved...

Roberto Winkler, the man who had saved our dinghy, said that ours was the first yacht he had ever seen in Estero Pillán, and he had lived there all forty years of his life. I doubt if any other yachts had been in most of the places where we anchored. Our draft of only 1.4 metres allowed us to go into some incredibly out-of-the-way places, feeling our way between mudbanks and rocks into minute coves, always seeking, recording and photographing birds. It was exciting and enjoyable work, and we came to know the area well. On Chiloé, and the many islands close by, there were more people, more houses, more churches, more boats – and more birds. It would seem that, generally speaking, the Chilotes have a good attitude towards birds, and do not persecute them.

After many adventures we headed back to Puerto Montt. Crossing Seno Reloncaví again we noted flocks of Thin-billed prions – another species we had not expected so far inland. Not far inside the southern end of Canal Tenglo is the Puerto Montt Yacht Club, and we thought we would stop there instead of going to Angelmó as before. Being winter, there was no sign of life and no boats on the water – just a few yachts hauled out on a slipway. We anchored close off the club in the dark, and during the night it blew a gale which caught us in a very exposed position. *Totorore* dragged her anchor but then stopped and seemed safe enough. In the morning we found that our anchor had caught on the wire cable used for hauling out the slipway cradle, but luckily we had not done it any harm, so we slipped it off and went back to our old berth alongside an Armada vessel at Angelmó. In fact we were outside two Armada vessels, and the *Negofol*, and it was a nuisance having to clamber across them and up a long ladder to go ashore, but we did know that *Totorore* was safe. At night one of their crew members would always turn on lights for us to negotiate the ladders.

Wednesday 24 August

This time we have come into a rainy spell at Puerto Montt, which gives me a chance to work on my paper about the birds seen during out Pacific crossing. It is never easy to do this sort of work on board, especially as I have to draw maps, and I really do not have the best facilities for that sort of thing. Also, I need complete peace and quiet to be able to concentrate, and that is difficult to get in a small boat. Dear old Jim, he never stops talking. If he does, it is because he is singing. Then the moment he puts his head down on a pillow he drops off to sleep and starts snoring! Patrick in the *Negofol* told us that last night he heard a very loud noise and could not think what on earth it was, but I knew!

...Patrick and Pierette came aboard for dinner. Jim made a really super meal with a ready-cooked chicken he had bought and good fresh vegetables, followed by one of his special desserts he makes with dried pineapple and tinned pawpaw, a chocolate sauce (melted bar of chocolate) and New Zealand tinned cream (saved for very special occasions) flavoured with rum...Wine here is good and very cheap...Pierrette said she would type out my bird paper for me, which is a great offer, especially as she does not speak English. We converse in a mixture of French and Spanish. Patrick told us that they had a friend called Andreas who is a keen ornithologist and would like to meet us.

Saturday 27 October

Andreas von Meyer came down to see us today. Patrick had told him about us, but he had also seen the article in the paper. He is young and bearded, and is studying agriculture at the University of Osorno so comes home only at weekends. He is a nice chap, but we did not know what to make of him at first. He never smiles, and when he speaks he does not move his lips. He has a limp, and does not swing his arms when he walks, which gives him an odd gait. His family call him Nipsy. Possibly he had polio when he was young, but we do not like to ask! He was most interested in our expedition and the birds we had seen, and we could tell that he was very knowledgeable. At first he did not believe that we had seen Inca terns at Puerto Montt...it seems that they could be another indication of the effect of the Niño Current.

Andreas said he would pick us up at 1800 hours to take us to a beach to see some birds. He came in an old Chevrolet utility, and on the way he also picked up Luis Espinosa, the only other keen bird man in Puerto Montt. Later, he picked up his niece Lily and a friend, and they rode on the tray outside...they must have felt cold, because we were cold enough inside the cab! We drove along the beach road, and then up to the von Meyer house at Pelluco. Jim and I were embarrassed because we were dressed for the beach, and here we were invited to dinner. It was a lovely old house, on a beef and dairy farm of about 140 hectares, and had a super view over Seno Reloncaví. Andreas's mother Barbara is a tall, strong-looking woman who speaks good English, as does Julia, his sister, but his father is old and failing and although he is still tall and straight, his sight and hearing are poor. His speech is a mixture of German, Spanish and English, and it is difficult to converse. The family came from Germany 27 years ago and

53

started the farm. Now they have lofty trees around the old house...there are 28 cows, all milked by hand, and they do a milk run into Puerto Montt with a horse and cart. Julia seems to take care of most of the farm work, although several hired hands live in houses on the property. Barbara looks after the chickens in a big run, just behind the house. On some fruit trees in the fowl run we saw Night-herons roosting, which pleased Jim enormously...

The next day we went for a tramp over a bird-rich estuary with Andreas and Luis and made tentative arrangements for both of them to join us for a small part of our expedition. Jim and I both realised how much we could learn from them, and they would be delighted to have a rare opportunity to travel to new places.

At that stage we had no idea of what an important part both Andreas and his sister Julia were later to play in the *Totorore* expedition, and they could not have ever imagined the fantastic and often dangerous adventures which they would experience with us in the next two years.

Flamingos

Chapter Five

Birds and Bad Anchorages

Canal Chacao – Bahía de Ancud – Est. Pudeto – Puerto Montt –
Isla Lagartija – Isla Guafo – Isla Ypún – Isla Guamblín –
Isla Tenquehuén – Laguna San Rafaél – Río Aysén

Jim and I sailed *Totorore* out of Puerto Montt at 1930 hours on 31st August bound
for Isla Metalqui, a small but extremely interesting island off the west coast of Isla
Chiloé. Here I hoped to find Little shearwaters; they are winter breeders, and
although some had been in that vicinity a few years before, there was no breeding
record for this species anywhere in Chile. We anchored for part of the first night
in a little nook of an island named Abtao, to catch the tide for Canal Chacao in
the morning.

Thursday 1 September
. . . It was raining with very poor visibility as we sailed into Canal Chacao.
Suddenly out of the rain loomed a large warship. It is a narrow channel
passing the Remolinas rocks, so we sailed well over to the side and as she
passed us we dipped our ensign to her in salute. Then we saw another
following, flying the Stars and Stripes. And then another! One by one they
appeared out of the dark bank of rain. Altogether there were seven ships –
four American and three Chilean – an impressive-looking fleet. Being
quite close to them, we tried again, dipping our ensign to the last two
Chilean ships. Their response was immediate and heart-warming. Not only
did they dip their ensigns in return, but their officers and crews waved to
us and cheered!
　We headed towards Isla Doña Sebastiana at the western entrance to the
Chacao, which looked likely breeding habitat for sea birds, but the weather
turned less friendly and in the disturbed wind-against-current situation Jim
felt sick again. I had to realise that Jim's state of health could not stand
work on the exposed outside coast, and unhappily abandoned the Isla
Metalqui project. However, what we found instead was of important
significance.
　In the shelter of Bahía de Ancud we came across huge flocks of
birds. . . all sorts of cormorants, terns including Inca terns, penguins,
grebes, boobies, pelicans, gulls, and one fulmar: twenty different species of
sea bird seen in just half an hour. Most fantastic of all, we counted about

3000 Red-legged cormorants! This species has never before been recorded in flocks of more than 30, usually being seen only singly or in much smaller groups. This we think could be yet another indiction of the upset of the natural order caused by the Niño Current.

For several days we explored the bays and coves in the area, often hampered by strong winds and rain. On one walk across to the west coast we saw our very first Kelp geese, standing on a breaker-drenched rock, well offshore. We had been told that Estero Pudeto, a small inlet on the eastern side of the peninsula and site of the town of Ancud, was full of waterfowl of various sorts. It is not well charted, and there is a bar at the entrance which can be dangerous at times. With some apprehension and a little trepidation, we approached the bar at about 1800 hours on 5 September, in wind force 5 with squalls of hail and rain.

...Seeing a fishing boat going in we thought it wise to follow her. Because of the rainy weather over the last few days we still had the cockpit tent rigged up, and I steered standing up, to see over the tent, and pushing the tiller with my foot. The fishing boat almost disappeared in a welter of foam as she rolled her way violently into the heavily broken water on the bar. I don't know about Jim, but my heart missed a beat or two! Did she draw as much as we did?

We were into the big swells rolling us in, and it was too late to turn back...Jim was on the foredeck, standing by in case we needed to drop the anchor. He was holding tightly onto the mast pulpit. 'Hell!' was all he said.

The entrance channel over the bar is narrow, between the high bluff of the peninsula and a bank of mud and rocks...When we arrived at the most frightening part among the actual breakers I found it extremely difficult to steer. The breakers came from astern, but the tide was ebbing very strongly against us, and I had to push the tiller hard over from one side to the other frequently to avoid broaching and being rolled over in the breakers. I looked astern once, but that was enough!

And then the tiller broke! Please God, help us! Luckily it still held enough for me to be able to nurse her through across the bar, where all we had to contend with was the current. That was bad enough. The fishing boat, hardly making way, was swinging around on a most erratic course and it was difficult to follow.

There was a heart-rending graunching and we went aground. The force of the current, rushing out at about five knots, slewed *Totorore* beam on and she heeled to a desperate angle, the engine making a terrible clatter so that I thought it was giving up the ghost, or that the propeller had come loose. I yelled to Jim to let go the anchor, while I hopped quickly below to stop the engine before it disintegrated. I was scared stiff that we were going to be swept quickly back into those terrible breakers.

A big swell lifted her and she swung again bow to the current. A larger launch struggled past us and signalled that we should follow her, so we tried again. Back on an even keel, the engine, although very hot, seemed to run well enough, so Jim hauled up the anchor, and with throttle fully opened and another swell under her, *Totorore* started to move. The boat ahead twisted and turned and we did not know whether it was necessary to follow a channel, or that she too was finding it difficult to steer.

There were swirls and eddies and whirlpools...the current was too strong for us, and we were making no progress at all. Then a large and powerful craft came down towards us at a tremendous speed, turned astern of us, then came back abreast and offered us a rope...Soon we were safely anchored, and Jim made us strong coffee, which we both needed. Whew!

Drifting under the bridge and up into the estuary in the dinghy on the ingoing tide, Jim had an exciting time photographing ducks, geese and waders in large numbers and from very close range. I had to go to the Armada office in Ancud to show our zarpe from Puerto Montt, which took me several hours, and was dismayed when told that before we left the whole area we must call back in to get another zarpe. The last thing we wanted to do was come back into Pudeto! This was one of the reasons we tried to avoid centres of population and officialdom. Later on and farther south there were no settlements at all, and it was much easier.

The weather and the sea were better when we crossed the bar on the way out, and we did some further work in Bahía Ancud. The next day we anchored in a tiny fishing harbour protected by a small breakwater, right in front of the town of Ancud itself. The fishermen there said it was a dangerous place and we should not stay, so as soon as I had the zarpe we left. The wind and sea were rising, and we could see what the fishermen meant.

Working our way slowly back towards Puerto Montt, we stopped to anchor in several different places to look at birds. One of these was a fascinating small island named Lagartija (Lizard) because of a long reef seen at low water, stretching out like a tail. There were about 800 Blue-eyed cormorants roosting on the rocks, and more on top of the cliffs which surrounded most of the island, the summit of which was well wooded. Some 35 Magellan or 'Rock' shags were nesting on tiny ledges on the cliffs, and on a spit of sand were 32 Pelicans and about 200 Black-backed or Dominican gulls. Not sure of the tide, I stayed to look after *Totorore* while Jim rowed ashore with his camera. As the reef dried out various waders flew in, and when Jim came back he said that he had never seen so many different kinds all at once.

Saturday 10 September
...Back at Puerto Montt, all is hustle and bustle in preparation for the annual Armada-sponsored race of the 'lanchas de vela,' the sailing cargo vessels, due to start tomorrow at 1000 hours. This is a long race of over 800 miles, all the way to the famous Laguna San Rafaél and back, in eight stages with a compulsory stop of ten hours between them, and a prize for the winner of each stage. It is a gruelling race for the four men in each crew, because when the winds are light they propel their heavy craft with long oars. Today, the lanchas were being given their provisions – generous quantities of fresh vegetables, eggs, flour, tea and even *Yerba mate*. The two French yachts in port, *Negofol* and another named *Jolie Brise*, have been asked to accompany the race to give it more publicity and provide more of a spectacle, and probably to act as rescue boats as well, should any of the lanchas get into trouble. The yachts were also given the same quantity of stores, and US$600 for their trouble. A small Armada vessel

will also go with them. The crews of the lanchas know their own waters close to Chiloé better than anybody else, but outside of their known area they need guidance because they have neither compasses nor charts, so really the race is a big undertaking for them.

Sunday 11 September
The lanchas are looking very smart and clean, all freshly painted for this great race. It is the tenth anniversary of the political coup which brought General Pinochet into power.

We were amused to see a new lancha close by to us still being completed only two hours before the start of the race. One man was sawing planks, another was planing them, and a further two were bending and nailing them into place, forming the bulwarks, and an extension aft as a stern platform right around the rudder stock. A friend was busily stitching sails. They were doing a great job, and putting their hearts and souls into it...

After a few speeches at the Armada steps, and a serious briefing for the crews, the race started. It was a great sight, with 36 boats. We followed them out, taking with us Andreas and his nephew and niece, Pancho and Lily, all enjoying the holiday atmosphere as we weaved in and out of the competing boats.

We are fascinated by the seaweed industry here. We see launches coming in laden with bales of it, stringy-looking red stuff, and we often see people raking it up into small boats or horse-drawn carts at low water. I am not sure how you cook it, but it is sold in many shops and markets, and is a common food. They call it *cochayuyo*.

Luis Espinosa brought his wife Harriet down to the boat to meet us. Her English is not very good; when she was trying to invite us to use the shower in their house she illustrated her point by picking up a stainless steel pot-scourer from our sink and pretending to scrub herself with it. We laughed. Golly, were we as bad as that?

Luis worked in a dairy factory and was going to have a holiday on Monday 19 September, Chile's Independence Day, so that gave him a long weekend and a chance to come for a jaunt. It had to be somewhere close, so we decided on Isla Lagartija, picking him up at Isla Calbuco which he could reach by bus over a causeway.

Jay Nelson arrived during the week to join us. He was young and very keen, and had been working for the US Wildlife Department in Alaska, mainly with birds. Having much experience of taking seabird population censuses, we knew he would be a great help.

I had my usual hassles with the Armada over not keeping in radio contact; sorting it all out and testing our set on different frequencies took a lot of time. We left Puerto Montt at 1930 hours on Friday 16 September and after anchoring in a cove for a few hours during the night to get some sleep, we arrived at Lagartija at 0800 hours. We all went ashore, and while Jim and Jay set up camp on the island – with two tents so that Jim could snore at a safe distance from the others – I went to look for the burrows Jim had previously noted up on top.

58

There were several hundred Magellanic penguins standing out on the spit. We had not seen these handsome birds out of the water before; they do not breed in the vicinity, so we wondered why they had gathered on the spit. Perhaps it had once been a breeding place, possibly many centuries before, and instinct still led them there on their migratory route back to the south?

They are large, dinner-jacketed birds standing about 71 cm in height, and have a habit of braying like a donkey, which can sound delightfully mournful but is disturbing when one is trying to sleep. In Chile the Magellanic penguin is called 'Pajaro niño', the Child bird. There were also Dolphin gulls on the island, often seen around colonies of breeding cormorants or penguins where they steal eggs and also eat carrion.

In the afternoon I left Jim and Jay on the island and sailed abut nine miles to collect Luis who had come by bus, over a causeway, to the fishing village on Isla Calbuco. He was waiting on the beach, so we were soon back at Lagartija. During the three days we were there we mist-netted small birds and compiled an impressive species list for the island, tape-recorded the call of the Plumbeous rail, which we were to hear frequently farther south, and Jim and Luis took photographs of many different waders.

Monday 19 September

...While we were preparing lunch we saw a lone figure rowing out from a distant island; he came ashore in a large wooden boat which he beached then climbed up the grassy slope to our camp. He just stood looking at us. He had a broad, flat face and the features of an Indian – the most full-blooded I have seen yet. We greeted him and he did not say a word. Luis questioned him in Spanish, but his answers were monosyllabic and Luis told us that the man spoke very little Spanish, merely indicating that he had come to the island to see us. Jim had cooked a sort of hash with beans and fish, and handed a plateful to the Indian who ate it in silence, then watched as we ate ours. He handed over his empty plate and went back to his place on the edge of our camp site. We took him a cup of coffee which he drank without response and handed back his cup. For about twenty minutes he watched us packing up, then suddenly turned his back and walked away. We watched him rowing quickly out to sea, with strong strokes, towards the island he had come from.

After we dropped Luis off on Calbuco to find his way home, Jim, Jay and I carried on southwards. We were about to tackle one of the major objectives of our expedition – to make a species list of the birds on Isla Guafo.

Lying well offshore about twenty miles south-west of Isla Chiloé, Isla Guafo is uninhabited except for Armada personnel who man the lighthouse. It measures about nine miles north to south, and eleven miles west to east, and is covered with almost impenetrable forest on low hills up to 240 metres. In spite of the presence of lighthouse keepers, and a small whaling station in Caleta Samuel earlier this century, very little was known about its avifauna. In the literature the possibility that Sooty shearwaters and/or Pink-footed shearwaters might nest there had been mentioned, and there were allusions to the presence of wild dogs, and even wild men! Altogether, the island had an irresistible reputation.

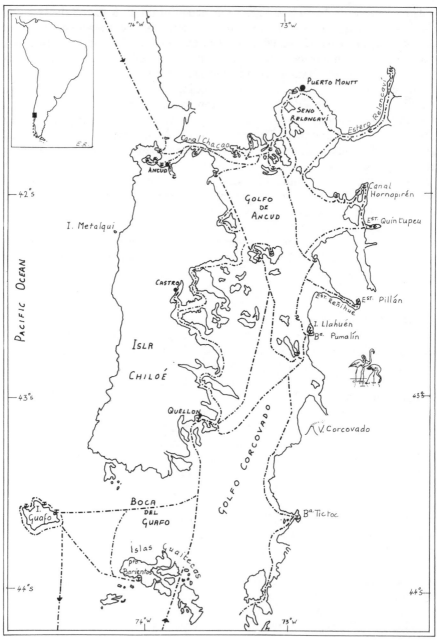

Map 7

It took us several days to reach Isla Guafo; we were weather-bound in Pumalín for three days, and then when we finally started out of the Golfo de Corcovado and across the Boca del Guafo, strong winds in the night forced us to run for shelter down to the Guaitecas Islands, where we anchored in Puerto Barrientos. In the morning, overhead clouds raced past from the east; we knew it was no good our

60

going to Guafo until the wind was from a westerly quarter, so we moved *Totorore* up into a pond-like basin under the trees, near a stream from which we collected water. Noisy parakeets, green with red on the face and in the tail, flocked above us, and Kelp geese foraged along the rocky shore, eating the green 'sea lettuce' type of weed. On Monday 26 September the wind was from the south-west so we sailed out to Guafo.

...The wind was still fresh and the sea was rough, so it was a slow and uncomfortable ride which put my crew to bed again. As we approached the off-lying island it was frequently hidden by rain, but I could see some off-lying rocks with terrific breakers, and when we were closer, the cliffs of the southern coast with dense forest above.

Caleta Samuel was well sheltered and we sailed in as far as depths would allow...Around the shore we counted 50 pairs of Kelp geese, lots of Oystercatchers, Steamer ducks and Teal, and could hear land birds in the bush. There were even caves to explore...

There was not much left of the old whaling station: a few rusting piles where there had been a jetty, and the remains of part of a concrete ramp. The bush is all secondary growth close around the cove, the big trees having been felled for firewood by the whalers.

We rowed the camping gear ashore and set up the tent in a small clearing among the trees. Down by the beach and hard up against a rocky ledge, we found the remains of a small shelter built of sticks and branches lashed together with synthetic cord, obviously erected some time ago by fishermen. This was a disappointing thought, as we did not expect fishermen to ever come here. Anyway it is very convenient for us and we spread our orange tarpaulin over it to make a food store and cookhouse...

After Jim had cooked us a good dinner on the campfire I returned aboard alone to sail to Quellón, the southern small port on the east coast of Chiloé, where I had arranged to meet Andreas. He is going to join us for this Guafo project, and we are all looking forward to having him with us.

Because of the many rocks and reefs on the other side, and the narrow channels between islands to reach Quellón I could not snatch even a wink of sleep all night, but with twin headsails poled out, *Totorore* made good speed.

I dropped anchor near the pier of the town at about 0930 hours and saw Andreas waiting for me. The rest of the morning I spent trying to appease el Capitan del Puerto. I had to write out a day-by-day account of where we had been, and where we are going to be until our return to Puerto Montt.

We sailed at 2140 hours, but the wind was light and the return voyage to Guafo was slow. Andreas was delighted to see a Royal albatross, a Salvin's mollymawk, a Cape pigeon, and lots of White-chinned petrels – all birds which he had not seen before.

Wednesday 28 September

...I took Andreas ashore with his tent and his gear and found that Jim had lunch ready for us. 'Well, how is it going?' I asked Jim and Jay. 'What do you want to hear?' countered Jim. 'Would Sooty shearwaters do?' enquired

Jay quietly. I was so excited that I could not sit still. What, where, when, how?

They had seen them in the evening, flying high, coming in from the sea right up the cove and disappearing far up into the hills as it became dark. Thousands of them. In the morning Jim was up early and saw them coming out again at about 0500 hours. . . This is the first confirmation of a breeding place away from the Cape Horn area, so we are really on to something big and significant, making all our efforts worthwhile.

I went for a walk along the southern shore to see some of the birds for myself. A Plumbeous rail, 'Piden', flew up from almost under my feet, and everywhere there were the almost tame Kelp geese in pairs. The gander is spotless white with black eyes and bill, and makes a pitiful little squeak when he flies, whereas the goose, chocolate brown above with black and white barring underneath, utters powerful honks. He, of course, is very conspicuous, whereas she, when sitting on a nest, is almost invisible, but when seen close by she is more beautiful than I can describe. I found a nest with three eggs in it, concealed by a light covering of vegetation. . . I cannot help but feel really warm towards these lovely birds.

I came to a cave in the sandstone cliffs and went inside to explore. Inside, I had to climb up a bank of very light, dusty sand which had obviously not been disturbed for a long time, and in this dust I saw some footprints like those of a cat, which was very disquieting. The cave had several branches to it, and in one I found a crude wooden cross. As my eyes became used to the gloom I could see what must have been the remains of a coffin, and in the middle was a human skeleton. I wondered who it could have been. . .

Sooty shearwaters

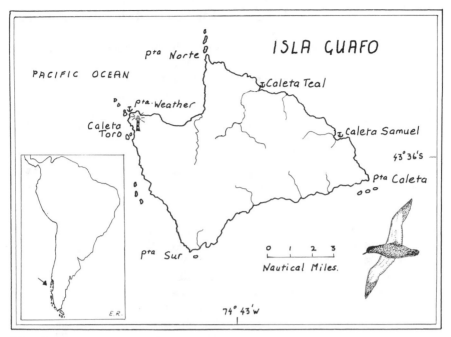

Map 8

While at Guafo we explored around the coasts in *Totorore*, and observed the incoming Sooty shearwaters from many different points, counting them and estimating the total size of the colony. Jay was experienced in this sort of thing, but I found it very difficult. Using machetes, we hacked our way into the interior to try to find the main concentration of nesting burrows which we expected to be in the hills. It was tough going because the undergrowth was dense and obstructed by fallen trees in every state of decay. We took it in turns to sleep in a small tent either in pairs or singly in as many places as possible, and as far into the forest as we could penetrate, to discover the shearwaters' destination.

At night, squatting beside our little tent in the damp dark forest, we would hear their blood-curdling cries as of anguished ghosts; every now and again one would crash through the canopy above and plummet noisily into the dense undergrowth which covered the forest floor. If one came close, we would endeavour to find it with our big torch and track it to its burrow, but successes were few. They seemed to just disappear, and the burrows were extraordinarily hard to find. The birds appeared to be courting and house-cleaning, and were not as regular in their visits as they would be later after their honeymoon period, when they would get down to the serious business of breeding. We never did find a dense centre of population, and could not be sure that they were not fairly evenly scattered over the whole island.

One day we set off to visit the lighthouse at Punta Weather, the north-western point of the island. The weather deteriorated as soon as we rounded North Cape, and seasickness affected the crew. Andreas was taken by surprise while down below and vomited over everything within a metre's radius, or so it seemed when I had to finish cleaning up afterwards! I decided that it was not the best day to go visiting, so we returned to Caleta Samuel.

Poor Andreas felt very embarrassed about it all. He still looked sick and cold when he went ashore, so I lent him a duvet to use in his tent. The tent had seen better days and had many holes ineffectively sealed with sticking-plaster. He was not at all well equipped, and I had to lend him wet-weather gear and boots. A very impractical fellow, he had a dry sense of humour and an astounding memory about anything to do with birds. We all liked him a lot and I later asked him to join us for two other parts of the expedition.

We put our net out regularly and kept ourseleves well supplied with fresh fish. Jim fixed up a smokehouse in the little cave behind our cooking shelter, and it worked well. He was a very useful chap to have around.

Tuesday 4 October

As the weather was good this morning, we motored around to the lighthouse, leaving Jay up in the forest by himself. We had to keep well outside the various rocks on the way so used the opportunity to take compass bearings and sextant angles of the highest hills, where we are hoping to find the biggest Sooty colonies. The lighthouse itself is set about 140 metres above the sea on a point with sheer cliffs all around it, and the landing place is close by, sheltered from the very heavy swell by a small island and a long line of big rocks over which the sea was breaking. We could see where there had once been concrete steps and a hand rail up the rocks at the landing place, but these had been washed away; on the cliffs there were sections of a wide ladder which once led all the way to the top, but parts of that were missing and none of it looked safe. Wire cables to a structure above indicated a flying-fox for hoisting stores.

There are six men up at the lighthouse and two came down to show us the way up. Leaving Jim aboard, as it was not a very secure anchorage among the boulders, Andreas and I went ashore and followed them along the rocks around the foot of the cliffs to where a track led up a very steep grassy slope behind the lighthouse. We found it rather scary, slippery and crumbly, with very little to hold onto. In one place there was a free-hanging rope which helped a bit, and in another the only thing to hang onto was a large Scotch thistle, which did not help at all . . .

Their accommodation block is spacious, but very unimaginative. Behind the lighthouse there is some rough grass on which they keep a tiny farm, with five cows, a bull, about twelve sheep and ten goats. I was concerned that some of these might spread to the rest of the island, but Andreas assured me that the forest was much too wet to attract them into it. They also had pet rabbits and chickens, but apparently none of them stray far away. The attitude of these chaps towards birds is to shoot at everything they see. They have one old .303 rifle and some bullets with 1912 stamped on them, and all the men have catapults.

There were the usual vultures, which especially like the ugly rubbish dump, straight over the edge of the cliff but with wind blown litter all over the place, and some Caracaras, carrion-hawks which apparently have a taste for baby chickens. We also saw some small birds – mainly Siskins and Rufous-collared sparrows. Some of the panes of glass in the lighthouse were broken and the petty officer told us that big birds did that, so I asked if some of us could spend one night up there to observe them.

Coming down the steep track was worse than going up, and Andreas said his legs were trembling all the way back to *Totorore*...After a welcome cup of tea we weighed anchor, and breasted out into a big swell through a gap between the rocks to complete our circumnavigation of the island...

Caleta Toro had been recommended to us as an anchorage in calm weather, but there is seldom any of that. Today it was full of broken water and looked fearsome. We did however see an interesting colony of Blue-eyed cormorants, nesting Dolphin gulls, and Sea-lions on a small island. What really caught our attention was a number of Fulmars flying around and actually landing on high rocks nearby. In these latitudes that is most unusual, although they do have predatory habits farther south.

Off Punta Norte, we were all excited to see some Red phalaropes, so we spent about an hour chasing after them for Jim to take photographs. Jim said they were like waders which had paddled out of their depths, and in many ways they are most unusual birds. There are only three species, and all breed in far northern latitudes and migrate south in the northern winter. They are about 20 cm long, are pretty and dainty, with perky, jerky movements, and have flexible lobes on their toes for swimming instead of the webbed feet of most sea birds, even though two species, the Red and the Red-necked, actually spend about ten months of the year at sea.

The female is larger and more richly coloured than the male. She arrives at the breeding place first and stakes out a territory which she defends, then displays to attract a male and courts him, telling him where to build a nest. When he has done that to her satisfaction she lays her eggs, leaving him the task of incubating them!

By the time we see them in the southern hemisphere, phalaropes are generally in their non-breeding plumage of grey above and white below, but among those we were watching were several with a reddish tinge underneath. They seemed to like the disturbed or breaking water in the channels between the groups of rocks, and whole rafts of them sitting on the water would suddenly fly up at the same instant and wheel about like Sanderlings, dropping back onto the water again with the same precise co-ordination. There were about 100 of them, which was more than had been previously recorded at one time as far south as this. About a week later we counted over 5,000!

Another bird which we saw at Punta Norte which was also far from its normal range was an American sheathbill. One flew around *Totorore* a few times in pigeon-like flight, then settled back near a Sea-lion colony on the long rocky spit off the point. They are omnivorous, and farther south we were always seeing them cleaning up around colonies of birds or seals, walking about, pecking at the ground like domestic poultry, eating the excreta.

Andreas and Jay spent a night at the lighthouse and saw even larger numbers of the Sooty shearwaters coming ashore at night. Jay counted 700 per minute for more than half an hour in one narrow sector. Meanwhile Jim surveyed the Punta Norte spit on foot, almost suffocated by the powerful stench of the Sea-lions. On the hillside close by he found a colony of Magellanic penguins. There were many burrows, and in some he noted that the birds were already sitting on eggs. Leaving Jim and Jay on the island, Andreas and I sailed back to Puerto Montt to take

Andreas home, and for me to take Roberto Schlatter back with me. We decided to stop at Castro to phone Roberto.

Wednesday 12 October

Just outside Castro, which is about seven miles up a narrow canal, we rounded a large light buoy on which was draped an enormous bull Sea-lion. He was far too big to fit on completely, so his head was stuck out underneath the frame supporting the light and his rear hung grotesquely over the edge on the other side. Two young females were there, one cuddled up to him on the top, the other playing skittishly in the water and trying to get up and join them...

Castro looked similar to the other small towns of Chiloé except that it was larger and had a bigger church. We rowed ashore, took our zarpe to the Armada, and then set off to find a telephone office. The whole town seemed rather dead, but then it was the time of the siesta...We wanted to buy some empanadas, which are like a sort of meat pasty, but could not find any. And then Andreas suddenly remembered that it was Christopher Columbus Day and a national holiday! No wonder everything was shut. A terrible waste of time, coming to Castro at all! Even if we had got through on the phone, Roberto would not have been at the university...

Andreas and I moored *Totorore* alongside an Armada launch at Angelmó, Puerto Montt, at 1330 hours on 13 October.

...When we arrived at the farm we found that the family were out for the day, but Andreas and the maid started to scratch up a meal for us. Andreas showed me to the bathroom and told me how to work the gas calafont to make hot water. I soaped myself all over, just as the water ran cold...

Julia's children, Pancho and Lily, came back from school and we all sat down at their big dining table. After the meal I picked up my large cup of coffee, and suddenly – splat! – the cup fell and I was left holding the handle. The cup broke, the saucer broke and hot coffee splashed across the white tablecloth and all over my best shore-going clothes. Pancho and Lily thought it was a terrific joke and nearly split their sides laughing, which made me laugh too, but poor Andreas was very embarrassed. First the cold shower, and then this, just when he had been trying so hard to please. The cup handle had broken off before and the children had glued it on again! When I did get to phone Roberto Schlatter I heard that he could not come for another week! I arranged to pick him up from Quellón on the 23rd but that means yet another trip to come and fetch him.

Between *Totorore* and the wharf was a French yacht, whose owners had gone to France, a large Armada patrol vessel, an Armada research vessel, and a big freighter. To climb to and from the shore across the smaller vessels and the freighter, from which hung a long rope ladder, took much time and effort, so working on my own to refill the diesel tanks and carrying twenty litre cans from a road service station by hand took me a whole exhausting day in constant rain.

I had been persuaded by Luis, who used to be a schoolteacher, to take an ex-pupil of his with me for the week and then back to Quellón when I called to pick

66

up Roberto Schlatter. Sergio Ohme was only eighteen and a very keen bird-watcher, so it was nice to give him such an opportunity. His mother and father had a van which was a great help when I had to buy the stores for the next phase of our expedition.

My heart really sank when I arrived back at *Totorore* in the rain and found the cockpit and after deck full of gear. A large drum of oil and two smaller ones, six wooden boxes of various sizes including a monster two metres long, and a large sack of wheat which had been put inside the cabin. All these items were marked 'Faro Guafo', Guafo lighthouse. The Armada had dumped them on board for us to take out there without having even asked me if I would! Under the circumstances I could hardly refuse, but in a boat the size of *Totorore* it was a terrible encumbrance, and I could only hope that we would have good weather. I had brought back mail from the men at the lighthouse and had told the Armada that if their families had mail ready we would take it to them, but I had not expected a load of cargo!

Sergio's mother came with us to a wholesale market to buy our fresh fruit and vegetables, picking over everything critically and making the vendors open up cases and sacks and tip the contents out so that she could throw out anything that did not look good. She did things I would not have dared to contemplate. To make it easier to load it all in the rain, and avoid climbing over all the other craft, we hired a rowing boat and brought the supplies alongside *Totorore*.

Sergio did not speak any English, but with my limited Spanish we managed to communicate surprisingly well. He was quite used to boats but had never steered by compass. Once he had the idea, he was very reliable, and in the more open stretches of water I was able to get some sleep. As soon as the weather became rough, though, poor Sergio was sick and stayed in his bunk the rest of the way. I often had to use the engine, which started to leak oil and exhaust gases rather badly. I did not suppose that the fumes in the cabin helped Sergio much, and I kept peeping into the cabin to make sure that he was still alive.

As usual, I arrived back at Guafo feeling very tired. Sergio was very happy to reach dry land again and went straight to a tent. Jay and Jim had explored more of the coast using the dinghy with the outboard motor, and Jim had found a dead Brown-breasted swallow, never before recorded in Chile.

Bad weather continued, and as we were unable to deliver the stores to the lighthouse, Jim tackled the jobs to be done on the engine. He understood diesels, which gave me confidence, and I knew that I would miss his experience when he was gone. While the engine was out of action we tried to beach *Totorore* at the head of the caleta using long lines and the dinghy with the outboard, but the wind was too strong and we failed. I wanted to change the propeller, which was two-bladed, to the more efficient three-bladed spare, and to check the stern bearing. We tried

South American Terns

again with more success the following morning, but it was not such a high tide as the previous one and because the keels sank into the mud, the propeller was never clear of the water.

Sergio enjoyed himself in spite of the rain, wandering far along the shores observing and photographing birds. He found a Kelp goose nest which already had three eggs; later a Black oystercatcher laid two more eggs in the nest while the goose was away. We wondered about the final outcome of that cuckoo-like behaviour but regrettably could not stay. We had seen practically no terns at all at Guafo, and were pleased when 23 Arctic terns came into Caleta Samuel while we were there. Sergio found a dead one, which we measured and Jay then skinned as a specimen.

Thursday 20 October

Although the sea still looked very rough outside and the wind fresh, I decided that we must try to take the stores to the lighthouse because we are running out of time if we are to collect Roberto on the 23rd at Quellón. I took Sergio with me, as it was his only opportunity to see the other end of the island; he is also young and big and strong, and would be good for handling the heavy cargo. We had to motor all the way against the wind, and after passing Punta Norte the swell was huge and breaking high onto the rocks over the Sea-lions. It took us two more hours to cover the last four miles to the lighthouse, and when we arrived there the conditions looked terrible. The wind was whistling between the island and the cliff in great squalls, whisking the sea up into writhing fountains, making it difficult to manoeuvre *Totorore* into the area at all...

We anchored about 80 metres offshore and I called the lighthouse on the VHF, and the operator asked me to bring *Totorore* alongside the rocks at the landing place! That made me laugh. The voice of inexperience! I would not put her alongside those rocks even in calm weather. I suggested that they float a light line out to us, using a buoy; Sergio donned his lifejacket while I tied the end of a 100-metre line to the dinghy and pushed him off to catch the small float. They were then able to haul him to the landing place and set up our heavy line, made fast to a rock.

From then on the whole operation went smoothly. Sergio is a sensible, capable boy and he did the job very well, taking the stores a little at a time. He got very wet, of course. The big drum we floated ashore, Sergio towing it astern of the dinghy, and the three men dragged it up the rocks on a rope.

Finally Sergio took them their mail and newspapers, and asked for the radio which we had said we would take back to Quellón. I was dismayed when I saw the size of it as they lowered it down into the dinghy. It was in a rough wooden case, with nails sticking out of it, and was very heavy! It had to come inside, out of the weather, and the only place it could fit was on a bunk. That is a nuisance because we are going 60 miles down the coast to Isla Ypún, and there are four of us. By the time we have brought back all our camping gear there won't be much room...

With Jim and Jay back on board, we sailed our overcrowded boat out into the night. Because of all the gear we had only two bunks available for sleeping, so two kept watch while two slept. It was raining, and the barometer was falling; I was scared that the weather would force us to seek shelter in one of the canals of the archipelago, but keeping to the coast was a shorter distance, and by the time we arrived at Ypún the sun was shining.

The ocean-facing Isla Ypún was of interest as a possible nesting place for pelagic sea birds; from my reading I had expected it to be rather barren, unlike the heavily wooded islands of Guafo and Guamblín. But it too was covered with dense forest, so it seemed hardly worthwhile to make an extensive study as Guamblín, farther out to sea, would no doubt be more rewarding. However Guamblín is very exposed and has no sheltered caletas, or coves, whereas Ypún has a fine deep inlet on the eastern side, Puerto Scotchwell. The word 'puerto' does not necessarily mean 'port' as we understand it, but rather a harbour which could be used by ships or even small craft. Most of such places called 'puerto' are uninhabited and have no man-made facilities at all. We decided to make Ypún our base for work in the area of Bahía Adventure.

We motored up to the head of the caleta and anchored close to where a small river emptied its brown peaty water across the shingle beach. In many parts the beach was separated from the forest by a belt of 'nalca', a succulent plant rather like giant rhubarb with enormous prickly leaves. One such leaf which Jay collected measured nearly 3 metres across: surely one of the biggest in the world! The stems turn a purplish colour and can then be eaten; they are said to be nutritious, so that one should never starve on these islands with shellfish and a variety of birds' eggs in season.

With a bushman's skill Jim lopped off tall straight saplings from the forest edge near the river and quickly erected a framework for a large cooking shelter. Assisted by Jay and Sergio, he covered it with our orange tarpaulin and made shelves. It was a lovely spot, close to the beach and the river, but protected by some bushes from the wind. A quick exploration revealed few birds except large numbers of Steamer ducks, with many of their well-worn tracks leading under dense thickets to their nests. Jim decided to return with Sergio and myself to Quellón, where he would leave us to see a little more of southern Chile before flying home to New Zealand.

Leaving Jay alone encamped on Ypún we followed an intricate course through the maze of islands in mostly sheltered waters. Sergio stayed outside steering during daylight hours, and with his sharp eyes never missed a bird. It was quite cold and he sat along the cockpit seat in his sleeping bag, wearing a poncho and a little German sailor's hat, flat and black. He looked a real character. We made many deviations to look at anything interesting, and were often accompanied by schools of Dusky dolphins.

On arrival at Quellón Roberto met us and the Armada sent a rowing boat to collect the radio from Guafo. Sergio left on the bus, and Jim moved into a small hotel for the night, to be joined by Roberto and myself for dinner before we returned aboard to set sail back to Ypún.

The islands to the south of the Golfo Corcovado, which we had come through on the way to Quellón, form the Archipiélago de Chonos. The Chonos used to inhabit the whole of this vast area of waterways and mountainous islands which stretches for 120 miles outside the coast. They lived in temporary camps and canoes, eating mostly shellfish and hunting wild fowl, otters and Sea-lions. The islands facing the ocean are mostly rocky and steep, while the inner islands are covered with luxuriant rain forest right up to the mountain tops, some of which rise to 1500 metres. We had occasion to pass through this archipelago several times, and each time we took a different route to make it more interesting.

This was Roberto's first time here and he loved it. There were colonies of cormorants to observe and we played with a beautiful pair of Killer whales, going round in circles watching one another.

Monday 24 October

...There seem to be many uncharted rocks in these canals, and the charts are of very small scale, so that one needs always to be very alert...Today we tried an exciting place in Isla Chaffers. It was a narrow channel, only about 25 metres wide at the entrance, and running between low vertical cliffs with impenetrable forest above. On the rock faces were incredible large daubs of red, yellow, green, blue and brown algae looking for all the world like the work of an exuberant modern artist. I had seen many examples of this colourful natural decoration around these islands, but never before so lavishly displayed. However I was too anxious to admire or photograph such wonders because the strong tidal flow was whisking us through the three-quarter-mile channel at great speed, and we had to keep a sharp eye for swirls of water which could indicate rocks.

In places we passed no more than three metres from the cliffs, and beautiful Rock shags, disturbed from their nests in small caves, flew out in alarm. Inside, we found ourselves in a large lake, one arm of which stretched away for a further five miles. In the smaller arm a long wooded island offered us shelter from wind, so we anchored close in its lee. Roberto straight away went ashore in the dinghy to see and hear the birds. When he came back he brought a heap of mussels which we had for supper. He said that there were so many big ones that it was obvious that nobody else had been to this place for years...

The next day, farther down the canals, we tried to take a short cut through a very narrow and beautiful canal between two islands, Isla Level and Isla Izaza. The canal, about eleven miles long, looked navigable on the chart, but when we came to the narrows in the middle we were stopped by insufficient water so had to turn around and go back the long way.

At Ypún Jay had done some good exploring but had not made any important bird discoveries. While I spent two days working on the engine, he and Roberto searched the coast farther north and endeavoured to reach an inland lake, They noted interesting land birds, all of which we recorded for the various universities in Chile, but apart from large numbers of Diving petrels offshore, nothing new to see. On the north-east coast Jay picked up a bottle with a message inside which read 'Thrown overboard from the American research ship *Atlantis II* 25 January 1976. Latitude 63°54'S Longitude 29°32'E, by Robert Munns, 2nd Mate, Woodshole Oceanographic Institute, Massachusetts, USA'. We calculated that it had travelled at least 9000 miles in the seven years and nine months since he entrusted it to the sea.

I was fed up with the frequent problems with the engine, and knew that there must be something seriously wrong with the installation. On this occasion another

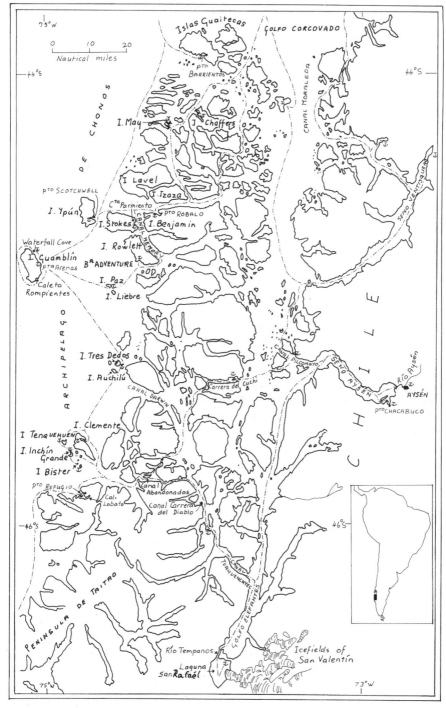

Map 9

71

bolt holding a bed bracket to the engine casting had sheared off inside the casting, right underneath again. The Dynastart would not work so we had to hand start the engine and this was becoming more difficult as time went on.

Friday 28 October

It's thick fog today but fairly calm, and the glass is high. We set off for Isla Guamblín while we had the opportunity. We found the southern channel out through the rock-strewn waters, seeing many Sooty shearwaters and Diving petrels, and now we are noticing a heavy swell as we sail the twenty miles across to Guamblín, hoping that we can land on the north-east coast...

We approached the island on the lee side, but the swell curled all the way around it, just like Más Afuera, and it looked as though we would not be able to land. After further examination we saw a gut in the rocks about 60 metres wide and leading right up to a beach of coarse sand. It seemed to be our only chance, so we tried it, and anchored with only a metre of water under our keels...

We had no sooner landed than we disturbed a Speckled teal from her nest in a bank of nalca between the beach and a swamp. She flew round and round several times and while we were watching, a Peregrine falcon stooped and caught her in mid air, right above our heads! A few feathers fluttered down as the falcon carried her off, and we could hear her quacking pitifully, making us feel guilty about having caused her untimely end. A Snipe flew off its nest almost at our feet, and we saw two eggs in the nest. Within a few minutes we had counted over twenty different species of bird, which is terrific. We only wished that Jim could have seen this lot. There is a waterfall down a cliff, and the stream is cleaner than at Ypún, so we set up a temporary camp next using a fly sheet to make a shelter for Roberto while Jay and I returned to Ypún to collect the rest of the gear.

Jay and I decided to take the whole framework for the cooking shelter on Ypún across to Guamblín where there were no convenient straight saplings. Getting it all on board was more of a job than we had imagined, because the poles were saplings of luma and arrayan, both very heavy woods which do not float. On our arrival back at Guamblín it was almost dark and we could not find Waterfall Cove, even though Roberto had put green leaves on his fire to make smoke to guide us. We anchored off for the night while Roberto slept badly in the shelter ashore, cold and badly bitten by midges from the swamp. For some reason his lips had swollen and he thought it could have been an allergy caused by some plant he may have cut for the fire.

On the following day we circumnavigated the island, but saw no other possible landing place. We spent the whole night drifting offshore using our pressure lamps to attract birds: with the mainsail set, we hoisted one lamp high up to the end of the spreader, and lashed the other to the coachroof, so that they both shone onto the white sail. Using a spotlight we brought aboard a Sooty shearwater, Common diving petrels, and lots of Wilson's storm petrels, from which we obtained lice and measurements. We had seen perhaps 1000 Sooty shearwaters coming in to land in the evening, but they were never in large numbers as at Guafo and we were unable to locate a single burrow.

72

When the weather permitted we used our net to catch robalo, a good eating fish about the size of mullet. A young Giant petrel always took a keen interest in the proceedings, the tamest any of us had ever seen.

We explored a great deal of the coast and made some tracks into the interior, where there did not seem to be many birds. Roberto and I managed a landing on Punta Arenas about three miles south of the camp. A large area of sand dunes with small lakes where we saw five different species of duck and several new land birds, as well as five Chilean skuas and twelve Turkey vultures. Everywhere of course was the 'Churrete' (*Cinclodes*), one form or another of which we were to see in all our travels round Chile. They are small to medium-sized birds of brown and grey colouring with a white eye streak, and are usually seen near water, bobbing and flicking their tails. Like the Rayoditos and the mouse-like Churrins, they became so familiar as to be part of our lives.

When we came back to *Totorore* the wind had changed and she had swung towards the rocks. It looked bad, with the sea much rougher than when we came ashore, and we had great difficulty in launching the dinghy, which half filled with water. Luckily Roberto did the right things when handling the windlass, and we got away with it. We certainly needed a cup of tea after that lot!

Our anchorage at Waterfall Cove was less than good from then on. The northerly wind blew across the gut, which necessitated dropping the anchor very close to the rocks on the northern side to have enough room to swing clear of the rocks opposite. Twice *Totorore* bumped heavily on the bottom, and as I found afterwards, damaged the rudder. In addition to the CQR, I laid out the Danforth anchor, but the close proximity of the rocks astern was a constant worry.

Jay arrived back from a solo tramp around the north coast and so we were all on board for what turned out to be a wild and uncomfortably anxious night. The wind started to blow into the cove from the north and *Totorore* became more lively.

Friday 4 November

This morning at low water the seas were breaking all around *Totorore*, and she started to bump again. Raising two anchors in a gale in the confined space was no easy task, especially with the windage of our twin furled-up headsails which caused the bow to sheer off downwind...by the time we were out into clear water away from the rocks, my clothes were damp with the cold sweat of fear and soaked with salt spray on the outside. Blowing as it was from the north, we thought that Caleta Rompientes (Breakers Cove) might be quite sheltered, but as we rounded Punta Arenas we were aware of huge breakers travelling northwards *against* the wind and sea, which tore the crests away in impressive plumes...Rather as we expected, the scene in Caleta Rompientes was horrendous and we could not even get near it. There was no option for us but to head for the canals, sailing under reefed jib.

With my two crew seasick I was not feeling particularly happy as we sailed across the turbulent Bahía Adventure in heavy rain with visibility down to about half a mile. In those conditions the radar is not much use until we are very close to land, as the scanner is seldom near horizontal. The scale of the chart is about five millimetres to a mile, so there is no accurate detail...the Pilot book does not describe these canals except to say 'Not recommended as they have not been examined.' As soon as we had passed the outer islands in the canal entrance it was comparatively calm, although some breakers in a heavy tide rip were a little alarming. Our little Seafarer echo sounder which I can bring out and mount under the dodger, visible from the cockpit, has been a real gem...

We found our way through a wilderness of islets, rocks, and shallows, to a delightfully sheltered haven in a small bay in Isla Rowlett. Above us, belts of rain were driving over the hills. The sense of peace and everything being suddenly still was a real joy. Soon the kettle was on, and we could relax.

Roberto went off in the dinghy to look for birds, and I rigged up the pipes to catch rainwater off the decks.

Saturday 5 November
Isla Paz and Isla Liebre, a mile apart, are similar islands of remarkable conical shape, about 350 metres high and well forested. Paz has a few spurs with only low vegetation, and these interested us. Heavy swell broke all around the steep rocky shores of the islands, but we found a tiny kelp-filled cove between two of the spurs and felt our way carefully into it. There was a big surge on the rocks, but the kelp in the centre of the cove kept it reasonably flat where we anchored in a very rocky and unreliable bottom, using twenty fathoms of chain in six fathoms of water. She lay beam-on to the swell which kept her rolling, with her stern about fifteen metres from the noisy waves on the rocks.

I kept ship while Jay and Roberto went ashore to explore. They made a difficult landing on a rock ledge, and then took to the scrub which was so dense that they had mostly to walk on top of it although it was about two metres high – or deep! When they came back they said that they had been unable to find burrows, so we decided to wait for dark and use our lights again...Magellanic diving petrels we saw going into the scrub, which constitutes circumstantial evidence of their breeding there...

Sunday 6 November
As usual in these conditions I had not put a nylon spring on the anchor chain so that I could hear any growling movement on the rocks to tell me if the anchor was dragging. Unfortunately this always makes a lot of noise which is transmitted up the chain to the hull, and nobody had much sleep. The wind started to blow into the cove from the north and *Totorore* became more lively...At about 0400 hours a violent snatch at the chain made a terrible noise. I stayed still for about half a minute listening, then leapt out into the cockpit and was immediately splashed by the sea breaking on the rocks! The anchor had let go, and I could see a big black rock only three metres away, with white foam spilling over it. 'Get up quickly, both of you – we are on the rocks!' I yelled to my companions who responded immediately, struggling out of their sleeping bags while I desperately tried to start the engine.

'Please God, help us now,' I prayed, swinging as hard as I could on the handle. I was quickly exhausted by my efforts and Jay attacked the task vigorously, but she would not fire. The noise of the breakers was terrifying and I expected the sickening crunch as the rudder destroyed itself on the rocks, but it must have been the backwash or the kelp which held her off.

When Jay was too puffed to continue, Roberto took over and at last she burst into life. Jay rushed forward to start winding in the chain on the windlass, only too conscious of the fact that our boat and probably our lives depended on quick action. I put the engine ahead to get away from the rocks and to take the weight off the chain to make it easier for Jay, but not wanting to override the chain and have her snub back. I was praying that the kelp would not foul the propeller, which was making awful noises as it chewed through it. By now the wind and sea had risen and she yawed wildly, answering the helm only slowly. I gave her full revs as Jay, after what seemed an eternity of time, shouted, 'It's up!' Fortunately I had noted the compass course to take in an emergency and headed confidently out, thanking God for our deliverance and rebuking myself for having risked our ship in this doubtful anchorage.

Again in a rough sea, and blinded by rain, we headed back for the canal we had left the day before, which was slightly easier than trying yet another unknown area. I wanted to go to Puerto Robalo, a cove in Isla Benjamín, protected from the swell by a group of small islands outside, but it took all day tacking against a strong wind in Canal Memory, so we anchored for the night in Caleta Parmiento on Isla Stokes. When we finally arrived at Puerto Robalo, we put the Johnson on the dinghy to try to get up the river to a lake about which we had been told.

Monday 7 November
. . . The mouth of the river looked dark and mysterious under the trees, and even above the outboard we could hear the rushing of water over the rapids higher up. The current was so strong that I did not think we had a chance of making it, but struggled slowly on. There were several narrows between boulders, and here the torrent was such that we could not gain an inch. Jay got out to lighten the dinghy and made his way on foot through the tangled vegetation along the banks. The dinghy yawed excitingly from side to side, as foot by foot we gained our way up the sloping, swirling water.

In the comparatively easier water above the narrows, submerged rocks spiralled the water into whirlpools which could easily have overturned us. We had just won through when suddenly the motor stopped; before we could do anything except hang grimly on to the dinghy, we were swept helplessly back down through the narrows again, the way we had come! Jay, up on the bank, watched amazed as we went shooting through the gorge below him, wishing that he had his camera to photograph us. A back eddy swirled us against the bank, and we managed to catch hold of a branch to avoid being carried all the way back to the caleta.

We managed to start the motor again and although it took about an hour and a half, we eventually completed the half-mile journey upriver to the calm lake above. It was from quarter to half a mile wide, and about three miles long. The birdlife was a little disappointing, but we saw Ashy-headed geese and Great grebes, and grebe's nest of floating rushes. What really did surprise and please us was to find three Chilean dolphins, which have rounded dorsal fins, swimming around in the lake, and we wondered at their coming up that shallow rocky river.

Going down the river stern first and using the oars only to guide us, we went at a thrilling speed and took only a few minutes to arrive back at *Totorore* before dark. At night we heard some owls calling in the forest – the first we have heard in this archipelago.

For Roberto to be back at the University on 11 November, we had no time to lose. Even though the weather was still bad we had somehow to get to Guamblín for him to collect his gear and to leave Jay encamped. This we accomplished with difficulty, but without mishap, and Roberto and I sailed northwards. On the last night we sailed right through and arrived at Quellón at 0500 hours on Friday 11 November, when I was able to get my head down for about three hours.

Roberto was genuinely grateful for his time with us and as he is one of the leading ornithologists in Chile, that made me feel that the last few weeks had been well worthwhile. His only regret was that I did not let him collect specimens. Dead birds, yes, but none were to be killed. We arranged for one of Roberto's students, Jorge Oporto, who was studying cetaceans, to take his place on board.

Friday 11 November

...When I took Roberto ashore to catch the bus, Jorge was there waiting. I took a liking to him straight away. He is very short, but seems full of energy, and was a tremendous help with the work on board, carrying cans of fuel from the service station up the road and taking one of our gas bottles – in a sack so that nobody could see what it was – in a bus to Castro to get it filled. He does not speak any English, which should help my Spanish.

Across the Gulf we can plainly see the mighty white spire of the volcano Corcovado, nearly 3000 metres high. This is always a sign of good weather soon to be followed by bad.

The next day I had to work on the engine. Jorge was seasick while we were still at anchor, which did not bode well.

Sunday 13 November

The only rest I had last night was in clear water where I could let Jorge take the helm, but my sleep was disturbed by the constant sound of him being sick. It is lucky that it is not rough...Once again I wonder at these endless islands and waterways with no boats, nor signs of any human habitation, especially on a nice day like this. Anywhere else in the world there would be pleasure boats...it's a bit uncanny.

I had wanted to press on direct to Guamblín, but when the wind freshened to twenty knots against us we ducked into a nice anchorage in between Isla May and another island to the north...

Monday 14 November

...We had the pleasurable company of seven beautiful Dusky dolphins, which delighted Jorge enormously. As cetaceans are his particular interest he took many photographs and notes of sea temperature, depth of water, exact locality, proximity of land, time periods between their risings, and so on. I was very glad for him.

76

We anchored at Waterfall Cove; Jay came out in the dinghy and was soaked when a sea broke over him. I cooked dinner while he gave me a report on his activities. He had made a water trap and caught ten mice which he thought could be a previously unknown species. He had also repaired the dinghy (while at Quellón we had used the spare).

The movement in *Totorore* became quite violent; Jorge was ill again, and Jay had to eat his dinner out in the fresh air in the cockpit. The nylon spring on the anchor chain parted, and with the lift of the big seas she struck the bottom three times with the skeg. I started the engine and shouted to Jorge to get up quickly and go ashore. Jay wound up the anchor, then while I tried to manoeuvre her to avoid hitting the rocks, he and Jorge packed Jorge's sleeping gear into a big plastic bag along with some bread and margarine, and the two of them got into the dinghy and cast off. Under a well-reefed jib, I set course for a wild, wet ride to Ypún.

Tuesday 15 November
Another sleepless night. I probably don't do my insides any good, but I find that in these circumstances I am a compulsive eater, just to keep myself awake. A biscuit and cheese, then an apple, a piece of chocolate, bread and honey, a handful of scroggin, an orange – and then if I can't think of anything else, I start again. In between, I have innumerable cups of coffee, occasionally interspersed with tea or Milo, and that is a bit of a nuisance because I am forever wanting to relieve myself.

Once again I had to face the worrying passage through the rocks of the southern pass to Ypún in the usual foul weather. Being on my own, I fetched out the Autohelm again, and before we arrived too close I took the sail off and motored so that the radar would stay more nearly horizontal and give a better picture. Even under bare poles she heeled considerably in the strong gusts, but I am getting more used to how the place looks on the screen and can pick the breakers over sunken rocks out of the clutter of broken water all around. With the naked eye it was quite hopeless, and in any case I could not see into the driving rain. Finally I arrived safely in Puerto Scotchwell and dropped the anchor at about 0400 hours.

I did not get out of my bunk until nearly 0830 hours, and then I cooked myself a pot of porridge. Seeing the sky looked much better, I set off back to Guamblín as soon as I had eaten. To save time I took the short cut between the small south-east island and Ypún, clearing the rocks without too many scares. Jay told me on the VHF that he and Jorge had the camp packed up and ready, so it took only an hour to get everything on board and stowed. We solemnly saluted Isla Guamblín and wished 'Hasta luego' as we set full sail southward towards our next objective, Isla Tenquehuén. Shortly after that we gybed, and my second woolly hat was knocked into the sea...

Sailing down the magnificent coast in fine weather was very pleasant, and at night we could still see the great backdrop of mountains by moonlight. It was not entirely appreciated by my crew who were both trying out the new 'behind-the-ear' seasickness remedies, which seemed to make them very sleepy. After anchoring for five hours in the lee of Isla Tres Dedos (Three Fingers) to give me a chance to sleep, we carried on towards Isla Tenquehuén.

For many miles around Isla Tenquehuén the sea is strewn with rocks sticking up out of the water in all sorts of jagged shapes and sizes, with surf boiling around them in beautiful but nightmarish scenes. By the time we arrived a moderate gale was blowing, with vicious squalls, and we were pleased to enter the shelter of the 2½ mile-long, narrow inlet, with its shores wooded to the water's edge, almost severing the northern part of the island.

Isla Tenquehuén is a forested, mountainous place 8½ miles long, with two peaks nearly 700 metres high. It is surrounded by a variety of smaller islands which we thought might be good sea bird breeding spots, but although we explored for nine adventurous days, we failed to find any burrows of pelagic petrels. There were the expected colonies of Blue-eyed cormorants, Rock shags, and Magellanic penguins, and one of South American terns, together with large numbers of Oystercatchers, Kelp geese and Steamer ducks. Kelp gulls were everywhere, and the forests had a good variety of land birds. On one island we were watched by a Great-horned owl, which followed us through the bush, calling loudly to let every other bird know that we were coming.

Thursday 17 November

. . . To begin with it was fairly easy, clambering over rocks. Then we came to an area of swamp with thick vegetation – low dense bushes, and patches of stunted trees with fallen and rotting trunks and branches tangled together and covered with incredible thicknesses of mosses and lichens. Some of the mosses were quite beautiful in themselves, with reddish browns and bright greens, while some were almost white, and fluffy. There were cushion plants with small daisy-like flowers, very pretty, which Jay said were a *Lycopodium* species, with which he is familiar in the Alaskan tundra. Occasionally we saw a flowering bush of some sort, including fuchsia, which added a dash of bright scarlet to attract the lovely little hummingbirds. However it was not always easy to appreciate the beauty. . . never sure when the surface would collapse and let us down into an evil-smelling bog.

Wilson's Storm Petrels

Our compass had led us to a truly enchanting caleta with a wide sandy beach backed by sand dunes and flowering bushes at its head, and bush-topped cliffs with an interesting rocky foreshore on each side...Sitting on a log to eat our lunch, we anxiously watched a pair of Kelp geese with six downy goslings take to the water. Mother forged out through the breaking sea, disappearing under each wave that rolled in, but the babies were bowled over willy-nilly and washed right back to the beach. It looked impossible for them to reach their mother out beyond the breakers, but all six eventually made it.

During the afternoon we entered caves, climbed cliffs, forced our way under or over dense scrub, and thoroughly searched the shores of the caleta. Walking back along the beach, Jay found a large brown onion. It was a most unlikely thing to find in a place like this where so few ships pass, even well outside. It looked all right, but how old was it, and how far had it come? We have just eaten it tonight, raw, with sea eggs which Jorge had gathered and prepared with lemon juice.

Systematically we visited each of the small islands as weather permitted, anchoring and staying for a day or so at the larger ones which offered some shelter in the frequent spells of strong winds.

Sunday 20 November
...During our wanderings in the bush we were entertained by a big male Magellanic woodpecker. He is about 45 cm long, nearly all black with a bright red head and neck. He was hammering noisily at the trees with his strong bill, and calling out loudly to us as he flew from tree to tree, as if to make sure that we really admired his splendour...

When we came back to the dinghy there were two penguins standing by it on the rocks. They are a bit wary, so I took some photographs from a distance. When I had finished my film eight of them appeared and allowed us to get very close. 'Asi es la vida!' (That's life!). Jorge looked for shellfish before we returned aboard. It is instinctive for a Chilean to do this: last night he had hung a sack of abalones over the side to keep them fresh, but the string had broken and they were lost. 'In the States, that would have been fifty bucks' worth,' said Jay ruefully.

Tuesday 22 November
...When we came around the north coast of this island [Inchín Grande] we were met by a very heavy swell, and the wind was again quite strong. After passing a fearful area of rocks with huge breaking seas over them, and our ship rolling heavily, we could see a bay about half a mile wide, open to the west, but sheltered by the barrier of rocks. Not knowing how deep it might be we anxiously headed in through the wild entrance. Once we had started there was no going back, as we could not possibly turn *Totorore* around until we were well inside.

Luckily it was quite deep, and we probed into a tiny caleta around a corner at the far end. Even in the rain it was absolutely beautiful! Four Ibises flew off the beach as we came in, and we were watched by Steamer ducks on the beach and two Turkey vultures on a branch high above us.

The caleta is completely landlocked, but not very deep – only about a fathom – and not much room to swing to an anchor, so we put out a stern line to a tree clinging to a nearly vertical wall of rock.

Now in the evening the wind is really piping, so we are rolling a bit. We had intended to move into the outer bay to spotlight for birds, but the weather is too bad...

It was going to be necessary for us to make a last call at Puerto Montt for some engine and other repairs, and to change the crew. Jay had to go back to Alaska to work, and I was hoping that Andreas would come with us for the next part of the expedition. However when we left the Tenquehuén area on 25 November I considered that we had not enough fuel to take us as far as Quellón. We could sail, but it would be slow. We decided instead to go to Aysén, on the continent; by way of a short holiday which we felt we deserved we would divert to Laguna San Rafaél and observe the birds near the glacier.

In such a maze of channels the route to be taken is abitrary, and we chose an intricate and tortuous track. Many wonders we saw on the way – mountains on Isla Clemente so full of quartz that they looked like marble; we saw a small rock hosting four species of cormorant, and five flamboyant Kingfishers in a group; we passed through channels with fascinating names like Abandonados, Carrera del Diablo and Tuahuencayec. One could travel in this wonderland for many years and still find a new and exciting place to stop for the night. To be so secured in such cosy little corners, with the foliage of trees sometimes brushing our rigging and only the sounds of birds in the bush and the inevitable rocky streams or waterfalls, gave us a feeling of warm intimacy with this wild land with which I was falling in love.

Close again to the mainland we were in view of the massive icefields of San Valentín which reach an altitude of over 4000 metres and push great tongues of ice down valleys and gorges, in some places reaching the sea. I saw my first glacier as we passed through the Golfo Elefantes; it was almost seven miles away, but the sight of it stirred my childhood longings for adventure and I could not help thinking about what the future held in store as our work took us farther south. What a thrill it was to see the first chunk of ice floating out into the gulf! The tide raced strongly through the tricky passage into Bahía Elefantes, and inside there were many large pieces of ice looking cold and blue, but melting rapidly in the warm water at 10 °C.

The water itself turned to a typical green ice-melt colour as we entered the Río Tempanos (Iceberg River), which was full of small bergs with above-water sizes from that of a car to the dimensions of a two-storied house, and we marvelled to see them against a background of lush forest. We had calculated our time of passage up the river so that we would enter the lagoon with the flood tide, going in the same direction as the ice, rather than meet it all coming out at great speed. We were more than surprised to see four Black-browed mollymawks in the river, and wondered whether they had really followed the intricate channels for about 100 miles from the open sea, or flown overland from the Gulf of Penas, which seemed most unlikely in that very few pelagic birds ever fly over land.

The weather became sunny and blue-skied by the time we arrived in Laguna San Rafaél, dominated by the great glacier with a two-mile jagged ice cliff where it breaks off into the lagoon. Sailing in and out among the bergs, we admired their amazing sculptured shapes and colours. There was some interesting bird life, and in the evening we noted a single Sooty shearwater flying over the lagoon, some twelve miles overland from the open sea. It flew straight up into the forested mountains; surely there could not be a colony there?

Jay and Jorge paddled around in the dinghy, sporting with the ice, and even climbing up onto a small berg. We anchored in an upwind corner of the lagoon so that we would not be bothered by floating ice. The last birds were singing in the trees, and the stars were beginning to appear, as we sipped our glacial ice-cooled drinks in the cockpit. In the morning we explored the glacier snout, but no closer than a quarter of a mile because I had been warned that huge masses of ice sometimes break off beneath the surface and suddenly shoot up out of the water. We were lucky enough to observe some tremendous ice falls from the glacier cliff, and one huge section like a multi-spired cathedral collapsed dramatically before our eyes with a thunderous roar and an almighty splash. The great chunks of ice debris were rolling and heaving, sinking and reappearing, for several minutes in the turmoil that followed.

With the wind against us we had to tack northwards for a grand sail down Seno Aysén over the last twenty miles with the twin headsails poled out. Under sail we headed across the bar to the Río Aysén, which runs through the town of Aysén, about six miles from the mouth. The only chart I had was a small one from the Armada catalogue, which I could read only with a magnifying glass.

Tuesday 29 November
...From the start I was concerned, as we found considerably less water over the bar than that shown on the chart. At one stage there was only 0.3m under our keels, but once across the bar all was well and we had ample depth. Very frequent heavy showers obscured our view of the spectacular snowy mountains, but we could appreciate the vivid green on the low banks which had an occasional house with a boat drawn up to it. By the tables, the tide should have been following us in, but the strong current against us indicated that there had been much rain upriver. We motored, following the banks on the outside of the bends, having seen only one beacon out of nine marked on the chart...

After about five very slow miles we passed a 200 metre cliff right close to the bank...suddenly we felt the bottom. The town of Aysén should have been in full view, the main street right next to the river. I kept checking the compass, and the bearings, and the surroundings. Nothing made sense.

After several abortive efforts, we drifted back to some men fishing on the bank. 'Over there,' they said, pointing...We could see the deep water where the current was strongest, but we were pushed astern and forced to creep along the edge of the unmarked channel across a wide expanse of rushing water with numerous obstructions producing fearsome swirls and overfalls.

Several times we stuck momentarily on the mud, but by easing the throttle we were soon washed clear again. The whole thing was completely beyond my comprehension. Where was Aysén? We went around bends across grassy plains with cows and scattered trees. We could see where the banks had been planted with grassy turfs and small trees in an effort to save them. Sometimes we were caught in whirlpools, and struggled with the

81

tiller before *Totorore* was swept beam-on into the fierce torrent. Often she heeled violently over, and I wondered if she would roll right over if we hit a tree in the full strength of the flood.

Eventually we saw a suspension bridge over the river ahead, and a fishing boat and a yacht moored to a bank near a wharf...We thought the town must be ahead, but we were heading north instead of south! Close by the fishing boat we ran out of depth again and stuck on the mud. 'Where can we go?' we shouted to the man aboard. He indicated the wharf. Full astern, and we edged over to the wharf and made fast...An Armada officer came and took our zarpe...it had been a nerve-racking and bewildering four hours.

Eventually we were ready to go ashore and climbed up onto the new wharf. It was freshly coated with creosote – apparently we were the first to use it – and we got the wretched stuff all over our hands and clothes. Wandering up the unsealed roads, dodging the puddles, we passed houses and shops, small, wooden and mostly unpainted before we found the plaza, well laid out with young trees in full fresh foliage...A few better maintained buildings indicated government offices and banks.

After making enquiries we headed for the Grand Hotel de Aysén, the best in town. We were looking forward to our much-needed showers! Mine was no more than tepid, and a big disappointment. Jorge's was cold. The place seemed clean enough, but typically had paper peeling off the wall in the bathroom, the ceiling looking as though it might collapse, the shower pipe hanging on a string from a nail, and bare wires showing next to the light fitting. However we did feel cleaner and enjoyed our dinner with a glass of beer.

When we arrived back at *Totorore* a drunken Chilean followed us aboard. We asked him what he wanted and he promptly climbed the mast, right to the top! We were too tired to take much notice and went to bed. After a while we heard him climb back onto the wharf and stumble away.

Wednesday 30 November
About 0500 hours we were disturbed by movement of the boat as somebody climbed on board. Whoever it was probably thought that the boat was unattended. When we called out, he left. We were still too tired to even get up to see, but later when we got up on deck we found nothing missing, only some pretty red carnation-like flowers strewn in the cockpit...

El Capitan del Puerto was a charming fellow who spoke good English. I asked him if I could see the latest chart of the river, and he produced the full-sized version of the one that I had in the catalogue! When I explained my confusion, he told us that the course of the river had changed and flooded the town about twenty years before, so it was now in a completely different place, and farther back.

The river had become wider and shallower, and the bar was now so shallow that only very small craft could cross it. Before the big flood ships of up to 1500 tons were common, and Aysén was a regular port of call for coastal ships. As no ships could now use the river, nobody had bothered to change either the chart or the

82

Pilot! At least that explained it, but I was still surprised that even the British Pilot, (mine had corrections up to 1978) still gave the old erroneous information.

The main reason for our going to Aysén was to take aboard diesel fuel but when I asked the Capitan about it he said that we should buy it at Chacabuco, which is now the main port and is in a small bay a few miles south of the rivermouth. I said that we did not even have enough fuel left to get us there, so he very kindly lent us a car with a driver to take our empty cans to the road service station several miles away. To save our going to Chacabuco, Jorge made four trips with the driver and completely filled our tanks.

After a brief call in to Quellón to pick up mail we carried on to Puerto Montt and arrived back at Angelmó on 4 December. Jay offered to stay for a couple of days to assist with cleaning the bottom and repainting the anti-fouling, so we beached *Totorore* on Isla Tenglo at the top of the tide. When that job was completed, Jay left. He had been an excellent and knowledgeable team member and a very good friend.

It was a very busy time for me, working on the engine, having the stern bearing relined with white metal, getting the Dynastart overhauled, changing the propeller to our big three-blader and attending to various other repair jobs needed before we set off for Punta Arenas. It was going to be a longish voyage because we had important bird survey work to do on the way, especially at Isla Byron just south of the Gulf of Penas where the weather was reputed to be terrible, and at Isla Duque de York farther south. The engine had been giving a great deal of trouble, and although I requested a reputable engineering company to check it over, the two young men whom they sent did not give me much confidence.

On top of the busy work programme I had other worries. The expedition seemed to be collapsing about my ears. A letter from Alan Cowan in Canberra told me that the French Government in Paris had refused to give us permission to do any bird surveys in the French-administered islands in the Indian Ocean, for which work Alan had been going to join us. A letter from Peter Harrison said that the South African Government would not give us a permit to work on islands in the Tristan group, and that Peter himself was unable to join us in 1984 as had been planned. On the telephone I spoke to Claudio Venegas at the Instituto de la Patagonia in Punta Arenas, to advise him when we would arrive to pick him up for our arranged visit to Isla Noir – one of the most challenging and exciting projects of the whole of our expedition. He calmly told me that he would not be coming with us, as he was going to Isla Noir with American Frank Todd from the Sea World in San Diego, by helicopter in that same month, December.

All these projects had been arranged and tentatively agreed to well over a year before, so I could not help feeling that the rug had been pulled from under my feet. To add to the difficulties, I learned that Chris Sale was still unable to join me, Andreas felt that he could not spare so much time away from the farm, and Jorge felt that he must leave me because he had no money to contribute towards his food. And I had practically no money either, and there was none left in the kitty back home.

I always found that my heaviest times were when *Totorore*, was in port. On this occasion I drew courage from the thought of our most important discovery so far – the Sooty shearwaters breeding on Guafo – which made me realise that the expedition was definitely serving a useful purpose and must go on. I prayed for guidance, worked hard, and carried on with faith. Marjorie had taught me that

83

if what I was doing was right then the necessary help would manifest itself.

Things did start to change. Some donations to the expedition came in, and Marjorie was able to send me some money to pay the repair bills and buy stores. I had a talk with Jorge and asked him if he would come to Punta Arenas at no expense to himself, but told him that we would have to go without luxuries and would need to catch plenty of fish and shellfish to supplement our rations. The von Meyer family asked me to dinner at Pelluco one evening, and there I saw evidence of the strength of character and the positive outlook of Andreas's sister, Julia. She completely overruled all Andreas's reasons for not being able to come with me, saying that it was a unique opportunity for him which he could not possibly miss. Andreas had been worried about the farm's water supply, because it was an unusually dry spell for the area and their pump was broken down. Julia said that his staying home would not make it rain, and she would have somebody in to repair the pump. To lessen the time that Andreas would be away from the farm, she herself would come with me, if I agreed, for the first part of the voyage, and then change over with Andreas. Furthermore she would supply us with meat, fresh fruit and vegetables for the voyage. I was delighted. I had a full crew once more, and everything was again going well. It occurred to me that Julia might be seasick, but as I had not yet had a crew member who did not suffer from that malady, it could not make much difference.

To bring our stores and gear aboard from the office of our good agent friends, we hired a horse and cart. The cart was loose and wobbly, and like so many of the carts in Puerto Montt, the large wooden wheels looked as though they were about to fall off. It seems that the owners wait for this to happen before they do anything about the worn bearings.

At last all was ready, and even the lengthy proceedings with the Armada at an end. Jorge and Julia were aboard and the farm pump at Pelluco was working again. The only place where it would be feasible for Andreas to join us and Julia to return home was Chacabuco, where there was a road to Aysén and thence to Coihaique which has an airport with a regular plane service to Puerto Montt. At 1800 hours on 14 December, *Totorore* sailed away from Puerto Montt for the last time on the expedition.

Kelp goose

Chapter Six

Wet and Wild West Coasts

*Chacabuco — Christmas in the canals — Puerto Slight — Isla Byron —
Isla Duque de York — Isla Diego de Almagro*

The general feeling on board *Totorore* as we sailed southwards was lighthearted and happy. Thirty-six year old Julia was enjoying a brief holiday from the weight of her responsibilities on the farm, and applied herself to learning as much as she could with schoolgirlish enthusiasm. Jorge was looking forward to seeing more dolphins, and hopefully whales, and was pleased to have somebody with whom he could converse.

We sailed by day and often half the night, anchoring in some delightful spot to get some sleep. Julia put Jorge and me to shame by going for a swim early every morning before we weighed anchor, but even in the fine weather the two of us could not be tempted to join her. Because we made good speed we had some time in hand for our rendezvous with Andreas and used it to make a diversion up a canal leading well into the interior to Seno Ventisquero where we had been told there was a hot spring. This was a little disappointing because we had to wait for the tide to uncover it before we could use it; even then it was in a very small hole into which only one of us could fit at a time, but it was fun anyway.

Julia was cooking the dinner that evening when I heard her shout, 'There's water coming into the boat! It came right over my foot!' Sure enough, it was coming in fast, and was well over the sole. To reassure my anxious crew, I first of all pumped the water out and then had a look. Although we were sailing at the time, I knew it would be something to do with the engine. I found that the stern gland had shaken loose; another bolt holding a bed-bracket to the block had sheared off, and this time it was even more difficult to get at, entailing lifting the engine off its bed and removing the flywheel. To keep our rendezvous with Andreas I decided to press on and do something about it at Chacabuco. In the meantime, feeling decidedly unhappy about the constant troubles which were sent to try me, I tightened up the gland with some extra packing and resolved to use the engine only in an emergency.

Monday 19 December
Chacabuco Bay is well known for the violence of the williwaws which come down off the mountains. [A feature of high coastal areas in the Roaring

85

Forties, williwaws are multi-directional squalls of short duration, frequently reaching hurricane force.] At Chacabuco there is a small settlement, some large oil tanks, a concrete ramp for stern-loading ships, and two very dilapidated steel wharves. In spite of the fact that Aysén is closed as a port, the Armada headquarters is still there rather than at Chacabuco, so for zarpe purposes we had to call them on the VHF to come to see us. They instructed us to go along side the 'Muelle Nueva', the New Wharf, and wait. In the squally conditions, which were worsening, it was hard to tell which of the two rusty-looking structures could be called new. We chose the one which had the least number of ugly and dangerous projections...I could see some wooden piles, which looked safer for us. No sooner were we alongside than a great squall laid *Totorore* hard over against the wharf and the starboard cap shroud caught on a projection up above. We pushed and shoved, and with full revs and pounding hearts cleared the wharf. It is always difficult to get away from a lee berth and the conditions made it nasty. Only after we had anchored close off the concrete ramp did we notice that the spreader root fitting on the mast was broken...

After making arrangements for an engineer to visit us the next day I enquired about taking diesel fuel. Oh no, we would have to go to Aysén for that! At Aysén we had been told that we would have to go to Chacabuco...Eventually we had a drum brought to us from Aysén by road, which was very expensive...

The engineer was a Frenchman, Pierre Bodin. We were all most impressed with the way he tackled the job, doing the work himself and so unlike the white-coated foreman in Valparaiso. His assistant, who must have been an apprentice, passed him tools or lent a bit of muscle when required. It amazed me that in such an out-of-the-way place we could find a really capable engineer...If he had been in Valparaiso I would have been spared months of worry, weeks of extra work and delay and large amounts of money. 'Nunca es tarde,' as the Chileans say, 'Better late than never.'

Tuesday 20 December
...We should have sailed today, but this is time well spent and will probably save a great deal of anxiety in the future. Andreas arrived from Aysén by taxi, full of woes about the farm at Pelluco, so it will be good for him to be away with us for a spell...

Wednesday 21 December
To relieve the congestion on board, Julia, Andreas and Jorge went off in the dinghy to find a stream to do some washing – I was grateful that they took mine too. The wind is getting up again so I insisted that they all wore lifejackets. In the afternoon our ship was covered from end to end with garments which dried quite well in spite of showers.

Julia had brought us a 'Pan de Pascua' (Christmas bread) which is more like a fruit cake than bread, for us to eat on Christmas Day, but we felt obliged to produce it for morning and afternoon tea while Pierre and his 'muchacho' were with us. The boy was not very intelligent or efficient and Pierre was giving him a hard time. I felt sorry for him, so kept slipping him pieces of the bread until the wretched fellow was sick into the cockpit.

'You terrible boy,' shouted Pierre in Spanish. 'You must be sick over the side, not into the boat!' At that the greenfaced and miserable boy promptly vomited over the side – straight into our dinghy!

Thursday 22 December
We had a bad night with Force 10 squalls and worse, and I don't think any of us slept well. Around 0600 hours we were very close to the stone wall and in desperation I tried to sail her off, our engine still out of action. It was impossible. We had 40 fathoms of chain out, and the squalls kept coming at us from all sides, laying *Totorore* far over each time, catching the jib aback, and putting us in a very dangerous position. We never managed to get the anchor aweigh. Across the bay we could see a ship like a large landing craft with a bow ramp sheltering from the gale. I called her up on the VHF and asked for assistance. She came down to us with her bow ramp down, and her crew hove us a line from it...She towed us ahead as we wound up our anchor chain, then took us over to the other side of the bay...When we were safely anchored I called up the master to thank him. He replied that it was nothing, and wished us buen viaje and a happy Christmas! Yet another reassuring indication of this true Chilean brotherhood of the sea...

We were all concerned for Julia who had to catch her plane from Coihaique at 1700 hours and did not want to miss it and her family Christmas celebrations...Luckily the squalls became less frequent in the afternoon and we were able to sail back to the ramp and get Julia ashore. We were sorry to see her go – she was bright company, a good crew, and, very important, a good cook!

Pierre had fabricated an extra-heavy bracket to avoid further trouble with the engine mounting brackets, fitting it between the flywheel and the block. He also welded up our broken spreader fitting. The barometer was falling and I had no wish to spend a williwaw Christmas in Chacabuco, so we thankfully weighed anchor at midday on Christmas Eve.

Out in Seno Aysén the wind freshened to 40 knots with driving rain, but our engine was sound and the three-bladed propeller gave us the power to forge ahead. In Canal Pilcomayo we passed a large container ship which loomed up out of the rain and exchanged 'Happy Christmases' with her on the VHF. The sea was wild as we crossed the four-mile-wide Canal Moraleda, but we had the pleasure of seeing large numbers of Black-browed mollymawks and nineteen Pink-footed shearwaters, which was very unexpected, and exciting.

After we had entered the unsurveyed and seldom used Canal Carrera del Cuchi, the wind dropped right away. We found our way into an inlet on the northern side and passed among so many small wooded islands and rocks that we wondered if we could find our passage out in the morning.

Sunday 25 December 1983
Christmas Day, and raining with poor visibility. We sailed out into the channels again in the cold grey light with warm thoughts of those at home, and rain trickling down our necks. A Steamer duck with seven small

ducklings in line astern all paddled splashily away from us, to our great amusement.

On the chart a narrow channel between Isla Palumbo and Isla Quemada looked passable: about 3.5 miles long, and with only one really narrow place near the start, which we negotiated without difficulty...

Instead of the exit about 200 metres wide as on the chart, it was more like 30 metres, and about half a mile long. What made it worse was the current going through in our direction at about six knots. With trembling hand and beating heart, I headed her in. The current swirled us around alarmingly, and I had to keep the engine going quite strongly to maintain steerage and avoid fouling the mast in the overhanging trees...As we passed over rocks the depth on the echo-sounder registered at a bare 1.5 metres, which had me sweating! We had no brakes, and could only hope that we could see the extra swirls around rocks that had less water over them. Jorge and Andreas were both up in the bow keeping a lookout, although Andreas could not help himself from watching for birds. Eventually we shot out at the other end, swirling round in a whirlpool...

We crossed Canal Darwin, a shipping route, but I prefer unfrequented places so we soon dived back into the more interesting and little-known channels between hundreds of unnamed islands. The wind freshened again, and fierce williwaws blasted at us from the mountains, laying *Totorore* far over at times...We joked about our 'regalos de Navidad' (Christmas presents) as each one struck us. I can't help loving this place even in this weather. There is a magnificent beauty in the shades of grey of the rain, the swirling clouds over the dark mountains, and the grey sea with white broken wave-crests...

We finally arrived at Puerto Refugio, tired from a rough passage; even in the bay, protected by islands from the ocean beyond, a big sea followed us in. At the head of the bay is a curved inlet called Caleta Lobato where the sea flattened right down. The inlet is sheltered all around by high mountains, the upper parts bare rock, and close by a tremendous waterfall roars down from among the trees. There are still squalls, but we feel secure with 30 fathoms of chain on our big Bruce anchor in only five fathoms of water. It was already 2100 hours when we anchored but we still enjoyed our Christmas dinner.

A few days ago Jorge had gone ashore on an island and come back with a small sapling of the beautifully shaped and coloured Huenque tree, which he put in a tin and lashed onto the centre swinging part of our cabin table. Last night he produced tinsel and glass baubles from his locker, which he had secreted away to decorate his Christmas tree. It was quite touching to see the care which he took...

We each had two glasses of whisky before dinner, which consisted of our dried and salted pork with potatoes and carrots. I would have added onions but neither of my Chilean crew likes them. Jorge had boiled the pork for a long time, but it was hard to cut and I had to lend him a saw. We had to hold it with both hands and tear at it with our teeth and all the strength we could muster in our jaws, and could not help growling like dogs with bones...the considerable work chewing each hard-won morsel before it could be swallowed precluded any form of conversation. Both Andreas and

Jorge, who must be used to it, appeared to enjoy it. They call it 'Charqui', which brings to mind the name 'jerky' used by Australians and by bushmen in New Zealand. It was followed by my special 'postre', or sweet, consisting of Julia's fruit loaf with pawpaw conserve and a sauce made of chocolate instant pudding into which I had mixed some rum...

Nobody suggested that our salt pork and boiled potatoes was not a fine Christmas feast; I think the whisky assisted with the illusion, and in the cabin it was warm and dry...we drank a toast to our families far away, and went to our bunks thinking of home.

The next day we were weatherbound in Caleta Lobato, knowing that the outer coast would be too dangerous. Jorge and Andreas went in the dinghy to look for birds and to do some fishing, even though it was pouring with rain. When the wind changed and blew right into our inlet and they did not come back, I became worried. One of the oars had broken, and paddling back with a single oar was a slow and tiring process. They were both soaked and cold on their return, so I gave them each a cup of hot laced coffee.

When the weather improved we sailed on down the exposed coast of the Taitao Peninsula, the only part of the whole Chilean Archipelago where there is no sheltered inside route, rolling violently in the swell. We saw more Pink-footed shearwaters, and in one bay a pair of Pied-billed grebes, thus extending the known range of both species. As we passed the Cabo Raper lighthouse, perched on a cliffy headland, we were accompanied by thousands of Sooty shearwaters. We called the lighthouse keepers and asked if two of us could spend a night at the lighthouse to observe the birds when we arrived on the other side of the peninsula.

Wednesday 28 December
...With some excitement we approached the Golfo de Penas, the infamous and dreaded 'Gulf of Sorrows'...The massive Cabo Tres Montes loomed high ahead of us, and as we passed the great cape I blew a blast on the foghorn and we all cheered. The wind died on us completely and we wallowed in the swell; Andreas and Jorge reckoned that my blast had killed it.

After we had tucked *Totorore* into a landlocked cove in Puerto Barroso we hacked a track through the forest to the outer shore where we were well entertained by an unselfconscious trio of 'Chungungos' (sea otters). Their antics seemed to be pure play, and their lithe bodies moved with such grace that one could almost hear symphonic music when watching them. One of them climbed up onto a rock with a large crab, at least 30 cm across its legs, and played with it like a toy. Later he took it back into the water and lying on his back, clutched it to his chest. I could not help feeling rather sorry for the crab. What was so delightful was that the Chungungos completely ignored us, probably because the usual bad weather here keeps hunters away. In other places they are hunted extensively for their skins, and as a result are shy and hard to observe.

In the evening, Andreas told us about their farm. Apparently thieves are always a problem, and they have to bring their cows into a big barn and lock them up every night. Once four cows were stolen and Andreas and a farmhand were taken around by the carabineros in a jeep trying to locate the thieves. They came across three suspicious-looking men with long knives and lassos; when challenged, the men bolted. One was shot dead, one escaped, and the other was caught and sent to prison. Sometimes whole fences are stolen from the farm – the wire, and even the posts!

Rain made our twenty-mile sail around to Puerto Slight, only three miles from Cabo Raper lighthouse, far from pleasant, but we arrived in time to meet three keepers who had come to escort Andreas and Jorge to the lighthouse. I then took *Totorore* to a safer place in Caleta Buena and went for an exploratory walk ashore. In a rocky stream bed there had been a land slip, so I was able to climb well up the hill to see the magnificent view – a privilege that is seldom possible in these densely forested places.

Friday 30 December
I sailed back to rendezvous with my crew at Puerto Slight. A little wharf was derelict, as was a small railway which once led to the lighthouse. This seemed typical, and reminded me of Guafo – serviceable installations now neglected and ruined. There were two store sheds full of materials and furniture for a new house being built near the lighthouse, to replace one which was blown over the cliff last year. A track of rocks and mud led through a tunnel under the trees across the isthmus and up to the lighthouse on the other side. Soon I heard the sound of an engine, and a small tractor towing a trailer with my crew and three other men came jolting into view. I entertained two of them aboard *Totorore* while the other took Andreas and Jorge to see the skeleton of a Sei whale, farther along the beach. Apparently two or three strand there every year, and they are often seen passing the lighthouse.

Up at the lighthouse my lucky crew had enjoyed hot showers. Jorge went to see a large colony of Sea-lions and Andreas watched for birds. Between 1700 and 2300 hours Sooty shearwaters had passed the cape at an average rate of 400 per minute...As at Guafo there is a small farmlet near the lighthouse, and in the house they used to have a pet 'Pudu', a miniature deer, as a mascot but they had eaten it.

We were invited to celebrate New Year with the keepers – they were going to kill a calf – but I was anxious to press on while the weather is still good. Out in the gulf there was nowhere very suitable for a night's anchorage before Bahía San Quintín, where we sailed into a small sheltered corner of Caleta San Tomás at 0130 hours, the great glacier visible with a ghostly light in the darkness.

In the Golfo de Penas we explored parts of the coast and sailed well out into the gulf to see the birds, all in incredibly calm weather. Jorge caught a fine 'Sierra', which is a fish like a barracuda, about one metre long and very good to eat. It was not until we were approaching Isla Byron that the weather cut up rough, with poor visibility and rain.

Sunday 1 January 1984
...At last one of our major goals, and not any easy one. It is the least known and the least surveyed of all our intended islands for study, and

90

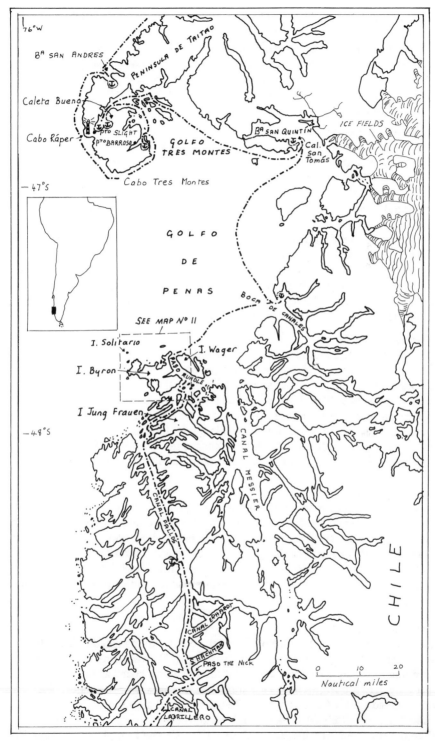

Map 10

91

there are no details available. The approaches are strewn with rocks and islets, and from a distance it does not look very high...

With Jorge in the bow we sailed on with just a heavily reefed jib, and only once had to start the engine to clear some bad rocks. The chart is so vague and incorrect that I had some difficulty in locating the entrance to Paso Rundle, between Isla Wager and Isla Byron. Eventually we found the way, and sailed thankfully into shelter.

Monday 2 January
Close to Isla Solitario, a wild and inaccessible rock island, we were thrilled to see nine Rockhopper penguins swimming and diving quite close to us...a little later we saw another five. Then Andreas said, 'Look at the third cormorant past the Chimango (common small carrion hawk) on top of the island!' and sure enough, it really looked like a penguin! Could it possibly be? It seemed too fantastic to think there might be some Rockhoppers breeding here, and it definitely was not a Magellanic penguin. With the considerable movement of the boat we could not hold our binoculars steady and came away only partly convinced. It might have been a Rock shag, sitting with his shoulders hunched. In any case, even without a colony, it is extraordinary to see Rockhoppers in the Golfo de Penas, far to the north of their previously known range.

Tuesday 3 January
Full of good intentions to make some onshore exploration, but with a falling barometer, a gale and pouring rain, our enthusiasm waned. We set up our cockpit tent, which is a tremendous asset, and did some maintenance jobs. The north wind has found us in here, and it is rather like being at sea, but I assure my crew that we are more comfortable than outside. Jorge was sick and retired to his bunk. I am always amazed at how he can fit into it, because with the bunkboard up it really looks full. Amongst other things in it he keeps a broom handle to poke Andreas when he snores...

Jorge collected specimens of a small rat, a frog and some tadpoles to take back to the university for study. In places the island was covered with dense impenetrable forest or scrub, and in other parts it was tundra with bogs and only low vegetation of mosses and lichens. The many lakes appeared to be almost lifeless, but we did find one with Ashy-headed geese, and a White-tufted grebe. On a sunny day we returned to Isla Solitario, and straight away saw two unmistakeable Rockhoppers on a ledge.

Thursday 5 January
Landing was difficult because of the swell, but Jorge managed to get ashore after being immersed up to his waist by a wave. He had some tricky rock climbing to do, and Andreas and I watched from on board as he crawled like a fly across a frightening face about ten metres above the water. We both agreed that it was not for us! He then crossed a rock bridge and gained the separate part of the island where the birds were, more rugged than the rest, and terminating in sheer cliffs. We saw him photographing penguins, and then trying to catch one. I had given him a sack, but I rather

wished that I had not because the penguins are very quick and his frantic leaps on the rocks suggested he would follow the penguins down a bouncy route with a long drop into the sea – the way two of them went. We saw him do a real rugby tackle, and then hold up a penguin by its bill and a flipper to show us...

To actually have a live Rockhopper to photograph and measure in this place was beyond my wildest hopes...we extracted him from the sack, and Andreas, wearing gloves, held him while I took measurements. Occasionally he tried to bite, but really he was surprisingly docile and let out few squawks of bad temper. When not being handled he just padded about on the cockpit seats, eyeing us in a friendly and curious way...

Jorge told us that he had seen eleven adults and six chicks, right on top where they could not be seen from below. The photographs will provide proof. Fantastic! Not a big colony, but an extremely interesting new record. It really makes me think about how many things we must miss...When we popped our little friend over the side he shot away like a torpedo.

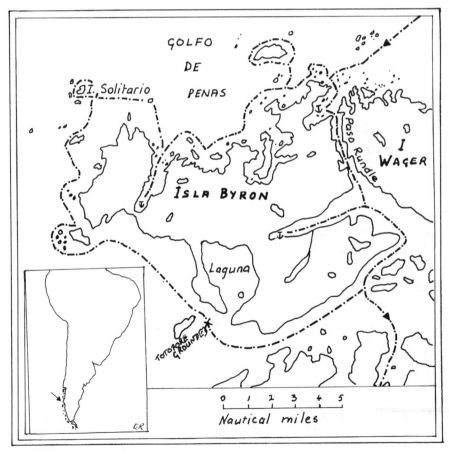

Map 11

To complete our inspection of the coastal areas from the sea, we circumnavigated Byron while we had the chance. The south coast was even less surveyed than the north, and the vague shape on the chart bore very little resemblance to the reality.

...With Jorge at the masthead we threaded our way between the rocks, and as we passed through a channel between a long, low island and the sand beaches on a bank surrounding a vast area of wetlands on Byron, the soundings steadily decreased. I could see breakers well ahead, but in the lee of the island there was neither swell nor breakers, so I thought there must be a channel.

To slow her down, I took all sail off except a small jib, and we felt our way along with very little water beneath our keels. Suddenly she bumped several times, fortunately on sand; Jorge pointed out a deeper channel but we could not reach it and she stuck fast, bumping heavily as the bigger swells now came at her round the island.

It was most unpleasant, and very worrying. The tide seemed to be dropping and the wind freshening, and I had horrible visions of *Totorore* being later battered to pieces in the unforgiving breakers. We put our big Bruce anchor and chain into the dinghy for Jorge to row out, but then a bigger swell lifted *Totorore* and swung her around towards the land again. I gave the engine full throttle and we moved, bump by bump and hopefully back the way we had come.

It was no use. The tide had fallen, and there was no way back. The seas were beginning to break around us; we had to cross the bank, which extended for about two miles and was studded with rocks. Moving only as each sea lifted her, the boat edged jarringly ahead and after an hour and a half we finally made it to deep water. 'Grace a Dios,' I said to my companions, and they agreed.

A long inlet leads from the east coast right into the centre of the island, a good safe place for *Totorore* and an excellent base for exploratory excursions. It was a joy to be able to walk over hills from which we could see all around, instead of always being blind to the view in smothering forest. We could see a lagoon about three miles wide, open to the sea at one point and bordered by a sandy beach. It just had to be a good place for wading birds.

Sunday 8 January

...Following the track we had already cut through the narrow forest fringe, we soon came out onto the open wetlands and squelched our way between the numerous ponds and bogs, using floating clumps of cushiony moss-like plants as stepping stones. A false step and we sank to our thighs in cold muddy water...On the shore of the lagoon it was easier going, being low tide; we walked across wide sandflats, sometimes wading in shallow water and sometimes stumbling over rocks. The wind was bitterly cold and brought with it stinging showers of hail or heavy rain, whipping up white wavelets over the shallow lagoon.

There were plenty of birds to keep us interested. Lots of Winter plovers, Baird's sandpipers, Sanderlings, Speckled teal, a Snipe, and most

94

interestingly, hundreds of Red phalaropes. Apart from our own observations at Guafo, this is the first real confirmation of these south of Chiloé. They were so tame that we could approach to within about two metres and saw that they were behaving just like waders, even mixing with the Sanderlings and Baird's sandpipers. They were well scattered along the shore, and often flew up and away across the island...

There were several rivers to wade and by the time we reached the gap where the lagoon opens to the sea, which looked very rough outside, we were pretty tired. We did not arrive back at *Totorore* until 2030 hours and as we rowed out to her, Jorge shouted out 'Té or café?' A welcome call! Climbing aboard, we could smell the dried pork and rice dinner which he was cooking, but the dominant smell was more like that of a wet dog as we removed our sodden trousers and socks in the cockpit. Two hot cups of tea and dry clothes, and we fell upon our reference books and felt much better. A good walk and a good day. I have not been getting much exercise, and I really needed that and the mental relaxation that went with it.

Monday 9 January

Raining again. We motored through the maze of uncharted islands in the northern group of Jung Frauen, one eye on the sounder, hand on the throttle: rather fun, really...We could have gone outside the lot, but it was still rough in the open sea and we preferred the shelter.

...I felt quite sad as I looked for the last time at Byron through a veil of rain. Above the wet green forest belt I could see the brown hills and mountains and thought of the lonely open tundra-like wastes in between. We were probably the first people to land on it for many years, and maybe the last for years to come. Again I felt frustrated at not having seen all of it, nor having uncovered all of its secrets. Our visit was too brief, but I feel that if we stayed longer we might miss too much on Duque de York, with most breeding birds fledging already...

Down Canals Fallos and Ladrillero we sailed in the rain. Apart from Jung Frauen islands, many names were suggestive of early German navigators – Canal Erhardt, Seno Hachman, Isla Stubbenkammer, Monte Siegfried – and a few Russians or Poles: Cabo Ligowsky, Cabo Boguslawski. There were also some English names – Paso 'The Nick', for example. We kept seeing Red phalaropes right through the canals, and many Sooty shearwaters, which increased to enormous numbers when we came out into Golfo Ladrillero for a short spell of open-coast sailing. The scientific name for Sooty shearwaters is *Puffinus griseus*, which we normally shortened to 'Griseus'. So used did he become to saying this that when Andreas was passed a cup of tea or a biscuit he would absently reply 'Griseus' instead of 'Gracias'. I found it very difficult to feed Andreas and Jorge because there were so many foods they would not eat, such as porridge and onions. I liked to use Vegemite, a tasty yeast extract, as a spread on bread or as a flavouring in stews or soups, but Andreas disliked it intensely. Once, when I took the lid off the pot, he said 'The smell makes me like a bull to shudder!' For most of the rest of the expedition, I and my crew referred to Vegemite as 'Bull Shudder'.

95

One evening, anchored in Bahía Flotten off Canal Picton we spotted an Alacaluf house among the trees on an island, and determined to visit it in the morning.

Wednesday 11 January
...We rowed ashore in the pouring rain, having joked about spreading tacks on the deck last night, in the manner of Joshua Slocum, and whether arrows would puncture our dinghy. Now we were nearing the island we really did wonder what sort of a reception we might receive from the very isolated, now rare, and apparently shy people. We found the dwelling empty, but it looked reasonably new and had obviously been occupied recently. It reminded me of the early Maori whares of New Zealand. Thatched with rushes over a framework of straight saplings, it comprised a simple gabled roof; well sheltered by trees, one end was open. Inside was an open fireplace in a hole in the centre of the earth floor, lined with round stones. Above was a large shelf. The beds were on the floor, framed by logs and filled with cushiony fibrous roots, just as the Maoris had used 'mingimingi', a climbing fern. It looked like a pleasant spot, but not in the winter...

Isla Duque de York is a mountainous island about twenty miles long and twelve wide, much indented with inlets and bays. The south and west coasts are exposed to the open ocean and are ceaselessly battered by the westerly winds. These winds also bring rain, and Duque de York has one of the heaviest annual rainfalls in the world, nine metres! We were not very surprised that there did not seem to be many land birds – what sort of bird would want to live here?

Thursday 12 January
Motoring up Canal Oeste the wind increased to gale force and the rain and spray made it difficult to appreciate the cliffy grandeur of the huge island on our port side, a violet colour when we could see it. We entered this two-mile-long unsurveyed fjord, about a quarter of a mile wide, near the western end of the canal...innumerable waterfalls cascade into the fjord, and a big one spills over a ledge only about 35 metres up, so we guess that there is a lake up there which must be explored...

Jorge had caught another Sierra today and we fried it for dinner. While we were eating it the first of innumerable violent williwaws hit us with tremendous force and plates and cutlery went flying. *Totorore* heeled far over and the wind screamed, but above it we could hear the loud growl of the anchor chain dragging over the rocky bottom. I did not like it at all, and neither did my crew. What a welcome to Duque de York! And we had already named the fjord Seno Totorore!

Friday 13 January
We are keeping anchor watches, and I am writing this until 0200 hours, when I call Jorge. This is a heck of a date to be worrying about the anchor holding, or the chain breaking in these terrible squalls...

By 1000 hours the squalls had almost ceased, so we moved over to explore the waterfall and the lake above, but saw no birds. Just north of Duque de York is

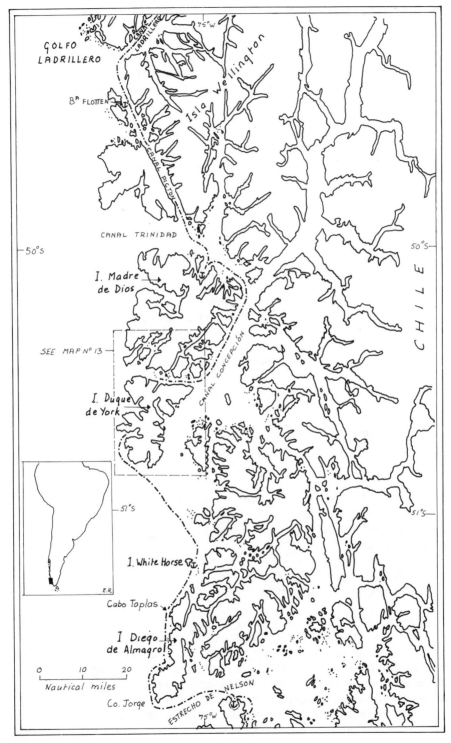

Map 12

97

an island named Guarello where there is a limestone mine operated by a staff of about sixty men in the only inhabited place for hundreds of miles. I wanted to see if we could buy some diesel fuel from the mine since we were only eight miles away. As we sailed across to Bahía Corbeta Papudo we thought we could see snow on the mountains, but it was the colour of the limestone itself of which the whole island and most of the much larger island of Madre de Dios consist. All the miners have to do is blast it, break it up into small pieces and load it into ships.

...The mine itself and the living accommodation are not too hideous, and do not greatly detract from the beauty of the bay and its surrounding mountains. We were well received by the Administrator and his staff, who proudly showed us all around the whole establishment and invited us to stay in their luxuriously appointed accommodation where each man has his own room with bathroom attached! There is accommodation for 100 men, with an enormous kitchen, separate bakery, and a modern laundry with permanent staff, all joined by centrally heated corridors. We saw a large gymnasium, and every possible sport facility. The doctor showed us his hospital with every imaginable piece of equipment − but no patients. He is very voluble, and we think he is a little mad! It is all so incredible...in this faraway, isolated place it just does not seem real!

After hot showers we joined the seven administrative staff members for dinner, the most sumptuous meal I have had for a very long time. It was served by a white-coated Italian waiter, with plenty of excellent wine. Afterwards they showed us a video film of birds in the Chilean National Parks. Jorge and Andreas slept ashore, and I returned to look after *Totorore*.

Saturday 14 January
Today we were driven to the top of the mountain and shown over the efficiently operated mine. The limestone is blasted and bulldozed from the mountain top and pushed down a deep pit shaft where it falls to enormous crushers and graders inside the centre of the mountain. From there it is brought along conveyor belts, through a long tunnel, straight into the bulk loader which empties it into the ships' holds. Everything is powered by electricity suplied by big diesel generators, taken from a German battleship many years ago.

I was anxious to get to work on the west coast of Duque de York while the weather was good, but after we had bought our diesel and filled our tanks, the electrician offered to have a look at our faulty Dynastart...

For the two-and-a-half weeks we stayed at Duque de York it rained every day. We anchored in a host of inlets and coves and climbed bleak mountains, floundered across bogs, tramped along shores, and found few birds. The heavy swell on the west coast never once eased enough for us to make a close examination of much of the shoreline; on several occasions we tried to approach, but the big breakers started far offshore, sometimes in 10 fathoms depth.

One day when we were far into the island in Seno Francisco, we could not get our trusty Bruce anchor to hold on the rocky bottom in the strong williwaws. Even when we had two good sternlines to trees, the squalls coming from different

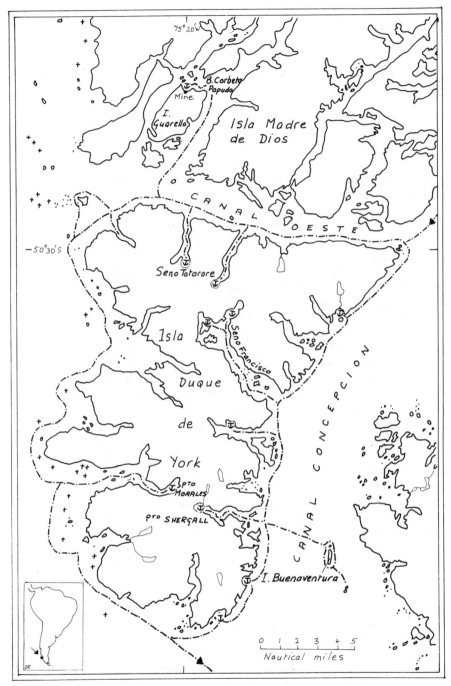

Map 13

directions pushed *Totorore* shorewards. It was then that we first tried our system of tandem anchors, using our CQR kedge anchor with six metres of chain shackled to the crown of the Bruce. It worked wonders and we continued to use it like that from then on.

Entering Puerto Shergall we were extremely surprised to find a yacht already at anchor; the first we had seen since Puerto Montt.

Wednesday 18 January

...In case she had one (she did not) I tried to call *Mazeppa* on the VHF. I was astounded to hear *Totorore* mentioned in a conversation, and listening carefully I heard a fishing boat spell out our name to the Armada at Punta Arenas! She is the boat we had seen in Canal Trinidad a week ago, and was reporting us. To be able to hear Punta Arenas, about 220 miles away across innumerable high mountains, was an incredible freak reception, apart from the coincidence of listening in to a report about ourselves. [Normally the VHF range is barely 30 miles.] I called Punta Arenas immediately afterwards and gave our position, and then advised our ETA at Punta Arenas. The wretched operator did not even express surprise!

Before embarking on our shore expedition we rowed over to *Mazeppa* to say hello and were invited to a meal in the evening. When we arrived back at *Totorore* from our walk at about 2000 hours, wet and tired as usual, we were in a bit of a quandary: how to make ourselves a little more presentable to visit the other yacht? We are very conscious of our smelly gumboots, and thinking of how unpleasant it would be if we all removed our boots in their cabin, we put on clean socks and shoes instead, in spite of the fact that we would get them, and our trousers, wet in the dinghy going across. Anyway, we need not have bothered...Yannick Trancart and his crew, Joe Adams from California, certainly would not have cared! We had a swig or two of brandy straight from the bottle and enjoyed a plate of rice with them – at least I had an enamel plate, Andreas a saucepan lid, and Yannick ate his out of the saucepan...

He has been sailing his steel boat around the world with one other crew member – Joe is his third – for three years. She is fifteen metres long and is a schooner of the Damien class, with a large drop-keel for which the wire raising-cables run horizontally across the main living space at about stomach height. To my way of thinking, they are doing things the hard way – they do not even have a dinghy, so seldom go ashore except in the big ports. They have no self-steering gear, no radio, no electric lights, and no echo-sounder. They spoke of the bad night last night when they came in here and could scarcely make way against the gale, with their 70 horsepower diesel, and Joe heaving the lead all the way in. They have a 45-kilogram CQR anchor, but it dragged.

Joe produced some nice hot scones – a luxury for us – and Yannick kept us interested with tales of his travels. The original purpose of his voyage was a cultural exchange with China, which he said had been satisfactorily concluded. He told us about his week's stay in the crater of St Paul's Island, and the incredible hospitality he received at Kerguelen, for which he gave me two charts...he and Joe are going to sail direct to Antarctica...

100

Sunday 22 January

Close to our stern I can see some flowers of the Coicopihue, very similar to the Copihue which is the national flower of Chile. It is a most remarkable climber with small hard leaves and a lot of beautiful pink bell-shaped flowers about six centimetres long, and in full bloom this month. It can be seen on the shores, or climbing high on trees in the forest and over rotting fallen trunks and moss-covered branches, on low bushes or tree stumps in the swampy places, and even a few flowers on little sprigs struggling to survive among the rocks high up on the mountains. It is heartwarming to see them everywhere, especially when one is cold and wet and everything else looks so dismal.

Perhaps our most exciting find in this area was on Isla Buenaventura, a steep and almost inaccessible small island, 100 metres high, on the other side of Canal Concepción from Duque de York. On its steep slopes there was a large colony of Rockhopper penguins, and mixed in with them, a smaller colony of Macaroni penguins! There were even Magellanic penguins on the same island, and Rock shags, and a very large colony of Blue-eyed cormorants. The important scientific fact which emerged from our observations was that the fledging Blue-eyed cormorants looked exactly like King cormorants, and this is what has obviously given rise to the considerable differences of opinion among ornithlogists concerning the geographical range of the two species. The discovery of breeding Macaronis was additionally important new data on a species which until only a few years earlier had not been known to breed in Chile at all.

On 29 January we left wet Duque de York and sailed south, off the wild outer coast, and anchored for the night in the lee of Isla White Horse. I wanted to have a look at the coast of Isla Diego de Almagro, an island about the same size as Duque de York and similarly projecting out into the ocean. Having failed to find any albatrosses on Duque de York I still thought there might be a chance of there being some on Diego. The Armada had forbidden us to go to that island, for undisclosed reasons, but I could see no harm in our observing the coast as we sailed past.

Monday 30 January

...Dodging big breakers over rocks, we thought how lucky we were to have such a good day as this for seeing Diego de Almagro...As we passed the first capes of the island it rained and we could not see much, so went in very close to Cabo Toplas and its rocky offshore islet. Reaching for my binoculars I said to Andreas, 'What are those white spots on the island?' 'They look like Black-backed gulls.' 'No, it is too far away to be able to see Black-backs.' Then I got my binoculars focussed on them and shouted, 'They are Black-brows. Hooray!' It was a tremendous moment – a moment of triumph. Andreas and I literally jumped for joy. This is just what we had been hoping for, for weeks! There have been so many flying around that we felt they must have a breeding place somewhere near. The closest previously known breeding place is on Ildefonso Island, in the Drake Passage, about 350 miles away...

We went right into the wild backwash off the rocks to have a close look and make sure. They were definitely Black-browed mollymawks, five

101

adults and two chicks on nests. There were more of these beautiful albatrosses flying around, so we passed through the turbulent gap between the island and Diego, and as the other side came into view we whooped and slapped each other on the back. Even Jorge caught the mood. Dozens – and then hundreds! A most unlikely-looking habitat in parts, being on steep well vegetated cliffs, with some of the nests only about fifteen metres above the sea. Fantastic! Had the weather been as bad as usual we would have been in the inside canals and never seen these at all...

Carrying on down the coast of Diego de Almagro we passed other widely separated capes with Black-brows, and estimated a total of 30,000 birds for the whole island.

In the Estrecho de Nelson (Nelson Strait) there was not much wind and we were sailing slowly when suddenly Jorge cried out, 'Ballenas!' (Whales!) Action stations! Jorge went to the masthead with his camera and I started the engine to motor in pursuit. Altogether there were seven, but we only came near to three. They were Humpbacks and they showed themselves beautifully, so that we saw their huge heads, and tails with white underneath. This was a real bonus for Jorge, and indeed for all of us. We were also noticing Fur seals now instead of Sea-lions, and quite large numbers frequently followed us, porpoising like penguins. The Chileans call them 'lobos de dos pelos', Sea-lions with two skins.

Because of the uncertainty of the weather and lack of shelter, we did not continue down the outer coast but dived into the canals. We spent a night in the Grupo Cuarenta Díaz islands (Forty Days) so called because a relief vessel with stores for the Evangelistas lighthouse close by once had had to wait there for this length of time during exceptionally bad weather before she could go out to the lighthouse. On Wednesday 1 February 1984 we entered the Magellan Strait: a new phase of our expedition was about to start.

Pudu

102

Dwarfed by the lovely brigantine *Breeze*, *Totorore* lies in the historic Stone Store Basin at Kerikeri before the start of the expedition.

Apart from the sailing, it was good to be out among the birds. Myself in the Southern Ocean. *Mike Hurst*

White Island is an active volcano. While we were photographing this, a sudden wind change blew the vaporous gases in our direction, nauseating us with the stench of sulphurous fumes.

Sailing down the west coast of Más Afuera was a wonderful visual experience, and we looked with awe at the enormous cliffs.

We heard Bill shout a joyous "Oi, oi, oi!" as he released the Cook's petrel which he had taken from a burrow. *John Atkinson*

Peruvian pelican. *Jim Watt*

Our landing place at Quebrada Casas, an untidy collection of huts used by cray fishermen in the season, but now deserted.

A village in Estero Reloncaví. *Jim Watt*

Two Steamer ducks paddle splashily away, beating the water with alternate wings. *Jim Watt*

Chilean flamingoes. *Jim Watt*

Isla Guafo. Covered with almost impenetrable forest. *Jim Watt*

Green-backed fire-crown hummingbird. *Jim Watt*

Andreas von Meyer '...an outstanding memory about anything to do with birds.'

Dolphin gulls. Found only in southern South America and the Falklands, these gulls frequent colonies of penguins and cormorants from which they steal eggs. *Jim Watt*

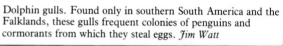

Roberto Schlatter who is one of the leading ornithologists in Chile – I was grateful for his enthusiasm and encouragement.

Black oystercatcher, a pair of Kelp geese (white gander), and a Turkey vulture on Guafo. *Jim Watt*

Magellanic oystercatcher. Their melancholy cry seems so fitting on lonely beaches. *Jay Nelson*

Laguna San Rafaél. It was fun sailing in and out among the icebergs and admiring the variety of their sculptured shapes and colours. *Jay Nelson*

Sailing in San Rafaél. *Jay Nelson*

I enjoy a hot spring in Seno Ventisquero.
Julia von Meyer

Exploring in Duque de York. Jorge and Andreas land to hack their way through the dripping forest.

Isla Noir is a wild place, difficult of access.

An exciting moment when we find our
first Giant petrel nests. Andreas on Noir.

A tiny gap between the rocks led us into this
mirror smooth haven, in Isla Desolación!

Isla Guarello. We were very impressed by the
ultra modern facilities in this faraway, isolated
place.

Caleta Julia. The rafagas hurtled at us, and I wondered how the anchor could possibly hold. *Anthea Goodwin*

In a caleta off Canal Beagle. We gazed in awe at the stupendous display of beauty all around us.

Anthea Goodwin ascending to camp on the peak of Cape Horn.

Moving slowly with the engine, the ice crackled around the bow and pieces tinkled as they skittered away across the surface. Julia.

Chapter Seven

Discoveries in Dangerous Waters

Magellan Strait – Bahía Wodsworth – Seno Helado – Punta Arenas –
Isla Noir – Back to Punta Arenas

The very name of the Magellan Strait stirs the imagination almost as much as that of Cape Horn, conjuring up pictures of bluff-bowed, square-rigged ships struggling against foul weather and fierce storms. Looking across the Strait I could visualise great Spanish galleons, and Indian canoes paddling along the shores. Since the opening of the Panama Canal, the volume of shipping which uses the Strait has been much reduced. It is however still a very important waterway, and the oil rigs sprouting up in the eastern part of the Strait have brought an appreciable resurgence of shipping, now mostly tankers. Travelling in the Strait we saw on average one ocean-going ship every day.

Our first stop in the Magellan Strait was in Bahía Wodsworth, Isla Desolación.

Wednesday 1 February
...The inlet is backed by a dark and sombre mountain wall, with a spectacular waterfall 260 metres high. Once inside, we followed the shore round to the other side of Peninsula Jorge to the bottom of the fall. What a wonderful sight! We are in a closed private lake – such a small entrance that I bet no other yacht has ever been here before us. The water is what the Chileans call 'Como una taza de leche', like a cup of milk...

We kept a continuous record while in the Strait of all the birds we saw, noting Great shearwaters – a new record – White-chinned petrels and Sooty shearwaters, though frequently our eyes wandered to the magnificent mountains, waterfalls and glaciers.

Tuesday 2 February
...Andreas sucks happily at his maté through a sculptured silver 'bombilla', a pipe which has a strainer at the bottom specially for maté. Made in a bowl, the chopped leaves of maté are soaked in hot water, like tea, but swell and fill the bowl. The liquid is then sucked up through the bombilla from the bottom. Normally the bowl is passed around those present and each has a suck or two, more hot water being poured on as necessary. Roberto had brought his own, and sometimes Jay and I shared it to be sociable. Julia had one too, but Jorge takes it only very occasionally.

It is very much a South American social custom; maté is a mild drug, said to be a stimulant...Andreas says that he takes it to avoid indigestion.

...We have come into the territory of the King cormorants, and we examined many colonies. One particularly amazing sight was in Canal David, where we came across a gathering of over 1000 Black-browed mollymawks and over 100 Chilean skuas and, incredibly, a single Blue petrel. We could not understand why one of the most pelagic of all ocean birds should be so far into the channels, about 50 miles from the open sea.

Friday 3 February

...We started to see lumps of floating ice, which became more numerous as we followed large flocks of King cormorants, flying low over the water in straight lines or V-formations, into Seno Helado (Icy Inlet). We had to slow down to about one knot as we dodged in and out...in places the growlers were so thick that we could not avoid touching them. Eventually we arrived in the basin at the glacier face, where a mighty wall of jagged blue ice, divided into two arms by a massive rock, reached high up into a vast icefield which stretched away out of sight into the clouds...making loud cracking and groaning noises on either side of us. Occasionally, with a thunderous roar a great avalanche of ice tumbled down into the basin, but there were no huge bergs calving off the glacier as there were at San Rafaél. On the big rock between the two arms of ice was a very large colony of King cormorants – we could not count how many thousands – to which the flocks we had seen had been coming. Close by, squeezed into a nearly horizontal crack in a cliff of rock, was a colony of seals, with three Striated caracaras in attendance – one of the world's least-known birds of prey. Altogether a fantastic place!

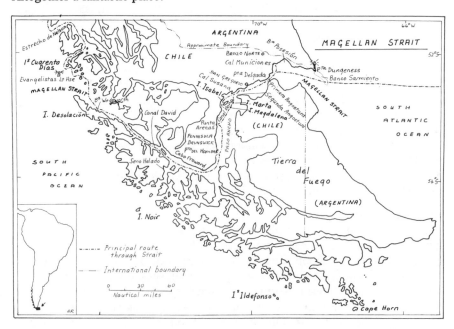

Map 14

Saturday 4 February

Ahead looms the great and fabled Cabo Froward, the southernmost point of the whole American continent. Another milestone! On the other side everything is supposed to change – different weather, scenery, trees, birds...Tomorrow night we should arrive at Punta Arenas...Apart from looking forward to receiving mail from home, I am dreading being in port again.

As we sailed north up this eastern part of the Magellan Strait hills gradually took the place of mountains and the land rounded down and became flatter and less interesting. Civilisation was not a welcome sight. In the morning we could see Fuerte Bulnes, the wooden fort and settlement reconstructed and commemorating the Spanish expedition which had been abandoned there in 1585 and the colonists starved to death, giving rise to the name Puerto del Hambre, Port of Hunger.

The temperature was only 2 °C as we weighed anchor and sailed gently up the Strait to Punta Arenas, which we could see from far off, although it did not look as big as the population of nearly 100,000 would suggest. There is only one pier, 380 metres long, which provides alongside berths for commercial and naval vessels, launches, fishing boats and – if there is any space left to spare – yachts.

We anchored near a French yacht which was heaving wildly in the swell rolling up from the south, and rowed across in our dinghy to seek information. Her bearded skipper and his wife greeted us in a mixture of Spanish and French which I found difficult to understand. They were not encouraging. 'You see that big sunken fishing boat alongside? She was wrecked last week, smashed against the pier by the waves! This is a horrible place.' The skipper spoke quickly, excitedly, with much gesticulation. Before we were finally finished with Punta Arenas, I had to agree with him.

It seems that in summer the winds blow strongly during the day and slacken off during the night. We stayed at anchor for a few days, but shore-going by dinghy was difficult and dangerous so eventually we went alongside a large fishing boat at the pier. This was more convenient, but still far from satisfactory because the boats were constantly coming and going, and shifting their berths.

My next crew member was Anthea Goodwin, a good friend, 52 years old and librarian of the Ornithological Society of New Zealand. Anthea was due to arrive at Punta Arenas on 3 March, and as I wanted to make good use of the time available before that, I managed to persuade both Jorge and Andreas to stay with me until then. Andreas came with me to meet Claudio Venegas at the Instituto de la Patagonia, but found he had gone away for a holiday. The Director of the Instituto told us that Claudio's trip to Isla Noir with Frank Todd had not come off; instead, he had hired a fishing boat to take himself and an assistant there, but conditions were so bad that they had landed only at the eastern end of the island. The scrub was dense and they were unable to penetrate to the interior – Claudio had said that he never wanted to see the island again!

Thanks to Brooms in Valparaiso, Agencias Maritimas Broom y Cía in Punta Arenas had been expecting us. The manager received us well and assured us of assistance. Frequently we were given the use of the taxi which was under contract to the Company and its driver became a good friend.

I was anxious to get away down to Isla Noir, which I knew would be an exciting and challenging project, but it was difficult to be in a hurry in Punta Arenas. There

105

was much to be done before we could leave – repairs, refuelling, storing, and the obtaining of a permit from the Armada. Fortunately Capitan Vasquez, who had been the radio communications officer in Valparaiso, was now Capitan del Puerto in Punta Arenas. By the time we were finished my chart was marked with a complicated pattern showing many places which were totally forbidden to us, and waterways through which we were allowed to pass but in which we could not anchor. It was then that I discovered we had already violated some of the forbidden places!

A German yacht, *Arca*, moored alongside us, and we met Alex and Dagma Wopper, her crew. Alex had built the steel yacht himself, and had made her very strong for work in ice because they were heading up to Alaska and then through the North West Passage in the opposite direction to that taken by Willy de Roos. I was full of admiration for their adventurous spirit, and envied their immaculate 38 horsepower BMW engine, which in four years of cruising had never given any trouble of any sort. *Arca* was the third yacht which Alex had built, and in his first of 6.5 metres he had sailed in one of the solo trans-Atlantic races.

On Sunday 12 February we sailed south from Punta Arenas down Paso Ancho, the part of the Magellan Strait which is nearly twenty miles wide, and back around Cabo Froward into the wilder, wetter, windier parts among the snow-capped mountains.

We anchored for the first night in the very secluded Caleta Cascada (Waterfall Cove). In the morning, on starting the engine I discovered that a bolt holding the rocker cover had sheared off, and we had lost a lot of oil. It was a composite bolt, also holding the rockers underneath, and I had no spare. We had to improvise by securing the cover with cords and wooden wedges, and hoped that it would last until we arrived back at Punta Arenas.

To reach Noir we had to pass through a complicated system of canals much encumbered with islands and rocks, culminating in one of the least surveyed areas of the whole region in Bahía Stokes. We entered Bahía Simon from the Magellan Strait, and proceeded thence to Angostura Toms, the narrows, where the tidal stream was against us and we took an hour to push through a half mile. After that, navigation was straightforward as we sped down Canal Barbara in the 'no stopping or anchoring' zone, into what I interpreted as being a small free area between two that were totally forbidden. Nevertheless, I had my doubts. A pleasant anchorage beckoned in Caleta Herrera, so in we went, joking about seeing periscopes and having a white flag in readiness for a declaration of surrender.

I notice in my diary that I had started to call williwaws 'rafagas', which is what my Spanish-speaking companions called them.

Tuesday 14 February

...We left our quiet caleta soon after 0700 hours and enjoyed a good sail through the uncharted area towards Isla Lort. Trying to find the caleta mentioned in the Pilot as suitable for sealing boats, we found ourselves in a maze of islands with thick beds of kelp between. Had I known what it was going to be like I would have kept outside, but once in, all we could do was keep going. We found the caleta at midday...all the caletas in this part of the world will be subject to rafagas, I am sure, but it is good to find one sheltered from the big seas...I named it Caleta Marjorie, after my very dear wife.

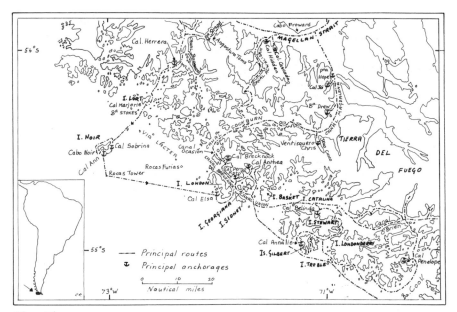

Map 15

Sailing away from Isla Lort we kept well to the north to avoid the worst of the Vía Láctea (the Milky Way), the notorious area of rocks and broken water extending nearly ten miles offshore. The wind was freshening rapidly and with the heavy swell the sea became rough, which makes it much harder to see which breakers are rocks. At about 1600 hours we were close off the north-east point of Isla Noir. Most of the north coast appeared to be steep cliffs, and looked very rugged. As we approached, violent rafagas tore the surface off the sea and laid *Totorore* well over with the sea over the cockpit coamings. I was afraid for the jib, which although rolled up leaving only a very small area seemed to be badly strained...

I started the engine and used full revs to get round the coast to the south-western end where there is a caleta which looked more sheltered, passing the caleta in the eastern end where Claudio Venegas had landed, and which we called Caleta Sobrina after the taxi-driver's niece whom Jorge rather fancied.

The weather was shocking, literally, and the rafagas were of hurricane force. Like tornadoes they blotted out visibility and flattened the sea with white spume. Each time one headed for us at the speed of an express train somebody shouted 'Cuidado!' (Watch out!) and we crouched low in the cockpit, hanging on tightly, and hoping and praying that we would be still intact after it had passed. It was a wearing, tiring business. We noted the large numbers of Giant petrels flying around, and thought there must be a colony somewhere. There were lots of Rockhoppers swimming in groups of about twenty or so.

Fearfully we approached the entrance to the caleta, making very slow speed against the wind and knocked back severely by the squalls. The entrance appeared to be blocked by rocks and kelp. I did not like the idea

107

of manoeuvring among the rocks but the thought of a night outside in this wild place did not appeal, and I dared not try to get back through the Milky Way. Inside the caleta we could see the clouds of spray whirling about, so knew that there were rafagas in there, too.

We managed to get through the first barriers of big rocks and came to the final entrance. It is about 25 metres wide between low rocks, and then opens out to about 35 metres for a distance of some 70 metres. Beyond that was the caleta, and what seemed to be another barrier of rocks and thick kelp right across. I didn't like the look of it at all. Fortunately the south-west point of the island, Cabo Noir, was protecting us from the swell...

When there was a spell between rafagas, I gave her full revs to maintain steerage and with a pleading prayer headed in. The soundings dropped to two metres. Jorge and Andreas were in the bow – Andreas standing by the anchor, Jorge looking for rocks. A shrieking squall hit us when we were still in the narrows. She would not respond to the helm and swung quickly towards the rocky bank. I could not hear the engine above the noise and thought it had stopped. 'Let go the anchor!' I shouted as loudly as I could. It was just as well that they did not hear me, as the engine was still going; desperately I pushed the control hard astern just as she hit an underwater rock and heeled dangerously over. 'Dear God, help me out of this one, please!' She seemed to be stuck on one keel and the next gust turned her right round, broadside to the channel and heading the other way. Another squall and she wrenched free; as I frantically worked the gear lever she blew back out of the passage and into a space where there was just room enough to turn her round again and head up towards the wind.

That left us all a bit shaken, but I decided to give it one more go. Again we got nearly through, although I could not for the life of me see where to go after that...another rafaga laid us over out of control and by a miracle and one metre we missed the above-water rocks and were blown back out of the passage. I was not prepared to try a third time to get into this one which we named Caleta Ann, and returned to the eastern end of the island.

Caleta Sobrina did not seem very big when we arrived inside, and rafagas hurled themselves at us from the high, steep hills all around. We noticed large colonies of Rockhoppers in the tussock and on rocks along the coast outside, and all around the caleta, but were too preoccupied to study them. Trying to find a sheltered corner we headed for a rocky gut with a beach at the end but it shoaled too rapidly and I had difficulty in getting back out again. We anchored in the middle, allowing clearance from the only above-water rock, inconveniently placed well out in the caleta. Using our tandem anchors we put down 25 fathoms of chain in four fathoms of water at 2000 hours...

As the squalls kept coming from different directions *Totorore* was twisting and turning, as did my insides. I would have liked to pay out more chain but there was not enough swinging room, and at one stage we were dangerously close to a rocky point. I did not want another anchor and chain down as it would tangle with the first; if anything were to happen to our present anchor, our only hope would be to start the engine as quickly as possible.

I told my crew to go to bed and get some sleep. About 2200 hours I woke them for dinner – a soup with rice, onion, cabbage and salami followed by a tin of kiwifruit. They seemed to enjoy it and then went back to bed. . .It is now 0100 hours. I keep looking at the shore with the spotlight, and she seems to be secure. Between the rafagas I can hear the penguins squawking and calling. Before dark, which was early tonight with the heavy overcast, a Blackish cinclodes came and settled briefly on the spare poling-out spar, and I saw a Striated caracara around the penguins. If only the weather plays fair, I think it will be an interesting island. . .

Wednesday 15 February
. . .When some of these rafagas hit us we see clear green in all the ports on one side of the cabin as they go right underwater. . .It is a beautiful green, whereas the top of the water is mostly dark grey, and white in the rafagas. Out to sea the huge columns of spray are so dense they look like waterspouts. It is much easier to put up with the discomforts of violent squalls in daytime when one can see what is happening, and we let the day pass. . .

All three of us have been having trouble with cold hands, mainly because whatever gloves we wear, they always get wet. We refer to our gloves as 'unseamanlikes'; Bill Tilman, the great mountaineer/sailor whom we all admired, once said that he considered gloves in this light. Given the ice-bound places he visited, he must have been an extremely hardy character. . .

The following day we circumnavigated Noir, seeing many large colonies of Rockhoppers in gullies along the cliffs of the north coast. In the shelter of Cabo Noir there was a great splashing of porpoising penguins around *Totorore* and we thought they looked like Macaronis, so determined to seek out their colony. Violent rafagas again prevented our entering Caleta Ann, so we returned to Sobrina.

Friday 17 February
Sometimes it is almost a surprise that we have survived another night. This morning we started making plans and preparations for Jorge and Andreas to camp ashore as soon as the weather allows. It would seem that we must make a positive move as we are wasting so much precious time. I told Jorge to go up high as soon as possible, find a sheltered spot to set up camp and work from there. I want them to explore the hilltops (about 300 metres) and the clifftops, looking for Giant petrel nests. As they will probably be *giganteus*, the more southerly species, the nests should be in a colony in a fairly flat open space. . .

We moved in towards the little stony beach in the rocky channel and off they went in the dinghy. It took two trips to get everything ashore. . .Regrettably the radio batteries seem flat, so I told them I would look out for them at the same place on Monday. . .

I have just had a look out on the hill and seen my two yellow-coated stalwarts trying to get through the scrub above the penguin tussocks. Now I can see that it is very dense and practically hiding them from my view. . .

About 1700 hours I was disappointed to hear a shout; my heart sank as I saw Andreas and Jorge returning to *Totorore*, rowing hard after leaving the shelter of the point and before the next rafagas hit us. They said it was impossible, although there were very interesting birds on the shore, and they had seen seven Striated caracaras, some of them feeding large chicks. I felt that if they could not get through the scrub at least they could have camped on the shore and studied the birds in that area, thus accomplishing something! It had been a rare opportunity to get everything ashore in safety, and all that time was now wasted...this has happened before on this expedition, so little has been done when I myself have been absent. The problem now is how long can we wait for better weather? and if it is always like this, what chance have we at Ildefonso?

We were watching about 20 Giant petrels near the rocks and noticed some white-headed and breasted birds – obviously Southerns – and then saw a large Sea-lion on the rocks with a Rockhopper in his mouth, which he was swinging from side to side. He seemed to be molested by about eight Skuas, and even the Giant petrels were interested in what he had, so he slipped back into the water.

Saturday, 18 February

Fewer rafagas this morning in spite of a low barometer, so we decided to have another go at the other end of the island and see if we could get into Caleta Ann. The temperature was 5 °C and the wind chill factor brought it well below freezing...

When there seemed to be an easing of the wind I motored in close to the pass and Jorge and Andreas went off with the dinghy to sound out the way through with a hand leadline. I thought it worth a try, as the open sea looked terrible...On the rocks outside were many Magellanic penguins coming and going in the scrub on top. Knowing that I would lose control in the narrow pass if caught by a rafaga I deemed it prudent to wait for a lull before taking the plunge and entering the pass. We anchored again in a bed of kelp, with about 1.5 metres under us, and waited.

While we were waiting we did some cleaning and emptying of the bilges. With the oil leak from the engine and the violent rafagas laying us over, the lower lockers on both sides had everything coated with black oil.

After about two hours it seemed comparatively quiet in the caleta, so we weighed anchor and headed in. It looked awful. I had to keep her moving fast to maintain steerage and try to follow Jorge's directions from the bow, passing no more than two metres from a rock in the middle, and then making a right-angled turn to port. We had just cleared the rock when a rafaga hit us. Tiller hard over and throttle lever as far ahead as it would go, it seemed an age before *Totorore* responded to Jorge's anxious shouting and outstretched arm pointing the other way. It was almost impossible to see. Shielding my eyes from the wind and spray, I kept full revolutions and struggled to keep her bow up. We were all scared. Eventually the depth on the sounder increased. 'Adentro – Hooray!' I shouted, and we all laughed with relief.

The depth over most of the caleta, which is about a quarter of a mile across, is between three and six metres, but it was difficult to find a sheltered corner where we could run lines to the shore because it shoaled rapidly as one approached the banks. At about 1530 hours we settled for a place near a small beach...

What excited me most was the apparent signs of Giant petrels nesting on the hilltops. With binoculars we really thought we could see some landing up there. The problem is, how on earth to get up there through this really abominable scrub. I feel we are onto something very important, so we must manage somehow...We got into this caleta, so we must get up.

Sunday 19 February

...We anchored and moored with lines again on the eastern side of the caleta, inspite of a low barometer. It is becoming apparent that neither the barometer nor the hygrometer give any indication of the weather we can expect, and the best days are usually on a low barometer, the worst when it is high. Somebody must always stay aboard if we are going to be away for any length of time; when making our plans last night Andreas said, 'It will be important that you should go to look for the Giant petrels' nests, as you never give up!'

Leaving Jorge to look after *Totorore*, with instructions to cast off and anchor out in the centre of the caleta if the wind increased in strength, Andreas and I went ashore with a tent, survival gear and food in case it was too difficult to get back aboard...

From the start it was tough going. What looks like grass swaying in the breeze is actually the tops of rushes which poke through the canopy of dense scrub, which is somewhere between 1.5 and 2.5 metres off the ground itself. Some of the bushes were tangled prickly things, some were tight and cushiony – they were the best to walk on, with the rushes providing handholds. Practice makes perfect, but we never attained that degree of skill and kept tripping and falling...When one disappeared below the canopy it was a painful, time-consuming business trying to get back on top, as the branches tangled around legs and arms, sometimes preventing all movement. It seemed an impossible and exhausting task, and progress was extremely slow.

At an altitude of about 100 metres we started noticing little patches covered with feathers where small birds had been killed by the Skuas or other birds of prey. These became quite numerous, and when we saw a Skua seated on a firm matted platform, we approached to see if it was a midden. The bird allowed us to come within a couple of metres, and we were able to admire its rich rufous and cinnamon colour. Sure enough, when it flew away we found a collection of disgorged pellets of feathers and small bones, and were lucky enough to find a skull of a small petrel...

As we plodded wearily upwards we came across more and more of the middens, and made quite a collection of parts of birds, all obviously of the same species, which caused us to speculate on what it was. It certainly looked like a prion. This was most exciting, as there are no records of prions nesting in Chile.

We stopped to eat our lunch and were looking aloft at the Giant petrels, some of which were definitely landing high up in the scrub, when we heard a low crooning noise from underneath us. It sounded suspiciously like a petrel in a burrow! We parted the scrub and peered down into the darkness below, all wet and mossy. After a long wait we heard it again, but from a different place, and a little later from right under where Andreas was sitting. This time he went in head first and squirmed his way to the bottom. I couldn't help laughing at his white boots sticking up out of the top of the bush. Even though he was stuck and couldn't move, he said he could see lots of burrows...it was obviously a real warren. I decided that really we should come back and bring some tools, so that we could cut some of the scrub and see what was underneath.

Our main task was to find the Giant petrels nesting, if indeed they were, but doubts were beginning to surface. Certainly they were landing up on the hilltop, and mostly in one place, but they seemed to swoop past often without stopping. Could it be that there was something dead up there which interested them? It seemed unlikely, as they are true birds of the sea and would not be expected over land unless they were breeding. The only way to find out was to go and see. We struggled on.

Sometimes the Giant petrels swooped so low over us we could hear the wind singing through their pinions...At about 190 metres on the altimeter we were just examining another Skua midden when I saw a Giant petrel chick only ten metres away, almost hidden by the rushes. I was so excited I almost threw my arms around Andreas. This was what we had longed to find! I could hardly believe it was true. The nearest known breeding place is in the Falkland Islands. They also breed in South Sandwich and South Orkney islands – all Antarctic islands. And now, here they are in Chile! I said a prayer of thanks for our good fortune...Imagine Claudio Venegas saying he did not want to come back!

Just beyond the chick, which was sitting on the mound nest of vegetable matter, was another about three metres away, and another beyond that. I took a photograph of the first one then asked Andreas to move in close so as to be in the picture. He was scared of being spat at by the chicks, which can eject foul-smelling oil at anybody who approaches too close. Opening their bills, they began to make retching noises and sure enough they tried to spit. Their range turned out to be only about 1.5 metres, so Andreas was able to stand just far enough away to be safe...

The view improved as we gained height, and when we reached the ridge we could see almost the whole island. Away to the south were the Rocas Tower – steep high rocks about ten miles distant. For the first time we could see the big mountainous islands around the canals we had left behind and beyond them the snowy peaks of Tierra del Fuego...Far below we watched Striated caracaras, of various ages, swooping up the hillside on the updrafts. There were several lakes, and a large, unknown and unmapped caleta, just as big as ours, between us and Caleta Sobrina.

We made our way to the top of the highest peak on the island, where my altimeter showed 335 metres. We could see more Giant petrel chicks, but they were scattered over very large areas of the hillside, mostly farther to the north of where we stood. Some were in groups of up to about twenty, but not the large colony we had expected. We were able to count over 200, but we think there were many more as they were difficult to see in the scrub. Towards the northern cliffs we could see another penguin colony stretching high up the hillside above the edge of the cliff itself, at that point only about 80 metres high...

Another colony looked even more intriguing, on a low flat isthmus leading to the wild and rocky south-west point of Cabo Noir. Might it be a different species? King penguins, or Gentoo...dare I even think of such an astounding possibility? One thing is certain, and that is that we cannot leave this island until we have found out!

It was becoming extremely cold in the wind up on the top, and getting late, so we started down again, choosing a route which from the top looked much easier, as indeed for the first half of the descent it was. Then we ran into trouble with the worst scrub we had encountered...We could hardly manage a step without falling into the awful stuff, and as we became more tired it was more and more difficult to get out again. I tried hard to keep Andreas's spirits up, and my own too. 'If we can't make it before dark' I said, 'we will get into our survival bags in one of these dark holes out of the wind and wait until morning.'...unfortunately our clothes were wet with sweat inside our heavy rain gear, and I knew that would prove harmful if we stopped our exertions, in the cold of the night...

There was no doubt about it, we were becoming dangerously tired. In holes out of the wind it seemed quite warm and cosy; I closed my eyes and thought how nice it would be to just stay there and go to sleep. I kept calling out to Andreas, who was having similar thoughts. Often I could not see him. When I heard 'Ach!' or 'Aaagh!' or similar grunts and growls, I knew that all was well. When I heard nothing I was scared; like me, he was having little rests.

Somehow we made the shore just as it was getting dark. Jorge picked us up in the dinghy and it was an effort to climb on board *Totorore*. Too tired to take off our packs and rain gear we sat in the cockpit and Jorge passed us cups of hot tea. After my third cup I felt decidedly better, and with a dinner of macaroni fired up by cayenne pepper inside us, I declared that as there was little wind it was an exceedingly rare opportunity to hoist the mainsail and exhibit our pressure lamps to find out what the birds were, nesting up there in the scrub. The idea was not greeted with wild enthusiasm...

We put the lights outside, hoisted the sail, and were amazed at the immediate response. There were birds flying all around us, bumping into the sail and falling to the deck. Many just landed in the water close by. We could have caught fifty without any trouble, but we caught nine quickly, popped them into bags and boxes inside the cabin, and lowered the sail as the wind was beginning to blow again. We doused the lights but they were still attracted by the cabin lights, and we heard some bump on the boat outside.

They were Thin-billed prions and we measured them one by one. Pretty, gentle little birds, they were easy to handle. We recorded length and width of beak, length of each wing from the carpal joint, length of tail, tarsus and mid toe. After measuring and weighing them we released them, keeping back three for taking lice. It was about half-past one in the morning when we were finished, and I was just too tired to get my camera and flash organised to take any photographs of any of the prions...

Tuesday 21 February

The wind now coming from the south-west, we moved over to that corner of the caleta and anchored without shore lines. Jorge rowed us ashore about mid morning, and we set off overland to have a look at the penguin colony we had noted near Cabo Noir... The weather was kind with only a few showers, but the wind was cold. Quite often we disturbed a penguin which let out a fearful loud braying noise which made us jump, but then remained quiet, so I did not manage any recordings on my tape.

We came to a very large caleta filled with rocks and no good for *Totorore*, and as the tide was low we waded across at its head without trouble, following the rocky shore around as far as we could before diving back into the scrub to take a direct route. We disturbed Speckled teal on rocky pools, and small groups of Ashy-headed geese. Rails, all brown with long down-curved beaks, were very common, some wading and feeding from the sea, others walking on top of the scrub. We had seen them on top of the mountain, and heard them everywhere, but were very surprised to find them later in the penguin colony, eating a dead penguin. We also saw several otters, and heard others twittering like birds.

From a distance we could see penguins on rocks around the small bay we were approaching, which had a grey shingle beach at its head. We focussed our binoculars, and could not help feeling disappointed. They were Macaronis, not the King penguins, or Chinstraps we had hoped for. There were many bones and remains of penguins along the shore, and Andreas made a collection of skulls. The sound of their braying came to us above the scrub and we watched to see the main entrance. Soon we saw comings and goings at the mouth of a small dirty stream leading under the bushes, so we bent low and followed it for about 70 metres to the colony...

A large irregular area cleared out of the scrub, about two metres high, was packed solid with penguins, each only just out of pecking reach of his neighbour. Sloping gently upwards, it was wet and smelly. About half the birds were in various stages of moult, some of them looking as though they had fur coats on, others decidedly scruffy. When one decided to go down the track to the sea, his passing through the mob caused a great commotion as all those he came close to squawked and pecked him, and that often excited a similar reaction in others close by, so that there was always a fight going on.

A Striated caracara was eating a dead penguin near the main entrance. The penguins themselves backed off a little when we came in, causing a bit of a chain reaction, but when we walked very slowly among them they merely parted to let us pass, and then closed in around us, eyeing us curiously. They are much bigger than Rockhoppers, and we were interested to see that it was a pure colony, with no other species visible among them. It was difficult to assess numbers in a short time, but by counting a small section we estimated about 25,000 birds. I took a few photographs but it was raining, and the wind and rain also upset my tape-recording....

Actually, our discovery was important, because it is the only known unmixed colony of Macaroni penguins in Chile.

It was 1830 hours when we left, and we knew we would be hard put to

114

get back before dark. We followed the shore as far as we could and then were forced into the scrub which was particularly high and dense. Progress was alarmingly slow. The shore seemed a better prospect but the tide was much higher than when we had come, and we frequently met impassable rock faces and vertical sided gullies...We were both very tired, and fell frequently. I filled one of my boots with water, which I was to regret later. The sky was getting dark, and cold showers became more frequent.

Finally we came to the side of the large caleta and our hearts sank. The full tide was now right up into the scrub, leaving no rocks as stepping stones, and the scrub was practically impassable even in daylight. Andreas said that Jorge would be worried if we did not return, and I agreed but said there was absolutely nothing we could do about it. We had with us our plastic survival bags, a few trail biscuits, a few milk biscuits, and a small flask of water – nothing else. It was an unpleasant prospect, and I felt ashamed of being so unprepared for an emergency. In the morning it had seemed such an easy jaunt...

The thick tangled scrub was wet and muddy underneath. Close by was a small islet in the caleta, about four metres high with a bush at one end of its narrow ridge, and clumps of rushes with a few other prickly plants. It was the best that was offering, and we were able to reach it by scrambling over rocks. I said to Andreas, 'These bags will not keep us warm, but they will keep us alive, and that is all we can expect!' A hail shower peppered us as we made our preparations...the rushes were our only shelter from the wind, sparse as they were.

There was just room for us to lie side by side. We ate a few milk biscuits, though neither of us felt hungry and both were cold already in our damp clothes. Our packs we emptied of cameras and tape-recording gear, the skull of a sea lion for Jorge, penguin skulls, and sundry articles useless for our present needs; we used them as pillows to keep our heads off the cold wet ground. It was dark when we wriggled into the bags, wearing all our clothes and our wet weather gear, including gumboots. 'Buenos noches. Please wake me with a cup of coffee in the morning.' Then began one of the longest nights I have ever known.

Our beds were hard and uneven, consisting mainly of wet spongy moss over a rock base with odd roots sticking up...The wind made the bags flap noisily and the tops of the rushes played a constant tattoo on the outside. When one of us moved, which was often, his bag squeaked a protest. Being cold to start with, we soon felt absolutely frozen. Both my feet were cold, but the one with the sodden sock really hurt. I wondered about frostbite...

My hips felt as though I was lying on a block of ice, and the cold got at my kidneys; three times I had to get up to relieve myself. It was an unhappy business, getting out of the plastic bag and feeling the wind go right through my clothing, freezing my hands numb so that I had problems with the zips. Once Andreas got up and fell on the slippery slope, his legs still in the plastic bag. He tangled with a dead bush and I could not help laughing at his exclamations. 'Como esta, Andreas?' (How are you, Andreas?) 'Más o menos,' he said, 'More or less.' I was glad he still had a sense of humour.

Andreas actually managed a short sleep as I heard him snoring, but I could not sleep at all. We spoke to each other frequently during the night. Between the showers it was really quite beautiful, with a gibbous moon and the Southern Cross above us...We were glad when the Magellanic penguins around us stopped calling, as it meant they had gone to bed and we knew that it was getting late. Neither of us had a watch. I said my prayers many times, and tried to think warm thoughts, but it was not easy. I tried deep breathing, and counting my breaths, but it did not make me sleep, then the yoga warming position, which helped a little but did not warm my hips, my waist, my feet or my hands.

I was constantly flexing muscles, trying to wriggle my toes, hunching my shoulders. The 'survival in the water' position with knees brought up to one's chest might have been good, but there was no room with Andreas next to me...Andreas said 'It will be the first time I have ever wanted to get up in the morning'. Joking became more difficult.

Wednesday 22 February

At long last we saw the first lightening of the sky and rose stiffly from our plastic bags. With numb and useless fingers we repacked our packs. We wanted to cross the caleta while the tide was still low and we could go across the rocks, but we found that we were awkward and unsteady on our frozen feet, and kept stumbling. Realising the danger of falling into the water while we were so unsteady, we walked the long way round the head of the caleta on the rocky shore...We had a quick swig of cold water from the flask, but the trail bread was finished and a milk biscuit made us feel sick. The effort of forcing a way through that scrub nearly finished me – I felt weak and dizzy, and was dangerously near to the limit of my endurance...

When we could finally see *Totorore's* mast, even that last hundred metres of bushes and bog seemed too much and it took a supreme effort to get there. We shouted from the shore and a worried Jorge rowed over to pick us up. He had stayed up until 0100 hours with every available light displayed – the two pressure lamps, two spotlights – and had attracted clouds of prions. He kept blowing on the foghorn, and trying to call Punta Arenas on the radio to ask for emergency help. Fortunately, they had not answered.

Back on board Jorge gave us boiled eggs and toast and three cups of coffee, and we both soon felt restored...We then all three snuggled into our warm sleeping bags and slept until 1330 hours, when Jorge produced a lunch of hot beans and our recovery was complete. I could not have been as bad as I felt, to recover so quickly; there were only a few aching joints and bad memories to show for our night's adventure...

I went ashore after lunch to obtain photographs and tape recordings of the Magellanic penguins along the shores of our caleta. The weather had deteriorated, so my attempts met with limited success. I could have happily spent a whole year on Isla Noir, there seemed to be so much work that could be done there. We had no more than scratched the surface, exciting though our discoveries had been, but our time was short and we had to push on to have a look at other islands while we had the chance, so on Friday 24 February we decided we should leave.

Our route took us close past Rocas Tower, with seals right on the tops, and then past the many Rocas Furias, the name which describes them well. On the way we saw seven more phalaropes; these looked like the Red phalaropes we had watched farther north and we wondered at their being so far south. That night we sheltered in Caleta Elsa (which I named after our eldest daughter) among low rocky islands south of Isla London.

As soon as we could, we ran up into the canals again where it was more sheltered. and followed the main shipping route down to Isla Stewart, where we met our first snow for the year. The high mountains on the island looked white and beautiful as we squeezed our way into the narrow cleft of Seno Belinda (second daughter) two miles into their heart. These southern islands had very little vegetation except in a few well sheltered gullies, and most were almost entirely bare rock. Poking around their inhospitable coasts and climbing over them was fun but we made no outstanding discoveries.

We did spend one night in a rather risky spot in Caleta Annalie (third daughter) on the west coast of the biggest Gilbert island, hoping to use our lights to attract the birds but we drew a blank. Isla Treble, in a small group of islands south of the big Isla Londonderry, was particularly attractive with three high pinnacles close together, visible from a great distance. Around the peaks circled five mighty Condors, the largest of all flying birds. Seen close up, their naked heads and necks with big wattles are rather ugly, but when flying they look absolutely magnificent. They wear a fluffy white collar, which together with the light grey or white area on top of the wings is conspicuous against the black of the rest of the plumage. We assumed that they were nesting up on the peaks, and that they probably existed on carrion from a seal colony out on rocks nearby.

Something which disturbed us considerably at Isla Treble was the sight of a deserted Magellanic penguin colony. Fishermen at Punta Arenas had told us of the illegal practice by the Centolla (King crab) fishermen, of baiting the crab pots with penguins, seals, and even dolphins. I had alerted the International Council for Bird Preservation to make them aware of this threat to penguins, and we were looking out for evidence. This was the first of such empty colonies we found, but in no way could we prove that the birds had all been killed by fishermen.

Monday 27 February

...We had not seen any fishing boats until we anchored in Caleta Penelope (fourth daughter), another deep, dark inlet between high mountain walls in the eastern end of Isla Londonderry. Soon after our arrival we heard a diesel motor, and around a point puttered a small craft which ploughed through the kelp towards us and came alongside. Her ensign was an unrecognisable vestige of exhaust-blackened rag and the rest of the boat was in keeping, but the four crew were cheerful and friendly. They were a tough-looking lot, wearing only shirts and jeans, and making us shiver just to look at them. They told us that they stay in this inlet from November to March, fishing for the Centollas, and a larger vessel calls once a month to bring them stores and collect their catch. We looked at the crude little box on the stern in which they lived and did not envy them. They gave us some

117

large lumps of rough-looking rock, but under the weed and other growth were shells of *Pyura chilensis*, the flesh of which is red like meat, and called *piure*. It is said to be a strong food, and to make you strong, which prompted some ribald jokes.

We made our way slowly back through the canals towards Punta Arenas, often motoring against headwinds, taking a different route from the way we had come and still avoiding the main shipping tracks clearly marked on the charts. In the Magellan Strait, east and north of Cabo Froward, we observed an interesting migratory movement of Magellanic Diving petrels. They were flying southwards, well spaced out and about a metre above the water. Diving petrels usually fly for a short distance and then dive, but we did not see a single one of the many hundreds which passed us dive at all. They flew straight and purposefully, and we wondered where were they going. If it were northwards, being autumn, then instinct must have told them to fly south first to round Cabo Froward and then up the western canals. Why did they not fly north up the Strait and out at the eastern end?

As we approached Punta Arenas we saw a truly amazing sight, which took us a while to identify. At first all we could see was a steel tower showing over the horizon; as we watched it grew taller until we could hardly believe our eyes! Then gradually a ship appeared over the horizon underneath this gigantic tower and we could see that it was a massive oil rig, more than 100 metres high, transported on a partly submersible vessel flying the Norwegian flag. Projecting about twelve metres over each side of the ship, the rig looked most unstable; we wondered what it must be like in the deep ocean swells, and thought that the windage alone must be enormous. Later, when she was lying at anchor off Punta Arenas, we heard that her anchor chain had parted and tugs and other craft had to go quickly to her rescue.

On arrival at Punta Arenas, Andreas telephoned home and Julia told him that she would like to take his place on board. That settled one of my problems, although I did have some slight feeling of apprehension at the thought of having two ladies for a crew. As it turned out, I need not have worried.

Otter

Chapter Eight

Camp on Cape Horn

*Canal Magdalena — Canal Ocasión — Caleta Julia — Islas Ildefonso —
Cape Horn — Cape Horn Islands — Collision with Los Gansos rocks —
Canal Beagle — Glaciers*

Andreas and Jorge left to go home, and I met Anthea and Julia on different days
at Punta Arenas Airport, so we were again a full crew. Our stay in port was
frustratingly prolonged by bad luck and bureaucracy, both of which took a great
deal of effort and help from Brooms, to overcome. In addition were the usual hassles
of bad weather in a bad port, with consequent minor damage to *Totorore* from
adjacent fishing boats, loss of fenders and mooring lines.

A more serious incident occurred when all three of us risked being ashore at the
same time, even though it was for only an hour. When we came back to *Totorore*
we found that she had been moved along the pier by somebody in our absence,
and her mast had struck and broken a large light fitting which projected from a
lamp-post out over some landing steps. We were visited by a foreman, and then
the pier manager, who told us that we would have to pay for it, but that the cost
would not be known until it had been repaired. In the evening an Armada officer
came on board and said that we would be forbidden to sail until the account had
been settled. In principle I had to agree that it was all fair enough, because we are
responsible for our vessel at all times; but I was not in a position to be able to pay
the 32,000 pesos (about US$350) which was mentioned as being the probable cost
and I objected to the delay to our work programme while waiting for the lamp to
be repaired. After many days of negotiation I had a brainwave. Production in the
right place of a letter from our then Prime Minister, Mr Muldoon, and a letter of
introduction from our New Zealand Ambassador to Chile, worked wonders. We
were let off all charges, 'for New Zealand'! It was a great relief.

I will not dwell at length on the bureaucratic delay, although it was equally
serious. It concerned our permit for work in the Cape Horn islands. I had made
out our itinerary and it had been finally approved by my friend Capitan Vasquez,
but at the last minute an Armada secretary pointed out that our original permit
for ornithological research in Chilean waters issued in Valparaiso, expired in April,
and that to extend it I must re-apply, giving six months notice! I had been unaware
of a time limit, so was badly shaken by this complete upset in our plans. I wriggled
and squirmed, argued and pleaded, and enlisted the help of Brooms not only in
Punta Arenas but also in Valparaiso. The authorities in Valparaiso said that I must

mark on a chart our intended route and our position each day – an obviously impossible task. I finally produced something to satisfy them, and when my application for work in six months time had been acknowledged I was in a better position to ask Capitan Vasquez for an interim extension to our present permit so that we could sail for Cape Horn. The zarpe was then granted. Following the upset of later plans by the French, our Committee back home thought it would be a good idea if we did some more work in Chile, and as I had already arranged to go to Falklands and South Georgia for about six months, our programme started to resume some shape.

We were all very happy to leave Punta Arenas, in itself a pleasant small city with friendly inhabitants, but as a port for a small vessel no good at all.

As we sailed down the Strait by night dolphins played around us, their white bellies showing clearly in the moonlight. My two new crew members were delighted by this and indeed by everything else we saw, and we soon felt more relaxed and ready to face the challenges of Cape Horn. On the way south we stopped in a variety of beautiful and interesting places, usually entering in the dark to give us practice at working together. I watched the radar and gave instructions to either Anthea or Julia at the helm, while the other stood by the anchor. Some of the places were tricky, and it was important to develop our teamwork so that in an emergency we each knew that the others would do the right thing. For the same reason, we took *Totorore* by day through narrow passages inside some of the islands, keeping a good lookout for rocks – Anthea at the spreaders on the mast, Julia in the pulpit, and myself at the helm and watching the echo-sounder. Generally kelp is a fair indication of rocks, but when we have to push through the kelp itself it is more dangerous, because the echo-sounder records the kelp rather than the seabed or rocks.

After leaving the Magellan Strait south of Cabo Froward, our route was Canals Magdalena, Cockburn, Ocasión, and Brecknock. Before we left each of our overnight anchorages, Anthea and Julia went ashore with the dinghy to explore and note down birds. I was very pleased with them, and appreciated their enthusiasm and willingness to be of maximum help. I suspect they were both determined to prove that they were as capable in a boat as any man, and they certainly succeeded. Anthea, who had been looking forward to this opportunity since before the expedition had started, was as excited as a schoolgirl and kept saying, 'I can't believe that I am really here!'

After we left Caleta 'Anthea', north of Isla Georgiana, the weather looked good enough for us to take an outside course, so we headed to pass south of Islas Stewart and Gilberts and spent a night at Isla Treble, where this time we saw only a single Condor. The open sea made both Anthea and Julia seasick; in fact, after our long stay in port, I did not like staying too long down below myself. I waited until my crew were in their bunks before I cooked my dinner of salt pork, so that the smell would not upset them.

Sunday 18 March

... The wind started to get up a bit, but we had a good twin-headsail run down. There were not many birds, and rain frequently blotted out the islands. By the time we were approaching Cabo Catedral de York, on Isla Waterman, it was getting dark, and the sea and swell together gave us a wild ride. Anthea and Julia vied with each other to take the helm, as they feel cold and wet when they are not steering, but it was not easy with a big

120

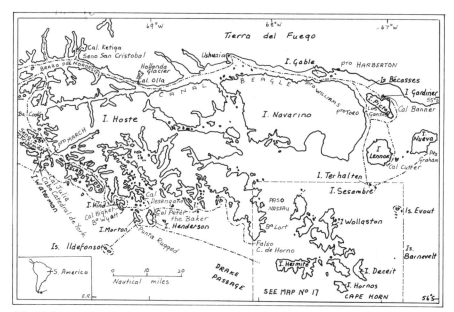

Map 16

following sea. We were just able to see the impressive-looking cape and the jagged and towering spires for which Captain Cook had given it its name...

Monday 19 March
...My crew are now well and truly initiated into the world of rafagas. Just as we were getting up, they started to hurl themselves at us with extraordinary fury; Anthea and Julia, although very scared, marvelled at the lovely greenish-blue colour under the surface of the sea as seen through the ports each time *Totorore* was knocked over.

The wind generator started to rattle and shake the Eiffel Tower with a most alarming noise, and I knew that a blade had blown off and I would have to secure it. Although the temperature was still warm at 6°C, my fingers soon became numb...

How easy it is to be slack when you are wet and tired! Today I found even the smallest jobs very difficult in the strong wind, and had to hang on very tightly to avoid being blown overboard. Down below, my two willing crew were coping well with unsecured items suddenly taking flight, and soon had a good hot breakfast waiting for me when I came in. They are in good spirits, and I think rather enjoying the experience...

The rafagas continued all day, increasing in violence and frequency – and even in duration, which was the most worrying of all. This place rivals Caleta Sobrina in Isla Noir...It certainly is not a good day for venturing forth.

Tuesday 20 March
My crew did not call me for my anchor watch and I slept through until 0600 hours...

121

I woke them with breakfast in bed (a very rare treat!) and we weighed anchor about 0900 hours to have a look into the inner part of Caleta 'Julia' in case we ever came back. The inner channel was narrow but quite deep, and easy without the wind...but nothing like on the chart. After that we motored through a small kelp-filled pass into Puerto March.

We found ourselves in a delightful anchorage with many small islands, and rocks covered by kelp. It was well charted, having been surveyed by Captain Fitzroy in HMS *Beagle* in 1830, and as we passed across we could just picture her anchored there, with a whaler in the bay being propelled by rough-looking oarsmen and a leadsman up in the bow calling out soundings. Steamer ducks would have been fanning out away from them, just as they were from us. It is so easy to feel romantic about such things in this lovely setting, seen through drizzle and completely unchanged and seldom visited since that day...

Islas Morton were the next on our list of principal study areas; it was here, we had been told, that several large colonies of penguins had been completely wiped out by the Centolla fishermen.

Tuesday 20 March
...A loud braying from the shore greeted our arrival, and many groups of Magellanic penguins stood watching us as we passed by, looking out for good caletas. On the sheltered side of Isla Morton itself the scrub is thick, and there are areas of stunted coigüe trees (Magellan beech). It was obvious that there were penguin burrows and tracks right through all of it.

This was nothing very new to Julia, but for Anthea it was the first time she had ever seen a penguin out of the water...I was pleased too, because it meant that the fishermen had not killed them all. The dense scrub was obviously the reason, and when we came to the more open areas of burrows we found that they were all empty.

The Morton Islands were a good refuge in which to wait for a fine-weather opportunity to visit the exposed islands of Ildefonso, lying about eleven miles south-west. We were able to observe several decimated penguin colonies and make a checklist of all birds seen in the group. Anthea and Julia took the opportunity to bathe and do some washing in a stream, but the water was too cold for me and I preferred to heat up a saucepan of water on our stove.

Friday 23 March
We arose early this morning to get out to Ildefonso in good weather and marvelled at the beautiful dawn. We could see Saturn, Mars, Jupiter, and Venus in a nearly straight line, and the Scorpion and other old starry friends so very seldom seen down here in the overcast skies. We heard the penguins waking up, and also Churrins and the musical Rails greeting the day as the soft rosy tints spread into the sky from above Henderson Island across the bay.

Our luck still holds, in spite of a rapidly falling barometer...on our way across the eleven-mile stretch to Ildefonso it clouded over and the wind freshened to a good sailing breeze, so that we made good time under just a jib. A Royal albatross went sailing by, and we saw two Grey-headed mollymawks, which made me think of Andreas, who had so much wanted to see one. There is the exciting possibility that they might be breeding on Ildefonso, along with the Black-brows which we know are there.

As we approached we could see great cracks and crevices in the rocky cliffs of the islands, of which there are about five, and many large rocks, all in a line about three-and-a-half miles long. There were also big caves, many of which went right through to the other side like huge tunnels. On the steep slopes on the tops we could see dense tussock, and everywhere among them Black-browed mollymawk chicks now fully grown and flapping their wings in exercise. They looked highly comic, with wings all floppy and seemingly not jointed in the normal way of birds' wings... Above and around them circled adult Black-brows and dozens of Striated caracaras – more than I had ever seen before. In one place I counted 22 in flight at once.

We took off the sails and we motored slowly down the windward coast. It was absolutely fantastic! What a joy to find such a place abounding with life! Anthea could not stop exclaiming at how much she appreciated being there... Just what she had dreamed about, she said.

On the very steep rocky slopes above the kelp were crêches of Rockhopper juveniles, and above them high on the hills hundreds of adults, often in the tussock among the Black-brows. On one very large rock in the centre of the group we found a colony of about 500 seals, with so many youngsters among them that it sounded like a large nursery, with a great variety of calls from squeaks to grunts. We watched them doing thrilling waterslides down the rocks in the receding breakers, rolling and tumbling with reckless abandon. In the water they porpoised around us, occasionally sticking their heads high up to look at us curiously.

Among the seals we saw the Blackish cinclodes, the little brown bird called Churrete which seems often to frequent these colonies of seals, but best of all we saw some more Sheathbills. I had only seen a single one before and that was the one at Guafo. Altogether we counted ten of these pigeon-like scavengers, visitors from Antarctica. Another similar-sized colony of seals was on the rocky lower ledges of the southernmost island where a huge cave behind them amplified the sound, giving it a deep and hollow resonance. To cap it all, we had ten dolphins gambolling around us! I had thought to make a landing, but it looked a pretty formidable challenge at the best of times...

Many Giant petrels were flying around...I really do think that there is a good possibility that some may be breeding up on the tops. I did not spot any Grey-headed mollymawks on nests – but it seemed too much of a coincidence that we saw them here flying around the islands, and they do often breed among Black-brows. Perhaps next summer we might find some? I now have a very good idea of what we will be up against when we do eventually return to make a more thorough survey.

The next day we 'ran our easting down' in a good sailing breeze, with our twin headsails poled out. We went racing across a blue sea with sparkling whitecaps under patches of blue sky, in warming sunshine. Not what we had expected only

40 miles from Cape Horn! Two Southern fulmars, among the first to come north from Antartica with winter approaching, graced the scene, and three Orcas, or Killer whales, passed us going in the opposite direction. Rain fell as we rounded the fascinating rhinoceros-horn-shaped Falso Cabo de Hornos (False Cape Horn) with its beautiful many-coloured rocks and cliffs, and anchored for the night in Bahía Lort on huge Isla Hoste. Across the Paso Nassau we could see the mountains of the Cape Horn Islands, with heavy grey rainclouds above, and our pulses quickened with anticipation.

Sunday 25 March

The hills around us were dusted with fresh snow and a little sleet fell as we weighed anchor with the thermometer showing 1 °C. There was a tremendous tangle of kelp on the small anchor ahead, and we had to use the dinghy to cut it free so that we could lift it. Outside, the south wind headed us and we had to motor-sail across to the end of Isla Hermite, but after rounding it we were able to lay course for Cape Horn...

We kept close to the coast where we could, and carefully examined the deeply-fissured rocky cliffs for signs of penguins or other sea birds, but saw mainly cormorants and Kelp geese...it was great sailing, with only a small reef in the main and jib...

Right now we are passing Cape Horn, the great Cape Horn itself, and it is a very exciting moment! We are inside the outer rocks, which are quite close to the Cape, and we can see this huge mass sticking up, a high conical shape, cliffs with green on the top, a wonderful setting. There was a veil of rain but that has cleared away and now we can see the tussock up there, and a certain amount of vegetation on the side. There are enormous

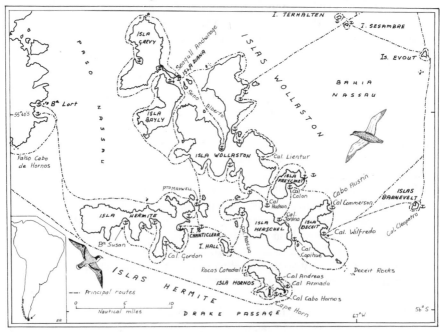

Map 17

breakers at the bottom of the dark grey rocky cliffs, and it looks absolutely magnificent! A white lighthouse stands near the bottom of the mountain slope and just to the east of it. As it came abeam with Anthea at the helm, Julia blew three blasts on our foghorn and I reverently dipped our ensign three times in salute to this mighty monument to the thousands of sailors who have drowned in the stormy waters of Drake Passage.

About two miles north-east of Cape Horn on the same island, Isla Hornos, is another cape, long and comparatively low, on which we could see some crude huts, a radio aerial, and a Chilean flag flying from a mast; and we knew that it must be the Armada coastwatchers' base. The huts right on the skyline were very conspicuous, which made their camouflaged exteriors rather absurd. We called the base on the VHF and reported our presence, adding that we would be working in the area for about three weeks and would visit them the following day. We then carried on up the lee side of Isla Hornos and anchored in a small corner south of a cape half way up the east coast of the island. We called the place Andreas, as it was his birthday.

We decided to visit the Armada station by walking overland to it, instead of sailing there, so in the morning we rowed ashore and made a wet landing on the boulder beach. Anthea stayed to look after *Totorore*, and Julia and I made our way through the thick scrub and over the hills towards the south-east point. On the heights it was very cold, with driving hail or light snow, and we had some dramatic views of the Cape Horn mountain from a different angle.

Monday 26 March

. . . The approaches to the station were a maze of barbed-wire fences and entanglements, with many trip-wires about fifteen centimetres above the ground. No doubt they would have been an obstacle at night, but it is no trouble to us to negotiate them by day. There was no sign of life in the log-cabin-like buildings with iron roofs, and only a metallic clanking noise, as a large radar scanner revolved, indicated that there was anybody in residence. A dog barked once, but we did not see it. We squelched across a peaty bog, past a board sign which said 'Bienvenido a Cabo de Hornos', and onto the wooden duckboards around the accommodation hut. I banged loudly three times on the door but there was no reply, so I tried again. Nothing. I peered through a window and right next to the door I could see a pair of green-clad legs and black boots, and concluded that the guard inside was fast asleep. This was about 1445 hours, obviously still siesta time. 'Muy Chileno!' said Julia. 'Very Chilean!' We wandered past the radar shed and had a look at the minute chapel. Inside, the illusion was rather spoiled by opened ammunition cases and long belts of shells, with bits and pieces of guns in front of the altar, which was decorated with plastic flowers. A figure of the Madonna surveyed the scene.

Outside, we walked past an emplacement with a small gun like an Oerlikon, all covered up, and then spotted a very surprised man by the door of the cabin. Without a word he bolted inside, no doubt to waken the others; soon two more appeared and greeted us. They asked us to come inside and we stepped into a pleasant little mess room which we found unbearably hot, with a large gas heater turned full on. A large photograph of President Pinochet hung on one wall and a map of Isla Hornos made of wood on another.

Various doors opened and more men appeared, rubbing their eyes. The petty officer in charge, in Armada black, was very friendly but obviously put out that we had literally caught them napping. He said we should have radioed that we were coming, as it was very dangerous to cross the barbed-wire entanglements and we might have been shot! We could not help smiling.

Julia and I took off our wet boots and socks, and one of the men took them away to dry while others brought us their jandals to wear in the meantime. While we were drinking coffee and enjoying fresh bread, the 'Jefe' (chief) asked us many questions and filled in a form with our names and nationalities. Then he produced an enormous visitors' book. It seems that Cabo de Hornos is almost a tourist attraction! When the *Lindblad Explorer* or the *World Discoverer* happen past, they land all their passengers here for a visit.

Claudio Venegas had told us that two years previously an Armada officer had located a colony of 2000 Chinstrap penguins at Cape Horn and we wanted to investigate the report. The men confirmed their presence on the point just below the station, and offered to lead us to them, but to our dismay they brought with them their hairy old dog. Chaska just loved chasing penguins, and we soon saw that they were Magellanic and not Chinstraps.

The next day we sailed into the tiny sheltered caleta right next to the station and climbed the steps they had made to the top of the cliff. Anthea came with me to make a more thorough search of the area for Chinstraps and we followed the oozy, smelly penguin trails though the tussocks right down to the bottom. It was a large hilly area, full of burrows and very slippery, so it was a relief to walk across a narrow causeway of boulders to a near-island. However the grass on top was burnt, and the men told us that it had caught fire during shooting practice! If Chinstraps had ever been there, which we doubted, it was obvious that they would have been driven off.

On 28 March we motored around the south-east point against a 25-knot breeze and into a wide bay between the point and Cape Horn, finding a good lee from all northerly and westerly winds. Before we anchored, we saw a penguin lying on its back with its white tummy up; in close we realised that it was a Gentoo. What excitement! It was the first Gentoo that any of us had ever seen, and it was in the very place that the only two ever recorded in Chile had been seen a few years before. Could there possibly be a small colony among the Magellanics?

Apart from looking for Gentoo and Chinstrap penguins we wanted to find Sooty shearwater burrows in the stunted coigüe scrub on the sheltered side of the mountain. When we landed in the dinghy, Julia and I found that the boulders on the beach were larger than they had looked from a distance and were very slippery, with deep spaces between. Julia had both her boots full of water before we managed to drag the dinghy clear of the breakers and we realised then that we must always take dry clothes with us in watertight bags.

There were Magellanic penguin burrows in the scrub from the shore to about 80 metres up the hill. On this first day we carried on up the mountainside and had a real struggle in the more dense scrub higher up, almost as bad as on Noir. Far down below, we could see *Totorore* rolling in the swell, and above us, often shrouded in rain, was the jagged peak of Cape Horn. There were no further burrows.

Wednesday 28 March

...Back on the beach we saw that the sea had got up and the breakers were worse than this morning. It was low tide, and there were more slippery boulders exposed by the receding waves...the dinghy flipped right over with me underneath it and although I managed to grab one oar the other floated out of reach. Holding the boat, both of us fell again on the slippery rocks when the next wave struck. I watched the floating oar, expecting each wave to bring it back in, but it worked its way along the shore, getting farther away. How foolish I was not to have had it lashed in the boat! While Julia held the dinghy, I went scrambling over the rocks, trying to keep the oar in view, but it was beginning to get dark and when I last saw it the oar was quite a way out.

I dared not paddle downwind after it because it was still in the big waves. For a moment I considered remaining on shore but I knew it would be dangerous, as we were both soaked to the skin and night temperatures have been only 1-2 °C. Apart from that, Anthea would have been terribly worried, and we might have to wait for days.

Julia kept her head and was very practical. Fortunately the water was not too cold at about 9 °C, but the wind was decidedly chilling and we had both lost our woolly hats. We carried the boat farther along the shore to a more upwind position; as we were already wet, it did not matter too much having to stand up to our waists in the sea. It certainly made it very much easier to hold the boat until the right moment to get aboard and start paddling, me on my knees with the one oar.

The waves partly filled the boat but we managed to get clear of the breakers before a rafaga came. While it was still I could make progress, but could not hold against the wind; I had a welcome rest from the exertion of paddling while Julia held grimly on to some kelp to anchor us. In this manner we progressed towards *Totorore*. I shouted out to Anthea to put the kettle on, but this proved a bit premature...

All was well until we had to leave the kelp to cover the last 50 metres. We almost made it when a great rafaga tore us away toward the open sea. 'Dear God help us now, give me strength,' I prayed as I paddled desperately. A very worried Anthea was wondering how to buoy and slip the anchor! I shouted to her to throw us a floating line and she struggled to get one out of the locker, but the wind allowed us to paddle almost within reach again before it whirled us away once more.

I could not have continued paddling much longer when Anthea grabbed the end of the oar which I thrust out towards her...A cheap lesson to treat Cape Horn with more respect...

We took it in turns to 'keep ship', so that one of us always stayed on board; when weather permitted, the other two continued exploring Isla Hornos and making a checklist of avian species. Landings were never easy, but the relaunchings to come back to *Totorore* were worse. The state of the surf was unpredictable; apart from the obvious lesson about lashing the oars, we learned to take off nearly all our clothes and pack them into watertight containers and bags, wearing just our wet-weather gear and wetsuit boots. The worst part was changing on the shelterless beach in the cold wind, especially when we had come down from the mountain already cold and wet and the sight of great curling breakers on the shore had struck terror into our hearts.

On one occasion when I was coming back with Anthea the dinghy flipped over three times. The plastic bags with all our gear were badly holed on the rocks and the contents soaked, so that we had a very large pile of wet gear to deal with when we finally reached *Totorore*. This became a great problem as we were running out of dry clothes to wear. I lit the cabin heater for the first time since we had left New Zealand, but it did little to dry out the salt-wet clothing draped about.

When we had done all else that we could, there remained only the actual peak of Cape Horn itself. It is only 405 metres high, and the ridge along the eastern cliffs was reasonably easy to follow, after which a steep walk in low but tangled vegetation from the landward side gave access to the peak. It was Anthea's and Julia's turn for an expedition, and after a bad landing they took the tent with them and set it up as a base right on the highest point. The weather was kind to them, and from the top they enjoyed glorious views in all directions. In the evening when they returned they had a very rough time of it on the beach and came back somewhat battered and bruised, as well as soaked. 'Ah well,' I thought. 'That's that. Now we can leave this place of horrible wet landings.' I was mistaken. My crew told me that right up on the peak, in tussock grass, they had discovered petrel burrows, and even heard the cooing noise of some sort of petrel in one of them. The news left me excited, determined – and rather afraid. The others were less than enthusiastic, which was understandable under the circumstances, but this is what we had come for and we had to see it through.

Sunday 1 April

It took us all morning, and more, to organise our gear and pack it all up as best we could for a wet landing. Then we had to unpack everything on the beach and stow it into our packs for climbing. It was already 1530 hours before we finally started upwards...we had to press on hard with our heavy packs, which I found quite exhausting. By the time we reached the saddle above the lake, the cloud had come down around us; we were lucky that we knew the way, and were able to follow yesterday's tracks. With poor visibility we could find no sheltered place for the tent anywhere close enough to be able to get back from the peak safely in the dark, so we went all the way up.

The wind on top was strong and it was cold, and the swirling cloud around us soaked everything quickly. It was almost dark when we started to erect the tent and completely dark by the time we had finished. Everything we put down had to have a rock on it.

With the torch held down by a stone, we struggled with the tent. The pegs were useless as the ground was either soft moss or hard rock, so each corner tab had to have a rock on it, and when we tried to put the rods through, to give it its shape, it billowed out and nearly flew away with us hanging on to it, dangerously close to the edge which dropped away sheer on three sides of us. We almost gave up and considered crawling into the tent, flat on the ground.

It was becoming serious. We thought of the makers' claim that the tent had been used on Everest in 100-mile-an-hour winds, but erecting it is the problem when it is windy.

Julia crawled inside and tried to get our temporary home a little organised, while I continued piling rocks around the base. Eventually I felt I could do no more and crawled inside too. With one side collapsed from a broken rod, the tent was small inside and flapping wildly, but it soon felt cosy with the hurricane lamp alight and was absolute paradise compared with outside. It was too dangerous to try to light the primus, so we enjoyed a meal of fruit leather, still in perfect condition after a year and a half...We also ate trail bread with sweetened condensed milk, and felt renewed strength.

After we had togged up with all the clothes we could get on, we called Anthea on the radio to tell her that we were going outside to look for birds, and then crawled out with the big torch, the hand net and the hurricane lamp, which we dared not leave alight in the tent. Standing still in the wind was difficult as the gusts nearly knocked us over, but straight away we could see birds flying. One hit Julia just as the wind blew the hurricane lamp out, and she was unable to catch it. Once we were wedged into the tussock it was easier, but quite difficult manoeuvring to follow the birds with the beam from the big torch. The swirling mists of cloud passing through the beam created a large circle of light which was ideal for the birds, although it did restrict the distance one could see.

In comparative lulls we could hear birds calling all around us, but could not tell if it was from the tussock or from the air. The first two birds I saw briefly in the light were dark, possibly Sooty shearwaters, but after that they were small, white underneath and blue on top, obviously prions or Blue petrels...this was what we had come for...

The birds flew very close above the light but so fast that we never managed to catch one in the net. I hoped that we could use the light to bring one down to land near us in the tussock but they veered off so quickly we could barely get a good look.

We searched the little passages between the tussocks and the entrances to the burrows, hoping to find a bird sitting quietly waiting to be picked up. But the main entrances were over the edge and it was dangerous in the very strong wind...Several times Julia cried out, 'Cuidado! Look behind you, there is nothing there!' Shining the torch down into the nothingness, we clung tighter to the friendly tussocks.

We stayed out for two hours and it was 2230 hours when we crawled back into our haven in the wildly flapping tent. Everything was damp but inside our sleeping bags with our clothes on we soon felt warm again. The ground below was very cold and Julia insisted that I should use the polyurethane roll, as we only had one...

Julia managed to sleep quite well – I heard gentle snores from the depths of her bag – but I had a rotten night. Sometimes the tent flapped with loud reports like rifle shots and the ground shook beneath us. In the morning we could not light the primus because of the wind and had to go without a hot drink. Later, I dug down into some of the burrows in the tussock and saw one bird which scuttled away before I could grab it with my frozen hands, but I was pretty sure that it was a Blue petrel. For positive confirmation we would have to actually catch one, which meant another night on the mountain, hopefully in better weather. In the meantime I carefully repaired the burrows I had damaged. On our way down, we tucked the camping gear into a niche in the rocks in what looked like a better spot...

For two days we were stormbound in Caleta Cabo de Hornos, and could not go ashore. While waiting, we speculated on the birds up on the peak. Both prions and Blue petrels should have left the burrows by now, but we had read that Blue petrels sometimes occupy burrows during the winter months without breeding. The fact that there were no Skuas around suggested that they too had left, but we were surprised not to have found any middens – places where Skuas habitually take their catches to eat, leaving pellets, bones and wings – from earlier in the season. We had seen two Peregrine falcons around the cliffs, and some Striated caracaras, but no Blue petrel remains. Nor had we seen a single Blue petrel offshore when sailing, and could only think that they came in after dark from far out at sea, returning again before daylight – unless they spent the whole day inside the burrows.

The weather was still discouraging when Anthea and I climbed back up Cape Horn mountain to set up camp again. The air temperature was only just above freezing and there were some nasty rain squalls, but we felt that we could not wait forever. The new camp site was much better and more sheltered than on the peak itself, and we trod down some scrub to make an insulating layer under the tent. Loosening rocks to anchor the tent and fly was troublesome, but eventually we felt it was secure enough to leave it while we went up on the peak.

Thursday 5 April
...Having donned extra Damart underwear, sweaters, scarves, and gloves, we set off once more to face the top of Cape Horn, carrying a piece of bamboo and a boathook to use as poles for our mist net, in which we hoped to catch a petrel, and finding them very useful as staves for support against the sleet-filled wind which threatened to blow us over the edge. A very different world from our sheltered campsite! We also carried the pressure lamp, searchlight, and a garden bird net to drape over the tussocks.

On arrival at the top we found this task more easily said than done in the strong wind, and it was frighteningly dangerous working over the edge where the main burrow entrances seemed to be...it was dark before we were ready to try the mist net. That proved to be an almost impossible job. First, we secured the bamboo upright among the rocks, well guyed with cord to other rocks, and then tried to tie one end of the mist net to it. Barely able to stand in the wind, and with frozen fingers, we soon got into a terrible mess; the net caught on us and everything else around. It caught the catch on the searchlight which released the sealed beam unit, and this fell to the ground. I pounced on it before it could blow away, and Anthea helped me to fit it back in. To our great surprise and relief, it worked. We then set up the boathook for the other end of the net, but it was a sorry tangle, and we could do little with it apart from a short section in the middle which we spread by weighting it with rocks.

Meanwhile we noticed large numbers of petrels flying around us, calling with dove-like cooing noises. We lit the pressure lamp – which took a long time, even though we did it behind a big rock with me leaning right over it with my raincoat stretched on either side. When it finally burned brightly it was very gratifying, and we set it down with supporting rocks on the ground near the net, and stood by with our hand net to catch our first petrel. Then the mantle fell off the lamp, extinguishing it...

We stood by with the searchlight, but although many of the petrels swooped close, none came near enough to be caught...While I continued to try to 'bring one down' with the searchlight, Anthea went off to check the net over the tussocks. Soon she came staggering back with a bird clutched to her, shouting excitedly 'I've got one!' She had seen it under the net, sitting quietly just inside the burrow with its tail out, so she grabbed it. We put it in a sack inside one of the packs, collected up our gear, and thankfully retreated from the cold wind. On the way down we passed a large rock with daisy-like plants at its base from which came a loud cooing, and the bird in our pack, which we had seen to be definitely a Blue petrel, answered the call...

Back in the more friendly world of our tent, our rechargeable portable searchlight ran out of power, having lasted just long enough to get us off the peak. Our other rechargeable torch also expired up there. In the warming glow of the small hurricane lamp we measured our Blue petrel. A very pretty little bird, recognisable from a prion by his dark cap and white-tipped tail, he was rather lively and bit Anthea vigorously, drawing blood. We then deloused him...and put him to bed in the sack in the porch of the tent, to await having his photograph taken in the morning.

The last mishap of the day came when I upset a tin of condensed milk, making a nasty sticky mess. It was midnight when we crawled into our sleeping bags, complete with our goros (woolly hats), and lay down to sleep listening to the Blue petrels calling with their delightfully soft voices as they flew around the mountain. 'Dear little things,' murmured Anthea as she dozed off...

Friday 6 April

At about 0400 hours I heard our captive scrabbling vigorously in his bag and thought that the strong instinct to leave the burrow and fly out to sea was working on him, and hoped that when we released him in daylight he would not fall victim to the Peregrine falcons...I made preparations to photograph our bird, carefully measuring out the focussing distance at which Anthea should hold him. Anthea carefully untied the sack and put in her hand. A look of amazement came over her face. 'He's not in there!' she said. We couldn't help laughing. I had just called Julia on the VHF to tell her that we were about to photograph our Blue petrel: it just shows how one can never be sure of anything...The bag had not been tied too tightly to make sure that the bird had plenty of air, and the clever little blighter had squeezed his way out...

131

It took two trips to get all our gear back down to the beach, and on the way we investigated several other clumps of tussock and found many more burrows with Blue-petrel feathers. The weather deteriorated before we had everything stacked up on the beach, and we were both worried by the breakers. Nearby were a few pitiful remains of the Australian single-handed yacht *Dorado* which had been wrecked there just before Christmas. Her owner, injured in the wreck, had managed to get ashore and took sixteen hours to make his way painfully around the bay to the Armada station. The 'jefe' there had radioed the Armada at Puerto Williams, in Canal Beagle, and they had sent a helicopter to pick him up.

After yet another traumatic launching of our dinghy, with the heaviest load we had ever carried, Anthea and I made it safely back. Julia said that the waves looked so bad she was afraid even to watch us! Certainly by this time we had all had enough, but were well satisfied with the results of our efforts. It makes one think how much can be behind the simple statements in bird books: 'Blue petrels nest on Cape Horn'. What a hard-won fact!

While we were in Chile 1983 and 1984, there was a long-standing confrontation between Chile and Argentina over ownership of three islands at the eastern end of Canal Beagle. For this reason, there were seven Armada stations scattered over the Cape Horn islands, each with a number of Armada infantrymen to keep watch for any possible Argentinian landings. The young men in these stations were always friendly and hospitable, and whenever they saw *Totorore*, passing by would call us on the VHF and invite us to share a meal. Sometimes we stopped for lunch or dinner at one of the stations but Anthea and I with our limited Spanish found it quite a strain, as did Julia who had to do all the talking. It was always also unbearably hot. Each station had about ten men, except the headquarters at Caleta Hudson on Isla Herschel, which had 28 men and the only officer, who commanded all stations.

At Caleta Hudson, Teniente (Lieutenant) Tulio Rojas became a good friend. He was interested in our ship and in our work, and could not do enough for us. The caleta itself was a delightful spot, almost circular and with a lovely beach of golden sand. The buildings, most of which were up on the hill above, were camouflaged and unobtrusive, and really it looked more like a holiday resort than a military establishment. It was the only station with its own water transport, having two large inflatables powered by huge outboard motors, and in these Tulio and his men patrolled regularly around the nearer islands. They obviously had much more fun than the men on the other bases, especially those which were too far away for it to be safe for the inflatable to visit them. The general impression at Caleta Hudson was one of efficiency under the leadership of a keen young officer, and it was quite apparent that they would never be caught napping like the men on Isla Hornos!

We circumnavigated all islands, including the Wollaston group, and made many excursions ashore up into the mountains and to visit lakes. Wollaston has particularly beautiful mountains, rich in colour with cloaks of golden brown ñirre trees between snowy peaks and the dark green forests of coigüe lower down. The caleta named Lientur on the east coast offered excellent shelter, a good stream for bathing and washing clothes, and a picturesque outlook.

At Isla Freycinet and Isla Hall we found more colonies of Blue petrels in burrows, as well as on smaller islets round about, all needing to be examined the following summer. We continued to look for Sooty shearwater burrows but the search was made more difficult by heavy falls of snow.

When we first arrived we had seen many small land birds, such as Wrens, Ground tyrants and Yellow-bridled finches, but apart from a few Chilean swallows which surprised us, most of the birds seemed to disappear when the snow came. The snow also covered the wild celery which was commonly encountered on the islands and had become a regular part of our diet. One big advantage of the snow, we found, was that it levelled out the unevenness of the ground and filled up holes, making it much easier to walk. Julia enjoyed making snowmen in the cockpit.

Strong winds and frequent gales were what we came to expect around the Cape Horn islands, and several times we were asked on the radio how we were in the 'mal tiempo' (bad weather) by one of the Armada stations, who seemed to be genuinely concerned for our welfare. It always amused us to hear them refer to the stations on the other islands as other 'countries', which is how they must have seemed to some of them in their isolation. If we had time when we were weatherbound near a station we would invite all the men on board for a cup of coffee, which they always appreciated.

On another visit to the south-east cape of Isla Hornos we had the incredible good fortune to find the oar which we had lost at Cape Horn, lying on the low causeway across to the island off the cape. It was being washed by waves from both sides and could so easily have been carried away to the deep ocean.

In several places we saw whales, and identified Orcas, Fin whales and Sei whales, one of which we found dead on a beach on Isla Wollaston. There were also a few Commersons dolphins, and plenty of Dusky dolphins. One cove on Isla Herschel always had dolphins, so we called it Caleta Tonina, which means dolphin. They continued to play around *Totorore* even after we had anchored, their slow and languorous movements being a joy to watch through the portholes in the bottom of the hull. In Seno Alberto, a large, almost enclosed, inlet in the north of Isla Wollaston, we were followed by literally hundreds of young seals which gambolled playfully after us wherever we went.

We were a happy team. Anthea and Julia shared a common interest in their love of trees and flowers, and plants of any sort down to the lowliest of mosses, in addition to their overriding interest in the birds which we were studying. I enjoyed seeing them poring together over some tiny herb, high up on a windswept mountainside. 'Poor little thing,' Anthea would say. On board I frequently had to exercise tolerance when I found the cabin table and bunks littered with sticks and leaves, flowers and seeds, and sometimes 'pretty stones' or shells.

On Easter Day we had been driven out of a precarious anchorage at Isla Hall by bad weather, and had tried to battle our way north against a gale to reach Puerto Maxwell. After several hours of getting nowhere, we were forced to run for shelter into a caleta in the north west coast of Isla Herschel, which we named Caleta Pascua (Easter).

Sunday 22 April

...Not having had much sleep last night, and not expecting to get much tonight either, we decided to take an afternoon siesta. When we arose for a cup of tea at 1730 hours it was nearly dark. Julia said, 'I am the Easter Rabbit, and for each of you I have hidden three Easter eggs, which you must find!'

We eventually discovered our three cleverly hidden eggs, beautifully decorated hen eggs, emptied through a small hole in the bottom and filled carefully with tiny pieces of delicious nut chocolate... Julia said they always did that at home, not only for her children, but also for her mother and father.

The only major island in the group which we had been forbidden to visit was Isla Deceit, which looked to us like a good bird island. Having invited our friend Tulio to come for a sail, we suggested that he might like to visit his station at Caleta Wilfredo on Isla Deceit and he readily agreed. Since the last time that we had visited Herschel, one of the men had been repairing our spare dinghy. He made a splendid job of it, and it was ready for us when we called to pick up Tulio, who brought with him a big bag full of lovely fresh bread and some cans of diesel fuel.

Friday 27 April
...We had a fast sail under jib alone through a west-north-west wind with driving snow which blotted out the islands from time to time. We were well wrapped up against the bitter weather, but Tulio was quite happy in his thin infantry-green clothing, with a light camouflaged cape which kept flapping in the wind and allowed him to get very wet. He had not brought anything with him in the way of an overnight bag, although the plan was that he should spend the night at the station at Deceit, and then walk right over the snow-covered mountain to the west coast of the island and if weather permitted radio for one of the inflatables to come across from Herschel to pick him up. 'Muy duro,' he said, 'Very tough.' We agreed with him, but later I did lend him a dry pair of trousers.

When we came around the fantastically shaped Islotes Deceit, with truly dramatic rocks, the weather and sea were bad and the light was failing. With the wind ahead we had to motor up the west coast of Deceit, and found our way into tiny Caleta Wilfredo in the dark by radar. The lights of the Armada hut looked very close, as did the breakers on the stony beach and the rocks on both sides! The station called us on VHF and when Tulio answered, the operator asked him if he could speak Spanish! They were very keen that we should join them for dinner, but we did not like the look of the breakers on the beach and considered it unsafe to try landing in the dark. We decided to wait until the morning, letting Tulio sleep in the quarter berth...

Our exercise tramping over the islands kept us all in remarkably good health in spite of frequent dunkings in cold water, and often wearing wet clothes. We were really fit, although I did envy the agility and nimbleness of my companions, especially Anthea who was only four years younger than I. Both of them were definitely tougher and more adaptable than I was, and never complained about being cold or uncomfortable. To see them washing clothes, mine included, in streams of ice-melt water from the mountains which made my own hands numb and useless in just a few minutes, filled me with admiration. And when they immersed themselves completely in the same water and even washed their hair, I began to wonder if they were superhuman! They were too polite to say what they thought of me, but nothing would have induced me to follow their example.

Both women were good cooks, and we all did justice to the excellent meals they produced. Anthea called our scraping of our plates, to make sure we left nothing, the '*Totorore* Signature Tune'. Generally, if we had managed to hole up in a good anchorage reasonably early, we made dinner a rather special occasion. It was quite comfortable sitting at our little cabin table, with the warm glow from our oil lamp as we wished each other 'Salud!' and sipped our good Chilean wine. Often we enjoyed music from one of the small selection of cassettes I had brought. One of our favourites was appropriately the theme music from the film *Flight of the Condor*.

On our way north to return to Punta Arenas we had a look first at Isla Barnevelt, some eighteen miles north-east of Cape Horn; fairly low, it was about a mile long, and had more tussock on it than we had seen anywhere else in Chile. The Magellanic penguins had departed, but we did see seventeen Sheathbills on rocks near the shore. It looked so promising that I noted it as a 'must' for a visit next summer. I also wanted to have a close look at Isla Evout, fifteen miles to the north, one of the places where Black-browed mollymawks were said to be breeding. Unfortunately the weather turned sour, and in a rough sea and sleet we could not see anything on the island as we passed. To the north lay Isla Lennox, one of the Chilean islands concerned in the dispute with Argentina, which were all prohibited to us, but we found ourselves forced to seek shelter in a small caleta on the south-east corner named Caleta Cutter. Hoping that we would not be mistaken for an Argentinian assault vessel, we sailed boldly in with our navigation lights on. Nobody answered our call on the VHF so we were unable to excuse our presence.

We had understood that Isla Lennox was farmed, to maintain a Chilean presence on the island, but in the morning we could see no signs of human habitation around our caleta except a short fence. Two Condors flew overhead, and as we left we saw a large colony of King cormorants on rocks, attended by 34 Sheathbills. Farther up the west coast we saw an Armada station with two huts and a Chilean flag, but nothing else. Progress was slow against head winds which became stronger as the day advanced, and we headed over towards the channel between Isla Picton, another disputed island, and the very large island of Navarino, which forms one side of the eastern half of Canal Beagle.

Sunday 29 April
...The barometer is falling fast and I am thinking now about going into Puerto Toro, on the east coast of Navarino. It does not look particularly good, and there is a settlement there, but there is nowhere else much to go.

It was dark before we came close to the point where a lighthouse stood blinking cheerfully at us. The wind increased to strong gale and we were motoring hard, keeping *Totorore* head to wind, or trying to. I was not too happy about the situation – the puerto did not look as though it would provide much shelter, and I worried about how to get in and anchor without ending up on the rocky shore, especially as the engine was tending to stall when the throttle was eased.

With Julia at the helm, steering by compass, and Anthea in the cockpit standing by, I went below to watch the radar. I gave Julia a course very slightly to starboard to take us clear of two large rocks called Los Gansos, but not so far that the bow would blow off downwind and give us many extra hours of battling to get back again. Outside, it was impossible to see anything, except occasionally the flashing light from the lighthouse, because of the driving spray. On the radar, though, I had a good picture, and could clearly see the cape, the cliffy shore, and just off it, Los Gansos.

Still a safe distance off I felt a very urgent need to relieve myself. When I came back to the radar I was confused. The scale seemed all haywire. My tired brain took a while to register what the radar was telling me – that in the two minutes I had been away, we must have taken a great sheer to port, straight for Los Gansos! In a panic I leapt for the hatchway but I was too late: a sickening, heart-rending jar threw me off my feet. 'Los Gansos!' A second crash followed and we felt the bow of the ship lift high into the air, announcing that we had indeed arrived. A stench of Sea-lions and cormorants assailed my nostrils; the wind howled in the rigging, the wild sea roared about us and *Totorore* shuddered. We were shaken, confused and terrified.

I seized the throttle lever and pushed it full astern. 'Que dirección?' cried out Julia, lapsing into Spanish in her excitement. 'Keep the tiller straight, and hold it tight,' I shouted, trying to make myself heard above the breaking sea. 'Dear Father,' I prayed aloud, 'please help us out of this one!' For a while she hung there, the keels fortunately having ridden up on a sloping rock, probably polished smooth by sea lions. Then another big wave lifted her and the wind caught the bow and pushed her off. In the darkness we could see the white of the breakers – a fearful sight! I kept looking below to see if water was coming in but all seemed well and the engine was still working, the throttle open as wide as it would go; the rudder seemed intact. I was breathing my thanks to God, when Julia shouted that she would not answer the helm and we were heading back towards the rocks! I grabbed the tiller and pushed it hard over the other way, praying that she would come round fast enough to not hit the rocks a second time. After what seemed a very long time I managed to get her up head to wind again, well clear.

Gradually we relaxed a little and realised how fortunate we had been that we had hit the rocks on the lee side and not on the weather side, which would most certainly have been the end of *Totorore*, the expedition, and probably ourselves.

An hour passed, and we were still too close to Los Gansos. 'What is that light?' I shouted. 'Is it a launch?' It seemed to be crossing ahead of us, very fast, and then it went out. The VHF came to life. It was Puerto Toro; a boat was coming out to show us the way in. I said that we did not want it, that we had radar. After a while a black shape appeared close alongside and an anxious voice shouted, 'Follow us!' but of course we could not. The radio repeated that we must follow the boat, which would lead us to the wharf. 'Tell him that we will not go to the wharf, but will anchor,' I demanded of Julia.

We had made enough headway to start edging gradually over towards the puerto. When we were still a quarter of a mile away the boat came back. 'You must follow us!' they shouted urgently. 'You are heading for the rocks!' Anthea and Julia were trying to get the anchors ready in the decidedly difficult conditions up forward. 'No se puede!' (I can't!) I shouted back. 'Rocas!' they yelled. I knew they were wrong, as they could not see that we were moving crabwise across the wind and not in the direction we were heading. If we altered too much to port as they wanted us to, we really would be swept down onto rocks before we could regain control. Anthea took the tiller while I went to have another look in the radar. We were beginning to feel less wind and sea in the lee of the land. By now we could see the lights of houses in the bay and it was all rather confusing.

Watching the sounder, when I judged that we were close enough I yelled 'Let go!' and the chain rattled out. We could now see that the boat was one of the large Armada inflatables with five men. It came alongside and an officer boarded us. 'Come to the wharf,' he said. 'It is very good there.' I explained my reluctance and he said he understood, as he was a yachtsman himself.

The barometer had fallen to 967 millibars and the wind whistled around *Totorore*, but it was nothing compared with the rafagas we had experienced elsewhere. I checked the bilges several times but there was nothing visible from inside the boat, so I thought I would wait until I could get *Totorore* out of the water at Punta Arenas.

The scenery in Canal Beagle was enthralling; sunshine brought out the autumn colours in the forests around the snowy peaks and right down to the blue water's edge. We saw several estancias on both sides, and a few settlements with Chilean or Argentinian flags.

There were no ships to be seen, and not a single patrol boat of any sort, unlike what we had expected. Passing Isla Gable – an Argentinian island which has cliff faces looking like gables – in the middle of the canal, we moved in close to a beach where we saw a large concentration of cormorants. A gruff voice on the VHF asked who we were and what were we doing. When we explained that we were a New Zealand yacht and were looking at the birds on the beach the voice wished us 'Bien viaje'. We had several calls from various Chilean stations along the canal, usually without our being able to see them, but they must have had information passed on about us, as most called us by name.

We could see Harberton on the Argentinian side and would have liked to stop to meet Natalie Goodall, the best known woman in Tierra del Fuego, with many interests similar to our own. But as we had neither Argentinian visa nor clearance from Chile, we could not risk it. On the Chilean side we passed Puerto Williams, the Armada base for the area, which has quite a large settlement against a fantastic backdrop of forest and white mountains. We would have called in there for fuel, but the problem of zarpes put us off.

Tuesday 1 May

...When we sailed past the Argentine/Chile border on Tierra del Fuego we blew a blast on our foghorn and shouted 'Viva Chile!' A little farther on, close to the north shore, we were marvelling at the arrangment of colourful trees, just like a superior garden behind an attractive beach. 'Look! What is that animal?' called Anthea. Our first Guanaco was peacefully grazing, about 200 metres away. What pleasure it gave us to see these beautiful, graceful animals in such magnificent surroundings...

A mile or two farther on, we came across a family group of six including one very young calf...in general shape they are something like llamas, but are more slender and graceful, and are built for speed. Standing more than two metres from the ground to the tops of their heads, they have a proud appearance. With thick fur, a warm brown colour, white shirt-fronts and bellies and dark-coloured heads, they look well clad for the cold winters. Guanacos used to be common in Chile from the northern deserts to the cold south, up to 4000 metres, and were the main source of food and clothing for many of the Indian tribes. With the coming of white men and guns they soon disappeared from most areas and survive now only in the real wilderness of the south, especially in Tierra del Fuego...

As we entered Brazo del Noroeste, the continuation of Canal Beagle, and faced up to the wild eddies, fierce squalls and floating ice which the Pilot warned us about, we decided to head for Caleta Olla, formed by the terminal moraine of the beautiful Hollanda Glacier, descending from the very high mountains above us. Julia spotted a Condor high overhead. Then suddenly two more had come from astern, very low; one looked as though it wanted to land on *Totorore*, with its enormous wings outspread. Before I could get my camera, they soared away into the distance...this really has made it another great day.

We did not get far the next day. After the security of Caleta Olla we found that the wind was right ahead, and would cost us too much fuel to battle against it. After only about twenty miles we found a passage through the outer moraine rocks of a former huge glacier into an un-named inlet with several glaciers coming down in to its inner reaches. Frequently we had to stop while dense snow squalls passed, but inside it was very much calmer than out in the canal. We called the inlet Seno San Cristóbal after our patron saint whose small medallion rests above our cabin table. The inlet branched and we followed the eastern arm to have a good view of the nearest two glaciers. Our exploration was hampered by much floating ice, so we sought out a peaceful corner to have a good night's rest. We called the place Caleta Ketiga.

Thursday 3 May
...Thick snow lay all over *Totorore* and large lumps of ice from the glaciers had drifted all around her and then frozen in, the clear surface already about 12 mm thick. We gazed in awe at the stupendous display of beauty all around us. The trees on the hillsides close by looked too filigreed to be true; beyond, the white mountains and gleaming glaciers against a clear sky completed the picture. Not a sound, not a movement anywhere. It was so tranquil, so perfect, that even to speak to each other seemed a desecration...

I could not help wondering how much ice it would take to freeze *Totorore* in so that she could not move. This was our first experience of fast ice, as it is called, and even though it was obviously quite local, it did cause me to think about how we will fare in South Georgia in winter, where there will be much more ice than here. The temperature this morning is −5 °C but without any wind it is quite pleasant.

We pulled up the anchor, laughing to see the chain coming up through a hole in the ice, then the anchor itself shattering the sheet as though it were glass. Moving slowly with the engine, the ice crackled around the bow and pieces tinkled as they skittered away across the surface. The open track we left astern slowly closed up again. It was fun, but also a little worrying, not knowing much about ice at this stage; when we saw that our escape route out of the inlet was completely blocked by larger pieces, we did think it possible that we might be there for a long stay. Slowly but carefully we pushed our way through, and were back out in the canal at 1300 hours.

It is always difficult in a small sailing vessel to stick to a rigid timetable, which for us meant catching or meeting planes at times of crew changes. On this occasion, Anthea had booked a flight out of Punta Arenas to return home to New Zealand on 8 May, and to arrive by that date we had to press on against weather in which normally we would have preferred to remain in shelter. Having taken some rather doubtful short cuts, we were making good time back up through the canals.

Friday 4 May

...We sneaked through a gap between Isla Catalina and Isla Stewart and made our way through the myriad rocks to pass south of Isla Basket. The wind increased to 30 knots and the sea was rough with heavy obscuring showers of hail or rain, so progess was slow and wet. When we motored into Canal Brecknock, the wind came down the canal against us in aggressive squalls, and as we were passing the outer rocks of Islas Nelson and I was wondering at what unearthly hour we would reach Caleta Brecknock, there was a loud bang and the whole boat gave a jolt. Anthea pulled the throttle lever into neutral. 'Must be kelp,' she said. 'It felt more like a log,' I replied. 'I hope we have not damaged the propeller.' Then Julia, down below, said, 'I can smell something from the engine!' I lifted the cover of the engine case and the alternator was hanging loose; it had chewed up its own belt and some of the sound-proofing foam inside the case and was now bearing on the flywheel. I stopped the engine, and told Anthea to put the helm hard astarboard to let the wind blow us clear of Nelson rocks. After removing the alternator and tidying up, I restarted the engine.

In the dirty weather and pitch dark we had to find an anchorage quickly as the radar's heavy power consumption would soon flatten the batteries now that the engine was not charging them. An unsurveyed area of Peninsula Brecknock on Tierra del Fuego looked quite promising but as we approached, the rafagas came out to meet us in a most daunting manner. I am always anxious when heading into tight corners which are not charted, in the dark, and this was no exception. It became narrower and more intricate, and still we had not found anchoring soundings. I slowed her down, but Anthea could not hold the course each time a freezing rafaga with hail or sleet tore across the caleta and I had to speed up again. As soon as the sounder showed ten fathoms I yelled 'Let go!' just as another rafaga struck us. She paid off so quickly that by the time the anchors were on the bottom we were in deeper water, and when we had brought up to 40 fathoms of chain, the depth was 25 fathoms. Not very good at all, but it was 2330 hours and we felt whacked! I set the alarm and rose frequently during the night to have a look, especially every time a severe rafaga struck and the chain rumbled on the rocky bottom. In fact we did not drag, but none of us got much sleep. We called the caleta, Perno Roto (Broken Bolt), because that was the reason for our being there.

Saturday 5 May

The mountains around us were mostly bare granite...with tools sliding around us as *Totorore* heeled to the squalls, I tackled the engine job and found that the bolt holding the alternator bracket had sheared off inside the block. It took all morning and most of the afternoon to get it all working again. Asi es la vida!

We were cutting it fine for Anthea to catch her plane, but as both of my crew would be leaving at Punta Arenas, I wanted to find somewhere really special for our 'last caleta' together and chose Caleta Hidden, off the Magellan Strait. To reach it, we came up through Canal Acwalisnan, with its two treacherous passages through which the tides race at great speed. They were not particularly difficult, but progress was slow against the strong tide. The water was turbulent, looking like rapids over rocks, and it was hard to tell which was the deep channel – where the water ran smoothly, or where it looked most disturbed? We settled for the latter, and although a heavy snow squall spoilt our vision half way through the first one all was well, and we finally arrived outside Caleta Hidden at 1820 hours in the dark and snow.

Sunday 6 May
...In the middle of the entrance is a large rock with a channel on either side. I chose the south channel as it is narrow and I thought might be deeper...In the dark it looked impossibly narrow, with black rocks on one side and a wall of trees on the other. Slowly, oh so slowly, we sniffed our way through – Anthea in the bow, Julia watching the sounder, and me at the helm. A goose honked in alarm as we passed the rocks...

It was snowing hard again when we found a corner with only ten fathoms for anchoring, about 90 metres from the shore on both sides. Rafagas pushed us around, and it soon became obvious that the anchors were not holding...when my cold tired crew heaved the tandem anchors up again they found the chain on the small anchor wrapped around the Bruce...

Our memories of that fabulous Caleta Hidden will always be of the way we first saw it in the morning. *Totorore* was thickly covered with soft, fluffy snow, and the water all around her was like a mirror, reflecting the snow-covered trees and mountains.

We arrived at Punta Arenas at 2130 hours on 7 May; Anthea caught her plane the next morning and Julia hers the day after.

Guanaco

Chapter Nine

Falklands

Repairs in Punta Arenas — Eastern Magellan — Challenge on the high seas — Stanley — Kidney Island — Volunteer Beach — Western islands, circumnavigation.

Punta Arenas was the same as ever, except that the pier and the streets were slippery with ice. There was much to do, and as usual everything took an unbearably long time. I wanted to have *Totorore* slipped to repair bottom damage from our encounter with Los Gansos, but found it very difficult to make arrangements as there were few facilities other than those at Asmar, the Armada repair yard close to the pier. There were several slips there, capable of handling quite large vessels and protected by a breakwater consisting of the hulks of two old sailing ships. I was told that their work there was excellent but prohibitively expensive. Sergio Barria from Brooms introduced me to Victor Hernandez who had a small shipyard for fishing boats a few miles down the coast, but his slip was fully booked up for at least two weeks.

Although it was an expensive luxury, I telephoned Marjorie every time I arrived back in a port after being out on expedition for a few months. Hearing each other's voice kept us spiritually close, and I never really felt very far from my family, who continued to be supportive throughout the expedition. Marjorie told me that a good friend Malcolm Roberts would be arriving at Punta Arenas to join me in about two weeks. He was a farmer from Mangawhai, in New Zealand, and I knew he would be very practical and a great help in getting our repair work done. As we were short of another crew member, we planned to sail to Falkland Islands to assist Ian Strange, the resident ornithologist, who would join us for some work in the area. After that Malcolm and I should carry on to South Georgia to do some sea bird censusing for the British Antarctic Survey which we had arranged with John Croxall, director of their 'fur and feathers' department in Cambridge, England. A third crew member would be needed again, and we wondered how one could possibly travel there to join us.

In the meantime I was 'keeping ship' by myself, and it was not easy. Constantly shifting about at the pier meant that I could seldom do anything ashore, and some spells of very bad weather gave me sleepless nights and more damage to *Totorore*. One night in particular was extremely unpleasant. The sea came up so quickly that I had no time to cast off to go out to anchor. I had to stay put, as did the fishing boats we were mixed up with. I found it necessary to double up on bow and stern

141

lines and the forward and after springs, so that *Totorore* had eight good lines out to the boat alongside all the time. Our fenders had all been ruined, but luckily Jorge, my taxi driver friend, had brought me two old car tyres which were excellent. Seas were breaking over the stern and the bowsprit was dipping under. During the night, four of our mooring lines carried away and had to be replaced, and a large section of our exterior gunwale and rubbing strake was torn off. It was a night of heaving and crashing and splashing, and shouting and cursing, of oilskin-clad figures and flashing lights. In the morning the decks were covered with ice.

While waiting for Malcolm I was busy writing up bird reports and dealing with the involved bureaucratic processes of renewing my Chilean identity card and my visa. There was no real problem about the visa – in fact I was offered permanent Chilean citizenship if I wanted it – but it required so many different visits to the office uptown, and took so long, that it was difficult to accomplish under the circumstances. In addition, I had further reports to write for the Armada at Valparaiso regarding our future work in Chile. It was only the system which caused the problems; generally the officials with whom I had to deal were most helpful and agreeable.

In spite of the difficulties and delays I encountered there, I have fond memories of Punta Arenas as a city. When I first arrived I was surprised to find the southernmost city in the world looking just like a modern town anywhere else, and the heavily ponchoed, sombrero-topped people I had expected were missing. In the streets everyone was smartly dressed in fashionable clothes, and to my amazement nobody even seemed to own a raincoat! In the city centre there is a fine plaza with lovely trees and flowers, and a magnificent bronze sculpture of the great navigator Hernando de Magallanes. Below him, one on either side of his great pedestal, are seated two naked Indians, and in front a mermaid. The large foot of one of the Indians is polished bright where people kiss it – to be sure of coming back to Punta Arenas. I did so, but would have preferred to kiss the ample bosom of the mermaid. Perhaps it was just as well that it was too high to reach!

I went out to the airport and met Malcolm, looking very brown and wearing a short-sleeved shirt! He was quite amazed at how cold it was. I was relieved and glad to see him, and knew that as I had nearly finished my paperwork, we could concentrate on *Totorore*.

We arranged a day for slipping at the Hernandez shipyard, but when we arrived we found that a fishing boat needing emergency repairs had taken our place. For ten days we went down to the yard and back again, but always there was a reason why we could not slip. The tide was not high enough, or the wind was too strong. It was very frustrating, but we were not idle. Malcolm did some good work on the engine and repaired our jib furling drums which had been smashed one night at the pier. We used epoxy glue, and to enable it to work in the zero temperature we had to keep applying hot-water bottles to it. We added an extra perspex sheet to insulate our forward cabin ports, and Malcolm generously bought me a good Antarctic suit and us each a pair of thermal boots in preparation for South Georgia. Finally, after Victor Hernandez had made special modifications to his slipway cradle to accommodate our twin-keeled *Totorore*, she was hauled out of the water and stayed up for a full week.

The yard was too busy to assist us with the work, but we managed everything needed by ouselves and repaired the stem from which a large chunk had been torn by Los Gansos rocks. To start with, it was not very pleasant living on board on dry land becaused there was no toilet at the yard and no washing facilities. It snowed every day. Fortunately we soon made friends with Pedro Gomez, his wife Helen, and all their family, who lived in a house a short walk from the yard and always made us welcome. Pedro and another good friend, Ernesto, took a real interest in our expedition, and several times came to help us with our repair work. Victor Hernandez was very good to us, and even though he had made the alterations to his cradle specially for us, he charged us nothing at all – as we were friends of Brooms!

When we were happily afloat again, we started to get things together ready for sailing. Pedro was a tremendous help, chasing up parts and materials for last-minute jobs, and Helen did a great deal of typing for me along with all our washing. We enjoyed some very pleasant evenings at their house.

One day we were pleased to see the US Research Vessel *Hero* at the pier, having often read about her and seen pictures of her in books and journals about Antarctica. She was an old-fashioned, solidly built green-painted wooden vessel, with external steel plates on the bow for protection from ice, and could still carry sails in addition to her powerful diesel engines. A real character ship, and we were lucky to see her because it was her last voyage and she was due to be laid up on return to the US in September. Her first mate, Geoff Jenk, made us welcome aboard and showed us around. Later we were invited to dinner and were entertained by Captain Pieter Lenie, who had been master of *Hero* for ten years and was a great story-teller.

At midday on 13 June we sailed at last up the Magellan Strait bound for Falkland Islands. Passing Isla Isabel we saw our first Upland geese, which are very common in that pampas part of the country, but while at Punta Arenas we had always been too busy to go out and about and hoped to have a chance to see some next time.

The tides in the narrows of the Strait run very strongly and it is impossible for a low-powered vessel to make way against them, so when the tide turned against us we anchored close to the northern shore after creeping in behind a sheltering sandbank near Caleta Susana. At 0200 hours we moved out to catch the tide but had not gone far when we stuck fast on the sandbank, which according to our radar had extended by a good half mile from its charted position. I was rather concerned because the ebb was already flowing, and I did not like the idea of staying there all day, especially with the strong tide scouring out the fine sand from under the keels as it had done at Valdivia. She swung on the keels, and with the engine full ahead and Malcolm and myself out on the end of the bowsprit, she came clear and we went on our way.

The coast in the eastern Magellan Strait is low, flat and uninteresting, and was plainly visible by moonlight. There were some oil installations and flares, and a few ships passed us. The Primera Angostura (the first narrows) are well known for the strength of the tidal streams, and we went racing through at thirteen knots – a novel experience and rather fun. I reported to the Armada station at Punta Delgada as we sailed past. It was cold at $-5\,^{\circ}$C and the spray was freezing on the rigging and on the decks, which became dangerously slippery. It was a whole new dimension for me, this world of ice, and I was not sure how to handle it. How would I manage sailwork at sea? Gloves which we had been given by the mate of the *Hero* proved to be inadequate and did not keep our hands warm when holding the tiller.

For the next tide we anchored close to the shore in Bahía Posesión under the lee of some low cliffs. The wind was fresh from the north, and the sea had become rough, so I took her in as close as seemed prudent. In this I made an unforgivable

143

mistake, which makes me feel ashamed even to recount it. As the ebb had been flowing for six hours, I assumed that it was low water and could only rise, so that it was safe to anchor in three fathoms, about 1.5 cables off the beach of sand and stones. Had I done my homework properly and studied both the tide tables (which I had not bought) and the chart, on which is a note, I would have learnt that the tide can continue to fall for three hours after the stream has turned in the direction of the flood! It was not long before I discovered my error, but in the meantime I had other problems on my mind.

When I went to stop the engine I discovered a great deal of water in the bilge. While I stowed away gear and checked the rigging prior to our going deep sea, Malcolm looked over the engine and found that a plug in the bottom of the muffler tank had rusted through. That was not too serious, and was soon fixed with epoxy putty. Up the mast I made the alarming discovery that the bolt holding the tangs for the lower shrouds had pulled down and elongated its holes in the mast, which were cracking in that area. I could only conclude that it was caused by contact between the shroud and a fishing boat when rolling alongside at Punta Arenas, and I had to make the decision whether to lose yet another day and stop to repair it, or nurse her carefully across to Falklands, only about 400 miles away. I chose the latter course, with some misgivings because I never feel happy when there is anything wrong aloft, but feeling that psychologically any further delay would seem disastrous to both of us.

While stowing away the dinghy in the after locker, I suddenly noticed that the beach on the shore was uncovering considerably, and farther east the sea was breaking at the same distance from the shore as ourselves. It was time to shift farther out. Malcolm weighed anchor, and rather than use the engine before the epoxy putty had hardened, I set a small jib and we soon picked up speed in the fresh offshore wind. The sounder was reading 1.5 fathoms when there was a violent crash as one of our keels hit a submerged (and uncharted) rock. The shock caused a glass lamp chimney down below to jump out of its bracket and break itself on the sole, the noise of which added to the horror of the moment. *Totorore* did not seem to have suffered any damage, although such a collision must put a terrible strain on the whole boat. Shortly afterwards we anchored again in deeper water and completed our preparations for sailing while awaiting the turn of the tide.

I say that I am not superstitious, but I could not help thinking that bad things happen in threes, so that we should be all right from then on, following the engine leak, the shroud, and then the rock. Soon we were sailing briskly along past the flares of the oil rigs, ashore and at sea, of Tierra del Fuego, the Land of Fire, and out across the rough seas on the Banco Sarmiento and into the Atlantic Ocean.

Malcolm was rather off-colour during the trip across to Falklands, still getting his sea-legs, and spent most of the time in his bunk. I tried very hard, with my limited culinary skills, to provide attractive meals, but when I asked him if he liked anything I had prepared, the best compliment he ever gave my cooking was to say, 'It's food.' However I was feeling more relaxed, and stress-induced complaints which had developed at Punta Arenas, like a bad back and a nasty cough, disappeared as I could again enjoy bird-watching, which was particularly interesting while over the continental shelf.

Sunday 17 June
...at about 0300 hours I could tell that the jib had gone aback, and I got

144

up to do something about it. I was just putting on my boots and wet-weather trousers when I became aware of an extremely bright light in the cabin. Then I could hear an engine of some sort, so I jumped out into the cockpit and waved towards the blinding searchlight. I reached inside and switched on the VHF in time to hear 'Vessel on our starboard bow!' I answered, and switched to Channel 69 as instructed. After contact there was a long pause, and then a cultured, very English voice came over the set. 'This is the Captain, HMS *Andromeda*. What is the name of your vessel, and where are you bound?' Good old Royal Navy! When they switched off the searchlight I could see the dark shape of what looked like a fairly big ship. 'You look becalmed,' said the Captain. He asked me details about us, and then if they could contact anybody at Falklands for us, so I told him Dr Bourne in the RFA ship *Sir Lancelot*, as Bill had told us that he is now doctor with her and should be in Falklands while we are there. I asked where she is, but that is probably an official secret and he did not tell me, but said he would let Dr Bourne know that we are coming. I also asked him to contact Ian Strange and he said, 'Oh yes. We were going to take him to Beauchêne Island today, but there was a change of plans.' It was all very friendly, but very efficient. 'Jolly good show!'

In the evening it blew a gale when we were nearing the coast of West Falkland; about seven miles off we stood out to sea to keep clear during the hours of darkness. It was a wild uncomfortable night and I was worried about our sick shroud with all the heavy jolting which *Totorore* was subjected to. The radar was no good in those conditions, and in any case the huge seas intervened between us and the low, flat coast, but the Satellite Navigator was a gem and did a great job. I had learned from experience that I could not rely on it to within about 2.5 miles of a coast because of the variability of the datum positions of charts, especially the older ones, but even that much accuracy was a tremendous help to my confidence and all I needed.

When daytime came and the wind became more favourable and blew from the south-west, it seemed a good chance to run for Stanley. Malcolm however was not well and asked if we could shelter somewhere. I was reluctant, but really did need a good sleep myself, so we closed the coast of East Falkland and headed for Bull Cove.

Monday 18 June
...We were within only three miles of the land before we could see it at all, and it looked like a long, featureless sandbank, bleak and uninteresting. We ran in until just clear of the enormous breakers, tacking downwind under a small jib, then around Bull Peninsula outside the breakers. We were caught by one which broke over the stern and sent a lot of water down below, as I had the washboard out to keep popping down to look at the chart. She was surfing in on the big swell, and it was exhilarating. Once in the lee, the swell flattened out and it was just a matter of following the edge of the extensive kelp beds right into the cove, where we anchored in 2.5 fathoms soon after 1200 hours. The wind was still strong but over a flat sea. On the sandy beaches we could see large numbers of Kelp geese and

Black-backed gulls, and King cormorants swam and dived all around us. . . After a quick lunch we both turned in and slept until after dark.

We had a few jobs to do before we left, so did not get away from Bull Cove until 1000 hours and it was midnight when we entered Port Williams, leading to Port Stanley. It was not an easy approach because the weather was still bad, and the shoreline invisible to radar and eye. I was somewhat dismayed when I saw that neither of the lighthouses at the entrance was working. They had been put out of action during the war with Argentina two years before, but had not yet been restored. The glow of lights from Stanley was a big help, but I was conscious of such hazards as Billy Rock in the entrance, site of the wrecks of at least four good ships. Malcolm was rather unnerved by the whole thing and kept saying, 'It's all right for you – you are used to it!'

We came through the Narrows, which did have working light beacons, and entered Port Stanley, finally anchoring off the Government Jetty. We were surprised by the extent and brilliance of the lights of Stanley, which made it look a bigger place than we had imagined. The harbour and approaches contained many ships, boats and buoys.

In the morning we saw that the eastern end of the harbour near to the airport had a new port constructed on a vast system of pontoons, like Mulberry Harbour during the invasion of France in 1944, for the use of naval and military ships, and beyond that were huge floating buildings like blocks of flats, for military personnel. There was much activity as Harrier jets, Hercules transports, and huge helicopters came and went, while launches criss-crossed the harbour between the ships at anchor. The town itself looked quite small, with rows of simple houses facing the harbour in lines along the low hillside, their roofs painted in bright colours, and a church with a pyramid-roofed tower in the centre, close to the shore. We could see one small wharf for ships, and several rather derelict-looking jetties built on the wrecked remains of old sailing ships. Discounting the large numbers of British troops who were living at the end of the harbour, Stanley had a population of about 1000, which was roughly half the population of the whole of Falkland Islands.

We were instructed to go alongside a small island trading ship named 'Forrest' which was lying alongside the broken-down Government Jetty, and this we did after washing the evil-smelling mud from our anchor chain. We were boarded by the Harbour Master and two uniformed policemen. Formalities were minimal, and the officials friendly and helpful.

A letter from Bill Bourne advised us that RFA *Sir Lancelot*, then in San Carlos Water, would be back in Stanley in about five days, and would be sailing for a ten-day trip to South Georgia the day after. Would I care to go along? I had to turn down the offer because I could not leave *Totorore*, and in any case felt that a trip in a big ship would not be of benefit to the expedition. However, I was looking forward to meeting Bill again.

Malcolm and I enjoyed a good bird talk with Ian Strange and his wife, Maria, but were sorry to learn that Ian would be unable to accompany us in *Totorore* as he had a bad knee. He spoke at length about the complex conservation problems in the Falklands, and when we left him we were wondering how we could help the situation while we were there, and also what we could do about a third crew member.

146

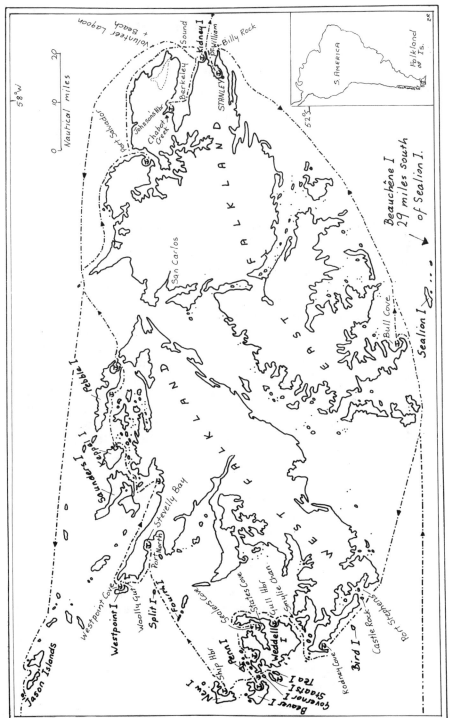

Map 18

Dr Andrew Douse, an English ornithologist who was working for the Government to assess the effect on pastoral agriculture of the Upland goose, came to see us. I had written to him just before the war with Argentina, but his house had been occupied and all his papers destroyed, so I had not received a reply. He asked us if we could do some preliminary offshore island survey work for the Falkland Islands Foundation, a charity organisation registered in the UK to promote and support the conservation of the ecology in the Falkland Islands. The majority of the islands had once been well covered with tussock, which made them ideal seabird habitat, but overgrazing by sheep and cattle had destroyed most of this. What the Foundation wanted to know was which islands were not too far gone and would be worth saving as wild-life reserves, bearing in mind that the economy of the Islands depended on the production of wool. This type of work was so completely within the aims of the expedition that we were delighted to be able to make a small contribution, even though there would be few birds to be found on the islands in winter. What we could do was report on the vegetation cover, height of tussock, signs of regeneration, and if we saw any petrel burrows. Andy did say that if we could come back in the summer, we would even be paid for such work, but I had to decline the offer as our programme had already been mapped out. In the meantime, we needed the extra crew member to assist with the island survey work.

Happily, we were able to bring Andreas von Meyer across from Chile to join us for our work both in Falklands and in South Georgia. A small Danish cargo ship, with the unimaginative name *A.E.S.*, was on a regular run between Britain and the Falklands, and arrived at Stanley one week after we did. After discharging her cargo she was going to Punta Arenas to pick up a load of timber – the first direct contact with Chile since the war two years before, and apparently a trial run, as it was thought that under the Danish flag she would not provoke any action from the Argentinians when approaching the Magellan Strait. I went aboard to see the master and asked him if it would be possible for Andreas to travel back with them on the return voyage. Following complicated and time-consuming negotiations with the agent, Falkland Islands Company, and messages to and from Puerto Montt through friendly ham radio operators, it was finally arranged.

While I was busy at Stanley with the various administration problems, Malcolm was doing a sterling job on our repairs. The Public Works Department, right next to the Government Jetty, allowed him to use their workshop, and I was able to purchase rivets from them for him to use on the mast when he reinforced it. In addition, he took complete charge of the engine, which had continued to be troublesome. My daughter Annalie had written to tell me that I should still love the engine even when it went wrong, and I tried to follow that good teaching but was only mildly successful. Malcolm, however, certainly lavished much loving care upon it, to which it readily responded. He tackled major jobs such as renewing crankshaft oil seals, which necessitated removal of the flywheel and lifting the engine, and overhauling the fuel pump. He fitted rubber engine mounts, which he had brought from New Zealand with him, and that made a tremendous difference both to the engine and to ourselves, with a considerable reduction of noise and vibration.

Between repair jobs and other commitments we managed a couple of jaunts not far from Stanley. The first was to Kidney Island, one of the very few which have never been grazed, and is thus still completely covered by tussock grass. It is a nature reserve, and a breeding place for a very large number of bird species. I had read Eleanor Pettingill's book *Penguin Summer* many years before, and felt I knew the place already. I immediately recognised the little hut in which she and her husband, Olin, had stayed. Unfortunately some army people had used it, and apart from leaving much litter around the hut (which we cleared up), they had left the door open so that it had been occupied by Turkey vultures, which had made a terrible mess. The tussock was very healthy, standing about three metres high in places, and underneath the big bogs, or pedastals, the ground was littered with burrows, indicating what a fantastic place it would be for birds in the summer. Above the beach of East Falkland itself, opposite Kidney Island, there were hundreds of Gentoo penguins in a tightly packed colony, and more coming out of the sea farther along. That was the first colony which Malcolm and I had seen, but we did not dare go ashore because it was an area marked on the map which I had obtained from the police as being mined.

In Falkland Islands there was only one small colony of King penguins, at Volunteer Beach on the north-east coast, about twenty miles by sea from Stanley. As there is no sheltered anchorage or landing place, to reach the colony it was necessary to approach it overland from Johnson's Harbour, where Osman Smith, the owner of the sheep station, lived. We sailed up Berkeley Sound, past the fishing fleet of large Polish and Spanish trawlers which habitually anchor there, then across Johnson's Harbour into the shallow and kelp-filled Chabot Creek. I was surprised to see how big the settlement was – four quite large houses with many outbuildings and farm sheds, and a small jetty. Everything looked neat and tidy, the buildings all with red roofs, white walls and blue trim. It seemed rather bare, but then there are hardly any trees in Falkland Islands.

Osman met us and took us up to his house, warm and snug with its peat stove, where his housekeeper Marion gave us hot coffee and home-made buns and cakes. The first pair of King penguins had started to breed in 1947, and since then the numbers had gradually increased. Some lay in December, then the following year in January, and then because of the late fledging of the chicks, they miss a year. In the fourth year they start again in December, and so on, which is similar to the pattern of Kings in other places. To avoid their being unduly disturbed, Osman had insisted that parties of British troops coming by helicopter to see the Kings must never fly over the colony, and must land about two miles away and then walk. This rule was always respected. We had been impressed by the way the British forces had issued booklets to all their personnel with detailed information on the wildlife of the islands.

Tuesday 26 June
We rowed ashore through slushy ice, the oars making new holes at each stroke, and Osman accompanied us for a mile or so to make sure we were on the right track. It is what he calls a 'medium-sized' farm of 48,000 acres, and we had a ten-mile walk to Volunteer Beach where the Kings are, and also where there is a 'shanty', in which he said we could stay. Osman said that he would keep an eye on *Totorore*; it was one of those very rare occasions when we felt it was safe to leave her, because she is in a well sheltered cove with good mud holding ground.

The 'camp' (which means anywhere outside of Stanley) was like a moor, with very rough brown grassland and patches of 'diddle-dee', which is like

149

a dark-coloured heather. We made towards Mount Brisbane, rounded and only 180 metres high but with many rocky outcrops near the top. Fences were few, and we had only two gates to pass, one green and the other red. We could see that when not frozen, the ground would be boggy, and there were numerous small streams to cross. When we spotted the red roof of the shanty we were both pleased, as we were tired from carrying our heavy packs and were becoming creaky at the joints.

The shanty was not what we had expected – it was, rather, a delightful cottage painted like the houses at the settlement, with a brick chimney sticking up from the centre of the roof on which sat two Turkey vultures. Apparently it is used by shepherds. Inside was clean, tidy and very homely. The kitchen/living room and one bedroom were downstairs, and up a narrow staircase leading through a trapdoor were two more bedrooms, each with two beds. What a perfect little house! While I lit our primus for a quick cuppa, Malcolm started to get to know the 'Modern Mistress' peat range, which had two large kettles, to be filled from a roofwater tank just outside the door. There were some easy chairs and an ancient sofa, and an old-fashioned oil lamp on the table.

Leaving the shanty for a walk, we crossed the grassy sand dunes, riddled with the burrows of now absent Magellanic penguins. Huge rollers from the Southern Ocean create a spectacular surf, and we could see a big Sea-lion patrolling for penguins as they came in... All around us on the dunes were hundreds of Upland geese, and the smaller but equally good-looking Ruddy-headed geese, all as tame as domestic farmyard geese. The Uplands are similar to Kelp geese, but the ganders have striking black barring and the geese have lovely red-brown colours with yellow legs. They have long been considered a pest by the farmers and a bounty is paid for destroying them, which accounts for about 50,000 each year as they are so easy to shoot. Osman says he likes them, because where there are lots of geese his sheep do well. Whether it is the manuring of the ground, or the fact that in the spring the sheep eat the green goose droppings, he does not know...

On the walk across we had seen few birds, just an occasional Pipit. Now there were large numbers of Black-backed gulls and Sheathbills, and some Two-banded plovers, Meadow larks, and Thrushes. Near to the shores of Volunteer Lagoon, close to the shanty, were large groups of Gentoo penguins. These seem to be the only species of penguin which habitually come ashore each night right through the year even when they are not breeding. They are very handsome, with a white bar over the top of their heads and orange beaks and feet, and stand about 70 centimetres high. They seemed a little wary of us if we were closer than about 30 metres, so we guessed that they have been often disturbed. We then visited the King penguins, which we could hear calling from a hollow at the far end of the beach. There they were in all their glory, the magnificent adults with their silvery-grey backs and bright yellow ear patches setting off their 'Persil-white' shirt fronts. The chicks were large and round, brown and fluffy, like huge tea-pot cosies.

After the sun had set and we were meandering back towards the shanty we suddenly saw large numbers of Gentoos leaping out of the surf onto the beach where they gathered into a great crowd and then started up the dunes and along the green in a thin line, only two or three deep. Crouching low, we made our way to a sandy bunker where we squatted and watched the procession approaching and make its way past us. What an unforgettable, theatrical sight! They kept coming and coming – there were thousands of them – and the line stretched for over a mile from the beach to the colony. In front of us the advancing troops shone gold in the last reflections from the clear sky, and behind us they made impressive silhouettes, like an army on the move. Waddling without appearing to hurry, and yet moving surprisingly quickly, with orderly progression and few low cawing calls, they passed us on their way to the colony for the night. We were both spellbound, and did not notice how cold we were until the tail-enders had disappeared into the gloom.

The next day we caught a Gentoo on the beach with our hand net and took his measurements, and also endeavoured to take lice from him. Later we did the same with a King chick. Malcolm was really enjoying himself, because apart from the Little blue penguins at home, penguins were a novel experience for him, and to be able to actually hold a great cuddly teddy-bear chick in his arms really appealed. We counted a total of 83 chicks and 115 adults in the colony.

Bill Bourne was able to join us for dinner at Andy Douse's house on the one evening his ship was in Stanley, and it was good to be in touch with him again. He kept us entertained with his fund of stories and his dry humour, and when he left said he would like to join us for a spell later, if it could be arranged, but in any case would see us in South Georgia.

Ian Durie, an army friend of Andy's came to see us to see if he could possibly come with us for a day or two, when convenient, as he too was a keen bird watcher. We said we could probably fit him in somewhere, because we took an instant liking to him.

After making an appointment at Government House (which we noted had twelve Turkey vultures sitting on the roof!) we went to pay our respects to the Governor, Sir Rex Hunt, and to ask for formal permission to visit South Georgia. He was very busy so our interview was brief, but he invited us to see a film which he had made of South Georgia one evening before we left. I had to drag out my old reefer jacket and tie from under my bunk and ask Monica Alonso to press it for me. She and her husband Jorge and a friend Mario Zuvic were all from Chile, and became good friends of ours. The jacket and tie were useful again a few days later when Ian Durie, himself a lieutenant colonel, invited us to dinner at the officers' mess.

With most of the winds from the west, we had shifted our berth to the eastern end of the Government Jetty, where *Totorore* lay off comfortably. At the forward end the jetty had collapsed below the water and the decking was rotten, sloping away at a dangerous angle, especially when icy or wet. One night after we had had a very good dinner, we came out of the house to discover to our alarm, that the wind had freshened and was from the east! We hurried back to *Totorore* and found that she was heaving about and graunching herself badly against the jagged ends of timber and broken bolts of the jetty. An official sign on the jetty says 'Persons using this jetty do so at thier own risk'.(A similarly worded and spelt [sic] sign is above the East Jetty, farther along.) We had an anchor laid out upwind, but even so it was a difficult job to get clear of that damaging horror, and we were pleased

151

when we finally anchored out in the harbour. There was nasty damage to the gunwale and sheet track, as well as the pushpit and life-line stanchions. The strong easterly winds blew, with snow, for five days; we had been told that easterlies never blow for more than a few hours!

As our main island survey area was to be to the west of West Falkland, we sailed out into a still-rough sea on 7 July to take advantage of the easterly wind while it lasted, and kept going day and night down the coast and across the Sound. The scenery of the West Falkland was more spectacular, with some great cliffs and bluffs and high mountains, all covered with snow. Castle Rock, off Port Stephens, really did look like a castle. Bird Island, fortunately already a nature reserve, looked a perfect habitat with big cliffs of layered pancake formation, and good tussock cover. There we saw Striated caracaras, known locally as Johnny Rooks. This is the only place, other than the south Fuegian area, where they are to be found.

Not knowing the state of tide in the Smylie Channel, which leads up to the settlement on Weddell Island, and aware that it can run up to ten knots at times in a vicious race, I did not want to tackle it in the dark. We anchored for a night in Rodney Cove, surrounded by hundreds of Logger ducks (a species of Steamer duck), Crested ducks, and Kelp geese. In the morning we had the tide with us in the Smylie Channel, and after a quick look at some small partly grazed tussock islets, we entered Gull Harbour which is surrounded by low land but sheltered from the west by a range of rocky mountains topped by Mount Weddell at 383 metres. The settlement was typical with a few houses, several farm buildings including a woolshed, and a jetty, tucked into a cove in the north-west corner of the bay. Lying off the jetty at a buoy was a small fishing boat with a sail and a box-like cabin aft, named 'Nancy'. A small house up the hill had smoke coming from the chimney, but otherwise the settlement looked deserted.

Monday 9 July

After anchoring we rowed ashore and walked up past the usual gallows with its beef carcase hanging from it, towards the cottage with the smoking chimney. There we met Bill Davies and his wife Violet, who made us welcome with coffee and cake. They told us something about the farm, which is the whole of Weddell Island, covering 56,000 acres, and is part of the Hamilton Estate which also includes Beaver Island and Saunders Island, and many smaller islands in between. The estate is Argentinian owned, and the political situation is not clear. The business is controlled by a major shareholder now in Jersey, but there is talk of the estate being split up into smaller units. Bill is a worker on the farm and said he would have been interested in owning a small farm of his own, but who would want to invest in a farm now, with the future of the Falklands so uncertain? All the farms are in a similar state of reduced production, with considerably less manpower than previously. More than half the houses on the settlements are empty. Weddell Island now carried only 7,500 sheep, and those on the smaller islands had all been removed or killed because, apart from the little *Nancy*, they had no boat. The only other people living on this farm are Bob Ferguson, the manager, and his wife Thelma, who invited us to supper.

Over a warming whisky before an excellent meal of beef steak and mashed potatoes, Bob and Thelma told us more about their life in the camp. It is fairly isolated here on Weddell, being about 168 miles from Stanley, and during the invasion and occupation of Falklands they never even saw a single Argentinian. They have few visitors, but they keep in close touch with other settlements by radio. Most settlements have an airstrip, and a small plane runs a service to settlements from Stanley. The *Forrest* or another small ship call very occasionally to bring bulk stores or to take away wool. In days gone by there used to be a schooner, the *Weddell*, which moved stock around the islands for nine years without an engine! Her skipper, Bob told us, could smell his way up inlets and creeks in the dark or blinding snow, making full use of the tides he knew so well...We are constantly surprised at how few boats of any sort there are around these islands and harbours where one would have expected boatwork to be a large part of the people's lives. There is no fishing industry, and the huge foreign trawlers we see pay only harbour dues for anchoring in Falkland waters, with no other benefit to the Islands.

After dinner Thelma gave us a nice piece of teaberry pie, a favourite delicacy in the settlement. The teaberries are currant-sized, red and white, and grow on a low ground-creeping plant in the same open places as diddle-dee, which also has berries. These berries are eaten by the Patagonian foxes which are a terrible pest on this farm and others in this group of islands, where they were introduced by the original owner of the estate, John Hamilton, about 50 years ago. He probably had in mind the establishment of a fur industry, but it was never developed, and now the animals prey on lambs. As a result, lambing on the far side of the island gives only about 20% success. At the same time as the foxes, Hamilton introduced Guanacos to Staats Island, in the same group, and it seems that they are thriving on that one unfarmed island.

We heard through the settlement radio that Andreas had arrived at Stanley on the *A.E.S.* and would fly out to Weddell Island in the Islander aircraft the next day. We sailed out of Gull Harbour with a five kg hunk of beef hanging in the rigging, and a billy-can full of fresh milk. Wherever we went in Falklands we received the same warm hospitality and help.

Even with radar it was a hair-raising experience finding our way into States Cove for the first time at night, the route being littered with rocks and reefs, many of which do not appear on the small-scale chart. Once inside it was well sheltered and with an easy landing. Andreas duly arrived in the morning, and we all set off to the end of the peninsula to look for birds. I had not realised how much I missed his youthful enthusiasm, and his wide knowledge of birds, which with his strange humour made him such a good companion. He was not very practical, but Malcolm kept the balance, so between us all I felt that we made a good team.

We had lunch in a tiny shanty at Sealers' Cove, and were glad of the shelter it provided from the cold wind blowing across the open moorland. On the way back along the beach we came across a large number of skeletons and skins of Long-fin pilot whales which had stranded there a year before. We never saw any whales, but the lovely Commersons dolphins, locally called Puffing-pigs, were common, and so too were Dusky dolphins and Hourglass dolphins.

For a week we made a systematic survey of the many islands to the west of Weddell Island. It was interesting work, but disappointing to us to see the ravages

153

caused by overgrazing, with consequent erosion on most of the islands, which had made little recovery since the stock was removed after the schooner *Weddell* had been withdrawn from service. Rats were evident on many of them, and few islands had petrel burrows.

On Penn Island we saw several hundred Southern giant petrels in a tight group on and just above a beach, pairing and beginning to prepare for the nesting season, although in mid winter it did seem very early. They were touchy, so we kept our distance, but even when *Totorore* was still 200 metres away, many of them were uneasy and fidgety. It could have been because the islanders still raid their colonies for eggs, or it could have been the presence of several large Sea-lions just off the beach, and younger ones playing among them on the shore. In our dinghy we were able to drift quite close past them without creating a disturbance. Among them was only a single 'white-phase' bird.

We spent one night at Beaver Island, where there is a small settlement. The farm of about 10,000 acres on this very irregularly shaped island was carrying 2500 sheep, and run by Tony Felton and his 17-year-old daughter Faith, the only inhabitants, who offered us the usual hospitality. Tony told us that foxes take about 50% of their lambs, in spite of their constant war against them by shooting and trapping.

On Governor Island was another large group of Giant petrels, which were just as touchy as those on Penn; they flew up and did not settle again until after we had anchored. Not much farther south we stopped at Staats Island to see the Guanacos.

Thursday 17 July

...As we passed around the end of Staats Island with its great cliff walls down the west coast, we could see that the tussock had been badly eaten out, but to our surprised pleasure we spotted about a dozen Guanacos grazing on the slopes above us. The water was deep close in so we were able to have a really good look at those magnificent animals. They didn't seem unduly alarmed, but did make an unhurried departure. The wind howled up the channel between Staats and Tea Island so we tucked into a small bay on the north-east corner of the island close to a sandy beach...We were careful not to wear our rather brightly coloured wet-weather clothing so as not to be too conspicuous.

Above the beach was the shanty, in this case a rough hut with little furniture and no stove. Around the hut was obviously a favourite Guanaco camp, being in the bottom of a valley in which there was quite a lot of long grass. The hills themselves looked bare and the soil between the dead tussocks was soft, black and eroding. Much bare rock showed all over the island. We could see small groups of Guanacos on both sides of the valley, one of three that go right across the island...I went in one direction, down the east coast, and Malcolm and Andreas in another, and we agreed to meet back at the hut before dark. I had not walked more than 50 metres when I almost stumbled over a fox, a pretty silvery colour, which bounded away about fifteen metres and then turned to look at me. While I fumbled to get my camera he disappeared. Then I went stalking Guanacos...I crept along hidden by hillocks or mounds of grass, but muffed my best chance by not seeing one just the other side of a ridge, much closer than those I was stalking. He leapt away with a loud call of alarm which set all the others off

154

too, and they were soon out of camera range...I set up several more groups, and watched the main herd of about 70 making its way up the slopes of the next big valley. A couple of Peregrine falcons flew overhead and some pretty Black-throated finches flitted about in the long grass...

New Island was one of the most interesting islands we had seen, and one of the best bird islands. Most of it belonged to Ian Strange, and he had removed the sheep from his holding for purposes of conservation, but the other owner still ran sheep on the northern part. The island is about 5.5 miles long, north to south, and of very irregular shape, narrow in the middle. The highest hills are about 215 metres high, with many smaller hills and valleys; all along the west coast are the most spectacular cliffs to be found in the Falklands. The hills slope down towards the east coast which curls around to form several harbours, sheltered from all except easterly winds. On our walks we found a large colony of Gentoos, and sites of Black-browed mollymawk colonies, and a Rockhopper penguin colony which already had about 30 Rockhoppers in it, to Malcolm's delight. He chased one and having cornered it had a long talk to it. We were amazed at the vast numbers of Thin-billed prion burrows, in bare ground, grassland and tussock. So very different from the well-concealed burrows deep in scrub which we had found on Isla Noir! There were also burrows of White-chinned petrels. Since the removal of the sheep the tussock was recovering well and looked healthy, and there were more small birds than on the other islands – Tussock birds, Thrushes, Pipits, and in the single tree by the house, two Black-chinned siskins. To add to the interest were the rusting remains of the small whaling station which had been abandoned in 1916, consisting of a boiler and various steam engines and winches, and parts of a slipway. Where the machine shop had been were still an old lathe and drill press. Close to the settlement were two wrecks, one of a sailing ship which had been used as a hulk after burning out in Stanley in 1895, and the other a beached minesweeper, the *Protector*, which had been used as a sealer after the Second World War.

Ian Durie flew in to New Island in a helicopter to join us for a few days and brought with him a box of fresh stores. It had been our intention to take him with us to the now uninhabited Jason Islands, but a strong north-westerly wind spoilt that idea, and I decided to go instead to West Point Island, a distance of 37 miles.

Saturday 21 July
...Gradually the wind increased in strength and veered to north-north-west, making it difficult to lay the course with reefed jib and reefed main. I picked up Fourth Island on the radar, which is always working at a disadvantage when we are well heeled over, and found that we had sagged from our course much closer to it than intended. As there is a kelp bed marked on the chart about a mile from the island, I started the engine to motor-sail clear. By this time Andreas was feeling sick; so was Malcolm. To my surprise and disgust, so was I! The only one feeling fine was our passenger, a soldier! He had wisely taken a Stugeron tablet before we left.

It was indeed a dark and dirty night, and we could feel that we were in the kelp bed although the radar showed us over a mile off the island and the sounder gave fifteen fathoms. Suddenly there was smoke in the cabin and I immediately shut the engine off. When I opened the case I found that the engine was badly overheated. What a blow! We were going to need it for getting into West Point Cove in that wind on a dark night, especially with the strong tides which run through the passage. Malcolm felt too sick to look at the engine, and I didn't feel up to it either in the rough conditions. A voice on the VHF asked us who we were and where we were going, and as we could see no lights we assumed that it was the radar station up on the one of the mountains, keeping an eye on all movements in the area.

I cooked up a large stew in the pressure cooker but had to keep coming out into the cockpit for fresh air; when it was ready, Ian dished it up for just the two of us. Andreas was sick on his bunk, a smell which persisted in spite of washing it up. Malcolm had been at the helm for a long time and was cold; when he went below, he too was sick. While I took the helm, feeling much better for having had some stew, Ian watched the radar and the chart...We were lucky that he was not seasick too...

The tide carried us across the wind and we saw that we could not weather Split Island, so I had to search the chart for an easy anchorage where we might find shelter under sail. The wind had gradually come around to north, which made the situation more difficult. It was blowing a gale and the sea was very rough. The whole area is strewn with islands and rocks so I didn't have much choice.

We ran off to the east on a reach towards Port North, and then clawed our way into Stevelly Bay, in a long mountainous peninsula of West Falkland. The chart gave no indication of conditions as the scale is too small, but when we finally reached a depth of six fathoms, about two cables off the shore, Malcolm, who had revived, let go our tandem anchors and paid out our full 40 fathoms...Andreas surfaced and we all had a cup of coffee before turning in. It was 0300 hours.

The next morning Ian cooked us a good breakfast of bacon, eggs and sausages which he had brought with him – a nice change from my usual porridge. After Malcolm had checked the engine and found nothing to indicate why it had overheated, we weighed anchor and motored out again into the wild weather. It took us four-and-a-half hours to cover thirteen miles to the settlement on West Point Island with the tide against us in Woolly Gut.

On Monday we were greeted on the beach by about twenty Johnny Rooks which are remarkably tame on this island and have the reputation of being kleptomaniacs. A Johnny Rook once picked up a visitor's camera lying on the bank only a metre from him and carried it about twenty metres up into the air before dropping it! The visitor was not amused.

West Point Island is about 2700 acres and carried 3000 sheep, which was the best stocking rate we had encountered, though we could soon see why. The hills were covered with closely cropped green pasture, and there was little diddle-dee or teaberry as on the other islands; it really did look more like the fat lamb farms back in New Zealand. We visited another Black-browed mollymawk colony, empty like the others, and a Rockhopper colony. When we sat down for lunch we watched a pair of Peregrine falcons chasing away two Red-backed buzzards – the first we had seen here – and on the way back saw a flock of domestic geese which had become feral, and a pair of Snipe, one of which let us approach to within three metres.

At the house Neil and Mary Jennings showed us around the garden which had more trees, all macrocarpa, than we had seen anywhere else; with the shelter they gave, the garden was probably one of the best in the Falklands. In addition to the vegetable garden there were lawns and crazy paving, and even a rose bed. With his keen eyes, Andreas spotted a Rufous-collared sparrow, a rare vagrant in Falklands and completely unknown to Neil and Mary. During dinner, our new friends told us of their various experiences during the conflict with Argentina, still very much in the minds of Falkland Islanders.

Ian Durie had to return to his duties, so we dropped him off at Hill Cove where he was picked up by a helicopter. It was time for us to be on our way as we had much work to do in South Georgia, so we continued our circumnavigation with only the minimum of delay to allow for weather and bird-watching. We visited Keppel Island, Pebble Island (both at the settlement and at Ship Harbour) and Port Salvador. All these places had much to offer, but not the more spectacular scenery of the western isles.

It was not particularly pleasant to be back at Stanley with the bustle of military activity and the need to inform the Queen's Harbour Master of our every move, but we had to present our report on the islands to Andy and to make preparations for our departure to South Georgia – our first voyage into Antarctic waters. Back at the broken Government Jetty, the French yacht *Damien II* arrived from Buenos Aires, where she had been for repairs. She was going to Bluff Cove, where Sally, the wife of Jerome Poncet, the skipper, was having a baby. We knew she had spent much time in South Georgia, and that Sally had given birth to her second child there – in winter, which had amazed us. *Damien II* is a big red schooner, and I was very pleased to meet wild, mustachioed Jerome, even for such a brief time.

Before we left Stanley we were invited to Government House to see the film which Sir Rex had made, and to meet Cindy Buxton and Annie Price who had made their own professional film of South Georgia. It was a pleasant, informal evening.

On Friday 3 August we completed our jobs, obtained our clearance, said our goodbyes, and were ready to sail before dark. It was blowing a gale from the north-west, and when I called up the Queen's Harbour Master on the VHF to report our departure, he asked 'Are you aware of the weather?' 'I heard your forecast,' I replied, 'but at least the wind is in the right direction!'

Outside it was a horribly wild night, so we gave the Billy Rock which had claimed so many lives a wide berth. Then we set twin well reefed headsails for South Georgia. Good-bye Stanley! We did not expect to see it again for a long time. A shower of driving snow soon blotted out the lights, and we were on our way.

Patagonian Fox

Chapter Ten

Icebergs and Albatrosses

At sea − South Georgia − King Edward Point − Grytviken − Bird Island −
Holmestrand − Bird Island − Sea Leopard Fjord − Royal Bay − South-west coast −
Annenkov Island − Saddle Island − Undine Harbour − Bay of Isles −
Beached at Bird Island − 'Hannibal'

Of all the places I visited during the *Totorore* expedition, South Georgia stands out as the one I loved most. Lying about 1000 miles south-east of Falkland Islands, it is over 100 miles long and up to 30 miles in breadth, with thirteen mostly unclimbed peaks of over 2000 metres, one of which is almost 3000 metres. More than half of the surface is covered with permanent ice, and there are over 150 glaciers. At the western end there are many rocks and smaller islands, and the coast has numerous inlets and bays. All along the northern and eastern coasts are bays and fjords, in many of which a vessel can find shelter, but the south-western coast where the mighty swells batter unceasingly is very inhospitable. It is a land of breathtaking beauty and teeming wildlife, of sudden violent storms and sometimes calm clear days with sunshine. Although it is in 54½ °S latitude, South Georgia is south of the Antarctic Convergence and is considered an Antarctic island. By late winter the pack ice usually lies close south of the island, and in exceptional years it extends all around it and reaches far to the north. This then was the island to which we were sailing with growing excitement and anticipation.

For two days after leaving Stanley the weather was bad and the sea rough, but the wind direction was favourable. The next four days were gale from the south-east, the worst direction of all, and then the south, which is not much better. My two crew were confined to their bunks with seasickness, but Andreas started to recover as soon as the birds became more interesting. I had many an on-deck battle with sails by myself, soaked in water which was not far above freezing. When the weather was slightly better, Malcolm gamely stitched up the foot of the starboard jib from which the hem was parting.

Wednesday 8 August
Driving snow and a southerly gale continued without a break. A lot of water in the bilges, spilling above the sole, so I hove to on the port tack to make it easier to bail it out. I stayed in the cockpit emptying the buckets, which Malcolm handed out through the hatch, over the top of the heavy washboard. Poor fellow is still very sick and had to make a terrific effort.

Andreas is not really sick but still cannot eat. He did the actual bailing inside, getting rid of the water which the pumps cannot reach when she is lying over at a great angle of heel, as she is even when hove to.

If it were not for the trouble of my hands, which hurt a lot at night in bed – probably with arthritis – and always when working outside, I could really be enjoying this. Not the constant discomfort, which is very tiring, but just the fact of being here on our way to South Georgia. It is winter and we had to expect cold and rough seas. But seeing Kerguelen petrels, and especially the Antarctic petrel, have made it all worthwhile...

In the late afternoon I had a bad time of it when the wind increased suddenly to Force 10 and I had to reduce sail and heave to. First I found it hard to get the deeply reefed main right off as the wind in it made it hard to wind down. The tail of the halyard went over the side, as it so often does when uncleated, but this time it managed to half-hitch itself around the jib sheet lead-block, which was mostly under water. I lay down to clear it and got soaked. The next problem was to furl the jib; because on the same winch and cleat as the furling line I had the staysail sheet, as neither could be held by their jam-cleats in the strong wind. That took some sorting out on the storm-washed lee side and heavy water broke right over me – I'm very worried about our damaged life-line system... The air temperature was $-1\,°C$ and the sea temperature $3\,°C$ and I was very cold and thinking that I should get back down below to change. Suddenly there was a loud clatter and I saw the wind generator lift right out of its socket, still shaking the whole boat with the imbalance caused by having lost another blade. 'Did I just write this morning that I was enjoying this?' I thought grimly as I struggled to secure it with my numbed fingers in clumsy gloves...

Back inside I enjoyed a scalding cup of Milo, emptied my gumboots into the sink, stuffed them with clean woollen socks to dry them out, and changed as many of my clothes as I had dry replacements. A solid jet of water came down the Dorade ventilator above the galley stove. 'Now I really do believe what they say about the Southern Ocean,' said Malcolm.

I cooked a big stew with the pot tied firmly on the stove, and my two crew each ate a little out of an enamel mug. My heart goes out to Malcolm. He is feeling it badly that he cannot be of more help, but the poor fellow just cannot get over his seasickness, which has left him very weak. I think both he and Andreas are losing a lot of weight...

Antarctic petrels are prettily marked birds with a conspicuous black-and-white pattern. Their happy flight with its soaring and swooping is always a joy to watch. We started to see more of them – up to six at a time – which worried us a little, as they are never found far from ice.

Saturday 11 August
Ever conscious of the proximity of ice I sleep fitfully for short spells...at about 0245 hours I had a feeling that there was something amiss and as soon as I stuck my head out I imagined that I could smell ice. At first I saw nothing, because of the snow, but then the nearly full moon shone on the brilliant whiteness of an iceberg away to starboard. What an exciting moment, my first deep-sea iceberg! I woke my two sleepy crew to have a

look but the snow came down again and they could barely see it, so were not over-enthusiastic. I had said that we could eat our last tin of self-saucing pudding when we saw our first iceberg, but tonight suggested that we wait until Malcolm was better so that he might enjoy it too. Malcolm said it did not worry him, at which Andreas demanded 'Shall we have it now?' He has got his appetite back, even though I put an onion in the dinner...

Sunday 12 August
Just before Andreas took over the watch at midnight I saw a bright glow right ahead, so stayed up with him to have a look at this monster iceberg...a shower passed away and we saw it in all its wondrous beauty, with huge cliffs and rolling ski-slopes on the top, brilliant in the bright moonlight. The whole scene was marvellous beyond description, and we all felt extremely privileged to see it. There were many large pieces of ice floating about within a mile of the iceberg, and as we passed less than half a mile away from it we had to steer between them. Watching the distance from the berg on the radar and taking sextant angles, I calculated it to be a third of a mile long and 56 metres high...this, of course, is just a first taste of things to come...

The sea temperature has fallen slightly below zero, which is actually four degrees lower than normal, so I am rather expecting that ice at South Georgia will be abnormally heavy and probably very restricting as far as our work is concerned.

Before going anywhere else in South Georgia we were obliged to report to the authorities at King Edward Point in Cumberland Bay, about half way along the north-eastern coast. Since the conflict with Argentina, whose forces had occupied South Georgia, the administration of the island was by the British army major in command of a contingent of soldiers numbering about forty. They were the only human inhabitants of South Georgia, and they occupied the base which was formerly used by the British Antarctic Survey, or BAS as it is known. Meanwhile BAS were operating from a hut on Bird Island off the north-west coast, where three of their scientists were wintering over, and where we were to make ourselves known.

We passed by Bird Island in heavy snow, but by midday on 13 August the snow had gone and the sun shone, treating us to a visual feast as we sailed past the endless array of icy peaks, snowfields and glaciers. We noticed how deceptive distances were in the all-whiteness, with far-off capes looking close, and inlets and bays almost invisible. The day was 'out of the box', as we say in New Zealand.

Monday 13 August
It was dark when we arrived and there was a great deal of brash ice and floating bergy bits in King Edward Cove, which we had to push slowly through with crackling and grinding noises. On the hill above we could see Shackleton House, a huge rectangular building of wood with three stories, which used to be the base for the BAS team but now houses the detachment of the Coldstream Guards...Using our spotlight we made our way alongside the wharf on the other side of the point and were greeted by

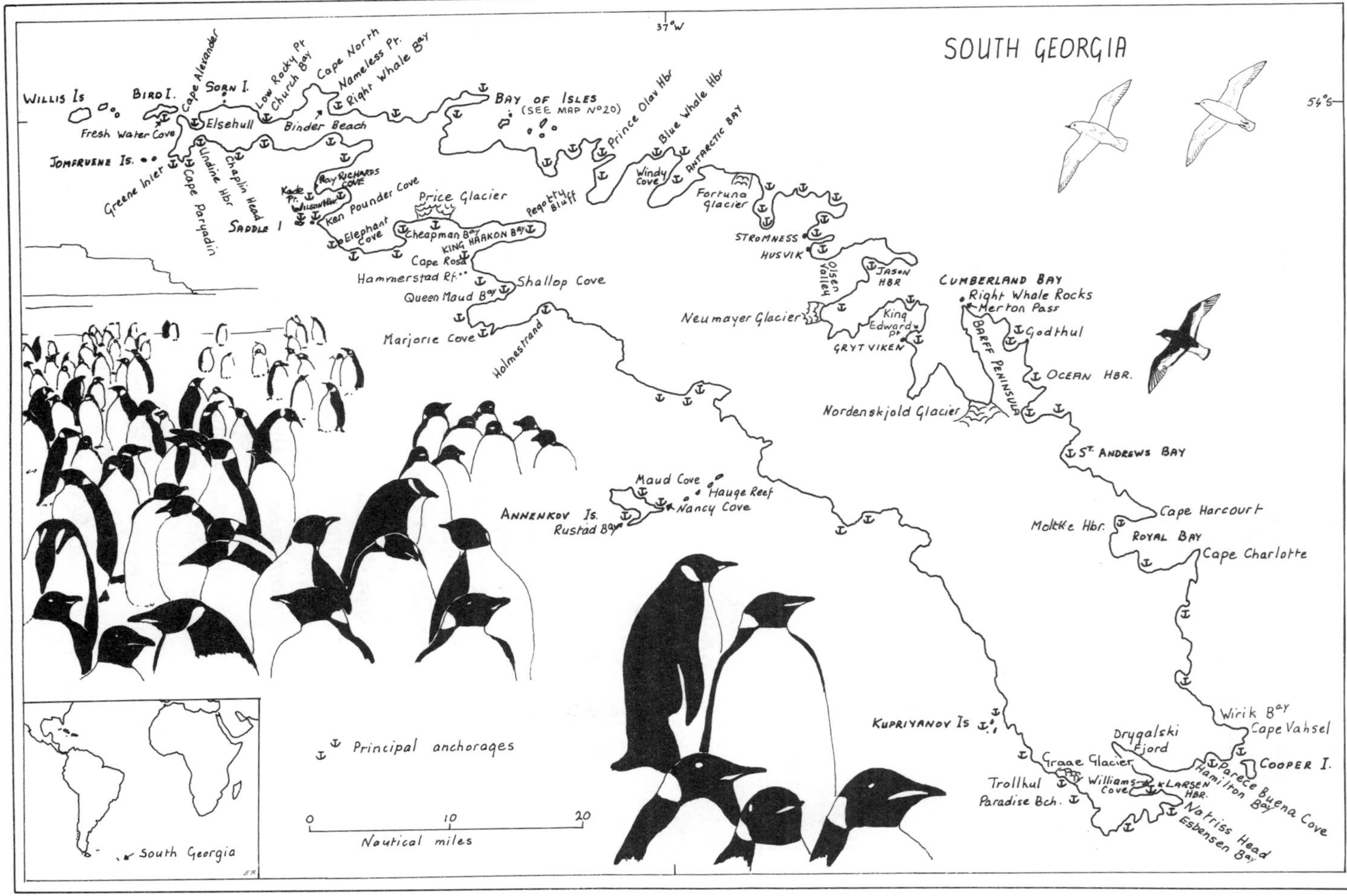

SOUTH GEORGIA

54°S

37°W

WILLIS IS
BIRD I.
Cape Alexander
Fresh Water Cove
SØEN I.
Elsehull
TØNEREVNE IS.
Grisbäk Inlet
Cape North
Low Rocky pt.
Cape Rocky
Chick Bay
Binder Beach
Right Whale Bay
NAGMELESS PT.
Cape Paryadin
Undine Hbr
Chaplin Head
SPROUL I.

Kade Richards
Roy Cove
Kade Harbour
ELEPHANT COVE
Red Slough Cove
Ken Richards
Gold Harbour
Cape Rook
HAAKON BAY
KING
Chapman Bay
Price Glacier
Bell Bluff
Hammersstad Pt.
Shallop Cove
Queen Maud Bay
Marjorie Cove
Holmestrand

BAY OF ISLES
(SEE MAP N°20)
Prince Olav Hbr
Blue Whale Hbr
Fortuna Glacier
Windy Cove
KØNIG BAY
STROMNESS
HUSVIK
Olsen Valley
BUTREKTIC BAY

Neumayer Glacier

Jason Hbr
King Edward Pt
GRYTVIKEN
Nordenskjold Glacier

CUMBERLAND BAY
Right Whale Rocks
Merton Pass
Godthul
OCEAN HBR.
BARFF PENINSULA
ST. ANDREWS BAY
Cape Harcourt
MOLKE HBR.
ROYAL BAY
Cape Charlotte

Maud Cove
Hauga Reef
Nancy Cove
ANNENKOV IS.
Rustad Bay

KUPRIYANOV IS.

Wirik Bay
Cape Vahsel
COOPER I.
Drygalski Fjord
Trosse Glacier
Trollkul
Williams Cove
LARSEN HBR.
Paradise Bch.
Hamilton Bay
Harcee Buena Cove
Natriss Head
Esbensen Bay

⚓ Principal anchorages

0   10   20
Nautical miles

South Georgia

Map 19

two army officers and several of the troops. They scrabbled under the snow, lying 60cm thick on the wharf, to find ringbolts to secure our lines, and then Major Peter Hicks and Captain Chris Cox came aboard to give us a clearance. They told us we had passed very close to the sunken Argentinian submarine *Sante Fé*, marked by a buoy which I had seen on the radar but I had thought was just another lump of ice.

As O.C. South Georgia, Peter Hicks is the Magistrate, the Postmaster, the Customs officer and the Harbour Master. Having formally attended to the paperwork and then stamped our passports, the two very friendly officers invited us up to Shackleton House for hot baths and a delicious and welcome supper, inviting us to have all our meals with them while we are here and asking if they could help us in any other way. I asked Peter if he could send a telegram home, to say that we had arrived.

Across the cove from King Edward Point is the derelict whaling station of Grytviken; established in 1904 it was the first of six shore-based stations, and it was one of the last to be finally abandoned, in 1965. At one time there were also eight floating factories at South Georgia, and various depots and items of shore equipment can still be seen in some of the coves.

When whaling at South Georgia first started, the whales were so plentiful that the catchers took all they could handle from Cumberland Bay itself. By 1917 the total number of whales caught at South Georgia amounted to 175,250. As whaling continued long after that, it is understandable that the number of whales which still roam the oceans is but a small percentage of the original populations, and some species – the Blue whales, Right whales and Humpback whales – are in danger of extinction.

Tuesday 14 August

We cast off and motored over to Grytviken to have a look at the old whaling station, mooring alongside the wharf close to a steam whale catcher, still afloat, which is apparently going to be restored by the Norwegians and taken back to Norway. Two others in not such good condition lay near another wharf. The buildings were all standing and we were impressed by the size and extent of the whole establishment. Deep snow covered everything; being new it was particularly difficult to walk across without skis or snowshoes, and drifts against the buildings often piled up to the roofs, so our progress through the ghost town was slow. It was fascinating to see the vast machine shops, foundries, storehouses, boiler sheds and the service houses for the community, which must have been quite large during the summer, when they were operational. There was a cinema, dated 1930, but that was one of the few buildings which had collapsed. A pretty little church was apparently also being restored. Abandoned by the Norwegians, the station was leased by the Japanese in 1963 and 1964 and left in very good working order. Since then sailors mostly from Russian and Polish trawlers have looted and smashed everything they possibly could. While we were there a military patrol skied through the village from out of the mountains.

When we left Grytviken we motored about seven miles across Cumberland Bay to have a close look at the huge Nordenskjold Glacier, the largest in South Georgia, with a two-mile face...we were able to pass only a quarter of a mile from the sculptured crags and columns – blue, green and white – in perfect safety, as it was too cold for much ice to be breaking off. We did see one massive tower come crashing down with a great roar, and we had constantly to steer around floating ice and small bergs. There were not very many birds in the bay, except large numbers of Cape pigeons and the usual Giant petrels, Black-backed gulls and cormorants, but we are seeing the pretty Antarctic terns and a few of the lovely white Snow petrels.

With temperatures down to $-10\,^{\circ}$C and the sea usually sub-zero, we began to know what it is like to work in cold conditions. Even small jobs like taking on fresh water became major tasks. Fortunately the water never froze in the tanks on board, although occasionally our cabin thermometer registered $0\,^{\circ}$C when the hatch was open, but we did have difficulty with frozen filler pipes to the tanks. We filled our cans from a large hydrant on the wharf which was always left running full bore, and had to be very quick in carrying and pouring in the water before it could turn to ice. To create warmth in the boat to keep the pipes clear meant running the engine, and keeping the kettle on the boil to pour down the filler to prevent blockages.

On our way back along the coast towards Bird Island the wind freshened against us to gale force and it was heavy going. We were forced to take shelter in Prince Olav Harbour, our ship and helmsman, Malcolm, thickly coated with ice from the spray. Ashore we could see another old whaling station, which had been abandoned in 1946, and the stranded hulk of a ship on the point. When I dived down into my bunk for a dry balaclava I found icicles on my sleeping bag, broken off from a stainless steel plate above where the bolts from the sheet winch come through.

Anxious to reach Bird Island before dark we pressed on without stopping, but always looking out for colonies of King penguins and signs of Wandering albatross. Sightings of both made us eager to get started with the work we had come to do. After passing through Bird Sound, a rough and rocky waterway about 0.3 miles wide separating Bird Island from South Georgia, we searched for the entrance to Freshwater Cove where BAS have their hut.

Thursday 16 August
...We found it hard to see where to venture in among the surf-swept rocks, and there were moments when my confidence was faltering as I headed *Totorore* into what looked like a dangerous cul-de-sac...from the looks on their faces, my companions were even more apprehensive than I was, but when at the last minute the hut came into view, we all cheered. The small, shallow, almost circular cove was full of thick brash and pancake ice through which we forced a way and dropped anchor in the centre.

Thursday 16 August
The three young men from BAS came out to the end of a small jetty to greet us...Malcolm had a job to row ashore with the lines. The ice was not firm enough to walk on or slide the dinghy over, and yet was heavy to push the dinghy through. Once the lines were set up it was a lot easier.

163

The cove is most attractive with a rocky beach, now covered by ice, snow and Fur seals, and surrounded by steep snowy tussock slopes. The hut is on the beach; inside was warm and comfortable with a good kitchen and a small bathroom. There was also a bunkroom with eight wooden bunks, a tiny dining room, and a laboratory/office/workroom with benches, desks, radio equipment and beautiful picture windows.

We met Robert Lidstone-Scott, the leader, Simon Pickering who is studying the Wandering albatrosses, and Mark O'Connell who works with both birds and seals. They gave us a nice meal with plenty of liquid refreshment and we talked until late about their very interesting work...

Friday 17 August
After breakfast we pulled our dinghy through the ice again and joined our new BAS friends for a walk over the hills. We found walking in the deep snowdrifts between the tussock very difficult, sometimes sinking up to our hips. In other places it was icy and slippery. They were wearing boots with crampons on, and I was wishing that I had brought some.

Everywhere there were Giant petrels of both species – *Macronectes giganteus* and *Macronectes halli* – and it helped us to distinguish between them, now realising that we must have made many mistakes at sea. On a knoll close above the hut, we came across the first Wandering albatross chick on its nest, looking very large and fluffy in its grey down. It clappered its beak at us, but it did allow us to handle it, to see the growth extent of the feathers under the down. There were nests all over the hills, widely scattered. Mark and Simon caught two adult birds which had come in to feed their chicks, and from these we took some lice. Somebody held the bill and somebody else ruffled the feathers of the head and picked out the lice with a pair of tweezers, to put into test tubes. Catching the birds was not too difficult, as they are awkward on land and the two experienced BAS men used sticks with crook wires on the ends to catch the birds by the necks. and then grab them with their hands.

We walked across frozen ponds then down to Johnson Cove, the western end of the island, also already crowded with seals and a colony of Gentoo penguins. Malcolm enjoyed scratching the back of an Elephant seal pup, but we had to be rather wary of the Fur seals, which are becoming aggressive as the breeding season approaches. Mark told us that in the summer they're a real hazard, as all the beaches and lower slopes are packed and several visitors from naval ships have been badly bitten.

Simon and Mark showed us where the Fairy prions and Blue petrels have their burrows, and as we walked back along the tops of the spectacular north coast cliffs, the places where Diving petrels nest, and a few burrows of the White-chinned petrels. Down below was a peninsula which will soon be populated by about 40,000 Macaroni penguins. Altogether a most enjoyable day, finished off with a nice hot shower and a good steak dinner...

Saturday 18 August
During the day a pair of large Leopard seals came into the cove and while one disported himself on the ice on the beach the other came over to make our acquaintance. In spite of their reputation I think they have kind faces,

164

and this one certainly seemed to be smiling at us. In the afternoon we invited the BAS team on board for coffee, and later went ashore for their special Saturday night dinner. And what a spread! We three from *Totorore* had second helpings of all five courses, followed by liqueurs. It was delicious and we felt really full, hoping that the cooks would be pleased by our appreciation of their work, and not just think us greedy.

Our principal work at South Georgia was to count the chicks of both Wandering albatrosses and King penguins in all the known colonies – except the Wanderers at Bird Island which were monitored by BAS – and to compare the numbers with previous counts. Most of the Wanderers had not been counted for seven years and even then many of the figures obtained were guesses from a ship offshore. Some of the records were dated as far back as 1970, and as there were about 30 different sites to visit for the Kings, and nearly as many for Wanderers, it was quite a challenge. It was to be the most complete survey of these species ever undertaken here, and we were very conscious of our responsibility. However it was a job we all enjoyed enormously; it was very straight-forward and we knew exactly what we had to do.

Visiting the different colonies involved a complete circumnavigation of South Georgia and trips to several offlying islands. Each place we went to was so different from the others that we could never lose interest. Landing from a dinghy in South Georgia is seldom easy, and on the more exposed coasts is decidedly difficult and often dangerous. We endeavoured to land as close as possible to each colony and then walk to it; this sometimes involved an all-day hike with mountain-climbing thrown in. Frequently the weather or ice prevented our landings at certain sites and we had to either take shelter or go elsewhere, to return another day.

It took us two months to cover all the colonies, except for three very large King penguin colonies in the Bay of Isles and St Andrew's Bay which we felt were too big for us to handle by ourselves. Although at the time it was not our intention, we returned to South Georgia the following year to make the first accurate count of those three.

Glaciers, which cover so much of South Georgia, are enormous masses of ice moving slowly but continuously down valleys, usually to end in the sea. They rasp away and carry with them rocks and other debris from the valley sides and floors; when the ice recedes as it has done on most of the South Georgia glaciers, deposits of this debris, which is called moraine, are left behind in the form of ridges along the sides – the lateral moraines – and at the maximum extent of the foot – the terminal moraine. We were to become very familiar with both forms, because the lateral moraine ridges, or moraine hills as we usually called them, seemed to be a favourite location of King penguin colonies.

The terminal moraines, or moraine barriers, were a mixed blessing. Almost every fjord, inlet or cove which had a glacier also had a moraine barrier, sometimes within a mile of the face and sometimes several miles from it; they were like rock walls stretching from one side to the other of the inlet, often wholly submerged. Some were dangerously shallow, and one had to explore carefully to find a gap. Usually the water was very deep right up to the barrier, and again inside. Advantages to us were that they were good protection from the sea and swell outside, and their basins were often the best landing places. Disadvantages were the difficulties of getting in and out, especially in bad weather, and the fact that the glacier basins were usually cluttered with ice.

Malcolm and I took it in turns to keep ship, so that lucky Andreas, who had not had enough experience to take the responsibility of *Totorore* by himself, was able to go on all the shore expeditions. Very conscientious, Andreas became an adept counter. Malcolm, who as a farmer was used to drafting sheep, developed a similar method for counting the penguin chicks.

Monday 20 August

...Passing several icebergs, we approached Cheapman Bay in visibility reduced by sleet which turned to snow. The coasts of the bay are mostly glacier faces and a long moraine barrier closes the inner part of the bay. We could see a large rock and a dead-straight line of kelp right across, so we approached it slowly and carefully, crossing where the kelp looked less dense. Soundings changed dramatically from 30 fathoms to six metres, and as we crossed the least depth we recorded was three metres...

Inside, the water was dead flat and icing over. Looking for maximum shelter we pushed on, but the pancake ice became heavier and more extensive. Although we found a good but narrow lead into a basin, not far from the glacier face, I decided that the risk of being iced in was too great and we came back out to a tiny cove with a small beach which looked inviting...

Walls of rock and ice rose sheer above us for several hundred metres, and the softly falling snow made it seem an incredible fairyland. Everywhere there were large lumps of floating ice to be avoided, but we anchored among them in a depth of only three metres and were immediately investigated by a big and handsome Leopard seal, which swam around and under *Totorore*, frequently lifting her head out of the water no more than two metres away, to regard us with a big grin on her face.

Tuesday 21 August

...We motored over towards Price Glacier edge, but stayed inside the moraine barrier for an easier landing and anchored close off the boulder beach. Andreas and I went ashore in the dinghy, determined to find the hidden King penguin colony...

After carrying the dinghy well up the beach we strapped on our snowshoes, which we had borrowed from Bird Island. To begin with we felt clumsy, but soon learnt the advantage of using them over the deep snow. Going uphill was warm work as there was no wind, and we had to strip off some of our outer garments. The snow glare was fierce so I used my goggles. We had a few tumbles with the snowshoes, and found steep slopes difficult...Icy patches were very hard to manage, and in one place I found myself skiing down quite a steep slope and wondered how I was going to be able to stop.

166

When we topped a ridge behind a spur which separated the two glaciers, we were able to look down on to a frozen lagoon surrounded by tussock, just behind the raised beach. There we saw a group of King penguins, which pleased and encouraged us. Maintaining our height we traversed the slopes, searching for tracks which would lead to the main colony...until we came to a hidden valley in the unvegetated moraine at the side of the great Price Glacier itself. At first we saw only a Giant petrel and a Sheathbill, and then a group of adult penguins. Hooray!! We had found it! As we came closer we could see another group, and then another, but where were the chicks?

It was not until we were almost among the groups that we finally saw them huddled together, with a small number of adult guardians, tucked behind a steep snow hillock. It was a huge group! However could we count them? The last record in January 1971 had given a total of 183 adults and eighteen chicks, with 50 of the adults incubating eggs. Obviously there had been a phenomenal increase.

We ate a lunch of milk biscuits, trail bread and a piece of chocolate while observing a Giant petrel devouring a dead chick, watched by a Sheathbill, and then started our counting...The adults were in six main groups on slopes above and around the chicks and were easy to count, but the chicks were so tightly packed that one's eye could not follow the lines along or across. We eventually agreed on a figure of 2275, which is probably within a hundred or so...

Occasionally a chick would break out from the crowd and waddle about ten metres up a slope to be fed by a newly arrived adult. After receiving the regurgitated food direct from the beak of its parent, it would waddle back to rejoin the crowd...

Wednesday 22 August
Some larger bergy bits floated past us during the night and one or two scraped alongside, but otherwise it was peaceful enough, except for some terrified noises from Malcolm, dreaming that he was trapped under the dinghy and a Leopard seal was about to take a bite out of him...

While we were still crossing King Haakon Bay, motor-sailing at seven to eight knots, the wind freshened suddenly to gale force and shortly afterwards the engine overheated and we had to switch off. In view of the numerous rocks, islets, icebergs and other floating ice which pepper the area I decided to seek shelter in Queen Maud Bay, so we hardened in the jib sheet and tried to weather the island to north of the long Hammerstad Reef. Icebergs got in the way so we couldn't make it, and paid off to pass to leeward of the reef. Violent squalls laid us well over, putting the cockpit coaming underwater and soaking us with freezing spray, but we gradually made it...I couldn't help thinking about my dear mother-in-law Maud, back home supporting us by making rugs to raffle to raise funds to keep the expedition going. If she could see us now she would probably say, 'It looks very uncomfortable.' She would be so right.

Friday 24 August
It was dull and murky when we left Horten after breakfast, dodging many

rocks and shoals over which the swell broke heavily. Keeping close into the coast we searched for possible albatross nesting sites on the tussock headlands, and for King penguins on the beaches. Entering a large bay almost entirely surrounded by glacier face, south-east of Holmestrand, we all felt the weird sensation of sliding downhill. It must have been some sort of optical illusion caused by the heavy dark sky astern, and the glare from the snowfield high above the glacier ahead of us, but it was really strange...

Approaching Holmestrand we could see that the whole bay was filled with ice, from small icebergs to fruitcake-sized pieces with a rustling, jostling, overall cover of smaller pieces in between...we pushed our way gently through with much grinding and crackling and leaving a clear trail astern, which gradually closed in again. In spite of all the ice, we could see breakers on the black shingled beach, or rather against the huge blocks of ice pushed up against the beach, so we forged our way behind some large rocks into a comparatively clear sheltered corner and anchored.

Andreas and I rowed ashore to the quietest spot...it was about half a mile and very slow, in spite of some good leads through the ice. Rowing in ice is like trying to row along a boulder beach with the oars jarring on the rock-like lumps. When we neared the beach the problem was to get past the car-sized blocks of ice which barred the way, and it took a while to force a passage towards some rocks...

Almost at our feet and mistaken by us for another rock was a sleepy and placid Weddell seal which watched us interestedly. It had a lovely face, almost human, and seemed to smile at us in friendship. We had never seen one before and they are uncommon here, but we did note five more during the day, as well as several Elephant seals, Leopard seals reclining on blocks of ice, and a few Fur seals.

Where we landed was about a mile from the glacier edge where we expected to find King penguins. Large numbers of Giant petrels were above the beach and up on a small hill nearby, the white-headed ones looking out of the tussock looked like Wanderer chicks. We soon wished that we had taken snowshoes because whenever we left the beach we sank deeply into the soft snow.

The King colony was conspicuous on a flat area about 150 metres from the beach, but before we approached it for the count we went to the end of the beach and climbed the moraine up to the glacier itself, then came back examining every hollow and valley and watching for penguin tracks. When we were quite convinced that there were no other Kings about we went straight to the colony which remained quietly all in one group. There were 38 chicks and 31 adults, which showed a healthy increase since they were discovered in 1975, when there were only fifteen chicks.

Andreas found the skull of a Weddell seal and brought it back for the BAS team, as well as other various bird bones and skulls for himself and some leopard seal teeth for Malcolm.

Launching the dinghy was difficult because of all the large moving blocks of ice, but we managed it safely...Malcolm prepared a good dinner with tasty dried mince and instant mashed potatoes, followed by stewed dried apples with instant pudding. When we had finished we were alarmed by the crunching, grumbling sound of ice on the move. The wind, though light, had changed and the whole field of loose ice surrounded us, heaving in the swell and grinding its way along the sides of *Totorore*...

We are anchored in the middle of an icefield. It is loose ice but there is no clear water to be seen between the pieces. Some are small, but some are the size of a table, and they're grinding their way past us. It's not very pleasant at all...There's a big berg not very far away. We're hoping that won't join the small bits and come down on us too...if we get frozen into this lot we might be here for quite a long time.

Saturday 25 August
As far as we could see we had suffered no damage, so we started to force our way out of the icefield. To deflect the larger growlers we left our main Bruce anchor awash, with the kedge on its six-metre chain hanging down from it to give it extra weight. As our anchor chain leads over a roller on the end of the bowsprit, the anchors were hanging well ahead of the bow...it took an hour and a half to get out and it was a great relief to be finally in clear water.

The wind was southerly and very cold but once north of Cape Rosa we felt the lee. Skirting the rocks we looked for the cove where Shackleton and his crew had landed in their seven-metre open boat *James Caird* after their epic journey from Elephant Island in 1916. The cove was there for us to see, with its shallow cave where those weary men had sheltered, but it was too small for *Totorore* to enter and we anchored in a similar cove farther along.

The cape is where Shackleton's men had taken Wandering albatross chicks to eat, and twice since then albatrosses have been observed there, although the last time, in 1976, only four pairs had been located. Our job is to see how many chicks are here now.

Having covered the whole cape area, we found a total of eight widely spaced nests with chicks. We passed Vincent Island, McCarthy Island and McNeish Island, each named after one of Shackleton's crew. We stopped and went ashore at Peggotty Bluff, where they had camped, and peered up into the mountains where Shackleton and two others had set out to reach the whaling station at Stromness. Everything must have looked exactly the same to them then as it did to us.

Wednesday 29 August
...We set off to leave Elephant Cove before 0900 hours. The sea in the entrance was in a terrible state of confusion, caused by the heavy swell rolling into the bottleneck, helped by the still-strong westerly wind. Steering was difficult and the motion of *Totorore* quite frantic...I had expected the seas to ease by the time we were a few miles offshore but they didn't, and it was extremely uncomfortable. We had to dodge large lumps of ice, and several times had breaking crests fill our cockpit. And then the engine stopped and the tell-tale smell of overheating came from the hatch. What a time for this to happen! While Andreas steered, and I set the jib, Malcolm went below to see what he could do. In the confused sea with

meeting waves fountaining around us it was difficult to sail, and with frequent squalls I didn't want to risk setting the mainsail...

We tried the port tack but the drift was taking us too rapidly towards the unforgiving coast. On starboard tack after half an hour it was obvious that we couldn't weather the rocks where the sea was behaving as if a series of depth charges was being dropped. I didn't like it at all. There was only one possible chance for us, and that was to sail back into Elephant Cove through that terrifying maelstrom in the entrance. I called Malcolm to come on deck and to leave the engine until we were back inside. Then we closed the hatch and headed in...It was exciting, and adrenalin flowed...

We had arranged to met Bill Bourne on Sunday 2 September at King Edward Point on his ship *Sir Lancelot*. Sailing down the north coast on 31 August we looked for a sheltered place with a colony to count as a stopping place on our way. The wind had been east-north-east, and a big swell was rolling in. As we entered the Bay of Isles the wind suddenly switched to the south-west, affording us a better passage.

Friday 31 August
...We headed across the bay towards Sea Leopard Fjord and as we entered the wind strengthened to gale force and whisked the sea surface up in freezing spray. I could see a few rocks showing up through the water and the kelp on the half-mile long moraine barrier, but it was almost impossible to look into the gale-driven snow and our speed was slowed right down.

When we were very close we came to a dense kelp bed with rapidly diminishing soundings and, just ahead, a long line of breakers. Malcolm, standing on the boom and hanging on to the mast, yelled that he could see a gap farther along. We ran an anxious route between the breaking reef and the thick kelp in an average depth of only three metres. When we came to the gap I headed her through but it seemed to narrow horribly and the breaking sea on rocks was close on both sides.

She was struggling to make way and I had the throttle as far open as it would go. Andreas was calling the soundings in feet: 'nine, eight, seven, six...It was like a countdown for a rocket launching. She seemed to steady at five and Malcolm shouted and pointed to port with his heavily mittened hand. His narrowed eyes could hardly be seen in the slit of his balaclava, with his storm hood pulled well down over the top. I tried edging slightly to port but dared not take her head off the wind as I would lose control, and the wicked-looking breakers with their rocky teeth were only twenty metres away...

'Six, five, four...'There was a crash as one of the keels struck a rock and she heeled over. She lifted on a wave and then hit again. I prayed to God to help us! She bumped, jolted, slewed her bow downwind towards the breakers. 'Please don't let the engine fail us now,' I pleaded. There was nothing for it but to try to bump our way over and in.

The wind tore sheets of water into the air and the surface was white. I was conscious of large lumps of ice drifting rapidly past us but they were the least of my worries. She stuck and then came free. 'And please save the rudder,' I added, as there was another sickening crunch from beneath our brave little boat. I don't know how many rocks she ground over, but little by little we made it.

In the other moraine basins we always found deep water inside, but this was the exception, with only about three metres. I headed over towards the glacier face, seeking shelter, but we came to another long line of kelp and much floating ice. We crossed the kelp, but inside it suddenly shelved to 1.6 metres. I stopped her and let her drop back. 'Let go,' I shouted to Malcolm, who threw over the small CQR and a few moments later, 'Let go the other one,' and down went the big Bruce. 'Give her fifteen fathoms.' 'Fifteen,' yelled Malcolm as he braked on the windlass, but she wouldn't bring up. 'Give her another ten.' Malcolm waved acknowledgment and out rattled the cable, but still she wouldn't hold.

Realising that at the rate we were dragging back towards the outer moraine we would soon be in trouble again, I told Andreas to go forward and help Malcolm heave the whole lot up again. They had a real struggle to get it aboard as the wind kept sheering the bow away, putting extra weight on it. I was trying to steer to help them, but also had to dodge ice. When finally it was up they saw that the Bruce had torn up a whole root of kelp, which effectively prevented the anchor from gripping...

Again we crept up towards the glacier face, this time at the other side, closer to the shore. The anchors held as the hurricane-force squalls screamed over us. 'That lot added ten years to my age!' said Malcolm, speaking for us all.

At King Edward Point we had a good bird talk with Bill Bourne in *Sir Lancelot* and a few drinks in the bar. He could not invite us to dinner in the saloon because we were not 'dressed'; instead, he joined us in the engineers' watchkeepers'

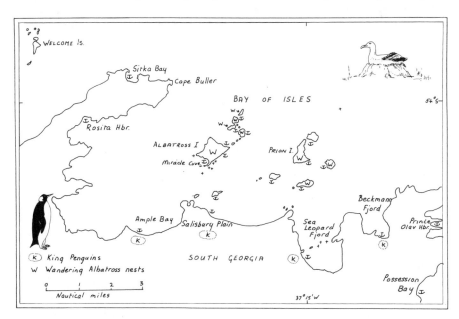

Map 20

171

messroom, where the roast pork was just as tasty. Bill gave us plenty of encouragement and advice and was interested in all we had to tell him.

A big Leopard seal was spending much of her time under and near the wharf and one of the signals men told us how she had attacked and torn a piece out of their inflatable boat. That story did not give us much confidence when rowing ashore in our dinghy, as the leopards were very common.

Our search for King penguin colonies took us down the south-east side of the island, systematically counting the birds in each colony. Chicks were more important than adults to us because they were stationary, unable to leave the colony until they fledged the following summer, and representing the production of the colony for the year. The number of adults at any one time was less significant, because it was constantly changing according to how many of them were away at sea. With the Wanderers it was different because only the chicks were on the nests; one or other of the parents would stop by briefly to feed their offspring only once every few days, so that on land we saw comparatively few adults. For them, the word 'colony' is used very loosely, because Wanderers are certainly not gregarious like most penguins and mollymawks, and generally their nests are spaced far apart. In some localities we found only one chick. It seemed that when several nests were in the same small area it was because it was a desirable site rather than a need to have company. The chicks looked so lonely sitting there by themselves for nine months!

Sunday 9 September

...The wind offshore was about 25 knots, but violent squalls hurtled at us from the mountains and covered the boat with spray which rapidly turned to ice. As we entered Royal Bay the wind came ahead and it was difficult to see to dodge the floating ice.

The King colony we were looking for was close to the Weddell Glacier and luckily the coast gave us a lee which made it possible to anchor near the beach. There was an area of tussock behind the beach and a low tussock hill at one end; there we spotted the main King colony, as well as several hundred adults on the beach. The wind was still strong and squally but the surf on the stony beach was not too bad, so during a brief lull Andreas and I rowed ashore. The wind was cold but the sun was shining out of a blue sky, which gave the whole scene a lively spring-like appearance.

From afar we could hear loud trumpeting from the adults and high-pitched whistles from the chicks, and guessed at large numbers. When we saw them we were amazed; there were many thousands of chicks! They were in several different groups with large numbers of attendant adults, more of which were scattered throughout the tussock in valleys and up on the hill. It was an incredible sight.

We carefully planned our operation. First of all we made our way forward, keeping very low and almost out of sight from the penguins, finally crawling on hands and knees which made our gloves and trousers extremely dirty because of all the guano, and reached a snowy tussock ridge which separated three groups from the remainder. We were able to count those, and then Andreas waited above a narrow connecting gully for me to go back and try to get the next group along, separated from the others, and then drive them through the corridor for him to count. All seemed to be going well at first; by moving very slowly I rounded up a group of about 2000 chicks and boxed them into a corner from which the corridor was the easiest escape.

Then the trouble started. They just would not go through. They tried hard to slip away and soon I was running from one side to another, wishing I had a good sheep dog to help me. A few adults stood in the corridor to bar the way. By pushing through the middle of the mob, I managed to get some of them into the corridor and chased chicks and adults to get the flow started, but then I had to hastily push my way through the mob to get behind to round up the others again. While I did that, those in the corridor turned round and came back! It really did seem as though the territory of the other groups, which we had counted already, was forbidden to them. There must be a definite social structure in these colonies which is quite beyond our understanding. Anyway, it was all tremendous fun!

Eventually I called Andreas to make his way round behind to help me. By this time the chicks were so used to me that I could no longer shoo them. They came right up to me, and then Andreas too, and actually pushed against our legs. We turned some of them round with our hands and propelled them in the right direction, which they seemed to take in good part and never once tried to peck us. But still they wouldn't go the way we wanted! Defeated, we gave up. We climbed up a steep bank with some difficulty, as the penguins' feet had compacted the snow into slippery ice, fouled with their guano. From a new vantage point we again started counting them group by group. It was trying and exhausting. Our final figure was about 12,000 chicks, and 7500 adults, which were very much easier to count.

The phenomenal increase in numbers in King penguins which we are discovering is thought to be mainly as a result of the massacre of the whales, leaving more krill for the fish and squid, which have multiplied at a great rate and provide more food for the penguins...

Having passed the south coast, where we were delayed by gales, we were extraordinarily lucky with the weather as we came up the magnificent and seldom visited south-west coast, where there is no shelter if the prevailing westerlies decide to blow.

Wednesday 12 September
We passed on up the coast, dodging the many rocks with which the offshore waters are strewn, and came as close as we could to Paradise Beach, where there should be a King colony. The swell conditions were obviously impossible for us to attempt a landing, so we carried on a further mile and a half to Trollhul, a cove backed by a mighty crevassed cliff of ice facing the Graae Glacier. Wide open to the west, it would be a death-trap in a westerly gale, so we kept our fingers crossed.

Surprisingly, the swell inside decreased...anchoring just outside the kelp in seven fathoms we were soon ashore to look for Albatross chicks. A big bull Elephant seal hauled himself up onto the beach behind us, to join dozens of others and hundreds of Fur seals which littered the tussock slopes. Elephant seals just sigh loudly, the way Malcolm does, but the Fur seals growl aggressively and sometimes charge. They are a real nuisance, as often they are thick on the only possible route and one must be constantly vigilant and carry a stick or stones to throw at them. In snowshoes it is easy to trip and fall over, and one would not want to do that when trying to avoid being bitten.

Starting a systematic search of the tussock slopes and cliffs and headlands, we soon discovered a large and healthy chick on the nest. Although we combed the rest of the area to the north-west we saw no more, except from a distance we could see two on the headland closest to the beach where we landed. The usual Giant petrels were everywhere and crowds of Gentoos occupied the lower slopes...

Back at our landing beach we climbed the narrow ridge up to the long peninsula on which we had seen the albatross chicks. We had not gone far along the top when we came to a narrow cut, making the outer part an island except for a rock causeway at the bottom. The sides of the ravine were vertical and we could see no way down, or for that matter up the other side, which although only about 20 metres high looked impassable. This was a real setback...

Taking off our snowshoes, we scrambled down to the rocks below, being careful to stay above the surge which occasionally swept up towards us...we climbed along the weed-slippery rocks and then upwards along the vertical face, seeking out hand and footholds as we went. I was not at all happy about it. I should have had an ice-axe to clear the tiny rocky ledges, which were dangerously slippery. I took off my gloves to get a better grip and tried clutching at some small clumps of tussock which were festooned with icicles, but they broke off too easily. My hands were soon very painful...

A couple of metres along and I could have made it, but there was so much ice that I baulked. It was not too far to fall, only about five metres, but the surging water below was $-0.5\,^{\circ}\text{C}$, with ice in it, and I knew that a tumble would be fatal. Andreas, following up behind, was full of foreboding. It was tempting to make a supreme effort to cross that difficult patch, but then how to get back? I was scared, and cold, but I started to sweat...

By the time we were back on the rocks below we both felt shaken and frustrated. So near, and yet so far. We have seen two albatross chicks up there and there are probably more. We must get up there to find out. There has got to be a way, so we will have a look tomorrow...

Thursday 13 September
Today was a wonderful day in all respects. The weather was glorious and we achieved what we set out to do. It was so calm that I felt it safe to leave *Totorore* unattended while we all went ashore, and Andreas and I set ourselves to get onto the headland to find the albatrosses, while Malcolm attempted to walk to Paradise Beach to find King penguins.

Taking crampons and snowshoes we searched for a way across the rocks but it was just not possible, so we carried the dinghy over a low isthmus and launched it on the other side. Somewhat harrassed by Fur seals, we launched the dinghy from a black sand beach among the rocks and rowed out into the heaving swell. We thought we could get into the middle of the ravine and make a landing there, but it was not as easy as it looked and the sea was breaking across the entrance.

Seizing a brief opportunity we rowed in, and the next foaming sea pushed us on with alarming rapidity. The vertical movement of the dinghy surging between the rock faces was about three metres and it was hard to keep control. I was afraid that part of the dinghy might catch on a rock ledge as the sea fell away and tip us out, but the backwash always kept us clear. However, as we got farther in it looked as though the cleft would be just too narrow...

Outside, we reconsidered the situation. Should we take the dinghy back and try to make a landing on the other side? After about twenty minutes, we took a chance and Andreas scrambled over the stern onto a ledge as the dinghy fell away from him and I rowed quickly out of harm's way.

Keeping clear of rocks and breakers I drifted offshore and pumped the dinghy which is leaking badly. Fur seals played around me, rolling over and over and rubbing their whiskery faces with their flippers. These are *Arctocephalus gazella*, different from the Chilean species *A. australis*.

Andreas came back well pleased. He jumped into the dinghy at the right moment, and as I rowed back to the beach he told me that there were five albatross chicks up on top.

On the beach we found Malcolm, who had returned after being blocked by a sheer ice cliff. He had walked along the face of the glacier with great jagged columns of ice above him, often overhanging, and had been caught by several waves which had soaked him to the waist. We found him drying some of his clothes in the bright sunshine, but he was pleased to change into fresh garments and have a hot drink as soon as we got back on board.

The swell being much reduced, we motored over to have another look at Paradise Beach. This time there was so much less broken water that we could see the rocks and thread a way between them, finding a nice spot well protected by an outer rocky barrier. It was still rather far from the beach but Malcolm was quite happy to row Andreas over to look at the Kings, which we had spotted at the far end of the beach. Since 1972 they had increased from ten adults, one of which was incubating, to 25 adults and 27 chicks. Very satisfactory. I was glad we had made the effort to come back.

In all of the Kupriyanov Islands we found a total of only six Wanderer chicks, and then headed up the coast towards Annenkov Island, for which we held high hopes.

Saturday 15 September

...It is a hard, rock-bound coast, glaciers alternating with massive and precipitous black headlands. There is absolutely nowhere to seek shelter. Indeed, it is so exposed that there is nowhere suitable for even the penguins. Below the clouds which hid the mountain peaks, the icefields above the glaciers shone with a weird, mauvish light. There are many strange icebergs: a cathedral, a fine gothic arch, and a huge and voluptuous female torso. Growlers and brash ice were everywhere, and farther offshore were more of the tabular icebergs, a mile or more long, from the Antarctic ice shelf.

It always amazes me how quickly these icefields advance; soon the whole area was packed full of grinding, grumbling growlers, heaving about in the swell and rolling against us with considerable force. We pushed our way slowly and painfully out to comparatively clear water, but to our disgust the pack ice farther south was breaking up and the pieces had arrived, some the size of *Totorore*. All we could do was push and nudge, with bumps and jars and fearful noises. Sometimes the impact stopped us dead.

I tried to steer clear of the largest pieces while Malcolm and Andreas endeavoured to push others from the bow with the boat hook and a dinghy oar...it was a nightmare journey across the twelve miles to Annenkov Island, but luckily the ice thinned out as we passed through the gap in the Hauge Reef. The wind had become moderate from the north-east and we anchored close to a rocky lee shore off the south-east point of the island in 7 fathoms of water, with 35 fathoms of chain and a nylon spring. Being on the northern side of the reef of rocks and islets we had not only come out of ice, but also the swell...

We pitched and rolled and tugged at the anchor cable noisily and uncomfortably, and the breakers on the rocks close astern gave me no peace of mind. However the lemon-flavoured sago pudding I made was much appreciated. With the spotlight we saw many Blue petrels flying around the cape; one flew right up the beam and actually hit the lamp in my hand.

Rugged Annenkov Island, four miles long and rising to 650 metres, really appealed to us. There was something about its isolation and magnificent loneliness that made it even more special, knowing that not very many people had been there before us. We found large numbers of Blue petrels in burrows, and also Diving petrels; previously their presence had not been confirmed. It was not an easy island to work but we enjoyed it, spending five days climbing its mountains and counting the Wanderer chicks.

Tuesday 18 September

...When Andreas and I rowed ashore we were attacked by large numbers of Fur seals. Andreas carried a broomstick and I used an oar, and we really had to whack them hard to discourage them from biting chunks out of us. The breeding season is starting and they are now fierce and resent intrusion. It certainly adds considerably to the hazards of landing in the already difficult surge...

Yesterday when Andreas was wildly swiping at the seals he hit Malcolm on the head, which was not greatly appreciated. One of the most difficult times is when we are struggling to carry the dinghy with all the gear over the rocks and are at a definite disadvantage. On this occasion Andreas suddenly shouted 'Look out!' as a seal charged me from behind and I dropped the dinghy and grabbed an oar just in time to deliver a blow before he got me...

176

Wherever we go we come across Giant petrels, and their neighing cackle is almost constantly in our ears — so much so that we find ourselves talking like that...Sometimes we find just a head of one on the snow, but a close approach reveals a pair of severe looking eyes glaring at us, and we see that the bird is sitting resignedly on its nest, completely buried under the snow.

It was another hard day of tramping and climbing and we kept our crampons on. The only trouble with this is that we tore our trousers, especially when we fell. There is quite a science in planning the day's operation to avoid backtracking. With so much snow, distances are very deceptive and sometimes it is hard to see whether the slopes one is walking on are steep or nearly flat. As far as possible we worked the ridges, climbing high up into the mountains, where it was just rocks, and then coming down the valleys. Up, down, up, down. Very energy-consuming but always with the encouragement of finding albatross chicks.

We saw several being fed by adults, and one had a pair of adults with it, which is unusual. The parents were bill-nibbling together and showing many signs of affection, which seemed rather nice as this year they will not breed, because the chick will not be fledged until too late. Unlike most people in our own society these days, Wandering albatrosses mate for life, and it is thought that their lifespan is about the same as our own.

Wednesday 19 September (anchored in the lee of an iceberg)
During the night there were some almighty avalanches off our iceberg with noises like tip-trucks offloading metal chips, followed by a boom and a series of waves to bounce *Totorore* about. Sometimes large chunks of ice followed and ground their way alongside. On one occasion it was so noisy that I hurriedly dressed and went out into the cockpit to have a look with the spotlight...what alarmed me was a small berg, much larger than *Totorore*, coming rapidly towards us from ahead.

My mind was racing. Should I get the others up? By the time they were dressed it would be too late. There was no time to raise the anchor. Should I buoy the cable and slip it? No time even for that...

CRUNCH!! It hit the bowsprit and stopped, heaving in the swell and thumping and crunching each time it struck again. Would it make the anchor drag? It must have pushed the chain down underneath. Then to my amazement it parted in the middle and a huge piece ground its way along each side of us. It was obviously a huge pile of loose pieces of ice which had crumbled off the berg...

Thursday 20 September
...There was much difficult soft snow but what was more troublesome was the fog which closed down upon us so that we were walking by compass. Not having a map made it difficult and it was eerie not being able to see the ridges and mountains. We found the frozen lake and skirted its northern shore hard up against a steep mountainside. The fog, or cloud, lifted for a while and we could vaguely see the towering black peaks above...

Near the lake we were surprised to see Gentoo penguins about 150 metres above the sea and quite a distance from it; also a group of 102 Skuas picking at Blue petrel remains on the snow. As we climbed slowly up the snow slopes the cloud thickened again and we both felt the glare effect...Andreas became sleepy and I was beginning to see spots. After some energy-sapping errors we eventually found the saddle; the cloud moved away and we were treated to a really spectacular view in all directions. To the west, below us, we could see the system of tussock ridges and valleys which had to be examined, but to reach them we had to cross some dangerous scree slopes which neither of us liked at all...

Our total count of Wandering albatross chicks for Annenkov was 168 for that year. As Wanderers breed only every second year, it would be necessary to count them the following year to assess the island's population. As it was, ours was the first accurate census ever taken there.

Wherever we went we found much activity among the Elephant seals, and the sound of their roars, grunts and barks, and the yaps of newborn pups, became so much a part of every anchorage that we probably would not have been able to sleep without it. The bulls had started hauling themselves out onto the beaches soon after our arrival at South Georgia. Later came the cows, to pup, gathered together in harems which were jealously guarded by the biggest bulls. Bloody fights were taking place on the beaches, the rivals rearing their massive bodies up to batter their chests and heads together, and slashing each other with their teeth, roaring the while. After only three weeks the pups were weaned and the cows were again mated. At Annenkov, Malcolm was lucky enough to see one of the metre-long pups being born. A raucous crowd of Giant petrels, Skuas and Sheathbills gathered to squabble over the placenta.

Saddle Island was another of our great challenges, mainly due to the difficulty of landing and of access to certain parts. Low cloud enveloped us on the saddle, and snow showers added to the difficulty of finding the chicks, but on the saddle itself we discovered 19, which with those on a ridge above brought the number up to 32, exceeding our wildest hopes. We had found none on the western end of the island and there remained only the eastern end to do, from which we were separated by a steep crag with nasty scree slopes. On the southern side, a deep chasm with sheer rock faces at its end barred the way.

Wednesday 26 September
...'I think we should go back to *Totorore* now, while we still can,' said Andreas, worried about the wind. I didn't like it very much either. The northern side had sheer cliffs with very steep tussock above, which could only be reached by crossing several more scree falls. 'Strictly for the birds,' I commented. Having done so much it seemed a shame not to complete the island so that we could have an accurate census. The wind was still behind us, so we knew *Totorore* would be all right, and I started off across the scree...

Andreas followed me, but I couldn't wait for him as we were running out of daylight hours and without crampons he was not managing too well. I worried when I lost sight of him, and called out, but my voice was carried away by the wind. Later, he told me that he had had a very bad time of it out on the scree when it started to slip under his feet, and he dared not go forward or back. Eventually he went up, but was not sure how he had finally found his way back to the saddle in the fog...

Meanwhile I made my nervous way around those steep slopes until I came to the other side of the gorge which had stopped me this morning. Good! I knew just where I was. All I had to do then was follow a tussock ridge down to the cape, meandering across to look on both sides to make sure I didn't miss any chicks. Giant petrels everywhere, some of them on eggs. I did find two more albatross chicks, so that was the island completed. Thirty-four! Now all I had to do was get back safely before dark. 'Strictly for the birds,' I said again aloud as I looked up at the difficult climb ahead of me...

The cloud thickened and I became worried as I could see so little. I could hear the sea on the rocks far below. There were some rocky outcrops barring the way and I had to decide whether to go above or below them. (Generally I tried to keep high to avoid getting too near the sheer cliffs below.) As I passed above one of them and close below another, a rock came loose from under my foot. It happened so suddenly that the tussock in my hand slipped from my grasp, my other foot's crampon tangled in tussock, and I fell outwards.

'This is it!', I thought with terror. I fell heavily and rolled down about three metres, desperately trying to clutch at something. I stopped lying down on my side across a couple of clumps of tussock, right on the edge of the lower outcrop. A peep revealed a sheer drop of another three metres with only a very steep tussock slope below, disappearing into the emptiness filled with fog. I prayed.

My leg was twisted underneath me and I thought I must have sprained my ankle. My hat had come off and I felt cold but hardly dared to move. Slowly, very slowly, I pulled myself into a sitting position and extricated my leg. My ankle hurt badly but I thought I could use it. I felt badly shaken, but told myself that if I stayed in the tussock and was careful, I would be safe...

Eventually I started to recognise where I was and began to descend into the deep gully where we had climbed to the saddle in the morning. Then the fog cleared a little and I could see *Totorore* out at anchor, just beyond the kelp, but now swinging inwards not far from the rocks. Andreas was standing by the dinghy waiting for me.

We were only just in time. The wind was freshening and the sea was surging over the rocks in an alarming manner. There were a few bad moments, but the backwash carried us out and clear...I struggled desperately to keep control as the waves spun us around; it was another hard row against the wind, trying to avoid the kelp and having to make a detour to pick up a dead bird floating on the sea for Andreas...

All is well that ends well, and for 34 chicks it was worth it...I asked Andreas to make tea and drank three cups. We anchored again in Ken Pounder Cove where we had ridden out a gale the night before last, so felt safe enough.

I wanted to continue wearing my wet clothes to dry them but soon felt so cold that I had to change and put on my Antarctic suit. My ankle is hurting a lot and I hope it will not incapacitate me, as we have still much to do before going to Bird Island for the Saturday night feast with wine...we told the boys that we are coming, to give them time to think up a really good menu!

Kade Point on the other side of Wilson Harbour was reputed to have Wanderers on it, but always appeared to be unapproachable because of the breakers, so on a calm day we sought a landing place to the north of it from which we could walk. In among daunting rocks and thick kelp we discovered a hidden cove which I named Ray Richards Cove after a good friend and expedition committee member. It was all rather a frightening experience both for me on board and my two stalwart crew who made a dangerous landing and did the counting, but when they came back, soaked and with the dinghy full of water, they were jubilant. They had found 26 chicks – far exceeding our wildest expectations.

On our way to Bird Island we saw that the Grey-headed mollymawks were back in their colonies on Cape Paryadin and Jomfruene Island, and knew that they would also have arrived at Bird Island to keep Rob Lidstone-Scott busy, as they are his particular study. We made it a little late but they waited for us and the meal was excellent.

On Sunday Simon helped me with my report to BAS and kindly put it on their word processor. We were constantly amazed at their equipment, such as fibreglass nests with weight-recording apparatus inside, for albatrosses. And yet in their own accommodation they did not even have a lavatory! The three dedicated young men spend 2½ years on Bird Island without a break, and were joined in their cramped quarters for several months each summer by five others. To answer the call of nature they had to go down to the water's edge regardless of the weather and face the danger of being disturbed or bitten by an aggressive Fur seal. When I suggested to Rob that even a small hut on piles over the water would provide a little comfort and shelter, he said, 'Oh no, we have too many huts around here already!' It was obviously a matter of priorities, and we had to admit that the Sheathbills made a very good job of cleaning up what was left behind on the beach.

Most of the scientists who work on Bird Island are landed there from a ship by helicopter, and taken off the same way at the end of their tour. Many of them never set foot on South Georgia's main island at all. We thus obtained permission from BAS to take Simon and Mark with us to count the Wanderer chicks on Cape Alexandra, just across the Sound from Bird Island. Having often watched the area through their binoculars, the two were very enthusiastic. To make room on board, we left Andreas at Bird Island with Rob.

Cape Alexandra is at the northern end of the peninsula of the four-mile Paryadin Ridge, and to reach it and the other Wanderer nesting sites on the slopes it was necessary to land in Undine Harbour on the eastern side, and go up over the mountains. Simon and Mark took our tent for a couple of days to do that part, while Malcolm and I made a survey of the whole of the Undine Harbour area, out to Chaplin Head. They found, as we did, that Fur seals had invaded most of the areas formerly used by the Wanderers, and that the tussock had been flattened down, even in the hills up to about 170 metres. Definitely at South Georgia the Fur seals were recovering very rapidly from their near-annihilation by the sealers in the last century, and like the King penguins, seemed to be enjoying a population explosion. This could also possibly be accounted for by the increase in krill, their staple food, following the destruction of the whales, but one wonders why the Wanderers are, regrettably, decreasing in numbers at the same time. It is doubtful if the invasion of some of their breeding territories by the seals would have a significant effect on their overall numbers, because they could move to other sites less affected, but it could be a factor which deserves further study. Simon and Mark found only five chicks, where an estimated 115 had been seen in 1977, and Malcolm and I found 20 where 66 had been counted, also in 1977.

Although a constant nuisance to us, and occasionally a hazard, we could not help feeling a degree of affection for Fur seals, and indeed for all seals. We found them always entertaining and amusing, and full of character. Naturally we had to protect ourselves from them when necessary, but tried hard not to molest or interfere with them.

Wednesday 3 October
On the causeway itself there were three bull Elephant seals taking up so much space that I had a job to get past. One of them did make a token lunge at me, but I reached the steep tussock spur of the other island safely. There were many Fur seals on that spur and I had to pass very close. I spoke gently to them...most of them growled threateningly, and some moved away. Others barely woke up. And then, when I was about ten metres up the spur, one young fellow changed his mind and came charging uphill from tussock to tussock, snarling viciously. I was amazed that he should not only attack me uphill, but that he could move so fast. He certainly meant business, so I swung my stick, knowing that I must not miss as there would not be time for a second chance, and hit him on the side of the head. He went out like a light, and with closed eyes fell backwards and rolled down, bump, bump, bump on the tussocks, until he landed on the rocks below and laid still.

From what Simon and Mark had told me I did not think I had done him any real harm...I carried on up and over the island and was rewarded by finding five more albatross chicks...On my way back down I saw my aggressive friend still where he had fallen, but now recovered and sitting up, barring my only route back to the beach. He looked a bit sorry for himself, and one closed eye had tears rolling down from it. He growled menancingly. I stopped only two metres from him, holding my stick ready. 'I am very sorry to have hit you, poor old chap,' I told him. 'But you were the aggressor, not me.' We confronted each other for a few minutes and I was glad when he exercised discretion and shuffled away.

When I was ready to push off in the dinghy into the surf, I had a small problem in the form of a nearly submerged Elephant seal bull in the narrow channel only ten metres from the beach. His head and tail protruded from the water, and his large eyes were watching me. Would he go away if I tried launching? Perhaps. But supposing he didn't? It was difficult enough getting off the beach without him. After a lot of snuffing and snorting he gradually sank from view and blew bubbles. When the bubbles stopped, I didn't know if he was still there, or at what depth. Was it safe to row out over the top of him? I waited for another five minutes, and as I saw no further bubbles or swirls in the water, I pushed off hopefully, and luckily did not see him again.

After we had returned Mark and Simon to Bird Island, we stayed for a few days while Malcolm decarbonised the engine and ground the valves, as it had been losing power. This gave Andreas and myself an opportunity to see something of the island's birds, which now that it was spring were there in excitingly large numbers. On a hillside immediately above Freshwater Cove where *Totorore* lay, Black-browed mollymawks were braying from their nests; lower down, White-chinned petrels were making their 'shoemaker noises' from inside their burrows. At night we could hear Diving petrels crooning gently. A short walk around the coast brought us to a gully where the lovely Light-mantled sooty albatrosses were nesting, and their loud and haunting cries echoed around the cliffs.

The Wanderer chicks, of which there were far more on Bird Island than all the rest of South Georgia and its other islands put together, were losing their down; half covered with fresh brown plumage, they made me think of poodles.

To complete our survey there were only a few colonies left to do, and we completed those on our way back to King Edward Point to obtain our clearance to sail for Punta Arenas. We spent a few days in the picturesque Bay of Isles, where we landed on eleven different islands and found a total of 182 Wanderer chicks, and then carried on to Stromness Bay to look for our last King colony, in the Olsen Valley. The tussock in that area had been practically eaten out by reindeer and we wondered how on earth they were surviving. We saw several herds in the distance, and their tracks were everywhere, even right through the old whaling stations. The herds had grown from two stags and five hinds which had been introduced from Norway by whalers as a source of fresh meat in 1912.

A similar number had been released on the other side of Cumberland Bay the year before, and we had seen some fine herds there, in good condition because they had a very much larger grazing area in which to roam. In both locations the herds are restricted from spreading to other parts of the island by huge crevassed glaciers.

In the Olsen Valley Andreas and I wandered far over barren ground littered with antlers looking for the King penguins which we eventually found in a small stream valley. On the way back to the beach we had to pass through an extensive area of Elephant seal wallows, which are deep holes in the ground created by the seals when they are moulting for six weeks to two months during the summer. They stay in the wallows in groups together for the whole period; as a result, the wallows gradually become deeper and fill up with ordure. It is quite revolting to see them in it, piled on top of one another, with often only their nostrils sticking out from the filth.

Projecting from one of the wallows we spotted some fine big antlers, and found that there were two pairs tangled together. The stags must have locked in mortal combat, fallen into the wallow, and perished. Andreas thought it would be fun to take them back to *Totorore* with us, and I agreed, but neither of us realised what a job it would turn out to be. One side of each pair, and the skulls, were deep in the mire which was still frozen, but stank abominably when we disturbed it. I loosened it with the boathook which I carried as a seal stick, and Andreas dug with a reindeer shoulderblade he had found. It took us an hour, and then we had to wash ourselves and our trophies thoroughly in the sea before we could take them aboard to show Malcolm. We lashed them up underneath the radar scanner where, in spite of weathering and being washed by spray, they continued to stink for weeks, rivalling the stench which came from the onion-bag full of bird skulls found by Andreas, which was lashed near the mast.

Alongside at King Edward Point. Despite the chilly appearance our reception by the British garrison was warm.

Striated caracara, called Johnny Rook in the Falklands where it is a cheeky thief. *Peter Harrison*

Counting albatross chicks at Cape Rosa. When Shackleton's crew first killed the chicks here to eat, they felt like murderers; afterwards they thought only of the delicious taste. Gerry. *Andreas von Meyer.*

It was a nightmare journey across the 12 miles to Annenkov.
Malcolm.

At Trollhul the whole scene was marvellous beyond description. We all felt extremely privileged to see it.

The Wandering albatross has the largest wingspan of any living bird – up to 351 cm.

Simon Pickering takes time off from his albatross studies to cuddle a King penguin chick.

Fur seal pup. Previously slaughtered to near extinction, Fur seals are again on the increase in South Georgia.

Gentoos at Holmestrand. We became very fond of these penguins, which seemed to be everywhere.

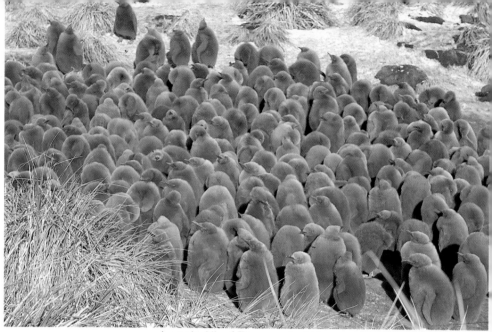
A cosy huddle of King penguin chicks.

Rockhopper penguins on Ildefonso.

The Elephant seal 'Hannibal' trying to bite *Totorore*.

From a proud ship flying across the ocean she had become, in just a few moments, a sad wallowing shambles. Malcolm.

Peter Harrison holding a fledgling Chilean skua. He was beside himself with pleasure.

Weddell seal. South Georgia is the only known breeding place away from the Antarctic ice-shelf. They can dive to depths of 600 metres in search of fish.

Ildefonso Islands. Gerry. *Alan Cowan*

Magellanic penguins on Isla Barnevelt. Their loud, donkey-like braying call is delightfully unforgettable.

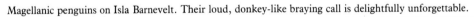

Chris had said 'I would like to anchor under a glacier'. We called this one, in Tierra del Fuego, Ventisquero Chris. *Chris Sale*

It is not everyone who can have a feather lined bath. What a glorious relaxing sensation it was! Joi and Gerry. *Chris Sale*

Wonderful South Georgia at its best. On such a day, the experience of just being there was quite overwhelming. *Totorore* in Antarctic Bay, and Julia walking across the ice.

In these surroundings, sailing was pure pleasure. Passing the Geike Glacier. *Chris Sale*

Heavily laden with fencing materials and scientific equipment, *Totorore* struggles out of Church Bay, South Georgia, in a strong gale. *Chris Sale*

In the dark we thought we had anchored under a cliff. In the morning we saw that it was an unstable cliff of ice. Joi and Chris, Trinity Island, Antarctica.

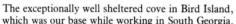

Mountain lunch-stop for Julia and Mark on Annenkov Island.

The exceptionally well sheltered cove in Bird Island, which was our base while working in South Georgia.

Back at King Edward Point we purchased more fuel, topped up our water tanks, and again enjoyed the hospitality of the Coldstream Guards. Peter Hicks stamped our passports, gave us our clearance papers, and wished us 'bon voyage'. Officially we left South Georgia, but in fact we were still there for another week.

A gale held us up for a day while we sheltered in Jason Harbour, Cumberland West Bay. The next day we sailed around to Prince Olav Harbour for the night. The engine was giving us a lot more trouble, constantly overheating, and nothing Malcolm did seemed to help. We decided that we had better spend a day or two at Bird Island to see if we could fix it before tackling a tough windward voyage back to Punta Arenas; this would give me a chance to finish our report and send it off to BAS.

We arrived at Bird Island in the late afternoon of Wednesday 17 October. By Friday evening we had done all that we could, and considered ourselves as ready for sea as we would ever be, allowing for the fact that our engine sadly lacked power. I decided that we would have one last good sleep, and set off in the morning.

During the night the wind came up strongly from the west and strong squalls rocked *Totorore*. At 0610 hours on Saturday morning the anchors suddenly let go and started to drag across the cove. Hurriedly starting the engine, we hove up the anchors, let go our stern line, motored out into the cove entrance, and dropped the anchors again to reset them.

Saturday 20 October

Around midday the weather looked reasonable and I said that we had better get our gear on to go ashore and say goodbye to the lads. Then 'Wham!' A hurricane-force squall laid *Totorore* over and plucked the anchors from the bottom! We all dived out into the freezing wind and blinding, stinging snow. I started the engine, and while Andreas took up the slack on the stern line to the jetty to keep it clear of the propeller, I headed her round away from the rocks as Malcolm wound up the anchor. The wind itself was strong gale, and the squalls, which were frequent, were far in excess of that. The biggest difficulty was to keep her heading up to the wind with our rather sick engine...In the nearly unmanageable conditions, we went careering around in the tiny cove.

And then the inevitable happened. Suddenly the engine stalled. 'It's caught!' shouted Andreas above the wind. 'Let go the anchor!' I yelled to Malcolm. In the wind and with his balaclava on, Malcolm could not hear me. I rushed forward 'Let it go again, quickly!' I shouted in his ear...The only safe thing to do was to let her drag back on to the beach, clear of rocks. The wind saw to the dragging part of it, and we took the line from the jetty to the starboard bow to control her direction by slackening or hauling on it as required.

Beaching her stern-first risks damaging the rudder, but we had no option. I dived below and frantically undid our morning's work of stowing and tidying in a few minutes, fetching out all our available lines: 100 metres of nylon rope, 16 mm diameter from forward, 40 metres of nylon, 12 mm, also forward, 100 metres of terylene, 12 mm, from under the cockpit, 100 metres terylene, 10 mm, from the same place, 100 metres of red floating line from the after locker. We had to get lines out in a hurry, to prevent her from broaching onto the beach. Malcolm got into the dinghy and was quickly blown ashore with the end of a line, where he began to walk around to the rocks at the entrance to the cove...

Malcolm had not gone far when he was delayed by a large bull Fur seal, which barred his way... Simon had seen the difficulty from the hut window and came to help; with his stick he kept the old bull and several others at bay while Malcolm got past. Then between them they dragged the rope along, their bodies bent low against the wind, and finally reached the rocks, where the swirling water made even more difficult the job of securing the rope. Andreas and I hove it taut on the windlass, then eased back on it, and also on the anchor chain, until she started to bump on the stony beach. With a fishing-float buoy, we floated another line ashore for Simon and Malcolm to double up.

The squalls tore the surface of the cove high into the air, blowing clouds of it up to the tussock ridge above the base as we laid out stern lines to a huge log high up on the beach. When all was fast there was nothing else we could do except endure the unpleasant bumping and scrunching from under the keels, and wait for the tide to go down...

We could hardly get into the cabin. A shambles of unstowed gear was strewn everywhere after my desperate efforts to get the spare rope out in a hurry. Looking at the absolutely impassable entrance, with its thunderous breakers and the furiously tumbling seas outside, we felt glad that we had not got out earlier as we would only have been blown farther away from Punta Arenas...

The gale continued most of Sunday, but by the evening it was easing so we refloated *Totorore* and anchored in the normal way, retaining our bow lines out to the rock.

Sunday 21 October

...A large young Elephant seal which had been patrolling the cove for several days, loudly telling everybody that it was his, watched everything we did. Rob had told us that 'Hannibal' had deliberately wrecked the shore end of their jetty a few days ago by rearing up several times and then flopping down onto it to crush it with his enormous weight. We had actually taken quite a liking to him, because he had such a naughty-looking face.

When Malcolm rowed over to the jetty, taking the stern line, Hannibal suddenly appeared close astern, looking as though he was going to attack the dinghy! Malcolm rowed as though his life depended on it, which, perhaps it did! and scrambled as quickly as he could up on to the end of the jetty, where Hannibal continued to menace him. He thrust the boathook right down into Hannibal's wide-open mouth, but it did not seem to deter him and he stayed there looking belligerent, as though he wanted to get up onto the jetty too. It was quite a while before he went away and Malcolm dared to lean over the end of the jetty to secure our stern line to a pipe underneath.

Andreas and I were in fits of laughter, even though it could have been a very serious situation. Later, we saw Hannibal chewing at our anchor chain and his bellowing disturbed the peace of the cove.

Monday 22 October

I was awoken early not only by hearing Hannibal's roar, but feeling it reverberating right through the boat. I went out into the cockpit and saw him actually trying to bite *Totorore*! When he saw me, he lunged up out of the water and seemed to want to come on board to get at me, poking his head at the space under the rail by the winch through which, luckily, it was too big to fit. Instead, he just rested his chin on the gunwale and roared some more. I could not help laughing. After each roar, he grinned happily.

I was not quite so amused when I looked over the other side. Foolishly we had left the dinghy in the water overnight and Hannibal had savaged it! All three flotation compartments were punctured, and even as I watched, he swam under *Totorore* and gave it another bite. We hauled our sorry dinghy onboard and drained the water out. I called up the boys in the hut on the VHF, asking them to let go our lines so that we could sail...Rob went down to the beach to lecture Hannibal, waving a reproving finger at him. The result was startling, especially for Rob. Hannibal came straight out of the water and up the beach, lolloping incredibly fast. Rob was forced to take to his heels.

When our lines were aboard, and our tandem anchors up, we waved goodbye to our friends and motored away out of the pass for the last time. I felt sad to be leaving this beautiful place which I had come to love in the all-too-short ten weeks of our stay, and wistfully watched the snowy peaks disappearing from view as a shower of snow blotted them out. No more Fur seal and Elephant seal noises; no more trumpeting of King penguins; no more clopping of albatross chick beaks; no more picking a nervous way across scree slopes; no more falling hip-deep into snowdrifts! The others felt it too. It had been a glorious, wonderful adventure.

Skua

185

Chapter Eleven

The Mast is Down!

At sea — Broken mast — Back to Falklands — Mast Repaired — to Punta Arenas —
Southern canals — Ildefonso — Cape Horn — Isla Picton — Puerto Williams

The first few days of a sea voyage are always the most trying, and we all usually tended to feel a little bit lethargic and queasy. This was no exception, and to add to the discomfort we were sailing hard on the wind. No sailor in his right mind could say that he enjoys beating to windward in the open ocean for days on end, especially when both air and sea temperature are only marginally above freezing, and we longed for a wind which would enable us to ease the sheets and sail free. After seven days we had actually sailed about 500 miles, but in the right direction had made good only 362 miles. Of course we had always known that in a boat as small as ours to sail against the 'Furious Fifties' would be a slow business, but the bird-watching was good and we were, surprisingly, seeing Atlantic petrels. We also saw two Scamperdown whales, which was a real bonus. Only about four metres long, and with a distinctive beak shape and colour, they were not hard to identify. They were the first whales I had seen since Cape Horn.

On the afternoon of 29 October the wind changed from west-south-west to east-south-east. Soon we were romping happily away at five knots on course, with the twin headsails poled out. The birds seemed to enjoy it too, and Andreas and I derived great pleasure from watching Atlantic petrels, Kerguelen petrels, and White-chinned petrels zooming around and over us in a fantastic flight display. In the night the wind increased to gale force, and the sea and swell built up accordingly, but she was going well and by noon our day's run was 112 miles. We knew that it could not last so I was determined to make as much westing as we could.

Thursday 30 October

I had reduced the jibs down to well-reefed size, and to give her maximum directional stability I pulled both the pole ends down to the bottom of the track on the mast, thus giving them more effective length and angling the foot of each sail slightly forward from the track. With the wind right aft, it was good sailing. When the wind started to tend towards the south, I eased the port sheet and hardened in the starboard, keeping the wind on the quarter as we maintained our course to the west. She was surging along in fine style, each massive sea lifting her stern, then hissing and roaring as it broke on both sides of her in a welter of foam. Sometimes she was thrown

186

way off course and broached, reeling as a sea broke over her and the sails flogged alarmingly. This was old stuff for me – I had sailed her like that many times. And then it happened.

At 1530 hours we were all inside the cabin. She was thrown by a big sea and there was a loud crack and a peculiar change of motion. 'The mast has gone!' shouted Malcolm. 'Where? At the spreaders?' I asked, hoping that we had something left to sail with. 'No, just above the boom' We pulled on our heavy-duty wet-weather gear, knowing that we were going to be outside for a long time. It really was a nuisance!

The sight was truly distressing. From a proud ship flying across the ocean she had become in just a few moments a sad, wallowing shambles. The mast was in the water with the headsails and luff spars and a tangle of rigging, all heaving dangerously up and down with the sea. The stump of the mast was unstepped, still attached, but the mast was bent like a safety pin just at the point where the two pole ends were still in the fitting on the track. So that is what did it! Too much thrust on the mast from the poles, which I had brought too low – lower than the strengthening doubler inside the mast. The rolled mainsail on the boom looked all right, but the leaping mast was putting tremendous strains on the goose-neck.

Our first job was to try to get the boom and poles off, and that alone took a long time. *Totorore* was behaving like a bucking bronco and we were in danger of being crushed by the mast. First we lashed the stump and the boom, and because the pole fittings were jammed up I had to hacksaw a section out of the broken track. It was cold work, and we were frequently drenched by a breaking sea. Malcolm helped me, and Andreas passed us tools. 'Oh dear!' said Andreas. We were too busy, and too desperate, to feel shock. We had to get this heaving wreckage under control before the sea pushed it through the side of our boat, and I was not prepared to jettison any part of it if it could be avoided.

The mast broke off its stump and seemed determined to kill me as I tried to work the broken end aft. It carried away lifeline stanchions and bent the pushpit, while Malcolm and Andreas were trying to get the top of it forward. We wanted to get it lashed fore and aft to take the murderous movement out of it, but it was a real struggle because the twisted and buckled luff spars on both the forestays and also the inner forestay made it difficult to handle, and with the three sails still in those spars it was all very heavy.

By dark we had it all secure alongside, mostly above the water. It had taken five hours, and we were exhausted.

In his comings and goings to fetch tools, Andreas had left the companionway washboard out and some of the breaking sea had gone down below. My bunk was soaked and pots and pans and a tin of milk had been knocked off the swinging stove. What a mess! I opened a few tins to cook a quick and not very good dinner, and then we all took to our bunks. None of us slept much. The motion and the noise were terrible.

I lay for hours, uncomfortable in the quick roll, and decidedly uncomfortable in my mind. I had a chance to consider the truths of the situation. It could have been worse. Nobody had been hurt. Our radar tower was still intact, complete with two smelly skulls and antlers. We still had a comparatively comfortable home with gas to cook on, and plenty of food and water. We would have to make for Stanley, our nearest port, only about 270 miles away. That was the most important first thing. Survival.

Stanley is to windward against the prevailing westerlies. Our engine was pretty dicky and would not give us much power. We could rig a jury mast with two poles, but we would never make to windward with it. Another gale would take us a long way back. I prayed to God for guidance. If only I had reduced sail even further! If only I had not sheeted the starboard jib so hard! If only I had left the poles higher up the mast, where it was doubled for extra strength!

I could not help thinking about my wife and family and how I should let them know as soon as possible that we were safe. But the aerial was gone, so it could not be before Stanley. And then there was Alan Cowan, due to meet me in two weeks at Punta Arenas...I kept churning these and other problems over and over in my mind.

Wednesday 31 October

The gale eased a bit this morning, but it was still dangerous work outside with the quick roll, water on deck, and the lifelines gone. We struggled to disentangle the jumble of wires and ropes and torn sails, and little by little we got it all aboard and secured. I'm constantly saddened by discovering new things smashed, destroyed or badly damaged, and knowing that I have no money to put it all right again.

I am worried about my crew, but Malcolm and Andreas are philosophic: 'We'll worry about what we'll do, when we get to Stanley.' They both worked very hard, and Andreas still found time to observe the birds, but I found it difficult, today, to share his interest.

By 1800 hours we were ready to go. The wind was only moderate, but the sea still big. The motor did not want to start and when finally it did, it gave no more than half power. 'I'll try fitting the spare fuel pump tomorrow, and see if that works,' said Malcolm...

I have an empty feeling. My little world is falling to pieces. I must snap out of it. Somehow I have got to get her sailing again to carry on the expedition. Strictly for the birds. During the afternoon, while we were working on deck, four Rockhopper penguins kept us company close by.

By the following morning I had managed to shake off my negative feelings and was filled with new determination. We were being amazingly lucky with the weather, so God was definitely on our side. It was up to me to do all I could to get us to Punta Arenas as soon as possible.

Shortly after 0800 hours the engine died completely. Malcolm fitted a new fuel pump, but that was not the trouble. He managed to get it going again for a few hours and that was all. As a last resort, I fetched out the spare injectors, one of which I believed to be still good. Malcolm fitted it in the forward cylinder and the engine made a miraculous recovery! Why had we not tried that ages ago? We were still dogged by the overheating problem, but by keeping the revs down we were able to nurse it along to the Falklands and were thankful when we finally saw the coast.

Saturday 3 November

...I was trying to call the Queen's Harbour Master, Stanley, on the VHF to report our arrival. Eventually the *Lumiere* answered, and asked if she could pass the message on for us. I said that we had been dismasted, and were calling in for repairs which we expected to take about two weeks. When they asked for our position and ETA I gave these as eight miles from the harbour entrance, and 1100 hours. I added rather cheekily, 'It is a good job that we are not Argentinians, because we have slipped in unobserved!' *Lumiere* answered, 'We are the forward observation post!' I was tempted to reply that they had not seen us, but instead said, 'My apologies. We consider ourselves observed.'

Back alongside in our old berth at the broken-down Government Jetty we learnt that the well-known British yachtsman, Chay Blyth, had left the previous day in his trimaran *Beefeater II* to round Cape Horn, following the route of the clipper ships to California.

I was immediately able to start making arrangements for our repairs. I went to the British Armed Forces Headquarters to see 'Snofi', as he was known, (the Senior Naval Officer, Falkland Islands), and was given a sympathetic hearing. He introduced me to the commander in charge of maintenance and repairs who said they would like to help but had no equipment for welding aluminium or stainless steel. He would let me know on the Monday if they could do anything for us. After that I went to the manager of the Falkland Islands Company, Terry Spruce, who was very friendly and said that his mechanics could help with our engine problems, but could do nothing for us about the mast. Meanwhile, Malcolm generously offered to stay for about ten days to help with the repairs before leaving to go home. Andreas wanted to go home too, but the only way for him to return to Chile would be via Ascension Island and England, which he could not possibly afford, so he was obliged to wait and come back with me in *Totorore*.

I phoned Marjorie to let her know that we were all safe. When she heard my voice she said 'How quick! We did not expect you so soon,' thinking we were at Punta Arenas. I told her about the mast and I asked her to obtain a secondhand sail from somewhere and send it and a spare I had at home to Chile for me, together with some rigging screws and other gear. There was no possible way in which anything could be sent to the Falklands.

Sunday 4 November

We slept in late and were quite surprised when a New Zealand voice called to us from the jetty. We told him to come back later and were eventually pleased to meet Alan Knowles, deputy leader of the New Zealand South Georgia Expedition from the Alpine Club in Wellington. He had flown into Stanley yesterday, and he and three other mountaineers, and a film crew of two, were aboard *Sir Lancelot*, now in port and sailing this afternoon. Alan told us that he was going to shout us breakfast at the Upland Goose Hotel, and had already ordered it for 0800 hours. What a treat! It was the best breakfast we had had for a long time, bacon and eggs and toast...

Their expedition plans to be in South Georgia for about six weeks and climb some of the mountaineering plums – the high unscaled peaks of the Allardyce Range...

189

We spent the day stripping down the gear from the mast. Many interested visitors came to see us, including our friends Jorge and Monica Alonso, and Mario Zuvic, all of whom offered to help in any way they could. Later, they did a great deal for us by passing messages to Chile on their ham radio, and Jorge rewired our navigation lights on top of the mast.

I tried to stop Alan Cowan from coming to Chile until we were ready, but he was unable to change his arrangements and would go there and wait for us. Knowing that put extra pressure on me to get our repairs finished as quickly as possible.

On Monday the FIC mechanics did what they could for us on our engine, and serviced the injectors and spares which we had with us, but advised us to send a telex ordering new nozzles, which I did. The FIC generously waived all charges for their labour. The naval commander I had spoken to came to tell us that they did, after all, have TIG welding equipment to repair our mast, and that we would need to go to the small dock at Navy Point, across the harbour. There, we were befriended by the bearded shipwright, Chief Petty Officer Tony Atkins. Many of the men became quite interested in our work and conservational motives and we had some good discussions. Thereafter we enjoyed the hospitality of the mess for all our meals.

Tony made an excellent job of our mast, shortening it by 35 centimetres and welding our spreaders back on. He did not have the proper equipment for stainless steel, but did what he could to repair our broken life-line stanchions and railing, and also brazed up the muffler tank on our engine. We did the rigging ourselves, and Malcolm straightened out our damaged luff spars by bending them between fenceposts. Meanwhile I had taken some of our damaged sails over to the 'Fipass', the big floating wharf system operated by the army, where a corporal patched them with khaki canvas on his heavy-duty sewing machine. It was not a sailmaker's job, but I was grateful for it, and the sails did get us back to Punta Arenas.

Malcolm had the satisfaction of seeing our mast standing up again before he went aboard the troopship *Uganda* to take him to Ascension Island, whence he flew to London on his way home to New Zealand. I really missed his practical ability and help when he had gone, but Andreas and I struggled on and finally were nearly ready to sail on Saturday 24 November, three weeks after our arrival at Falklands. We gave away our two sets of reindeer antlers, because Andreas said they had brought us bad luck. One went to the NCOs' mess at Navy Point, and the other to our good friends the Alonsos.

To complete our final onboard preparations, we sailed around to Kidney Island so that we could work at peace without any visitors to interrupt us. So close to Stanley, it could have been in a different world, and it was a real joy to be among birds again. While at Navy Point I had been too preoccupied to even notice the few birds around, although Andreas had kept them under observation, and we did have an occasional Sea-lion swimming around.

After dark we took a spotlight ashore and wandered about on the beach, looking at the birds and talking to the Shoemakers sitting in the entrances to their burrows. The next day Andreas returned ashore to make an island species list while I re-rigged our repaired 'Ivon', wired up all the rigging screws and fitted new furling lines for our jibs and staysail. During the day the wind freshened from the west, with gale-force gusts, so we stayed another night and watched the Sooty shearwaters circling around over the island at dusk.

We sailed at 0600 hours on 26 November, a little apprehensive at facing the westerlies with our rather makeshift rig. Several of our rigging screws were damaged, our sails were inexpertly patched and our repaired mast was untried. All went well to start with, but as soon as we started to beat against the wind along the north coast our troubles began. The big sail repaired by the army had not set well, and as soon as we put *Totorore* hard on the wind, the seam along the edge of the khaki tent material let go. Obviously the stitches had been too close for the terylene sail and had cut it. We tried motor-sailing, and then the engine overheated. Shortly after that, the main halyard jammed at the masthead, but we did have the pleasure of seeing four Orcas playing around and underneath us and it was nice to feel warm again – the sea had come up to 8 °C and the air had reached 10 °C.

After our bad start everything went well. We had a good sightseeing trip close past the Jason Islands, which on our previous visit we had been unable to reach. We were intrigued by a large colony of Black-browed mollymawks in an atypical habitat – a gentle rock slope between the shore and a belt of tussock – and which from a distance looked like a gannet colony. The weather was wonderful, and we thankfully entered the Magellan Strait at 2000 hours on 30 November, the dreaded windward passage behind us. On his own, Andreas had turned out to be a good and reliable crew, something he was able to prove again before we arrived at Punta Arenas two days later.

The engine overheated several times as we motor-sailed to windward among the oil rigs in Bahía Posesión, and I got no sleep all night. Malcolm had shown me how to remove the top hose and with the engine idling wait until the water came through again before replacing it. To do this without stopping the engine usually meant being nearly scalded, but the method worked, and not once did the engine stop of its own accord. When we came to the Primera Angostura (First Narrows) the wind freshened to a gale against us and the sea got up. Although we had the last of the tide with us we could make no way and had to run back downwind, losing hard-won ground. The Armada at Punta Delgada advised us to shelter in Caleta Municiones, which was not marked on our chart and which we could not find as we plodded again upwind, following the coast. The sea was very short and steep, and progress painfully slow. After two hours we spoke to an oil rig tender, herself at anchor riding out the gale. She asked if we needed assistance, and why we had not anchored. I said that we were looking for Caleta Municiones, but could not find it. She replied that we were in it already! The vast, wide-open space, almost out of sight of the low land, certainly had not looked like a caleta to us. Allowing plenty of depth for the nine-metre tides we dropped anchor and gave it our full 40 fathoms of chain, plus a nylon spring. The wind was still 40 knots, and the bow kept dipping into the water and throwing it back over *Totorore* with reckless abandon. We had wasted six hours of time, effort and fuel, but we were glad that we were where we were, rather than outside drifting back towards the Falklands.

Sunday 2 December
...We had a good run right down to Segunda Angostura which we passed through as the tide was turning against us. The next stretch was among the shoals around the Islas Marta and Magdalena, to east of Isla Isabel. It looked straightforward enough, and as the wind was backing and freshening I decided to motor-sail hard on the wind across to the shelter of

Isabel, passing north of the shoal areas, and then use the passage between them and Isabel, called Canal La Reina.

North of Isla Marta the wind increased with frightening suddenness and the leech of our jib tore on a seam high up. I started to furl the sail when the engine died. The sea had become wild, and strong tidal swirls and eddies created great areas of violent turbulence over the shoals. 'No más aventuras, por favor!' (no more adventures, please!) pleaded Andreas. I opened the cover of the engine case and a sad sight met my eyes. The bolt made by Malcolm at Bird Island, which held the cover over the valves on the forward cylinder and also held the rocker pedestal, had sheared off, and oil had sprayed everywhere. What a disaster! I was fully aware of our danger. We were being swept very rapidly down onto the big breakers over the shoals, and beyond them, Isla Marta itself. *Totorore* would not go to windward without a jib, and now both were torn. It was far too windy to use the main, so I set a reefed staysail, and reefed the small jib which had just torn, hoping that the leech cord in it would hold it together sufficiently to get us clear of the shoals. Anchoring was out of the question at that moment, as the water was too deep and the sea too rough. We could have dropped anchor on the shoal, but the sea there looked murderous. That would be a last desperate resort.

Andreas took the tiller...He was worried, and so was I. The bow was frequently buried in the steep seas, and each time it happened *Totorore* stopped dead as though she had hit a rock, but she did cease her leeward drift towards the island. 'Do your best, and keep telling me where the island is!' I shouted above the wind.

I started the unpleasant and difficult job of removing the broken bolt. If I could only get it done quickly the engine might save us. Conditions for

Blue-eyed Cormorant

working were the worst. *Totorore* was leaping madly about with a nasty jarring, jolting movement which made even taking tools from the tool locker difficult, and finding somewhere to put them handy where they would not move about was almost impossible. The end of the bolt was down inside the head block, and after trying desperately to turn it with a hammer and screwdriver, I had eventually to resort to drilling a hole down into it and then unscrewing it with an 'easy-out'. 'How are we doing?' I asked Andreas frequently. 'How is the sail?' His answer was always the same. 'Más o menos' – more or less.

I sweated over my task. The engine was still hot and I stripped down to my vest – the first time for a long, long while. I prayed that the sail would hold out a little longer, just to get us clear. Once the broken end of the bolt was out, it did not take long to put a new bolt in. 'Hold your fingers crossed,' I said as I started the engine again. It came to life and we laughed with relief. Magdalena was close a-lee, but with the engine running strongly we soon slipped away clear of the danger.

The wind dropped to about 20 to 25 knots and I was able to furl the torn sail, and motor-sail down the coast under the staysail. 'Punta Arenas, here we come!' 'Don't say it – we are not there yet', retorted Andreas who was becoming superstitious. However we made it to the pier without incident at about 1900 hours...

Monday 3 December
We were pleased to meet our good friends at Brooms again, and found there an exciting large stack of mail. Alan Cowan came to find us at the pier and could be seen from far off, towering high above the crowd. In spite of having waited so long he was in good spirits; he had visited the beautiful National Park at El Paine, and then taken a trip down the canals to Puerto Williams in a coaster. Although not a boating man, he was fully aware of the fact that there would be work to do here in Punta Arenas before we could sail, and was not expecting us to be able to set forth immediately.

Andreas left to go home to Puerto Montt, but Alan stayed on in the comparative comfort of the pension where he had been living until we were ready to sail. That gave me space to clean up inside *Totorore* and carry out some repairs, but made the many shifts on and off the pier more difficult on my own.

Alan was able to do the running around for me in the town, buying stores and seeking out spare parts, all of which take time. Pedro and Helen were extremely helpful as always, and introduced us to a special South Chilean meal called 'cuarento', consisting of many different kinds of seafood and meat. On Sunday we sailed a few miles down the coast to anchor off Ernesto's and Marcia's house, on the beach, and joined them and other friends for a 'parrillada', or barbecue. We had to be well clothed to keep out the cold wind, but we enjoyed both the company and the delicious lamb chops from their own farm, as well as experiencing a little more of the Chilean way of life.

It was arranged that we should meet Peter Harrison at Puerto Williams early in the New Year, so Alan and I left Punta Arenas on 11 December for the South

Fuegian region to see what we could do by ourselves before Peter arrived. As it was the main breeding season for sea birds, our principal objective was to follow up the work we had started in the Cape Horn area in April, and learn more about the Sooty shearwaters.

Moving down the Strait under full sail we heeled steeply but I was pleased to see that Alan, too tall to stand up straight in *Totorore* and unused to boats, coped very well and actually cooked us a very good dinner. He was the only crew member I had had who was completely unaffected by seasickness, and held that distinction for the whole of the *Totorore* Expedition. Like certain others before him, he did not like my simple meals much and preferred to go to much trouble to prepare more elaborate fare, which did nothing to help me lose my reputation of having a good appetite.

We spent our first night in Puerto Hope in Canal Magdalena in a tiny cove called La Poza, the Puddle.

Wednesday 12 December
What a joy to wake up in such a beautiful place! La Poza is surrounded by forested mountains, with snowy peaks and icefields up above. A few Steamer ducks made characteristic noises, Swallows twittered over the water, and a pair of Upland geese foraged in the grass near the beach.

Passing through a very narrow channel studded with rocks, between some outer islands and a peninsula of Tierra del Fuego sticking out into Canal Cockburn, I asked Alan to keep an eye on the sounder. The cockpit 'Seafarer' is still out of action, and the larger Furuno echo sounder is in the cabin where I cannot see it from outside. He straight away called out 'Two metres!' I was mystified. It looked so deep, and I had been through here before. Then '1½ metres!' I slowed right down. 'One metre!' I put the engine full astern. The sun was dead ahead, in my eyes, with bright reflection on the water. I turned *Totorore* in a tight circle, going ahead and astern, then went back out of the channel. Before we were clear I stopped the engine and lowered the lead and line over the side. Deep water! I went inside and looked at the sounder. Alan, not familiar with echo sounders, had been reading the zero marker!

For several weeks it was incredibly calm and we were forced to motor most of the time, prompting Alan to comment, 'I thought you said this was a sailing boat!'

Thursday 13 December
Not even a faint zephyr rippled the mirror on which *Totorore* lay, and a thin mist hung over the crags and forest around us. We motored down the caleta, along the inlet, and out into Canal Cockburn, where the mist thickened to fog and we had to use the radar to find our way among the islands. We passed groups of Magellanic penguins, and scores of Black-browed mollymawks sitting on the water waiting for the wind. It was uncanny, the sea was so flat that not even a swell disturbed it...Through Canal Ocasión, Canal Brecknock, Canal Unión we went, and only when we were past Isla Sidney did the fog lift and we started to roll in the open ocean swell. But there was still not a breath of wind. We headed between

the breaking seas on rocks towards Isla Stewart, looking mountainous and barren. From now on we must be alert for signs of Sooty shearwaters...

The ocean coasts of the islands bordering the Drake Passage seemed to be the obvious places for pelagic petrels to nest, but although we explored extensively, and every night used our lights to try to attract any birds which were flying around, we discovered very little. The lack of wind discouraged most of the sea birds from flying, making offshore bird-watching not very lively, but at least we enjoyed the many and varied inlets and coves which we visited, and the passerines and other land birds which we found.

Sunday 16 December

It was after midday when we arrived at the Ildefonso islands...the upper slopes and vegetated cliffs were full of nesting Black-browed mollymawks, and the lower rock faces, some very steep, were alive with Rockhopper penguins. We were interested to see if there were any Macaronis among them, and sure enough we found one large group mixed with the Rockhoppers on the largest and south-eastern island. Then, carefully examining all the main concentrations of penguins we found smaller numbers of Macaronis scattered among the 'Rockies' everywhere.

We watched with amusement as the Rockies came ashore after porpoising up to the islands in large numbers. Out of a big wave there would suddenly emerge dozens of them struggling upwards in the thick, slippery kelp which clung to the rocks everywhere up to the high-tide mark. Then they would scramble hurriedly up the steep rock face until clear of the waves, stopping to preen themselves. Far above, we could see some making their way up tracks into the tussock and their nests among the Blackbrows.

In some places there were also cormorants nesting, all mixed up together. It was exciting to be among so many birds again, and we were both delighted with the opportunity afforded by the good weather. Fur seals gambolled around us and uttered hysterical squeals up on the rocks, the sound echoing back from the cliffs reminding us of children in an indoor swimming pool.

Finding Macaroni penguins here is a first. When we were here in March they must have already left. We also hoped to see Grey-headed mollymawks on nests to confirm breeding; Beck had seen one in 1918 – the last visit by an ornithologist, apart from our own previous call. Alan was sceptical as we had not seen any flying about, but then we spotted one on a tussock slope high up on the western end of the largest island. Hooray! A careful search revealed five more, and shortly afterwards we saw two flying...

As it was so calm we anchored there for the night, and saw hordes of Sooty shearwaters flying over the islands, indicating that they were breeding there.

On Isla Moreton I found many burrows, some recently dug, and trails like tunnels through the scrub. Alan and I had heard Sooty shearwater calls and I thought perhaps these were their burrows. Somehow they did not look like bird burrows, and the only droppings or feathers I could find were from the lovely Ashy-headed geese. I could not smell the musky scent of petrels, so in my ignorance I was puzzled. It was not likely petrel habitat as it was too flat, and had an overgrazed look about it, with many ponds and soft patches. Then I saw two Coipus, like beavers but with rat-like tails; often their dens have entrances underwater, like those of otters. Later we saw Coipus and their signs on the other islands and realised that they were quite common.

The islands of the Cape Horn group seemed the most promising, and everywhere we went we came across extensive rafts of Sooty shearwaters on the water, or huge flocks in flight, but although we tramped over many likely looking hills, and spent the midnight hours working with our spotlights, we could not locate any actual burrows. Alan was becoming impatient. 'Perhaps they have evolved into a state in which they no longer need to breed.' We paid a visit to Isla Hall, where we had found some Blue petrels in April, and poked into a small cove on the south-east corner of the island, close to the tussock-topped cliff where the petrels had been seen.

Friday 21 December

...I was surprised and pleased to find that the tussock on top, and the rocks below, were occupied by Rockhopper penguins. They extended well round the spur, and even into a cave from which their chatter sounded very different and amplified. We anchored close by and sat and watched. There were many Striated caracaras around the colony, and we frequently saw one fly away to a well vegetated cliff with something in its talons or beak, obviously to a nest with hungry young. Up in the tussock at the top I saw a bald head appear above a long neck with a white ruff. A Condor! Two of them flew up and circled around low over the colony. There was a Giant petrel also flying around, and suddenly a Peregrine falcon appeared and stooped upon it, driving it quickly away. Later we saw the Giant petrel harrying the Caracaras, which however did not take much notice...

My night work was however disappointing. I was certain that the lights would attract Blue petrels, as I knew they would be here now at the height of the breeding season, but I saw very few and did not catch any. I stayed up until 0200 hours and then gave up. If my two pressure lamps and two spotlights shining on the mainsail did not attract them, nothing would! The ones I saw seemed to come straight into their burrows without circling about, and I heard no calls. As the hours of darkness are short, perhaps they do not waste time when they are incubating and just come in for a quick change-over.

Until then no Rockhopper colonies had actually been located in the Cape Horn islands, where breeding had only been suspected. Later we found another colony on Isla Hornos itself, at the north-western end and including about five percent Macaroni penguins. We searched again for the once-reported Chinstrap penguins, again without finding any sign. Right out on the south-east point, which fortunately was difficult of access so that the Armada station dogs (Chasca had a new companion) could not reach it, we found a sizeable colony of South American terns, with two or three eggs in each nest. The birds flew off at our intrusion, so we did not stay long; luckily there were no predators around to pounce on the eggs. What did surprise us was the complete lack of aggression from the birds, very different from the Antarctic terns which would have been diving furiously at our heads.

From our anchorage in the caleta near the Armada station we could see six men bathing in a cascading stream, half way up the cliff, and from their squeals we could tell that they were finding the water understandably very cold.

Sunday 23 December
...We motored across to the Deceit Rocks, south-east of Isla Deceit, and started seeing Great shearwaters again. This was a real pleasure, as they are so beautiful. They are really Atlantic birds and not commonly reported here.

The Deceit Rocks are a variety of strange shapes with some sharp-pointed stacks; on the outermost islands, which had sheer cliffs and large caves, was a very big colony of King cormorants. We saw also a large number of Fur seals on the lower rocks and ledges, attended by Sheathbills and Dolphin gulls. Altogether delightful, and today remarkably approachable...We moved on up the coast of Isla Deceit, noting that the best and most likely places for Sooty shearwaters to come into the wooded hills were near the two Armada stations, but we really did not feel like getting ourselves involved again.

Late in the afternoon we anchored in Caleta Commerson, named by ourselves last trip, up at the north end of the island. Once we had cleared the scrub we came to a low flat tundra area of spongy moss and cushion plants, easy to walk on, and covering the isthmus which led between the hills across to the western coast...there were several passerines, and many Winter plovers, or Rufous-chested dotterels, which amused us with their busy activity, running here and there, peeping, and chasing each other. We heard a mystery bird calling with a repeated croak, sometimes followed by a 'churr', from out of the scrub. We tried following it, but could never catch up, and regardless of our speed over the ground, it, or they, stayed between ten and twenty metres ahead...It was quite incredible that any birds could remain so concealed.

Back on board we consulted all the literature but could find nothing that seemed to fit. We considered Canasteros, little ground-creeping birds, or Seed snipes which are a partridge type of bird, but none had the same call...the first requirement is a tape-recording, so we will have to come back.

Christmas Day 1984 (at Caleta Lientur, Isla Wollaston)
By way of a Christmas present to ourselves, we both had a really good bath in the stream which although still chilly was bearable and very invigorating...in the evening Alan cooked a risotto which we ate with Chilean tinned rabbit and Dutch tinned ham, followed by an apple crumble made with dried apples. This was the first time the oven had been used since we left New Zealand. It was a fine meal, washed down with good red wine. We talked of home, and speculated on how our families might be spending their Christmases...

Wednesday 26 December
...Alan and I went for a walk and climbed up the mountainside, peering under bushes and reaching into holes to see if they were burrows. Some certainly appeared to be, but not one showed any sign of occupancy...

Back on board after dinner I suddenly thought, 'What the heck! Time is getting short and we are not making much progress! Nothing ventured, nothing gained!' It was 2100 hours. I pulled out my pack, stuffed in the tent, big battery spotlight, sleeping bag, tape-recorder, some dry clothes and a flask of coffee, and rowed myself ashore. Climbing up the hill kept me warm, and once up near the large rock I had been aiming for, with a dense patch of stunted beech trees at its foot where I thought I would find Sooties, I spent quite a while looking for a clear level spot on which to set the tent.

In my hurry I had come up without an axe or saw to clear the branches or roots which obstructed every site, so I had to kick and pull, and finally managed to get the tent up with a very lumpy, uneven floor. Nevertheless it soon felt like a cosy home out of the wind, and by the time I was established in it, it was nearly dark. The first Sooties appeared at 2320 hours, flying silently and directly to I know not where. The first of the flood! But the flood never came. There were dribs and drabs, but not the large numbers I had hoped for. After midnight others flew around with their weird caterwauling noises. I tried to follow them with the spotlight but failed. I wanted to find where at least one came to earth, but none came down anywhere close. I played the tape-recording of Sooty calls but they took no notice...

Twice more after that I tried camping alone up in the hills in different places, and both times there were many more Sooties but still I never found a burrow. The birds just disappeared into the scrub.

Alan was getting bored with the Sooty project so we thought we would go back to Isla Deceit and try to track down our 'mystery bird'.

Saturday 29 December
Equipped with the tape-recorder and cameras, we set off ashore. It was not long before we again heard the call – 'kraak, kraak. Chrrrr.' We were on the track. I thought it was on the other side of a small gully, only 50 metres away. Alan thought it was farther – about 200 metres. We moved around in a wide circle to try to get behind the bird, or birds, and stop them from escaping into the dense forest on the hillside. At first the sound seemed to move farther away, and then it stopped altogether. Lying low, we thought. Exercising careful strategy we circled a small hillock; when we arrived in the area in which we had last heard it, we stopped still and waited for half an hour. Nothing. Perhaps we should come back in the late evening? I wondered about sleeping the night in the tent to trace it in the early morning. We started on a circuitous scrubby route back to our landing beach.

Suddenly we heard it again, much closer! I started to record, but there was not much volume. I cautiously approached. The sound moved farther away. We followed, Alan watching like a hawk with his binoculars.

'It's incredible,' he said. 'It melts away without even moving a blade of grass!' Across the soft moss I could move quietly, but in the scrub I had to cast caution to the wind, and crash through as best I could, trying to close the gap between me and the bird. A few times I seemed to be closer, and kept the recorder going, but always it moved away ahead. It started to rain, and was not at all pleasant. Wretched bird!

I waited miserably in the wet scrub. Alan had made a wide detour to get behind it, and possibly work it back towards me. No luck. Then he said, 'Way up in those trees is a pair of Caracaras. I saw them flying. Perhaps there is a nest!' We had a good look at them. They were Crested caracaras, with which we were familiar farther north, but here they were mainly replaced by Striated caracaras. As we both watched with binoculars we saw one throw back his head. 'Kraak, kraak. Chrrrrr!' Slowly the truth dawned on us: we had been hoodwinked all this time by a ventriloquist! How we both laughed...

In the course of our explorations we saw Great grebes which had never been recorded in these islands before, and a dead Black-necked swan. Searching along the north coast of Isla Grévy, the northernmost island in the group, we passed impressive cliffs which in one spot had the most remarkable columnar appearance I have even seen, looking like stack after stack of organ pipes. From there we carried on down to Seagull Anchorage, where Hal and Margaret Roth had been wrecked in their yacht *Whisper* on Isla Diana a few years before. What had amazed me particularly, from Hal's graphic account in his book *Two Against Cape Horn* was that the next day their second anchor had been found higher up the bank on the island than *Whisper* herself! We were much more fortunate and had a peaceful night, the silence being broken only by the braying of the Magellanic penguins and the grunting quacks of Steamer ducks.

Thursday 3 January
...on the north coast of Isla Picton is a caleta named Banner, not far from a lake on which I thought we might find interesting birds. Our zarpe did not mention that we could go there, but it seemed to me that if we asked the Armada personnel who were bound to be in residence – it was one of the disputed islands – then it would be all right.

We motored up through the gap between Islas Lennox and Picton, passing through thick kelp, then sailed up the east coast of Picton in rain. Caleta Banner was entirely different from what we were used to seeing, the trees in the surrounding forest being tall and not stunted. A delightful scene opened up before us, with a park-like quality. Sheltered by Isla Gardiner outside, the caleta was like a lake itself, and grassy patches on the shores looked ideal picnic spots in better weather.

The Armada station seemed very small, but had two quite modern-looking houses, as distinct from huts at the other stations we had seen. Two men came out to us in a wooden rowing boat; they lived here with their families, and obviously loved it. We went ashore with them to meet the wife and young children of one of them and enjoy a cup of coffee with fresh bread and butter. Juan, the petty officer in charge, offered to show us the way to the lake, saying that it was necessary to stick to one particular route, as much of the area was mined!

Perhaps this accounts for some places being prohibited...the previous trip, all these disputed islands were forbidden. I might have some explaining to do when we reached Puerto Williams!

199

We set off along a track through the forest, skirting the river. It was beautiful, in spite of the rain, and was just like being in a beech forest in New Zealand. In a small clearing we came to a derelict corrugated iron hut, and Juan told us that it was the house of the missionary Alan Gardiner who lived here in 1929 in his first house, the framework of which was just behind. Some of the walls were still standing and were made of heavy, hand-adzed planks. Inside the corrugated iron house there was still a bed frame, a table with an ancient enamelled coffee pot and other utensils, including a broken earthenware bottle...

The river narrowed to about twenty metres across, and then we came to a great dam which held the water up to a depth of about two metres. It consisted of trees and branches, and was obviously constructed rather than haphazardly thrown up by a flood. As we neared it we could see drowned trees in the flooded area beyond, and also that the trees and branches had been axed – or so we thought! 'Castores,' said Juan. The penny dropped. Beavers! I vaguely remembered reading about their having been introduced into Tierra del Fuego from Canada and how they had become a nuisance with their dams and the destruction of the forest.

We saw many more dams and also lodges – huge piles of wood with underwater entrances, sometimes into big earth mounds at the banks. All around were tree stumps cleanly chiselled off, and many newly gnawed trunks with huge chips adzed off by strong front teeth. We heard several at work, but saw only a few swimming along in the water before they dived out of sight.

Finally we reached the lake, which must be beautiful in fine weather. Although I spotted some Great grebes, the rain did not assist bird-watching and we went back to the caleta...

Friday 4 January

As we approached Puerto Williams we could see some sheep on a few grassy slopes, and some cattle being driven along a beach by a man on a horse. There were three motor-torpedo boats, and other small naval craft at the main jetty, and an old frigate, now out of commission and used as a workshop base, moored close by. Over the VHF we were instructed to go to the small jetty just beyond, and there we were met by an Armada officer who welcomed us to Puerto Williams. He told us to let him know if there was anything we needed, and he would make the arrangements. Again the courtesy, and the warm feeling of friendship which we have come to expect in these places...While we were completing formalities we heard an unmistakeably Kiwi voice, and were hailed by Keith Brookway, a young New Zealand doctor who had spent last year as house surgeon at Whangarei Hospital. He had spotted our port of registry, Whangarei, on *Totorore's* transom, and naturally came to see who we were...He and Bill McSweeny, another young doctor from Christchurch, are tramping and climbing around South America, back-packing and sleeping in a tent. They wish to go to Ushuaia, the other side of the Beagle Channel, in Argentina. So far they have been unable to find a way of getting there, although apparently there is an occasional small craft taking passengers. We would like to visit Ushuaia also – Alan has an Argentinian visa – and will see if it is possible for us to take them over...

Saturday 5 January

A sailor came down to our jetty early in the morning to tell me that the Armada at Punta Arenas wished to speak to me on the telephone, up at the lookout post. Wondering what could be the trouble, I was pleased that it was only to tell me that Peter Harrison would be arriving at Puerto Williams tomorrow...

Puerto Williams is a small town consisting almost entirely of Armada personnel with their families, and most of the services seemed to be run by uniformed Armada men. The total population is about 1200, so I was surprised to see as many shops as there were, in two neat squares. A monument made of the bow of the Armada vessel *Yelcho*, in which the Chilean pilot Pardo had rescured the crew of Shackleton's ship *Endurance* from Elephant Island in 1916, stood in front of the shopping centre. We bought some more eggs, cabbages, and a piece of fresh meat, and Alan was delighted to find a pair of jeans which actually fitted him. As he is 190.5 centimetres tall and has very long legs, that was a fluke indeed. He had brought only one pair of trousers and in spite of his constant attention with needle and cotton the seat had become dangerously thin! He had been considering cutting up one of his shirts to make a complete new seat, but now that will not be necessary.

Coipu

Chapter Twelve

Fuegian Summer

Ushuaia — Islas Terhalten, Sesambre — Isla Barnevelt — Islas Hall and Chanticleer — Ildefonso — Southern canals — Punta Arenas — Brazo Norte

Peter Harrison, English ornithologist, artist, author, and presently lecturer in the *Lindblad Explorer*, arrived at Puerto Williams in the pilot launch. There had been a change in the itinerary of the *Lindblad Explorer*, and instead of leaving her at Punta Arenas, he had been dropped off with the pilot at Cape Horn. It was immediately apparent that we were a compatible team, and Peter's knowledge and energy gave additional zest to our efforts. He was always 'rarin' to go'! To keep himself fit he did 200 situps every day, setting an example much admired, but not followed, by Alan and myself.

To obtain a permit for our further work, and to take our New Zealand friends to Ushuaia, we had to go to see the Comandante of Puerto Williams. It took a while to be granted an interview with this very important person, who, according to Keith and Bill, spoke very good English. When Alan and I were ushered into his presence, I said, 'How do you do, Sir.' He shook hands formally, but said in Spanish, 'When in Chile, we speak Spanish.' I said I would try, but asked him if he would help me out if I got into difficulties. That was the only time we saw even a ghost of a smile cross his face.

I said we had come to pay our respects, and to thank him for allowing us to stay at the very good wharf in that beautiful place. He nodded, and I presented our proposed itinerary and discussed it with him. Isla Evout was the only island we were not allowed to go to, he said. We could land on the small islands and rocks nearby, and we could sail close around it, but we must not land. We were allowed to go to Ushuaia, but would have to return to Puerto Williams to obtain clearance into Chile again before proceeding further.

It was only a few hours sail across the Strait to Ushuaia, where we all went ashore, unhindered by the guard on the dock gate. We walked through the pleasant little town to the Prefectura Naval to clear inwards and present our passports. We were received politely but had to wait for two hours before being told that Peter and I were not allowed ashore as we had no visas. Alan had an Argentinian visa, and of course the two doctors had theirs. I had thought that as ship's crew we would be able to obtain a temporary visa, but that was not possible. We could stay aboard *Totorore* out in the harbour as long as we liked.

As it turned out, I had to go back to the Prefectura with the papers the next day to clear outwards, and did some shopping with Alan on the way, so saw all I needed to of Ushuaia. We found handling Argentinian money quite confusing, with the denominations of the notes in millions of pesos. The inflation rate was said to be 2500 per cent per annum!

After going back to Puerto Williams for our papers, we had a good fast sail down Canal Beagle, passing rafts of White-chinned petrels and counting over 1000 of them, which was particularly interesting as they had not previously been recorded there. Before leaving the Beagle we anchored in the lee of the small Islas Bécasses, the Woodcock Islands, where the English ornithologist Percy Reynolds had landed some fifty years before, to make a comparison with his findings. His was also the last published paper on the birds of the Cape Horn islands, and we had already found several discrepancies which needed further investigation. Alan and Peter spent three hours ashore and took many photographs of nesting terns, Skuas and Magellan cormorants, and thoroughly enjoyed themselves.

About thirteen miles north-east of Isla Wollaston, across Bahía Nassau, there are two small islands about one mile apart named Terhalten and Sesambre, which had not been visited by an ornithologist before. As we approached Terhalten, the northernmost of the two, we saw increasing numbers of Rockhoppers both on the surface and porpoising.

Friday 11 January
...soon we could see dense lines of black-and-white cormorants along the top ridges. Then we saw the penguins on the rocks at the bottom, and going up into the tussock and dense scrub. There were mostly Rockhoppers, but also several thousand Magellanic, and close to the coast the sea was thickly covered with small marine creatures looking like reddish marbles, which both kinds of penguins seemed to be enjoying...I stayed to keep an eye on *Totorore* after rowing Alan and Peter ashore with the tent.

After a preliminary survey they came back to collect the rest of the camping gear and have an early dinner. They said that the going was difficult – either very steep, dense scrub, or horribly muddy and sticky where the penguins had invaded the tussock. At one end, the tussock had been flattened by the thousands of Fur seals which we had seen on a rocky cape. Right at the top was an extremely large colony of King cormorants – the biggest Peter had ever seen...

Alan and Peter had a list of 22 bird species for Terhalten, which was quite good for a small island, but had not seen any petrels during the night. Sesambre, without penguins, and with only a few seals and cormorants, looked more promising. The vegetation was more open and the tussock drier. A few Baird's sandpipers were on the rocky shore, which was like the tops of broken-off columns forming steps up to the vegetation above the normal wave height.

Saturday 12 January
...Again we anchored close off the north shore, out of the worst swell, and Alan and Peter went for a quick survey on top without taking any gear. At first they found the ascent difficult. It was steep, and the scrub dense, and

it took quite a long time to reach the top. There they found a wide flattish area of low empetrium, sort of heather-like plant, and azorella, which is easy to walk on, with large clumps of hebe covered with white flowers. Best of all, there were big areas of good healthy tussock, riddled with burrows! They seemed to belong to Sooty shearwaters. They also found two Skua nests with chicks. In the afternoon it was so calm that I joined them and spent several enjoyable hours browsing around this delightful island, never very far from *Totorore*, which I could see down below. Alan and Peter set up the tent in a good place near some burrows, then came back on board for dinner. I rowed them ashore again at about 2200 hours complete with spotlight, tape-recorder and delousing gear, then returned to look after *Totorore*.

Sunday 13 January
Getting Alan and Peter off the island was quite easy in the calm conditions, and they were pleased to tell me about the wonderful night they had had. The Sooties started coming in, in small numbers, at about 2330 hours, and then soon after midnight there were about 1000 flying around calling loudly and thumping into the ground, pretty well straight into the burrows. By mistake the hand net had been left behind and they took a full hour to catch one by hand, dashing up and down on the top of the island with the spotlight. It was quite a performance to hold the struggling, biting bird to delouse it...Alan said it was all tremendous fun!

Isla Evout is a much larger island, about half a mile across, and also much higher, lying ten miles south-east of Sesambre. Along with Ildefonso and Diego Ramirez Islands, it was one of the reported breeding places of the Black-browed mollymawks, which we wanted to see. We had been told that we were not allowed to land, and remembered the mines on Isla Picton; nonetheless it was very tempting in such calm weather. We circumnavigated the island closely, and examined it as thoroughly as we could from *Totorore*. On top was good tussock cover, probably full of Sooty shearwaters, but we could not tell. However we were quite convinced that there were no Black-brows breeding there, and on searching through the literature discovered that in his paper on the birds of Cape Horn, Percy Reynolds said that a friend had told him that Black-brows breed on Isla Evout! Nowadays such unsubstantiated evidence would hardly be accepted in a scientific journal. We were disappointed, but realised that even a negative record in a case like that was very important. Our discovery of the colony on Diego de Almagro farther north was more than compensation.

Our next island was Barnevelt, on which Anthea, Julia and I had been unable to land in April. At that time it was, strangely, also forbidden by the Armada, but now we were allowed to examine it. It is almost circular and about a mile across, with a wide bay on its northern side. The highest point is only about 100 metres and there are many offshore rocks above and below water.

Sunday 13 January
We followed on around the main island's east coast, and on a rockshelf leading up to a dense tussock slope we found a truly enormous colony of

Rockhoppers, stretching up to the top of the hill. Many thousands swam all around, close by. We searched thoroughly, but saw only two Macaroni penguins among them. Still looking for an anchorage protected from the west, we carried on until we found a small and impressive caleta tucked into the rocky cliffs. On one side a large columnar rock looked so like something from Egypt, with long carved faces on it, that we called the place Caleta Cleopatra. There was just enough swinging room, but we had to anchor in thick kelp, and several rocks showed above water rather too close for my liking.

We all went ashore today as our caleta seemed well sheltered from the fresh wind blowing outside... There were two gullies, and we had a choice between a steep one with a stream bed, and a less steep one with thicker scrub. Neither way was good, and the stream bed we chose was slippery on bare rock, or very crumbling scree, or just plain muddy.

At the top we could look across most of the island, and we saw that it was not all tussock as we had been led to believe. Most of it looked like long grass but was in fact rushes sticking up through a tangle of low scrub. It was rolling country with occasional streams and ponds, and on the other side we could see wide areas of dense green tussock, full of Magellanic penguins whose mournful braying could be easily heard from where we were. Alan and Peter set off in the direction of the Rockhopper colony we had seen and I started along the cliff tops to the west. Many Skuas circled overhead – at one time I counted sixteen. I also saw a Peregrine falcon and several Striated caracaras – all good signs for small petrels. I was looking for skua middens to give some indication of petrels here, as they would contain remains, with possibly a skull or two to aid identification. I could not find any, which surprised me. However, I made a point of examining small clumps of tussock on the cliff edges, and straight away I found little trails with feathers which looked like either Blue petrel or prion feathers. These extended back into grassy areas behind the actual tussock. Many of the tussock clumps were overhanging the cliff edges, and I had seen how easily tussock could come away from rocky bases, so I was very wary...

I found one exceptionally good cape, rather less dangerous than the others, and with the end patch of tussock completely riddled with burrows and much evidence of occupancy. I could not hear any cooings or crooning noises, and did not like to walk around any more for fear of crushing some bird inside one of the burrows, so I collected feathers to show the others and set off back after discovering two more smaller colonies of Rockhoppers. A dark grey Plumbeous rail flew up from under my feet with a shriek of alarm, but there were not many small birds to be seen, just a few Grass wrens and some Rayoditos...

After lunch I went back with Peter, carrying the tent and the bird net and trowel, and climbed back up to the top. By the time we reached the best place for burrows the wind was strong and cold with showers. We soon found the trails through the grass, and when I felt my foot sink through tussock into a burrow Peter came and scrabbled at it with his hands. We heard a squeaking sound and he drew out a beautiful little Blue petrel chick, almost fully feathered but with fluffy down still sticking to it. Peter was beside himself with pleasure. We both photographed the bird, then replaced it in its burrow and covered the hole we had made with grass and soil. Breeding of Blue petrels confirmed on Isla Barnevelt. Good.

Tuesday 15 January

...After seeing the concentration of White-chins in the Beagle Canal, I am still hoping to find a nesting colony somewhere around here. Our landing was a little tricky, as the swell was curling around the corner into our caleta and breaking fiercely on the rocks, but by being patient we both got ashore dry...we soon encountered the difficult tussock area, full of Magellanic penguins. In places it was over three metres high, with foul black mud underneath. Following penguin trails worked well in some places, but in others it was too dense, and one had to use tussocks as stepping stones. Some were firm, others springy, and some collapsed sideways, sliding us off into unknown spaces below. Once I fell waist deep into a very evil smelling pool, and still did not touch the bottom as I hung from the tussock with both hands, madly scrabbling with my knees and feet to extricate myself from the mud. We searched diligently but concluded that there were only penguins there.

We found a sheltered spot on a boulder beach to have our lunch and were surrounded by the penguins which were not at all afraid once they were used to us. During the afternoon, crossing the low scrub, we were rewarded by seeing a large and handsome Strickland's snipe which after a short flight allowed us to approach to within three metres for Peter to take photographs. At the extreme western end of the island we found a ternery where some more of the beautiful South American terns were nesting. There were many eggs lying around, usually in pairs, well camouflaged and hard to see as was a single newly hatched chick. A magnificent Black-chested buzzard eagle floated over the island in unhurried flight, ignoring the terns which mobbed him.

After looking at the other two Rockhopper colonies without finding any more Macaronis, we made our tired way back to the gully and down to the beach...

Wednesday 16 January

The barometer had taken a tumble, so we thought we had better head across to the Armada caleta near Cape Horn while we could. The wind was only moderate as we had a good look at the colonies of Blue-eyed shags, which are unusual around here, out on the rocky islets south-west of Barnevelt. From there we set full sail towards the outer Deceit Rocks to show Peter the large colony of King cormorants, and we enjoyed a good sail for about five miles before the wind started to increase to gale force, and I decided to head up towards Caleta Wilfredo in a good bay on the east side of Deceit. We motor-sailed with just the reefed jib and staysail, then took the staysail off and eventually all sail, plugging up dead to windward with just the engine.

We arrived within two miles and the sea started to smoke as the wind increased to Force 10. It was almost impossible to keep her head up as I struggled with the tiller...after an hour we were farther away, and the sea was very rough indeed...I told my crew that the open sea was the safest place, and rejected the suggestion that we could return to Caleta Cleopatra in Barnevelt...Both Alan and Peter coped very well, as they are unaccustomed to bad weather in boats as small as this. Finally, tired and wet, I lashed the helm after I had seen us pass the outer rock off Barnevelt, and went below. There was not enough power in the reefed staysail to put her about, and she held a good course.

I had to put the washboard in to keep out splashes from seas which broke into the cockpit, and frequently I looked out and up at the mast. Its bending and flexing made me anxious in view of its patched-up nature, but it held up all right. I felt decidedly off-colour, and so did Peter who did not want anything to eat, but Alan was fine. After we had safely cleared Isla Evout and its rocks, Alan boiled some eggs for himself and me, and we had also some semolina with stewed dried apples, after which I felt better. We all lay down to sleep – I had my alarm set every hour to check...

At about 0500 hrs we anchored in the lee of Cabo Graham on Isla Nueva – about 42 miles from Caleta Wilfredo which we had been heading for!

When the gale had blown itself out, we made our way back to the Cape Horn islands and continued our search for Sooty shearwater and Blue petrel burrows, and Grebe nests. Of Sooties we found quite a lot, and of Blue petrels we found thousands, especially on the two islands just west of Isla Hornos – Islas Hall and Chanticleer. On Isla Hall, Alan and Peter were up near the peaks sleeping in the tent for the night when a gale blew up and the tent collapsed on top of them, giving them yet another hilarious night to remember. Peter estimated the Blue petrel population on that island to be 50,000.

Friday 25 January
...At Isla Chanticleer, we anchored in a small indentation in the north coast...not only was the island absolutely riddled with Blue petrel burrows, but we saw two Condors sitting above a large cormorant colony before they flew away below us, giving us impressive views of their huge wings. Peter was particularly thrilled when we found two fledgling Chilean skuas. This was just what he wanted to verify plumage patterns for his sea bird book, and to take photographs for his next project. The cinnamon colour was absolutely beautiful, merging into the light brown on the head. Rufous and tawny markings under the wings made these very handsome birds...All the way to the top there were signs of Blue petrels – feathers and burrows – and in the tussock itself on the top and in other clumps round about there were literally hundreds of burrows...The steep climb made me sweat profusely but parts of the way back down again were hazardous enough to give me a cold sweat.

All the islands had so much to offer, and so much work still needing to be done on them, that it seemed a pity to leave them. Unfortunately our time was running short to get Peter back to Punta Arenas to rejoin the *Lindblad Explorer*, and Alan to catch his plane, so reluctantly we started to make our way back. I still wanted to have another go at Ildefonso, using Islas Morton as a shelter base.

Monday 28 January (anchored in Caleta 'Peter the Baker', Isla Henderson)
A cup of tea for my crew at 0520 hours for an early start, so that we could press on out to Ildefonso while the weather gave us the opportunity. Peter is keen to get up onto the islands, so he started winching up the anchor before he had even drunk his tea. Certainly it was calm, but the sky had a windy look about it and the barometer is falling. I got a shock when I started the engine. It is making a most awful noise as though it is falling to bits inside, and the tachometer needle swings wildly about. It seems to be running all right otherwise, but it certainly has me worried.

We got away at 0530 hours and motored through the beautiful rocky-looking Morton Islands. A Blackish cinclodes, like a small hen blackbird, came aboard and hopped about amazingly tame and unafraid. He stood on the edge of our cockpit dodger, and on the tiller close to my hand, then he actually stood on Peter's hand where it rested on the dodger. We tried feeding him with breadcrumbs, but he was not very interested. Out across the sea we can see the Ildefonso Islands now about ten miles away. These are perhaps the greatest challenge of this part of our voyage. . .having seen Peter's climbing ability, I now have more confidence in our being able to accomplish something here.

. . .It was a difficult landing onto a steep rock face with much kelp, and a surge up and down of about three metres, but Peter managed well. I rowed back to *Totorore* and Alan and I watched him climb up the rock face which neither Alan nor I felt we could tackle. 'No problem,' Peter had said. 'If a penguin can do it, I can!' He stopped to take photographs of Black-browed mollymawks, all the nests now occupied by well-grown chicks, and Rockhopper and Macaroni penguins which are now moulting. He was accompanied by inquisitive Caracaras and more friendly Blackish cinclodes. In some places we hardly liked to watch as it looked so dangerous, but like a spider he made his way up the cliff and into the enormous, lush-looking tussock. Even there, it was very steep, and we could see that it was going to be difficult. . .

After about three hours I rowed over to meet him. A bodily leap into the bottom of the dinghy as it dropped rapidly away from him and he was safe as I rowed hard away from the turbulent broken water next to the rock. Over hot soup Peter told us what he had found.

There was no sign of Sooty shearwaters, but he confirmed Blue petrels in abundance, estimating at least 5000 on that one island. A chick he dug out with the trowel seemed to be about a week behind those on Hall Island. I am very pleased with the care Peter takes when removing a bird from its burrow; after replacing it, he always repairs any damage he has done so that no harm will befall the bird. Alan is more scientific in his approach to ornithology, and humorously says that I am emotional and sentimental and that my attitude to birds is anthropomorphic and teleological! Probably he is right, but it is the way I enjoy it and I don't think I could ever be a scientist.

Peter counted over 8500 Black-browed chicks, and estimated about 12,000 Rockhoppers with a small number of Macaronis among them. With a falling barometer we were anxious to have a look at the first of the smaller central group of islands as quickly as possible, before the weather packed up. It was over those that I had seen most of the Sooty shearweaters on 16 December. I decided to row him over to the next island, rather than move *Totorore*...but it started to blow and we only just made it back. We pulled up and deflated the dinghy, and within five minutes the wind was blowing 40 knots from the north-west...

The twelve miles seemed a long way to Punta Rugged, the south cape of Isla Morton, which I hoped would give us shelter. We could see the squalls smoking off the cape, so while I struggled with the tiller, I instructed Alan and Peter, who had never done it before in heavy weather, how to reduce sail using the winch for the furling line. They did it very well – not easy with *Totorore* almost on her beam ends – and it was safer for rounding the cape itself. In the lee there were plenty of severe rafagas, but at least we were out of the rough sea.

Tuesday 29 January
...When we arrived at the Ildefonso islands again the swell was breaking high up their steep sides and we could see no possiblity of landing or of Peter's climbing the island we had missed out on yesterday...at the eastern end of the large south-east island, however, Peter thought a climb might be possible. There was certainly less surge there, but to Alan and me the cliff looked frighteningly difficult. 'No problem,' said Peter, 'as long as I have some handholds, I don't mind how vertical it is.' I was confident in his ability, but Alan certainly did not want to see him try.

I was none too happy about the weather as it was already blowing Force 4, and the position so exposed that any increase in wind would make landing and later recovery very difficult. It was a hard decision to make – I desperately wanted the information, time was getting short, and Peter was keen to give it a try. We could have done it, but I did not want to risk leaving Peter on a difficult island while we had to clear out with *Totorore*. 'No,' I said, finally. 'We will have to come back when there is less swell.'

In fact the wind did not increase, and the swell diminished as we sailed back to Morton Islands after having a look at the truly wild south-west coasts. It was a wrong decision I had made and I regretted it, but as Peter generously observed, 'It was the right decision, because it seemed right at the time.' Unfortunately the weather did not give us another chance. On 1 February, because the conditions were still bad for Ildefonso, we started heading back to Punta Arenas. I was worried about the engine which continued to give trouble, and we certainly needed it to make to windward in the narrow channels if we were not going to be late. Progress was slow with strong headwinds and rain, and when the weather finally improved on 6 February, we were in Bahía Drew, off Canal Magdelena, where we had anchored for the night.

This was one of the superbly beautiful and well sheltered places, and the route to its innermost recesses was so intricate that we doubted if anybody else ever went there. We were thus very surprised and a little disappointed to see a small fishing boat appear, a rough-looking craft powered by an outboard motor and with two men aboard. We waved to them, and they came after us, so I slowed down until they were close alongside.

One of them held up a crab – a beautiful big centolla. 'You want a crab?' he asked in English. 'How much?' I replied. 'Nada!' (nothing) he replied. 'Thank you very much.' We brought our boats alongside each other, and he showed us how to prepare the crab for eating. He simply put his foot on the carapace and holding the legs in his two hands tore the crab apart, neatly cleaning it at the same time. He gave us three, and we gave him a bar of chocolate and three bags of sugar. That night we dined on crab cooked to perfection by Peter, with a mayonnaise made by Alan. It was the first time I had been able to afford to eat it!

We arrived at Punta Arenas on 7 February and Alan moved back into the pension where he had stayed before while Peter stayed aboard with me until the *Lindblad Explorer* arrived. An agreement over the disputed islands had been reached between Chile and Argentina, and the atmosphere in Punta Arenas was more relaxed. There were no longer any armed guards at the dock gate, and we did not need passes to come or go.

Alain Caradec, whom we had met before on his yacht *Basile*, was back in Punta Arenas and we lay alongside her for a couple of days. *Basile* had been chartered by a party of mountaineers and a film team for an Antarctic expedition and she really looked the part, all loaded up with prefabricated huts, a sledge, a kayak, a mountain of other gear and on top of it all, a husky dog. Alain was busy and efficient, but had a constantly worried look, which hardly surprised me considering his responsibility for that lot! It was all very interesting, and started me thinking...

When *Basile* sailed, I moved alongside a large, traditionally constructed and rigged yacht named *Appledore 3*, built and owned by Herb Smith and his wife Doris, from Maine. They had with them their two young children and five paying crew, and were on a round-the-world cruise. Herb is a professional photographer and author, and showed me some of his work, which was very inspiring. I greatly admired them and their ship, and their enterprising venture: it was their third circumnavigation.

Before he left, Peter went uptown and bought himself a small box of watercolour paints, and while I was away he painted a beautiful cormorant's head on the flyleaf of my copy of his book *Seabirds, An Identification Manual*. 'To my good friend Gerry Clark. God speed you and the *Totorore*.' I am always proud to show that to people.

Punta Arenas was, as ever, a difficult and frustrating place for getting anything done, and apart from frequently having to shift *Totorore*, which suffered more damage as a result, and during bad weather, I was constantly up against the mañana (tomorrow) attitude. They were such nice people, but oh so unreliable. I was extremely glad when Chris Sale, young and strong, arrived from New Zealand to help me, and we started to make progress. Chris is a good friend and a boat builder, and had given me a lot of help when I was building *Totorore*.

One day we were visited by Jorge Glucevich, a director of Brooms, who was privately interested in collecting and exporting guano, and had already sent one shipment to New Zealand. He asked us if we knew of any good bird islands where he could take some samples. Thinking that it was a good chance for us to repay Brooms, I said we could take him to see Islas Marta and Magdalena, about twenty miles north, and where Andreas and I had nearly got into trouble in December. It provided a good opportunity also to repay our friends Pedro and Ernesto, who were very pleased to accompany us.

Tuesday 19 February

Our passengers got along extremely well together. Jorge, a grey-haired, distinguished gentleman of about 63, was full of humour. Although he speaks excellent English, and did so to Chris, he preferred that I should speak to him in Spanish and he gave me some helpful tips. Pedro and Ernesto were good fun, and altogether it was a happy day...

We went first to Isla Isabel, where Pedro had previously found his arrowheads, but the combination of fresh wind and strong tidal stream created a nasty sea so that landing at the beach was not possible. Instead, we headed north towards Isla Marta. Flat topped, it has a cliff about ten metres all around it; devoid of vegetation and really looks as though it is all guano – which excited Jorge considerably. We could see vast numbers of cormorants and some Magellanic penguins, as well as Dolphin gulls. On the lee side the sea did not seem too bad, and close to the north point we anchored right next to the Sea-lion colony.

There were about 200 Sea-lions, and most of them took to the water and gambolled around, poking their heads up high to look at us. Chris, Pedro and Jorge went ashore in the dinghy, while Ernesto and I stayed on board. We saw them photographing a single Elephant seal on the beach, and then they disappeared around to the other side to climb to the top. After about two hours they returned, Jorge with two bags of guano and a lot more all over himself and the wet-weather gear which we had lent him. He was very pleased, and said one bag was for me to take to my wife for the garden! I thanked him, but declined the offer, as we really could not spare the space...

While at Punta Arenas we several times enjoyed the hospitality of Claudio Venegas and his senora in their home at the Instituto de la Patagonia, which had the best hot water shower we had come across! During our absence Claudio had finally gone to Isla Noir with Frank Todd and we were interested to hear all about it, but in spite of many tentative plans Claudio, regrettably, was never able to join us for a trip.

Wednesday 20 February

...We were lying alongside a small fishing boat named *Ernestito* at the pier, and in the late afternoon a nasty swell rolled in from the south-east so that we had to cast off to go out to anchor. Chris climbed aboard the *Ernestito* to let go our mooring lines but could not undo the knot on the stern line, made by a fisherman when we came in. Our bow was caught by the wind and swung out just as Mario on *Ernestito* let go all of his lines. To protect our self-steering gear I had to push well off, so I let go the stern line from our end, leaving Chris on board *Ernestito*. 'I'll pick you up when we get around to the other side!' I shouted to him. Then I watched horrified, as *Ernestito* motored straight ahead into the shallows near the sea wall, where the sea was breaking. Chris was hanging on grimly on the afterdeck as she rolled and bumped heavily on the sandy bottom. I thought she was going to be rolled right over, and moved in as close as I dared, thinking to send her a line to try to tow her off. Luckily Mario managed to get her under control – he had been having trouble with his gears – and backed off from disaster, shaken but apparently undamaged. It was a frightening experience for Chris, who was only too pleased to come back aboard *Totorore* when we were around on the other side.

Saturday 23 February
...I was somewhat dismayed by the appearance of Luis Silva, who visited us in May last year and again each time we have been in Punta Arenas. He used to tell us how he was building a six-metre yacht, and now this time he brought his 'new' craft and moored her alongside us. She is named *Horizonte* (Horizon) and looked awful. Terribly rough and looking very old although she is brand new, her paint is all peeling off. We think he is definitely unbalanced, or 'loco' as they say here.

Luis said he wanted one of us to go for a sail with him as he needs to learn from somebody experienced. Neither of us would dare to go in that boat which is decidedly unsafe, and unseaworthy, being inadequately rigged and already leaking fast. He asked us to help him as his centreboard was stuck in its case and would not go up or down. Chris spent some time with him and we had to finish our own jobs in the dark. Then Luis went home and left his horrible little boat alongside us...

Sunday 24 February
Horizonte was listing over against us, and was obviously half full of water. As a truly enormous padlock secured the hatch – which amused us, as there was nothing inside to steal – we could not do anything to help her and just secured her alongside a fishing boat when we left.

In spite of everything, we had to admire Luis for having built his own yacht, obviously without any experience of boatbuilding or sailing, and with nobody in Punta Arenas to give him guidance. Some weeks afterwards I met him in a supermarket and he told me that he wanted to swap his boat for a car!

Desperate to get away from the congested port area, and needing to find somewhere to dry *Totorore* out to work on the bottom, we moved north a few miles to Bahía Catalina.

Tuesday 26 February
...We anchored close to a jetty in front of an ugly and very evil-smelling meatworks, with a fishery on either side of it. Dos Oceanos is to the north, and Pesquera Magallanes to the south. A large fishing vessel was alongside the jetty discharging 'centallons', a crab much smaller than the centolla, but which is the only one available at this season.

We rowed ashore to the beach, passing through hordes of Dominican or Kelp gulls (the same as the Black-backed gulls at home) and Chilean skuas, which were gathered around the gory effluent from the meatworks. The Dos Oceanos fishery had an enormous pile of leg shells and carapaces piled up on the beach outside the processing plant, and these were spread along the beach for miles in both directions. Beyond the low sheds were about fifteen fishing boats of various sizes hauled up above the tide for repairs, and two more under construction. These were of particular interest to Chris, a boatbuilder himself. We watched a man axing out a boat's forefoot from a grown piece of timber, and could not help being impressed by the boats themselves, built with such primitive methods. Certainly rough and ready, they do the job, although we both agreed that we would not feel very safe in them in the sort of weather one gets down south... The beach was littered with derelict, abandoned fishing boats, large and small, and we found several that were riddled with teredo.

Inside the processing sheds all looked clean and efficient, and many white-coated women were cleaning and packing the crabs. We walked along the beach past the meatworks to the other fishery, Pesquera de Magallanes. Next to a large fishing boat hulk we saw a ramp of steel with wooden sleepers, deeply scored, where many a fishing boat had been hauled up. The lower sleepers were steel pipes. This, we thought, would be a good place to dry out. The manager spoke good English and said they would be able to help us with repairs, and Sergio, his marine superintendent, said that they could pull *Totorore* right out of the water for us.

The next day, with some difficulty in crosswinds of about twenty knots, we managed to get *Totorore* onto the ramp at high tide and secured for the night. It was very uncomfortable because waves kept lifting the stern and dropping her down again with sickening force, and the water slapping underneath the hull was most disturbing.

Thursday 28 Feburay
When we dried out we had a good look around the hull, apart from the stern gear which was still in the water. All was sound except for a couple of minor damage spots, probably caused by ice. Fouling was not bad – just some rather black weed growth around the waterline, and on the keels and skeg. There were some deep scratches from the end of the mast when it was in the water, but really the condition of the paint was most impressive considering the ice we had pushed through. Very good stuff, that Barrier anti-fouling which we put on on the beach at Puerto Montt in December '83!

There seemed to be no sign of any of the promised activity to start hauling us up the ramp, so after partially cleaning the bottom we went to borrow two shovels and spent a couple of hours shovelling the sand off the ramp sleepers in readiness. While we worked, people came to look at *Totorore* and to ask questions. Some were fishermen from the boats alongside the jetty, and some from the fishery processing shed. A constant stream of white-coated, white-hatted women came out of the shed door with baskets of shells and other crab refuse to empty onto the beach, to the obvious delight of the noisy gulls. Varying from old and fat to young and pretty, they seemed to think that we were amusing – it may have been because when Chris bent over there was a gap between the back of his shirt and his trousers, showing part of his bare bottom. They called out 'Ola!' and waved to us, with much giggling, before going back into the shed.

Again I was impressed by the warm friendliness of the people. They certainly know how to behave, and we as a race could learn much from them. The fishermen are cheerfully hard-working and uncomplaining, and although wine is of good quality and cheap to buy, I have yet to see an objectionably intoxicated fisherman. In fact I have seen very few drunk people in all the time I have been in Chile.

213

The tide came in again, and the weather was bad, so we were forced to winch ourselves back off the ramp and go out to anchor. The following evening we tried again, and once more positioned *Totorore* on the ramp.

Friday 1 March
Soon we had a tow rope onto Sergio's four-wheel-drive pickup, ahead of which was a tractor, also ready to pull. They heaved and tugged, and *Totorore* bumped and shuddered on the lower steel pipes. Sergio was there in his leather jacket and large cowboy hat, directing operations. They tried again and again, but to no avail. She would not come any higher. 'No más!' (no more!) he shouted and ran to his pickup, cast off the tow line which one of his men made fast to the old hulk, and took off at great speed, throwing up clouds of spray. So that was that. More or less back to where we started and we had to suffer again the bumping on the ramp with each wave, as the tide receded.

In the morning we shovelled the sand away again and fitted bridles around the keels for the tow line. I went to find Sergio in the office and asked him when they were going to pull *Totorore* up. 'Now!' he said. I went back and waited with Chris, but nobody turned up. We tried unsuccessfully to jack up the keels to lay planks underneath, to help her slide. Meanwhile the wind came away strongly from northeast, which put us in a vulnerable position. As the sea got up we started to worry. We were unable to get her off the slip, and with an onshore wind *Totorore* would certainly suffer damage where she was.

Saturday 2 March
...Again I went to find Sergio and told him the seriousness of the situation. He came straight away, summoning his work gang and a large truck. They pulled out a heavy threefold purchase with wire cable and attached that to our bridles, and made the hauling part fast to the truck, which took up the strain. At the first attempt one of the ropes parted, so we doubled up on everything and tried again. This time she started to move rapidly up the ramp, bumping heavily between the sleepers. I was worried for the rudder, as the skeg dropped down between each pair of sleepers, but although it touched it suffered no damage. The jolting loosened the jam cleat on the starboard jib-furling line and the wind freed the sail which billowed out, flogging wildly and giving the impression that she was sailing up the ramp...

Another good pull and she was up at the top of the ramp on greased wooden sleepers. 'Enough!', shouted Sergio. 'No more!' With that, he leapt into his pickup, and with frenzied slipping of wheels and side skidding, took off around the sheds and out of sight as though the Devil was after him.

We were high and dry for six days and completed all the underwater work, as well as having our lifeline stanchions and rails repaired. The engineers from the Pesquera did that for us after we had hired the proper equipment from somewhere else. *Totorore* was at a steep angle on the ramp, which made it uncomfortable for Chris on his bunk with his head aft, much lower than his feet, so he turned around and slept with his head tucked away in the small recess where his legs usually went. The hum of the wind in our then finely tuned rigging was considerably amplified in there and disturbed his sleep. Up on the hard, the whole boat reverberated with the sound, like a bumblebee in a jar. One night it even disturbed the watchman's dog, which was barking madly, his front paws up on the starboard keel, and looking up the mast.

Persuading *Totorore* to come off the ramp was almost as much trouble as getting her up onto it, and it took Chris and me two days using jacks and wedges and levers. The manager of the packing shed came out frequently in his white coat to lend a hand or offer advice, saying 'Bien, bien!' every time she moved a few centimetres. Eventually she took off with a terrifying rush. 'Olé!' I was on board, and as the stern lifted in the water, the keels hit each of the steel pipes at a steeper angle, and the crashing and jolting was terrible. She shook and rattled and banged and I felt sure that she must start falling to pieces, and then suddenly she was afloat and all was quiet. Chris and 'Bien bien' on the shore were smiling happily.

When we returned to the port the beautiful sail training ship *Esmeralda*, which we had seen in Valparaiso, was alongside, her lofty masts towering high above everything else around. The next day she sailed, a wonderful sight with her cadets manning the yards on the foremast, loosing the sails, and hoisting full sail on her other three masts as well. We joined the fleet of small craft, fishing boats, tugs and launches which followed her out to see her off.

One night when we were having dinner with Pedro and Helen, Helen's mother Peggy Fell asked us when were we going to visit her out on their 10,000 hectare farm at Brazo Norte, on the Argentine border. She had been inviting us for a long time, but I always told her that there was nowhere safe for us to leave *Totorore* while we went away. Pedro, who worked in a senior position for ENAP, the Chilean oil company, said we could moor to a buoy at the oil installation at Cabo Negro, near to Isla Isabel. We both felt that we needed a break, and wanted to see something of the pampas and its birds.

Tuesday 19 March
We rose at 0530 hours to make all ready for our departure, putting another rope – this time a heavy nylon spring – out to the buoy, and making all shipshape and secure. Because the sea was rough we took clothing ashore in the dinghy in waterproof bags, and our cameras in a watertight distress flare canister. Pedro met us on the beach and helped us put the dinghy into his camioneta and then took us a few kilometres up the road to meet the ENAP bus.

The ride was about three hours and most interesting as we had never before seen the wide-open emptiness of the pampas. For mile after mile, as far as the eye could see, the plains of brown stunted grass rolled on, with just odd clumps of low grey and prickly bushes. Occasionally we saw a post-and-wire fence, or some widely scattered sheep, and more rarely an estancia with a house, a barn, a woolshed, a cookhouse and sundry other lesser buildings around it. What did thrill us was to see the Rheas, the South American ostriches which were more numerous than we had imagined. They were in loose groups, and could be seen sedately walking along pecking at the grass with deliberate thrusts of their long necks. Mostly grey in colour, when the bus came near they would suddenly run off flapping their wings, showing a lot of white like a flurry of lace petticoats.

The road was metalled and very rough in parts, and huge clouds of dust were swept off it by the dry wind. Inside the bus it was much too hot for comfort – they always keep the heaters up too high – and constant loud music made it a long and tiring journey. We stopped briefly at another oil terminal, San Gregorio, where several passengers alighted and disappeared into small buildings among the maze of tanks and pipes, right next to the Second Narrows of the eastern Magellan Strait, and then carried on to another terminal at Delgada, at the First Narrows. There we got out of the bus and waited an hour for Helen's brother Johnny to pick us up in the truck from Brazo Norte. We seemed to be at a residential camp for oil men, with an office, various cabins and a cookhouse, and a vast parking area partly protected from the constant wind by a lattice fence. We saw few people – a feature of these oil places.

Johnny arrived in his small truck with a water tank on the back, with which he had been carting water to sheep on the dry and distant parts of the farm. An occasional oil well broke the monotony of the landscape, but when we arrived at the estancia it was like coming into a different world. It lies in a shallow valley, only about twenty metres deep with a small river running between often vertical rock cliffs. This widens out to form almost green river flats – vegas – and beds of green rushes, and around the large old wooden house are trees – willows and poplars, and others with bright red berries. The house is in need of repairs and paint, but has a wondrous charm about it. Peggy's husband died a number of years ago, and the house and garden have gone back, but now Johnny has left school and will live there all the year, so will be able to start putting things to rights again.

Inside the house was warm, homely – and very Victorian. After a late lunch of roast lamb, we had a look around the garden, broken up into small plots by shelterbelts of trees, and with plenty of good vegetables growing in fine black soil. There were potatoes, carrots, turnips, beetroot and lettuce, and in a glass hothouse was still a good crop of tomatoes. In a small wire cage Johnny showed us his wildcat which had been caught in a fox trap. About twice the size of a domestic cat and coloured like a leopard, it hissed menacingly at us. He said that it would never be tamed. To feed it, he shot Upland geese, which were more than plentiful all over the vegas. They are a pest and in some seasons are there in their thousands.

Johnny drove us along the riverbanks as far as he could and then we walked through the gorge. What a fantastic bird-watchers' paradise! There were Speckled teal, Silver teal, White-tufted grebes, White-winged coots, beautiful Black-necked swans, and the unreal-looking pink Chilean flamingos. There was also a host of small birds, including Rufous-collared sparrows, the lovely Red-breasted meadow

Otter

larks, the green and yellow Sierra finches and many others. Snipes, too. One had only to climb up out of the gorge and walk 50 paces and it was all lost to view; one was again in the brown and dusty pampas stretching from horizon to horizon. We did see some birds up there which were new to me – Scaly-breasted earth creepers and Tawny-breasted dotterels. There were others which I failed to identify. We also saw a silvery brown fox and some hares. There are about 30 horses on the farm, of which about six are ridden; the rest run wild for most of the year and are kept for breeding.

Throughout our prolonged stay at Punta Arenas I was continually casting around to find a third crew member to accompany us back to New Zealand, and Marjorie was doing the same for us back home. Although for a long sea passage two of us would be adequate, we needed three for work on the islands on the way. Eventually I telephoned Andreas – always a lengthy business, because they were not on the telephone, and messages had to be relayed through a friend living in Puerto Montt, so that it took at least two days. Andreas could not come, but his sister Julia was able to help out if we could wait until May. Their father was ill, and by then she might be able to find somebody to look after him. In the meantime Marjorie told us of a 25-year-old New Zealand girl, then working in Santiago, who might like to come with us. Her name was Joi Rosoman and she came from Tauranga; when I phoned her she could not make up her mind as she had never done any sailing before. Eventually we decided to take her with us for a short trial trip to see if she liked it, or from our point of view, if she was up to it. If the answer were no on either count, we would by then know if Julia could join us.

Chris suggested that we could pop down to the Antarctic Peninsula, which I thought was a good idea as we could record the birds in the Drake Passage at a time of year for which there had been few observations. I doubted if we could actually reach the Peninsula because by April it could be expected to be ice-bound, but there was no harm in trying.

To obtain a zarpe to go to Antarctica I would have had to give the Armada six months notice, because *Totorore* was a registered research vessel and Chile claimed that part of Antarctica as her territory. For that reason I declared only that we would be working in the Drake Passage, and then return to Punta Arenas.

I had some misgivings when I went to the airport to meet Joi. On the phone she had sounded so naive, but I reminded myself that she must have spirit to agree to come to Antarctica for her very first voyage in a yacht! When I met her, her only baggage was a back-pack with a pipe frame: just what I had told her not to bring! She saw the look on my face and assured me that she was going to leave the pack with a friend in Punta Arenas.

Chatting with her in the bus I had my fears dispelled. She was so much like one of my own daughters, with similar interests and ideals, and was a vegetarian and a health-food faddist. A social worker by training and profession, she was teaching English to business people in Santiago. My first impressions – and they are important – were good. I was soon to discover that in Chris and Joi I had an excellent team with plenty of humour, so necessary when the going gets tough.

Chapter Thirteen

South to the Pack Ice

*Seno Chico — Collision with ice — Caleta Highet — Cape Horn — Drake Passage —
Deception Island — Antarctica — Pack ice — Drake Passage — Punta Arenas*

On 31 March, within an hour of Joi's arrival on board, we sailed off down the Strait
with a favourable wind. Joi started to learn to steer, but was soon seasick. However
she gamely stuck to the helm while Chris and I ate our evening meal below. After
that I sent her to bed, telling her that I would call her when we arrived at our
anchorage in the early morning.

Chris and I were enjoying the much-needed freedom of being away at last from
Punta Arenas. I particularly wanted my new crew members to see something of
the wonders of the Chilean fjords and canals while they had the chance, so chose
our route with care. The first night we went to another of those mysterious places
which we did not know if we could get into until we tried, as the chart did not
actually show an entrance gap. It was good practice for our teamwork, with me
at the radar, Chris at the helm, and Joi reading the echo-sounder.

In the morning we had the pleasure of looking around at one of the loveliest of
all caletas. Chris in particular was impressed as he had seen very little ice and snow
before, and here we were surrounded by snowy mountains, with a great blue glacier
high up in a valley and a magnificent waterfall cascading down through luxuriant
beech forest. Even I, who had seen so many of these incredibly beautiful sights,
was still moved by it and named it Caleta Joi.

After we had filled up our tanks from the waterfall, which we had waited to do
rather than take chlorinated water at Punta Arenas, we left and headed out for a
brisk sail down Canal Magdalena. I asked my crew what sort of an anchorage they
would like that night. Chris said, 'I would like to anchor under a glacier!' so we
headed for Seno Chico, a narrow fjord in Tierra del Fuego, at the southern end
of Canal Magdalena.

Monday 1 April
...Four miles inside the fjord there is a caleta with a big glacier at its
head...chunks of ice littered the approach, and when they became too
thick we found an anchorage about half a mile from the face where the
depth was only five fathoms. Chris kept fishing out big pieces of ice, and
once nearly fell in while he was doing it. The ice closed around us, moving
quite fast in the current, but there was nothing dangerous...

Tuesday 2 April

Not wanting to waste time we weighed anchor before breakfast and motored up towards the glacier, dodging large ice and pushing through the brash. Drizzle stopped and the sun came out. What an opportunity! Chris and Joi went off in the dinghy with cameras while I drifted slowly back and forth close to the towering glacier, which I named Ventisquero Chris. They landed on a rock and I sailed up past them. It was all good fun, but it took up most of the morning.

We had a brunch of bacon and eggs – Joi just had muesli – while motoring away down the Seno Chico and Joi took the tiller while Chris and I were eating. Suddenly there was an almighty crash, followed by another, and *Totorore* reared up and then heeled violently over! I grabbed for the throttle and stopped her. Out in the cockpit, Chris and I saw a large piece of ice, the size of a big car, now broken. There was not another piece of ice for half a mile in any direction, and Joi had to hit it! I scolded her, saying that when on the helm she was supposed to keep a lookout...Poor girl! A good lesson for her, anyway, and I am sure we will be able to rely on her in future.

Chris and I examined the bow and saw a nasty damaged area on the stem abaft and inside the bob-stay, which must have bent right back. The stay itself still felt secure, but we could not see the bottom fitting under water, or what possible underwater damage there might be. The boat was not making water, apparently, but we had hit very hard...a sorry finish to a fantastic interlude. In such surroundings it was impossible to be unhappy, so we pressed on. A pair of Fin whales added further interest, and seals gambolled around us. We saw Fulmars again, absent during the summer months, but only one Skua as most have already departed for the north.

With the wind usually favourable we had some grand sailing, thankful for the new sails which Marjorie had sent us, and with twin jibs poled out we sometimes reached ten knots – the top of our 'clock'. Chris laughed for the joy of it, but Joi was laid low and came to life only when we entered a caleta each night. Then she bounced back and was full of energy and gratifying 'oohs' and 'aahs' at the scenery. In one such place, tucked deep into the interior of Isla Stewart, she went ashore to bathe in a stream at the bottom of a waterfall of melt-water from the snowy peaks above, while Chris donned his wetsuit and examined the damage to our hull. Fortunately it seemed to be confined to about a metre of the stem, on the forefoot, but it looked ugly. He was unable to get any epoxy putty to stick underwater, having difficulty in handling it in his wetsuit gloves. We could only hope that it would last out until we could repair it on our return to Punta Arenas.

On another day we ducked into Bahía Wyatt in Isla Hind, to find shelter from a gale.

Saturday 6 April

The bay proved somewhat inhospitable with rafagas tearing across it...in one corner we saw a narrow passage less than two boat lengths across, which looked as though it led into a small lagoon.

Chris went to the masthead while I edged *Totorore* up. Inside we could see quite a large area, and for a while the wind passed right above us, leaving us in a calm space. The gap was full of kelp. It was just too tempting, as the sounding still showed fifteen fathoms. In we went. Half way through the passage the sounding reduced with frightening rapidity to less than two fathoms, just as a squall hit us. To steer I had to give her full revs, praying that the way ahead was clear of rocks. Joi had woken up, having slept right through starting the engine and motoring up through Morton Islands. Her face appeared at the hatch. 'Where are we?' she asked. Seeing the worried look on my face she glanced to both sides and saw the rock walls very close. 'Wow!' she exclaimed. We were through and inside, laughing gleefully...

I named this lovely caleta, Highet, after our former benevolent Minister of Internal Affairs who had made us a generous grant for our expedition from the small fund he had for his discretionary use.

Sunday 7 April

...Joi felt and looked much better, and even ate a good lunch. In the afternoon she was quite chirpy, but said 'Would you consider it mutiny if I said I did not want to go to Antarctica?' Although I am very sorry for her, with her seasickness, I do not feel that we can abandon our project and make this whole voyage a waste of time. We have been around these islands at this time of year before so there is nothing new for us, and I am wanting to see what birds are actually in the Drake Passage in a month when so many species are coming north...There really is not much in the way of alternatives. I am sure we could land her at one of the Armada stations – the men there would love that, I know – but I do not think the higher authorities would approve, and we can never be sure that we will be able to come back this way...All in all I am inclined to think she will just have to put up with it, poor kid...

Monday 8 April

Beating around Cape Horn was rather a slow business. The sea was blue and white, and the sky blue, so the great Cape looked very impressive. We saluted it as we passed by dipping the ensign and blowing a blast on our foghorn. I have rounded the Horn a number of times now, but I still get a thrill out of it. It was rather hilarious today because Joi was steering and several times was caught unawares by the variable winds from around the Cape, which took the big headsail aback and we went round in circles. I think the Cape looked down rather sternly at such frivolity, which had us in fits.

There was another setback when a bearing in the alternator collapsed. Foolishly I did not have a spare, because having renewed both bearings in December I had not expected to need one. The position looked serious; I realised that although we could get back to Punta Arenas without electricity, I doubted the wisdom of going south at this time of year, with the ice advancing rapidly, without the radar. We holed up in Caleta Lientur for a couple of days, while Chris exercised great patience and Kiwi ingenuity to make the bearing serviceable again. It sounded awful, but was doing its job, so we sailed on.

Thursday 11 April

...Blue petrels are everywhere, while Wandering albatrosses looking superb in full adult plumage fly majestically past. There are Black-brows and Grey-heads, White-chins, Giant petrels, and lots of little Wilson's storm petrels. A beautiful display of vibrant life over the edge of the continental shelf. I feel quite excited...who knows what adventures lie ahead? The others do not share my feelings yet. I asked Joi if I could get her anything, and she answered, 'Yes – some land!'

Friday 12 April

...Chris is fully recovered now and is back on form. Poor Joi is not better but she can occasionally manage a laugh, which is a good sign. Today she said with considerable feeling, 'I hate sailing!' I was almost sympathising after one particularly heavy sea crashed aboard and squirted between the hatch and the washboard, soaking my bunk and a variety of clothes lying on it, as well as the chart table and various charts and books in the chart drawer...

We were caught by another big bumper this afternoon which put a lot of water down the ventilators, wetting Chris's bunk and some of his clothes. Now that he is feeling better he just laughs loudly at everything, especially at the deluge which came down the galley vent, shot out from behind and under the stove, and wetted my legs and yet another pair of socks. I was just pouring out the Milo, and when I told him that most of it had gone into his boots he thought it was hilarious. Even Joi laughed.

On Saturday 13 April we crossed the 60th parallel, which was quite a milestone, and for me at any rate, a thrill.

Sunday 14 April

...Nippy at 0 °C. We had to take the poles off at about 0900 hours when the wind freshened from the north-east, but it came in foggy with poor visibility and an ominously heavy swell. The barometer continued to fall to an unbelievable low at 952 millibars, where it steadied after 1500 hours. The swell made *Totorore* roll abominably at times, and every now and again a big one splashed over her, giving us a fearful jolt inside. A nasty one took us by surprise while I was washing the breakfast dishes, rather late in the morning, and the dirty dishwater, at 1.5 °C, suddenly emptied itself out and landed on Joi's head, in her bunk. She sat up abruptly with a shout and was sick soon afterwards. We did what we could to mop up.

I'm even more apprehensive than ever now with such a low barometer...I keep studying the Pilot and chart looking for alternative places to seek shelter. Unfortunately there is really nowhere to go. All the islands are fringed with barriers of rock, and I have only one small-scale chart, quite useless if the visibility is bad. We are heading for Deception Island, but I can only hope the weather will allow us to get there. If this north-east wind builds up it could block the strait with ice...que sera sera.

Chris says he wishes he were anywhere but here...the humidity is 98% so everything feels cold and damp and that is not good for morale. But the birds are fantastic and a joy to watch as they wheel around the boat. Chris spotted a school of penguins porpoising along, but could not tell what they were. The Fulmars are here all the time, usually about five, and also a couple of Kerguelen petrels. I saw a Black-bellied storm petrel this morning.

Monday 15 April

...As we neared Deception Island, it looked very impressive with streaks of black cinders showing through the snow and heavy clouds over the peaks. On the lee side high black cliffs gave us shelter, but every now and again a squall would speed us along with the lee gunwale under. We took the sail off to motor against the wind through the pass into the crater – Neptune's Bellows – and saw hundreds of Cape pigeons flying around the cliffs where they have been nesting.

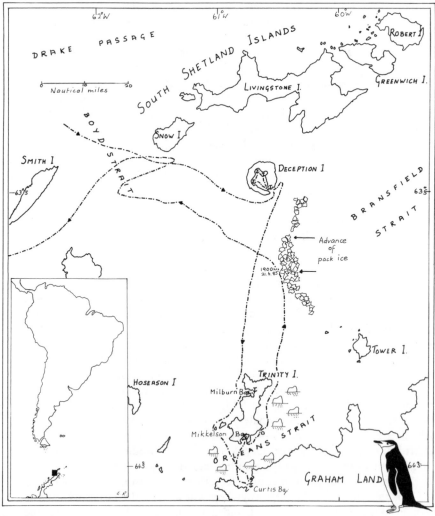

Map 21

In spite of the fresh squally wind it was good to be out of the big seas and swell, and we made our way into Whalers' Bay, just inside the entrance. It reminded me so much of South Georgia whaling stations with the wrecked buildings and rusting boilers and tanks standing out starkly against the white snow. The bay was deep, but close up to the scoria beach, littered with debris, Gentoo penguins and Fur seals, we found a spot shallow enough to anchor. The Pilot says that in the cinders anchors do not hold well, but I felt that it was safe for us all to go ashore as long as we kept *Totorore* in sight...

We landed on a beach to the east of the old station, accompanied by a splashing, porpoising mob of Gentoos which seemed very interested in us. The whaling station had not been large and was abandoned in 1931. The big volcanic eruption in 1969 destroyed much of what was left of it, and the BAS base next to it, as well as wiping out the Chilean base in Pendulum Cove up in the north end of the crater. Chris went for a jaunt over the ridges to check the type of terrain and see the view. I went over to the old aircraft hangar, where there was the remains of a British Antarctic Survey Aircraft, and then to the small Kroner Lake nearby, where there were reputed to be hot springs. A few Fur seals rushed at me aggressively with 'harrumph' noises, but after my South Georgia experiences I knew how easy it was to discourage them with a handful of scoria or a snowball. Gentoo penguins were everywhere. On the north side of the lake I could see steam issuing from the scoria beach and the water at the edge of the lake was almost warm. I dug a hole into the scoria with my hand, and the water at the bottom was as hot as I could bear. 'Aha,' I thought. 'I will bring a spade and dig a hole big enough to sit in!' Somehow it did not appeal as the wind was bitterly cold for undressing and dressing again...

Tuesday 16 April
...While we were having breakfast Chris said, 'There is something strange about this place. Look where the wind is coming from, and we are lying across it. And yet there is no current!' We looked out, and indeed the whaling station shore looked farther away. I put the echo-sounder on and it read 45 fathoms! Our tandem anchors were hanging up and down in the water, well off the bottom, but we had heard nothing and felt nothing, as though the anchors had eased themselves through slush. By the time we had our wet-weather gear on we had drifted dangerously close to the shore on the other side of the bay, under the high black cliffs.

It was lucky for us that this had not happened during the night, as we would have known nothing about it! When we re-anchored it was much closer to the whaling station beach, in only three metres of water. Chris was hankering to get up into the ice-covered mountains, so I asked him to have a look at Bailey Point on the outside coast where there is in the summer the largest known penguin colony in Antarctica...

Down below, much of the snow has been blown away and the thick cover of cinders looks dark and dismal. Joi stayed on board all day, busy with cleaning and cooking and mending, and luckily starting to take an interest in eating again. I went ashore in the afternoon to investigate the diesel drums we had found by the old BAS hut. After extricating several from the volcanic ash and cinders and finding them rusted through or full of water, I. nearly gave up. I opened a few more caps with the same results, and then tried tapping the remaining drums with my hammer. One which was particularly deeply covered with cinders sounded more solid. When I opened the cap I found it was still full to the top. Wonderful! I went back on board and fetched four empty jerry cans and then met Chris coming down off the mountains. He had enjoyed his day but it was hard going with deep crevasses in the ice, much layered with ash, and he had not been able to get down to the penguin colony.

It was dark when we filled our jerry cans with diesel from the drum. This was a real bonus, extending our working capacity in this area, which could be difficult with ice...

We had another hearty dinner, washed down with wine. I enjoy the company of my young friends, and nowadays there is plenty of laughter in the boat.

Wednesday 17 April
The cabin temperature in the morning was 4 °C, but outside was −5 °C and everywhere was again white with fresh snow. We motored around to Pendulum Cove where the Chilean station had been, and the twisted wreckage could still be seen above the steaming water of the cove. It was a new experience to smell the hot water around *Totorore*, like a bath and not at all sulphurous. Well offshore the temperature was 19 °C. After we had anchored we rowed ashore in the dinghy, feeling the heat of the water through the bottom of the boat increasing as we neared the beach. It was 42 °C on the surface and Gentoo penguins were apparently enjoying the unaccustomed heat on the beach and in the water.

The first big pool with a hot spring gave a measured temperature of 78 °C, much too hot for a bath; the next one was 40 °C, which felt great. Chris went off to photograph Gentoo penguins while Joi and I reclined in our luxurious hot bath. There was a nice hollow in the pool just big enough for us to lie down fully submerged, and the bottom was clean scoria lined with moulted penguin feathers. It is not everybody who can have a feather-lined bath! What a glorious relaxing sensation it was. Snow fell on our faces as we lay in bliss. It was hard to get out, but when we did we both felt a little faint. However, the steamy atmosphere around us was not too cold while we dried and dressed.

Chris had spotted a Gentoo penguin with a tag on its flipper, so at my suggestion he chased it while Joi and I helped to head it off. We thought we had it cornered up against the very hot pool, but to our astonishment it jumped right in! For a short while it just swam there, unconcerned, but then the hot water penetrated its dense coat of feathers and it shot out of the water like a rocket! Chris made a good flying tackle and caught it, grabbing it behind the head so it could not peck him with its sharp bill. We were rather worried for it, but it seemed to be all right. After we had read the number on the tag, Chris released it and it walked away, looking rather grumpy, and we saw it head up the hill alone to sulk.

A new small crater lagoon formed during the last eruption provided us with a pleasant protected place for lunch, after which we moved to umarole Bay and anchored close off the Argentinian base where there had ɔeen a radio station, and which was last occupied in 1974. It was quite a large and comparatively well kept establishment and was apparently still available for emergency use. There were some food stores there and most of the basics for living, but everything inside was wet. The windows had all been covered up, but we had a look around with a torch. Joi found a stack of old gramophone records, and was amused to find songs by Frank Sinatra and the Andrews Sisters in English.

On the snow between the buildings lay a Crab-eater seal, the first I had ever seen. I approached fairly close while Chris took a photograph from a safe distance; although the Crab-eater raised its head and showed its teeth

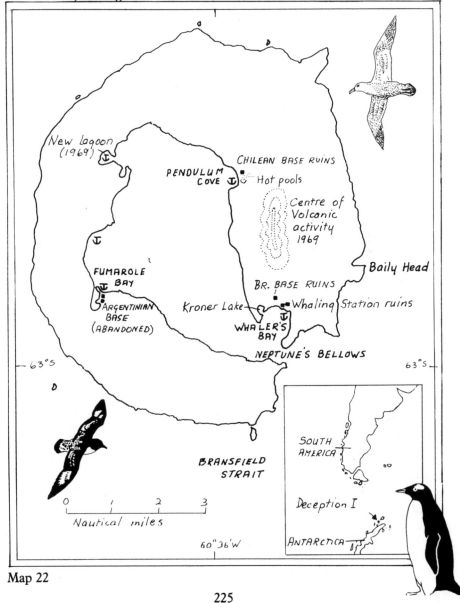

Map 22

225

while hissing, it certainly made no aggressive move toward me like the Fur seals do.

Not having seen any pack ice yet, we sailed due south for about 50 miles across the Bransfield Strait to Trinity Island, where we hoped to find an anchorage.

Thursday 18 April

...Before dark we saw Tower Island away to port, looking huge and white, and we thought at first that it was an iceberg. Then we did see a large blue iceberg straight ahead, and behind it the lower parts of the ice cliffs, with occasional rock faces, of Trinity Island itself. The wind freshened from the east and became squally as we ran down the west coast, looking out for rocks and ice...

It should snow in Antarctica, not rain! Snow is not so wetting and is much nicer. Chris stood in the pulpit with his goggles on, straining to see ice and direct us which way to go to avoid it. He got soaked. Joi took the tiller while I kept hopping in and out of the cabin, watching the radar and the sounder. 'I am frightened,' said Joi, shivering and looking up at the walls of ice towering above us on both sides, shining in the darkness. It was indeed rather scary, but it was exciting and good fun, as I tried to convince her. She thinks we are crazy and cannot understand how we can enjoy so much cold wet discomfort...I became rather worried when I could not find any soundings in which to anchor, as we were getting very close to the glacier at the head. Not wanting to anchor right under the glacier face where there is the risk of being struck or swamped by falling ice, I angled off into a small cove about a quarter of a mile away, thinking that icebergs calving from the glacier should be blown well clear. On one side of the cove we could see a high ice cliff – a glacier itself – and on the other a vertical black rock cliff with a sheer wall of ice on top.

Choosing the black rock side we approached to within 100 metres before soundings appeared at all. At ten fathoms we dropped the anchors and went astern on the engine. The chain rumbled and grumbled as the anchors dragged over the rocky bottom, and she appeared to be almost within spitting distance of the rocks when she brought up. 'What if all that ice falls down on us?' asked Joi.

We were all wet and cold and tired, so we had a cup of hot coffee laced with rum and then enjoyed Joi's excellent cooking for dinner. After dinner, she cut my hair, which had been bothering me by hanging down over my eyes from under my balaclava. For that reason I named the place Shearing Shed Cove.

Friday 19 April

A few tremendous icefalls around dawn brought vast quantities of ice around us and in spite of very poor visibility we could see that the ice cliff in our cove was about 30 metres high and was the most actively calving glacier face in the inlet...

We crossed Orleans Strait with a Force 5 south-east wind against us, throwing up spray which iced in the rigging. Snow and sleet reduced visibility so that we had to keep a keen lookout for ice, not easily seen in the choppy seas conditions. Large numbers of icebergs of all shapes and sizes were grounded in the Strait and it was hard to tell, even on the radar, which were icebergs and which were islands. Large, round, ice-covered Roe Island showed up in the middle of Curtiss Bay, surrounded by bergs and floating ice, through which we slowly pushed our way. As we proceeded farther into the bay and lost the swell the weather started to clear and we were treated to some magnificent views of mountains and glaciers...We even saw some blue sky, and sunshine on the icy peaks...

The trouble with this coast of the Palmer Peninsula is that there are very few sheltered anchorages, and if we could not get in here there was nowhere else. At the south-western end the cove was indeed full of ice, but the remainder had clear water...We were worried that all the coast around the cove consisted of glacier cliffs – about three miles of it, and we thought of all the ice which would be calving off during the night.

We chugged around in the clear water and were pleased to see an Adélie penguin on a small berg in the middle of the bay – our first...Finally we managed to drop anchor in ten fathoms, dangerously close to a glacier face with deep blue columns looking ready to break off.

Wanting to set foot on Antarctica itself before dark we rowed across, all three of us, to a small rocky headland covered with snow, sticking out between the glacier cliffs. I had thought that I would like to spend a night in a tent on the continent, but here there was no site for a tent and this lonely rocky headland rose steeply up into the ice above...

Just as we were about to relaunch our dinghy, we heard and saw another icefall, and watched the resulting waves rock *Totorore* and her surrounding field of ice. It was calm otherwise and we closed the hatch to try and warm up a bit, hoping that there would be no great traumatic adventure during the night. Heavy bumps meant that at least one of us would go out to see what had caused it...one was a fantastic shape, like an eagle with wings outspread. Meanwhile Joi cooked a cheesecake to celebrate our arrival in Antarctica. She is a good girl and joining in the spirit of the thing, although she is rather frightened – as are Chris and I, though more secretly.

Saturday 20 April

There were several thunderous avalanches of ice from the glacier cliffs around the bay but luckily for us, none from the one near our anchorage. Every time a big piece of ice hit us, Joi said 'Ouch.' Chris climbed onto a floe as long as *Totorore* and pushed us out of its way, but when it first hit us it made such a noise that we kept examining the bilges for leaks for some time afterwards. In the morning the whole bay was full of pack ice, but it was always on the move and we had no difficulty in finding leads to get out. We passed many groups of seals, mostly Crab-eaters, stretched out on ice floes; Leopard seals poked their heads out of the ice as we sailed past.

There was loose pack all the way across the Orleans Strait along with Orcas and Sei whales...We pushed up into Mikkelsen Bay in the south of Trinity Island...in the middle of the bay we could see a small island with a conspicuous orange-painted hut which we knew to be an Argentinian refuge hut. Ice would not allow us to go up to the head of the bay, so we anchored close to the island, packed up our lunch with a flask of hot soup, and went ashore.

The windows and doors of the hut were covered with sheets of corrugated iron, nailed over as protection from the weather. Dozens of Sheathbills were on the roof and the low hills of the small island were covered with Gentoo penguins. I returned aboard to collect a bar and a hammer to open one door and two windows of the hut so that we could eat our lunch out of the wind. The hut was in good condition and dry inside. We did not light the stove as there was not much fuel and ours was not an emergency need.

On the far side of the island we found many Weddell seals, a few Fur seals, lots of whale bones, and the remains of an old sealers' or whalers' boat. I decided that I would spend the night ashore in our tent as a practice run: I wanted to learn what it was like to sleep on the frozen snow. While I prepared my camping gear, Chris and Joi had great fun tobogganing down the icy hillsides on plastic sheets, with much laughter and shrieking, scattering penguins as they went.

Throughout the afternoon the penguins kept coming ashore until there were thousands of them, covering the whole island. They were very curious and if one of us stood still many of them came over to within a metre or so just to have a good look. Chris left his camera on a low tripod and it really looked as if a penguin was trying to take a photograph.

As it was getting dark, Chris and Joi helped me to set up the tent, and then I rowed them back on board and returned alone. The tent was on the far side, away from the hut, and was in a beautiful situation with a fantastic view. Penguins were close all around, and I could hear the sighs and snorts of seals. I retired early into the tent, read a short story by the light of a hurricane lamp – the first fiction I have read since I left New Zealand – cooked my dinner on the primus and went to bed about 2100 hours.

It was very cold in the tent, but as long as I kept on the polyurethane mat I was fine...The penguins went to sleep before I did, although at intervals throughout the night, one would wake up and utter its wheezy call. Fearful avalanches occurred on the coast opposite, sometimes followed by waves on the rocks of the island. A light wind shook the tent a little, and I was glad that it did not blow a gale...I pulled the drawstring of my sleeping bag tight, so that it left only a small hole for my nose...

Sunday 21 April

...For about three miles we twisted and turned, watched by sleepy Crab-eater seals on the floes. Bird life was plentiful, and we saw several colonies of Blue-eyed shags. The dainty Snow petrels were numerous around the icebergs, and they were joined by Antarctic terns and Cape pigeons...One mighty ice berg had a cutting through the middle of it through which we motored cautiously, full of wonder at the vertical walls of ice on either side and the beautiful light blue of the ice under the water below us. The least depth we found was three metres. It was a thrilling, though possibly unwise, experience.

At about 1500 hours we left the ice cliffs of Trinity Island astern and started off across the Bransfield Strait toward Deception Island, where we hoped to spend the rest of the night after anchoring at about 2200 hours and picking up some more diesel. The sky had cleared and visibility was good. Chris said suddenly, 'I think I can see the pack!' From the masthead he reported that it looked like a long line of ice reaching almost ahead, filling the eastern horizon. I decided to keep going and assess the situation when we were closer.

It was very dark but to starboard was the ghostly white light of the ice-blink. I had always wanted to see it, and now I knew what it was like. Joi and I were in the cockpit; Chris was cooking the dinner. 'There's a big bit,' said Joi, as we sailed past a bergy-bit barely ten metres away. 'There's another.' Chris put the radar on and Joi scanned ahead with the spotlight, with a whistle in her mouth to direct my steering. One peep to starboard, two to port. Chris made a hurriedly executed extension to the lead of the spotlight so that Joi could stand in the pulpit, forward; 'Peep' – 'Peep, peep.'

It started to snow. The wind was off the ice, and the swell flattened out. Chris saw the pack in the radar – a long wall of ice about one and half miles away. 'We'll follow it along and see if we can get around the end,' I said. We were motor-sailing, for manoeuvrability, but making only four knots for safety. 'I can't see which way to go!' shouted Joi in a frightened voice. Certainly there was a lot of ice, and it was impossible to avoid all the small bits. One which we hit passed underneath the boat. There was a 'clunk', and suddenly our propeller was not turning. As I thought, we had sheared the rubber coupling on the propeller shaft. Luckily the wind was off the ice!

By now I could get a pretty good picture of the ice front advancing down Bransfield Strait. Obviously it would reach Deception Island very soon. I thanked God we were not inside and blissfully unaware of the freezing net being drawn around to trap us in. I also thanked Him that we were not caught in Mikkelsen last night, as indeed we would have been tonight. Cutting it very fine! We would have been there until next January, or even February!

There was nothing for it now but to escape while the going was good, and sail out through Boyd Strait, south of Snow Island, the way we had come in. I could only hope that the pack was not also advancing down the outer coast, but it seemed unlikely. Meanwhile we had to get away from the ice, and that meant all three of us out in the freezing cold, trying to see through blinding snow to avoid hitting more loose floating ice. It was a nightmare. After an hour we saw no more ice close to us, and the radar put us well away from the pack. The snow had become so thick that trying to see ahead with the spotlight was a waste of time. Joi had done well out there with the light and I was pleased with her.

Tuesday 23 April

...I cannot seem to get warm, however many clothes I put on. But at least we are away and have escaped from the pack ice. There is still a strong possibility of meeting icebergs, but that is all. The adventure is over. And now is just the dreary chore of getting back to Punta Arenas, in adverse weather conditions...Chris repaired the broken shaft coupling today.

All in all, we are agreed that it was a wonderful experience, and we are the richer for having done it, even if we did not make any very exciting bird discoveries. For myself, it was a real privilege to see something of Antarctica, to feel it, smell it, to really experience it. I have seen superb photographs of it, but that is different from being there oneself. Photographs are usually taken in fine weather, when much of the haunting atmosphere is lost; we saw it in all kinds of weather, and were awed by it, frightened by it – and loved it.

Wednesday 24 April

It blew a gale during the night and twice I had to struggle into my wet-weather gear and face the ghastly freezing weather outside, with heavy seas breaking over the boat. Inside, the mighty thumps made Joi think we were back in the ice. It was very uncomfortable and none of us got much sleep.

In the morning the barometer fell to 955 millibars. I had just made a jug of milk for our coffee when a deluge of salt water came down the galley Dorade ventilator, and much of it landed in the jug, so I had to add it to last night's mashed potato and with eggs and flour make breakfast out of it. Towards noon it fell calm – the centre of the depression – and the confused sea had us rolling uncontrollably. Chris, who was feeling much better, was baling out the bilges; the way everything kept moving about, including the bucketful of oily water, made him laugh and laugh. I showed him my woolly hat which had been soaked by oily water, and then he found a wetsuit boot in a similar condition. It was a bad case of the giggles, and soon Joi and I were laughing too, and could not stop. Chris had tears rolling down his face...

In the middle of the afternoon the wind came away predictably from the north-west but I resisted the temptation to set the mainsail as I knew it would freshen. I saw an unfamiliar white bird sitting on the water; it flew up and I recognised it as an Egret. The bird flew toward us and made several attempts to land on the radar dome, which was too slippery. Then it managed to land amidships, near to our lashed-up inflatable dinghy, and snuggled down into a hollow. I caught the poor wee thing and handed it down to Chris. It was obviously an immature Cattle egret, all white with a bright yellow bill and rather dark legs. Chris showed it to Joi, who although she loves birds, has a phobia about having them too close. So Chris adopted it. He climbed back into his sleeping bag and took it in with him, to warm it up... Squeals and giggles later told us that the bird was becoming quite perky, and its claws and bill were penetrating his thick underwear...

Thursday 25 April

...We managed to force-feed our bird with sardines, but it regurgitated most of it. We also gave him, at Joi's suggestion, a couple of drops of homeopathic rescue remedy. It does seem quite lively and I think it is gaining strength. Chris and I were discussing force-feeding Joi if it becomes necessary. To prevent her regurgitating, we could tape up her mouth, but then it might come out of her nose. Joi was listening and thought we were cruel. I said; 'You have to be cruel to be kind.' She said, 'Just find me some land'. I assured her that I was trying to do just that.

Saturday 27 April
Our bird was dead this morning. A pity. Joi called me to her bunkside and said 'Gerry, I don't want to be fussy, but can't you do something to stop the boat going up and down?' I told her it would be better if we ran off before the wind, but there is no land in that direction, so really there is nothing I can do! She said it is driving her crazy. She is still very sick.

Sunday 28 April
...I was intrigued by the name of a little caleta on a peninsula of Isla Hoste. It is called Desengaño, which means 'disillusion'. Seeking the maximum shelter we crept through a narrow passage inside small islands, a passage I knew to be clear having been through it in daylight, and just before midnight we felt our way into the concealed caleta.

The sudden cessation of movement produced an incredible change in Joi. She was rather groggy on her feet, not having eaten for about six days, but had to get up to see the longed-for land by spotlight. She was such a happy chatterbox that Chris and I nearly had to tie a pillow over her head so that we could get some sleep. We were happy too. We had made it safely back from Antarctica, and the comfort of a night at anchor was very welcome.

For the last time *Totorore* made her way through the now familiar South Fuegian channels. We took the opportunity to spend each night in a different caleta, the only sadness being that we had not time to explore them all. We arrived back alongside the pier at Punta Arenas at 0600 hours on 6 May, 1985.

Cape Pigeon

Chapter Fourteen

Penguins and Miracles

Punta Arenas — Caleta Susana — At sea — South Georgia — Bird Island — Bay of Isles — St Andrews Bay — Bird Island and 'Gertie' — Annenkov — Bird Island — Miracle Cove

We had returned to Punta Arenas six days after the estimated arrival date on my 'tentative itinerary' which I had submitted to the Armada before we sailed at the end of March. This caused some consternation in high places and got us into a lot of trouble, which made me feel foolish as I could have so easily given a date very much later and nobody would have minded if we had come back earlier. I had not really expected the ice to allow us so much time in Antarctica, which accounted for the extra days, and as we had not obtained a permit to go there, I did not like to give that as the reason for our being late.

The Armada had alerted ships and aircraft, of which we had seen none at all, to keep a lookout for us and I had to write a letter of explanation and apology to the Comandante of the Armada at Punta Arenas and pay a fine of 'one hundred gold pesos', which in less archaic terminology turned out to be about US$30.00. Having had a rap on the knuckles, I thought the matter closed, but a few days later it took a more serious turn. They wanted to know exactly what we had been up to in the six missing days, and took it all very gravely. After endless interviews and interrogations they demanded to see our logbook. We got the impression that they were relieved to see that we had just been to Antarctica without visiting any foreign bases, and were indeed the harmless 'birders' we had always claimed to be.

Although Joi declared that her voyage with us had been 'the experience of a lifetime', and Chris and I had become fond of her and her cooking, her seasickness ruled her out as a more permanent crew member and she returned to her work in Santiago. Meanwhile, Julia's father had died and she would be able to come with us as soon as she had squared up her family affairs. As it turned out, our various engine repairs, for which we had difficulty in obtaining spare parts, delayed us anyway, and with drying out for more hull repairs, our hopefully brief stay at Punta Arenas extended to three weeks. In our search for engine spares, we contacted Hugo Carvallo, an importer who said he could obtain them direct from Germany.

Thursday 9 May
... sitting outside his office, Chris spotted a tuft of lining sticking out through a hole in my jacket. 'You look as though you are sprouting

feathers,' he remarked. 'Yes,' I said, 'it happens to ornithologists after a while.' That set Chris off giggling, and I could not help joining him. The lady secretary at the desk was giving us some very queer looks as he spluttered away out of control. I was scared that we would suddenly be ushered into Sr Carvallo's office and made a supreme effort to become serious...Luckily Chris stood up and said with difficulty, 'I will go out and buy some bread.'

Back on board I found that he had made me a birthday cake, covered with chocolate icing and sporting a candle...it was jolly good, even if it did have the consistency of a cannonball.

Pedro was able to tell us where to get things done, and had a new shaft coupling, designed by Chris, made for us by ENAP. Helen did a great deal of typing and translating for me, as she spoke excellent English. Peggy opened her house as before, so that we were always welcome to have showers there, or do our washing; her 'townhouse', where she and Johnny lived when not on the farm, was within walking distance of the port. With Ernesto and Marcia, these good friends made our enforced stays at Punta Arenas tolerable and at times pleasant, but we were impatient to be on our way and doing more bird work on the journey back to New Zealand.

To repair our ice-damaged bow Chris and I sought a place to dry out nearer to the Second Narrows where the tides have greater range, and ended up at Caleta Susana, about 36 miles from Punta Arenas. Almost circular and about half a mile across, the caleta is completely protected by a hook-shaped spit of dark stones which leaves only a narrow entrance on the north-eastern side. At high water it is full; at low water it nearly dries out with just a few shallow channels between the central mudbanks. When we arrived it was low water, and we could go no farther than just inside the entrance.

Sunday 19 May
...By this time it was dark, and cold, so we went below and cooked up our dinner. The tide was racing in, and after a while we reasoned that if we drifted with the tide, the strong stream would probably keep us in the deepest channel and we would be carried well up into the caleta...we hove up anchor, and carried on with our dinner inside the cabin. It was fun. Mother Nature in charge! Outside we could see nothing but a light on a fishing boat, and our compass showed that we were surging about in all directions. Sometimes we heard rustling noises as our keels brushed over stony patches, and occasionally we bumped lightly and stopped for a few minutes until the tide carried us on again. It was an eerie sensation, and I must admit that sometimes we had our doubts about the wisdom of it, but we couldn't stop laughing. Around 2100 hours we got the impression that we were being carried back out, so started the motor and moved southwards until we were well and truly stuck. Then we laid out an anchor ahead and went to bed.

As the tide fell, *Totorore* gradually heeled over to port. I kept telling Chris not to worry, she could only go until the bottom was on the mud, and that is where she stopped listing....

233

In the morning, at high water, we moved *Totorore* to a hard bank on the side of the caleta.

Monday 20 May

...There were literally hundreds of the lovely brown Patagonian crested ducks, and about 40 beautiful pink Flamingos on the bank farther along. I had always thought of Flamingos as being nearly tropical birds, and hardly expected to find them in the Magellan Strait! Steamer ducks paddled around, and some Upland geese honked and squeaked among hordes of Black-backed gulls. Six Night herons roosted on the mud close by.

Chris straight away got stuck into the work on the engine, which now leaks so much oil that we cannot keep up with it. We found that much was dripping from the sender for the oil pressure alarm, but also a lot was coming from behind the big plate which holds the forward crankshaft bearing. To remove that we had to lift the engine and take off the flywheel, engine mounts, and fuel pump. The flywheel itself took the rest of the morning as we do not have a puller. We were visited by a fisherman from a very large boat high and dry much farther up the caleta. He lives aboard her, by himself at the moment, and says that she has been there for six months and was pushed up there in a storm...

Tuesday 21 May

The extraordinary good weather holds, but at $-4°$ in the morning it is chilly...Chris carried on with the engine, while I worked on the bow as soon as the tide permitted. I was using epoxy putty, but found it difficult. The cold wind cut right through me, and my fingers really hurt. I was wearing rubber gloves, and to prevent the putty sticking I had to keep my gloves wet, but the water insisted on turning to ice...nor did I have a chance to do anything about the Furuno echo-sounder, the transducer for which is broken right off with just a couple of wires hanging out of the bottom of the boat from when we met the pack ice. We are lucky it did not cause a serious leak.

Chris completed the engine, but I did not finish the bow. There was no chance of making a proper job of it between tides, so all I could do was keep filling up the damaged area with epoxy putty, building it up. We had to return to Punta Arenas, so planned to make another stop at Caleta Susana to finish the job after we had obtained our final zarpe.

In Punta Arenas bad weather kept us at anchor much of the time, so it was hard to get anything done. Julia arrived on 24 May with a huge load of fresh fruit and vegetables which the tolerant airline had allowed her to carry as personal baggage, and which were so expensive in Punta Arenas.

Our good friends gave us a fine farewell dinner at Ernesto's and Marcia's house and the next day we said our goodbyes to everybody at Brooms who had looked after us so well. In the evening we cast off from the pier and sailed up the Strait, leaving the port which is so bad for yachts but which had been our base for the last sixteen months. Why did I have a lump in my throat as I looked back and watched the glow from its lights gradually disappear?

234

After two more days in Caleta Susana to complete the work on the bow we carried on through the eastern Magellan Strait to sail direct to South Georgia.

Friday 31 May
...We passed the lighthouse on the point of Dungeness around noon, making our report to the Armada there and being given their saludos and wishes for a buen viaje! Once outside and clear of the Sarmiento Bank, we set sail; *Totorore* is bounding eagerly over the waves. Goodbye Chile! We are homeward bound! No doubt many more adventures lie ahead of us in the thirteen thousand miles to sail before we reach New Zealand, but we are actually on our way...

To begin with I set a course north of the Falklands in order to avoid icebergs for as long as possible, but north-east winds made it easier to pass to the south of them instead. The weather was gentle with persistent light easterly winds and calms, and we passed slowly only ten miles south of the Falkland Islands without being seen or challenged and had the islands in sight for a whole day.

Wednesday 5 June
...Before daylight we started seeing fishing vessel lights and we passed through a line of them well spaced out. They were very large trawlers of various nationalities, all heading south as though they were working together. We heard some talking on the VHF and one at least was Chinese. A Bulgarian trawler (which surprised us) spoke to us but we did not catch her name. 'Where are you going?' she asked. I said South Georgia and the skipper replied, 'That is a very cold place with too much ice!' Later we saw a Hercules (Chris is good at recognising different aeroplanes) keeping an eye on the fishing fleet, but the crew did not appear to have noticed us. The birds were very numerous around the trawlers which made our counts difficult, but we saw nothing new...

Saturday 8 June
...We made our best days run for the trip so far, 139 miles. We all make a guess at the noon-to-noon distance and the winner has an extra piece of chocolate after dinner. Julia is the optimist and guesses the highest figure, so she was certainly the winner today...There were no icebergs to be seen, although there were plenty in this area when we arrived last year...

Sunday 9 June
We had promised ourselves a spongy pudding when we saw a whale or an iceberg, but so far we have missed out...

Monday 10 June
Shag Rocks did not show themselves as we passed well north in the horrible conditions of the very early hours. It was squally and rough, wet and cold. I took over the watch from Chris at 0030 hours and after about one hour all hell let loose on the foredeck. We had been broaching occasionally, and I had reduced the size of our poled-out twin headsails, but now they were flogging abominably and the poles were thrashing about in a frenzy. I could not understand what had happened and desperately

struggled to furl both sails. Chris got up to see if I needed any help, and Julia was awake too. Nobody could have slept through the violent shaking of the whole boat...

I saw that the carrier for the poles had slid right up the track on the mast, its halyard and downhaul having slipped out of the jam-cleats... There was still a small triangle of staysail set hard-sheeted amidships and so we continued to make five knots downwind without the headsails...

Tuesday 11 June
...We have made it back to dear old South Georgia. Whoopee! With the gale astern, and huge foaming wave crests surfing us ahead, we raced along the coast, which we saw only occasionally, and as usual I blessed our all-seeing radar. Around midday we turned into the Bay of Isles and took the poles off our twin headsails for the first time for a week...

Wednesday 12 June
...Crossing Stromness Bay we passed close to a big iceberg, which meant we could have one of our self-saucing puddings; it was amazing that it was the first we had seen this trip. When we came into Cumberland Bay we started seeing floating ice, and as it fell dark following a brilliant sunset we used the radar and the spotlight to avoid the larger pieces. VHF communication was intermittent due to the mountains, but we made contact with King Edward Point, and as we felt our way into the jetty we could see a group of soldiers waiting to take our lines. The jetty looked strange by spotlight, and we learned afterwards that a small naval ship had just about demolished it in strong winds some two weeks before...

Major Ian Davies came aboard and after paper formalities invited us to Shackleton House where we met the doctor and the various sergeants of this battalion of the Welsh Fusiliers who are now stationed here instead of the Coldstream Guards we met before. We were given an excellent dinner, plenty to drink and lovely hot baths...we learned that three weeks ago the whole cove was frozen over to a depth of 7.5 cm which would have prevented our entering...

The Army radio technician kindly repaired our faulty radio and we filled up our tanks with fresh water. After another night at the jetty we sailed back along the coast towards Bird Island.

Friday 14 June
...There was a fair amount of ice in Cumberland Bay as we made our way out, and we were most amused to see one large bergy bit of a very irregular shape, with caves and tunnels in it through which a number of young Fur seals were jumping and diving in and out and round about, obviously having a wonderful game.

Saturday 15 June
...Once outside, we had to motor hard against the south-westerly wind which threw freezing spray all over the boat. Ice soon festooned the rigging and lifelines and the helmsman too. In the cockpit we had to be well covered with no bare skin exposed to the wind, as the chill factor made the

temperature the equivalent of −28 °C. Chris and I used goggles so that we could see to windward, but ice kept forming on the outside, making it very hard to see anything at all. Luckily the floating ice was in localised areas, and most of the way was clear.

The wind reached gale force as we came into Bird Sound, and the heavy swell from the other side created wild conditions. Dense black clouds of snow swept across, blanking out visibility, but luckily it was not too bad as we started to enter the cove in Bird Island, where the BAS hut is. The swell made it look fearsome, and the gap between the breakers very small. *Totorore* slewed to one side and then the other, making it critical work at the tiller...

Outside it had been too wild and rough for Chris to get the anchors ready, so as soon as we were in the tiny cove he hacked and chipped at the ice all over the anchors, chain, windlass and ropes. Meanwhile I struggled to keep *Totorore* off the rocks onto which the wind seemed determined to push her, and with so little manoeuvring space. Full throttle and tiller hard over − will she make it, can we get round? Too close, no she can't! Oh yes, we are making it, but only just! The wind caught the bow again and away we went towards the other side,...at last we were able to motor hard out into the narrow entrance and drop the tandem anchors. The wind carried us back in the right direction towards the wee jetty − at other times it was never as helpful − and Julia got the dinghy ready...They landed on the beach, and when Julia climbed out of the dinghy Chris shouted 'Look out!' as an aggressive Fur seal came rapidly in to attack. With a thick balaclava on, she did not hear him, but luckily at that moment Rob suddenly appeared out of the snow with a big torch and diverted the seal...

Rob and Mark I knew, but Simon was away for the winter and the third member was Callan Duck, a young Scot studying the seals. Mark had one arm in a sling, nursing a broken collarbone − the result of a skiing accident. They made us welcome in the usual Bird Island manner...Rob said he knew we would make it there whatever the weather, as it was a Saturday. What a reputation to have! I must admit that it was true, and the dinner they put on justified the effort we had made...

We suggested that one or two of them might like to come with us to count penguins, by way of a break from Bird Island. This time, John Croxall had asked us to count the Kings in the three large colonies which we had missed last year.

Sunday 16 June
...We decided that Rob would come with us to the Ample Bay colony on Tuesday. Ice is still thick all over *Totorore*, and rowing back aboard was slow through the thick sludge of ice in the cove − just like rowing through stodgy porridge. On board the temperature in the cabin was −1 °C, and ice had formed wherever there was any condensation. The milk in the jug was lumps of ice.

Wednesday 19 June (Ample Bay in Bay of Isles)
...most of our work was on the ice which had been trampled hard by the penguins and become slippery, so we changed our snowshoes to crampons. Starting at the eastern end of the colony we counted a batch of chicks, then

237

separated them from the remainder, and set up a sight line with red sticks. Rob and Chris, with hand click counters, counted the chicks as Julia and I collected them and drove them across the line. To begin with it worked well, but soon those which had been counted wanted to come back again, sometimes the same way and sometimes round behind the tussock. We needed more drivers, so left Rob to do the counting while the three others of us ran around doing the shepherding.

It was jolly hard work. We waved our arms and shouted until we were hoarse, ran up and down, and were soon sweating. The chicks could be very obstinate, and there were always troublemakers who wanted to go in the opposite direction. They often had to be picked up and carried, as no other form of persuasion had any effect.

For about five hours we kept it up without a break. We could not stop, because as soon as we eased up those counted tried to join the uncounteds, and all our work would have been undone. When I could shout no more and was feeling just about run out I took over the counting and Rob leapt into action, threatening the penguin chicks with hell and damnation if they did not move. We kept shifting our sight sticks along the colony, always trying to maintain a space in the middle. Finally we concluded that there were, as near as we could make it, 7948 chicks.

With four of us on board it was rather crowded, so we took it in turns, two at a time, to sleep in the tent. Either Chris or I had to be on board each night in case a change of wind made it necessary to shift *Totorore* to a more sheltered place.

Before we started to count the chicks in the next colony near the mile-wide flat area called Salisbury Plain, we experimented with making simple fences to separate them, thinking how much it would help when we came to do the really big one at St Andrew's Bay.

Thursday 29 June

...Our first experiment was to set up a rope fence using wooden stakes and a light orange cord. To begin with the stakes could not be made secure. The ice, packed by thousands of penguin feet, was too hard, and rather thin over stony ground. In the soft snow the sticks were not firm enough. When either an adult or a wandering chick came up against the rope it instinctively pushed harder and harder, usually forcing the rope or ropes lower down the belly until the bird fell forward over the top, often getting caught by the legs for a while before standing up and proceeding on its way as it nothing had happened. Sometimes there would be several penguins pushing from opposite sides against each other, which held the fence up for a while, but eventually they managed to pass...

We tried to mark out a grid system with sticks, to count the chicks in one square and multiply by the number of squares, as is often done in very large colonies. However the variation in the density of the penguins throughout, the uneven mixing of adults which chicks, and the disturbances caused by ourselves when knocking marker posts in, and by Giant petrels running around, wings outspread, looking for weak or sick chicks to kill, made that method too inaccurate. Eventually we counted a group of nearly 1000 individually, and then from a vantage point up in the hills visually related that group to each of the other groups in the colony. Two of us did this independently, three times, and by pooling our results we estimated 14,000 chicks altogether. It had taken us three days.

To try to collect some suitable fencing material we paid a visit to Prince Olav Harbour and searched the old whaling station. There were plenty of possibilities there, with lengths of steel piping and bars, but it needed a lot of work to extricate it from the ice and snow and the only mesh we could find was too heavy, so we decided to collect something more suitable from Bird Island instead.

Tuesday 25 June

Julia pumped up the dinghy ready to take the stern lines ashore as a big Leopard seal came swimming around and under *Totorore*. Chris was very doubtful, but I kept assuring them that really Leopard seals were very friendly, even if one had bitten a chunk out of the army inflatable boat at King Edward Point! Eventually they set off in the dinghy through the slushy brash and pancake ice towards the jetty with some trepidation. Sure enough, the leopard followed them closely, sticking its head out frequently and regarding them with a fiendish grin. On board, Rob and I could hear Chris shouting 'Row! Row!' to Julia at the oars, who was struggling to push the dinghy through the heavy ice. They reached the jetty and Chris scrambled out hastily, reminding me of Malcolm last year when he was pursued by Hannibal, the naughty Elephant seal...

Julia took the second line ashore by herself but unfortunately it was not quite long enough, and before she reached the jetty she had to bend on another line. With the leopard poking its head up through the ice close alongside she was distracted, and fumbled over the two bowlines she was trying to make. She kept picking up the oar ready to bat the leopard on the head if it actually attacked, but said afterwards that she was not afraid as I had told her that if she loved it, it would not hurt her. I must admit that I was a little anxious myself...

Making the end of the line fast under the jetty, Julia sat in the stern of the dinghy, lifting the bow slightly out of the water. Suddenly the leopard's head appeared right under the bow! How easily it could have tipped her into the water! Mark threw a large snowball at it which gave it the huff and it moved away.

'Look, it has made a kill!' shouted Cal and we saw a large bull Fur seal being thrashed around in the water. It was a gory sight. The seal stayed alive for quite some time as it was torn to pieces. The strength of the leopard was very apparent from the way it could lift the whole seal clear out of the water in its jaws. A bull seal like that would probably weigh about 130 kilograms. It certainly gave us plenty to think about, but we felt that the leopard would not be hungry for a day or two at least...

That night as we were pulling the dinghy on board we had tug-of-war with a Leopard seal which left two holes for us to repair. It really had become something of a hazard to go ashore, even though it was only about 40 metres from the stern of *Totorore* to the end of the jetty. There were four Leopard seals in the cove and we always had to have a good look to see where they all were before putting the dinghy into the water. After a while we suspected that it was only one large female, 'Gertie', who was responsible for the mischief, but she did seem to be encouraging another one to play.

Thursday 27 June
...Just as it was getting dark I put the dinghy over the side to pull myself ashore and straight away I saw it lifting up out of the water. As I suspected, there was Gertie...I quickly pulled it back up again and did a few more jobs on board, waiting for her to go away...Later, when I could no longer see her around, I tried again.

As I was hauling myself through the heavy brash and pancake ice I suddenly felt the dinghy lifting from underneath! It was dark and I could only vaguely see Gertie biting at it and then disappearing under the ice. I did not have an oar or stick, or a spare hand to hold the torch, so just kept pulling on the rope as though my life depended on it – which maybe it did! I had to reach the shore quickly in my rapidly deflating boat, punctured in the two main buoyancy compartments. 'Gertie, stop it'! I shouted. 'Go away!'

After dinner, Chris patched seven more tooth holes and when we· returned on board the BAS boys came out with torches ready to throw stones if necessary to help us make a safe crossing. Gertie was up on the snow, fast asleep right next to the jetty. We did not disturb her and launched the dinghy on the other side and had no trouble. I still think that Gertie was playful rather than aggressive – like Hannibal had been...

For fenceposts for our penguin project we cut up lengths of angle iron and sawed points on them. These and a large roll of chicken-wire netting, and a heavy sledgehammer, we loaded onto *Totorore* to take to St Andrews Bay, about 80 miles away on the south-east coast. This time Callan came to help us.

Friday 28 June
It took us until after lunch to get ready to sail, and then I went ashore to collect Callan and his gear. Gertie was lying out in the kelp at the entrance to the cove, waiting for some hapless Fur seal to come in. Julia was pulling the dinghy on board with Callan helping her when suddenly there was a splash and Callan had fallen into the icy water! Nobody, including Callan, knew quite how he did it, but he shot back out of the water and on board with the speed of a Gentoo penguin. He is certainly very fit. Wearing a sort of float suit he did not feel very cold, but went below to change into dry clothes at my suggestion, although he would have been quite happy to have just carried on as he was.

Saturday 29 June
...Unbelievably beautiful! As we ran in close to the Fortuna Glacier we were given an added bonus when we saw four Southern right whales close in to the glacier face in amazingly shallow water...They gave us a wonderful display from about 50 metres away, and did not seem at all concerned at our presence. After seeing their knobbly heads we watched the curves of their backs before they sounded, lifting their tails with

massive flukes straight up out of the water. They appeared many times, and even seemed to follow us down the coast...

At the end of the glacier we again observed the King penguins, looking even more special in today's bright sunshine, and then we passed on with a whooshing bow wave as our big jib pulled us across the sparkling blue sea. Crossing the entrance to Cumberland Bay we could see the highest mountain range in South Georgia, towering above the mighty glaciers. Beyond, as we passed the Barff Peninsula, we saw several herds of reindeer, making their way across steep snow slopes. One herd of seventeen was close by the water's edge, probably eating kelp, and when they saw *Totorore* they took flight and went racing with enviable agility across the tussock hills and up into the white mountains, where their creamy-grey coats still showed up.

We were almost saturated with beauty, but could not help exclaiming when we came finally towards Ocean Harbour as the sun was setting. The icy peaks above glowed orange, and in the bay a sailing ship hulk with her lower masts standing, and the lovely lines of her hull still very apparent, added the final touch...we were indeed the luckiest of people.

After we had anchored and settled down, we came again into the cockpit to admire the moon, shining above the old wreck on the rocks and throwing shimmering reflections across the rapidly icing water towards us. It just could not be true – it was too improbable – too overwhelmingly perfect. What a day! Most definitely worthy of one of our special steamed fruit puddings!

At St Andrews Bay the only possible landing place was tucked into a corner behind a rocky spur at the northern end of the long beach. About half a mile inland we could see the BAS hut, which was to prove invaluable to us as a base. Having ferried our fencing and other materials ashore, Chris constructed a sledge for transporting it all about a mile across the glacial plain to the colony, where we set up a camp for working convenience and as a refuge from the potentially dangerous blizzards which sometimes swept across the Bay.

Monday 1 July

...From a distance the colony had looked large, but close up it was staggering. Most of the penguins, and all the chicks, were sprawled over about half a mile on the lower slopes of the moraine between Heaney Glacier and Cook Glacier, both of which had receded and left an extensive plain of outwash debris. Smaller groups and wandering trails of adults were scattered high up the moraine hills, over the plain, and along the shores for about two miles. It was an amazing sight which left us speechless with awe as we walked around the main colony, climbing up into the moraine hills and looking down onto the vast hordes spread below us. The noise was an almost deafening cacophony of trumpeting from the adults, and shrill piercing whistles from the chicks. It is by far the largest colony of penguins we have ever seen, and how impressively, soberingly, daunting! We thought about our proposed fence, and what a puny effort it would seem to be. I said, 'John Croxall must have had his tongue in his cheek when he asked us to count this lot!'

For quite some time we just looked and looked, shaking our heads disbelievingly. Then Julia spoke up. 'We must think positively.' How right! How easy it would have been to just give up at that stage and declare it to be an impossible task...

Most nights we were at St Andrews Bay we had dinner in the hut, which was much warmer with the Tilly lamp and the primus going than it was on board. There were actually three rooms; just inside the door at one end was a space for tools and hardware generally, as well as somewhere to leave outer clothing; in the middle of the hut a kitchen was chock-a-block with cases of food for emergency stores, and was therefore unuseable; lastly there was the bunk room. That measured about 2.5 metres square and contained two bunks, one above the other, and a table. Outside the hut was a heap of survival equipment, covered with a good tarpaulin and well lashed down. At the other end under the snow we found crates of old-stock food waiting to be dumped at sea the next time there was an opportunity. The tins were mostly rusted through, but we availed ourselves of anything which was still good including some glass jars of marmalade – Fortnum and Mason's, no less! For the two of us who were sleeping on board – again we took it in turns – it was always hard to have to leave the warm hut at night and trudge through the snow, make a wet dinghy launching, and return to lonely *Totorore*, cold from not having been lived in all day.

Wednesday 3 July
...At midday when we stopped for a cup of hot soup made by Julia in the tent, Cal suddenly spotted a different penguin among the masses. It was bigger and whiter and seemed to be being pushed around by the Kings. 'It must be an Emperor!' What excitement! Chris and Cal dashed off in pursuit and after a slippery chase separated and caught the heavy bird, bringing it back to the tent to be photographed. It was obviously a first-year bird, which, being pelagic are not often seen. When released it pottered quietly around the outside of the tent, and did not seem to be very concerned.

Counting the chicks in the colony was a long and involved process. To start with, we had to make a careful study of their habits, because we noticed how they huddled up close together in very bad weather but tended to wander about and spread out more when it was fine. We would not dream of disturbing them when extra movement could cause dangerous expenditure of energy at a time when it was more difficult for the parents to catch fish and come ashore to feed them. In any case, bad weather with blizzards made it impossible for us to work. We also concluded that the chicks were fairly faithful to their habitual place of repose, which fact was very important to us because we could not possibly count them all in one day.

Our planned strategy was to mark off the colony into three sections, and count each section separately. To do this we proposed to set up our fenceposts right across the centre of a section in one day, leaving the wire netting rolled up in readiness. The following day, or as soon as weather permitted, we would persuade all the chicks in that section to move to one side of the fence before quickly unrolling and securing the wire netting, leaving a one-metre gap in the centre for the chicks to pass through while we counted them. The first half would go through of their own

242

accord, back to where they had come from, but the second half would have to be gently herded. As soon as we had finished counting, the wire netting would be removed and everything returned to normal before nightfall.

We soon found that our 80 metres of fencing was nowhere nearly long enough, and however hard we tried there were not enough of us to prevent the chicks from 'escaping' around the ends. A factor much in our favour was that as soon as we started moving the penguins the adults filtered right out of the mob and remained safely at a distance until we were finished. Driving the fence standards into the hard ice was troublesome even though the wielder of the sledgehammer stood on a strong wooden box. Although we wore crampons the ice was so hard that we still found it slippery, and had many a fall into the guano when rushing to head off recalcitrant chicks.

Monday 8 July

A strong blizzard howled around the hut and it was obvious that we could do no penguin work today. Mid morning we contacted Chris and Cal on board and said that as the weather had eased Julia and I would make our way to the beach... We duly trudged across but the blizzard came down again with renewed violence... Clinging to each other, backs to wind, we could not move.

Suddenly out of the snow close to us came a long troop of King penguins, plodding resignedly and steadily along the ice above the beach, heads down and shoulders hunched. They looked absolutely wonderful, and I would have dearly loved to have been able to record them on film. They hardly faltered when the violent gusts struck them, and soon disappeared again into the driving snow.

It was a strangely moving experience which I shall remember for the rest of my life. For the few minutes that we shared that tiny space within the limits of our vision with those warm-blooded fellow creatures, my heart extended to them, and I felt at one with them in a way that I cannot explain.

Somehow we made it safely back to the hut, and in the afternoon when the weather had eased, we sailed *Totorore* out of the Bay to go to find more fencing materials.

... There were still some squalls with snow, but for most of our run around to King Edward Point the weather was pleasant enough... The garrison had been changed since our last visit and was from a different regiment. Two armed soldiers came down to escort us to Shackleton House, so we feverishly searched for something clean and tidy to change into, not wanting to go to dinner smelling of penguins. We looked forward to a warming drink before the meal...

The new O.C., whom I prefer not to name, introduced himself and offered us a cup of coffee. The major did not seem very happy in this wonderful place, and was unaware of its attractions. We talked with him for several hours, during which he made some offensive remarks about New Zealand, and about BAS biologists and ornithologists in general; he thought learning more about wildlife was a waste of time and money because he could see in it no benefit to mankind. In the course of conversation the major told us that he had been given, by his mother, a pair of electrically warmed socks...

It was nearly midnight when we arrived back on board, in fits of laughter. How ludicrous the situation was! Used as we were to the hospitality of the former garrisons we had really expected to receive the same treatment this night, but obviously it is very much a matter of the O.C.'s personality. To have spent so many hours seated just in front of the bar and not even been offered a drink other than a cup of coffee was unbelievably hilarious. We cooked ourselves a very late dinner and finished a bag of peanuts with our glasses of rum...

'Hotsocks' lent us ten steel fence standards and 50 metres of three-metre plastic camouflage netting. When he took away our windlass handle to be welded by the engineers and then brought a gang of Tommies to relay cans of water to top up our tanks, we began to think better of him. In search of further fencing materials, we paid a visit to Grytviken, visiting Sir Ernest Shackleton's grave, which is in a small cemetry on a slope overlooking the cove. It is marked by a simple rough-hewn block of stone, of which only the face with the inscription is polished smooth. We had been pleased to hear that when Russian research vessels call in, somebody always puts flowers on Sir Ernest's grave.

On our way back to St Andrews Bay, we stopped for a night at Godthul, a sheltered cove formerly used by whaling factory ships. Two partially ruined sheds, a tank and some old lighter-shaped boats were all that remained of the depot there. In the morning when we looked out we saw twelve fine-looking reindeer standing or lying in the snow between the two sheds, seeming quite domesticated. Above them, the snowclad hills were pink in the early light from a clear sky, giving the scene a fanciful Christmas card quality.

One of the sheds contained an interesting collection of hawsers and blocks, some of them enormous wooden blocks, double and three-fold, with their wire strops still served with tarred hemp. From a beach nearby, a Leopard seal sang to us, its weird trilling and unworldly song being similar to that of a whale, and surprising us with the purity of its notes.

We found that even with the additional materials, our penguin fences were still not long enough, so had to extend them by building walls of ice blocks, and digging deep straight-sided ditches. Julia, who was very good at this said that building those walls was what she enjoyed doing most of all during the whole of the time she was with us! When we had finally finished our count of chicks in the colony we had reached a total of nearly 34,000, which shows an enormous increase from 3500 to 4000 which were counted in 1976, and gave us much satisfaction. That night in the hut, Julia made us a big mince pie in a folding oven which fitted over the primus, using condemned Fortnum and Mason's mincemeat. It was by way of a special celebration, which we felt we deserved, and as a thank-you gesture to Callan, whose considerable energy and drive had been a mainstay of the project.

Our work was done and there remained only the return of the materials and gear we had borrowed. We spent three more days working at the hut so that we could leave it in a better state than that in which we had found it, burning large quantities of combustible rubbish and taking six bins full of bottles and tins well out to sea to dump. The survival stores and equipment under the tarpaulin were for use if the hut should burn down, but quite ridiculously were stacked up against the hut.

We helped Cal to move the whole lot to a new site about 40 metres away, which was much more difficult than it sounds, because the edges of the tarpaulin, and the many rope lashings securing it all to the pallets underneath, were frozen in solid ice. Finally, we loaded onto *Totorore* some large crates of scientific equipment which BAS had asked us to take to Bird Island.

Totorore was cluttered and overloaded when we left St Andrews Bay and made a difficult passage back towards Bird Island. For two nights and a day we sheltered in Godthul, and when we came out it was still blowing hard.

Sunday 21 July
...Sometimes the gusts reached Force 10 and we could not hold her up to the wind, even with maximum engine revs. We managed to avoid the many dangers of the north-east coast of the Barff Peninsula, but passing through the Merton Passage around the northernmost point to head into Cumberland Bay, we were met by a wind of increased fury with a truly wild sea and dense, driving spray. It could not have happened at a more inconvenient time. To starboard were the islets called the Right Whale Rocks, surrounded by heavy kelp, and on our port side a normally submerged rock which now showed itself in the huge breaking sea. I struggled with the tiller to keep her bow up to the wind but it was impossible, and she sheered violently to one side or the other. We had passed the rock when a squall of hurricane force laid *Totorore* over, lee deck awash, and the bow fell off to port...I tried to bring her up to the wind again but we were drifting rapidly down to the maelstrom over the rock. It was an anxious time for all of us. With pounding heart I put the helm up to pay her off towards the rock while there was still time. With the sea beam on she did not respond and it looked as though nothing could save us. But my hastily breathed prayer was answered at the last moment and we raced downwind in a flurry of spray, past the rock which was not much more than spitting distance away. 'We missed it!' I laughed shakily.

The gale held us up in King Edward Cove for two days, after which we searched Cumberland West Bay for King penguins. My crew had often expressed the wish to land on an iceberg and I had watched for a sensible opportunity. Offshore there was always too much swell, which made close contact dangerous.

Tuesday 23 July
...Among the numerous pieces of floating ice was one sizeable berg of interesting shape, with caves and hollows...I pushed the bowsprit gently up against it at a suitable place and all three crew climbed onto it. They were wearing crampons, but still found it dangerously slippery as the ice was too hard and polished for the spikes to dig in. Timidly they climbed all over it, hoping that I would come back for them. I had told them that if the wind got up I would not be able to take them off!
...When it was time, I put the bowsprit against the berg in an easier place, but they all found it a frightening experience getting down the difficult slope and falling forward to grab the furled sails on the forestays to

245

climb aboard...It was quite an experience, they said, to feel the slow roll of the berg beneath them when keeping their feet was already such a problem!

Friday 26 July

...In Sitka Bay a narrow beach between the rocks gave us a good landing place and we walked along to the largest cave. It was a fascinating place with several Fur seals of various sizes, and Elephant seal cows...We made friends with one small pup which just sniffed at Cal's and Julia's hands and scratched himself nervously with the end of one of his rear flippers. He almost let Julia scratch him, but one has to be careful as they move fast and even small ones can give a very nasty bite.

There was sudden commotion just outside the cave where Cal had caught a young Fur seal, much larger than the pup in the cave, by its rear flippers, and then grabbed it behind the head and thrown himself on top of it to pin it down on the snow (they are very strong). He had seen a tight nylon string around its neck, and Chris helped him cut it off. It seems that this is often the case – they get caught in big fishing nets, or put their heads through loops in cord or more often plastic banding tape, and frequently suffer a slow death through gradual strangulation. Often the cord becomes embedded in the flesh, causing a nasty festering wound. As soon as it was released the seal was determined to take it out on somebody and chased Chris at great speed.

Cal told us that every year they free about 50 seals of this kind of dangerous encumbrance on Bird Island alone, so we realise how many thousands must get caught elsewhere.

As we made our way back towards the dinghy, Chris spotted a larger one with a cord around its neck...Convinced that it was about to be killed by the people surrounding it, it kept making aggressive lunges at anybody who went too close. Chris tried to push its head down with the end of an oar (which it bit holes in) so that Cal could grab its rear flippers, but it was too quick and we had to run to avoid being bitten. Once Cal fell over backwards, but luckily the seal's attack had been directed at somebody else. Experienced at this type of game, Cal finally overcame the seal and held it down like the other one while Julia cut away the cord from its neck, having to pull it away where the skin had grown over it. Little realising what a kindness had been done to it, the seal was blind with rage on being released and we had to scatter – fast!

Sunday 28 July

...When daybreak came and visibility cleared a little I saw that we had dragged a long way down into the corner of Church Bay, where we had seen a big Gentoo colony. Squalls of hurricane force tore the sea to shreds and laid us over until the cabin ports were under water. It was a tricky and dangerous situation...

Passing through a very confused sea we came clear off the coast to try to round the bad rocks off Sorn Island, and the gale hit us full strength. Sometimes dense clouds of snow blotted out visibility, and then for brief moments we could see patches of blue sky. Cal spoke to Rob on the radio, and Rob said that it was very stormy, the iceberg had disintegrated, and the Sound was full of ice...

Gusts of Force 12 and more were fearsome to see, and when they forced us round beam on, *Totorore* lay over until the lee cockpit seat was under water. We were all very wet, and very cold. Hoping always that it would improve, we struggled on for two hours, but then seeing it was hopeless, we gave up and ran for it.

The nearest shelter we could find was Right Whale Bay, but to reach it we had to pass a mile off Cape North to avoid the breaking reef protruding out from it, and then come in towards the land with the wild sea on the beam. Some of our deck cargo came loose, and Chris steered off downwind while Cal went forward to secure it, but not before about five of the steel fenceposts had disappeared overboard...

Monday 29 July
...I called up Bird Island and told Rob to send a bottle of rum around to Elsehul so that we could put some in our coffee. He said they would strap a bottle to the back of a Fur seal and send him off...

Back at Bird Island, we thought that as we had taken the other two with us for a trip, and as Mark was now recovered from his collarbone injury, we should offer him a jaunt before we left South Georgia. When I asked him where he would like to go, he said he would like to help count the Wanderers on Annenkov Island. That came as a bit of a shock, because it would take much more time than we had intended to stay. However having had Cal with us for about a month we agreed, thinking also that it would be a good idea to count this year's demi-population of Wanderers on the island...

The weather was not the best for work on Annenkov, but in our first three days we counted all the Wanderer chicks on the northern half, anchoring each night in Maud Cove on the north-eastern side.

Sunday 4 August
...Counting the Wanderer chicks is rather like a game. From a distance they are not easy to see, and it is necessary to tramp over every likely spot, as they can be concealed in small hollows or among the tussock. Each one found gives quite a thrill – the more unexpected they are, the bigger the thrill. We walk around the nest to leave footprints, so that nobody else will count that bird, click the counter, and then can't help saying a few words to the chick: 'Hello! You're No. 32, and what a fine fellow you are! Yes, you are beautiful. Oh well, sorry, but I must be on my way...Good luck, and I hope you have a long and happy life soaring over the great Southern Ocean. Perhaps I'll see you around New Zealand one day.' The usual answer is 'clop, clop' from the great bill of the large and fluffy, bright-eyed chick...We found a total of 49 today.

Tuesday 6 August
...The swell was moderate and short, breaking heavily on the beach where hundreds of seals were cavorting as I rowed Mark and Julia ashore with our gear...Nearing the beach I found it difficult to go astern with the oars, as

the back-flow from each wave held us off. With Mark and Julia in the stern, and heavy packs and snowshoes in the bow, my rowing movements were restricted. As I tried to get in close a really huge breaker caught the bow and before we knew it we were airborne, the dinghy flipped end over end.

It is hard to follow exactly what happens on such occasions, but I found myself under water, under the dinghy, and then being rasped along the bottom on the shingle. When I surfaced I struggled out from under the dinghy and stood up, holding the dinghy. I could see Mark standing but not Julia, until she too stood up on the other side of the dinghy. 'Where is the other oar?' I shouted. 'It is still here,' said Julia. I was glad they were both lashed on.

We dragged the dinghy up the beach, unlashed the packs and snowshoes, and left them in a hole in the ice above the beach. 'We must go back to *Totorore* for dry clothes,' I said.

We were very cold with the sea at 0.3 °C. Viewed from the shore it was truly fearsome, much worse than when viewed from offshore. We carried the dinghy a few hundred metres north, but the rollers coming in there were enormous and we could never have launched it. There was nothing for it but to go out again in the same place as we had come in.

Mark volunteered to wait on the beach, as it is so much easier to row with only two of us. . . He helped us to launch, and then watched anxiously until we were clear of the rocky passage.

It was a relief to arrive back at *Totorore*. Chris had already put the kettle on and lit the heater. While he looked out dry clothes for Mark, Julia and I quickly changed, had a hot drink and climbed back into the dinghy, leaving Chris to deal with a pile of sodden clothing left in the cockpit.

As we rowed ashore we could see Mark jogging up and down the beach trying to keep warm, and chasing seals which were in their hundreds. We were lucky and made it back to the beach with the dinghy only half full and ourselves almost dry. Mark gratefully put on fresh clothes and at last we were ready to start work.

We split up to cover the area more quickly, and between us found a total of 21 chicks during the afternoon.

In the evening we found that the surf on the beach, instead of getting better had become worse.

. . .It was obviously suicidal to launch the dinghy, so we decided that we would have to stay ashore.

While Julia and Mark started to get the tent out of the sack, I walked along the shore looking to see if I could find a safer place where we might still try a launching. On the other side of a small islet. . .the breakers were less frequent, but it was a longer row to get clear of them. I went back to tell the others and we carried the dinghy over, waving our sticks at playful seals which thought it would be fun to bite us. Occasionally one really meant it and had to be fended off more seriously – usually just a tap under the chin. . .

When it looked right we pushed the dinghy out, climbed in, and I started to row as hard as I could. It was a mistake. A breaker caught us badly, rolled the dinghy upside down and we were soaked again!

Not at all good. The idea of a night ashore in wet clothes did not appeal. I thought it might be possible to launch off the rock shelf, beyond the worst breakers, and walked out to have a look. A bit tricky, but it could be done if I could get safely into the dinghy and then back on the oars until the stern was close enough, on top of a wave, for the others to jump in. While I watched, a big wave came over the top and with water up to my waist I was very nearly swept away. That squashed that idea. It was getting dark, so there was no time to be lost.

We found a place for the tent on a flat area of ice, in a seal- and penguin-filled gully. Mark went back for the packs. We cleared a seal from under one tussock, and a cow Elephant seal from under another. It was a superb site and we hardly felt the wind at all, which was lucky as it was dark by the time we were putting the tent up and only the whiteness of the ice helped us. Julia and Mark carried stones up from the beach to weigh the tent down as the ice was too hard for pegs.

We crawled into the tent, spread our single sleeping roll and sat on it. Julia fumbled in a pack and brought out some emergency rations. We could not help laughing, cold as we were. 'Here, have a biscuit.' 'Where is it?' 'In my hand.' 'Where is that?' 'Hey, that's *my* hand!' Julia found the flask which still had a little tea in it and rationed that out. A gulp each, and then there would be some for later. . .

Our position was pretty serious and we knew it. I was very pleased – I could not have had better companions with whom to share the coming ordeal.

We spread the empty vinyl packs on the floor to put something else between us and the ice. Luckily in sealed plastic bags we each had a dry pair of socks, and that was a big help. Inside the tent felt much warmer than outside, and we hoped that our body heat would dry our clothes, but we did feel very, very cold. I looked at my watch and told the others, 'It's seven o'clock'. We had hoped the time was passing more quickly.

We sang songs, Mark sang us some lovely Irish songs in a good brogue, and Julia sang German songs in her soft, sweet voice. I followed rather lamely with a little refrain in Malay, and then 'Good King Wenceslas' as I thought 'Though the frost was cruel' rather appropriate. After that we had poems, and I was impressed by Mark's memory. Julia's poems were in German or Spanish. It helped to take our minds off our freezing limbs.

Later, we saw a glare reflecting off the snowy bank on the other side of our gully and knew that Chris was still casting about with the spotlight from on board. I went outside to walk along the beach, hoping that he would see me in the light and know that we were all right. I did not go very far. The ice was slippery and the seals, probably alarmed in the dark, were aggressive and hard to see. . .Mark came out to join me, but as soon as we turned the corner to go along the main beach the freezing wind hit us and in our wet clothes it was painful. The spotlight had gone out, but we could see a light on board bouncing up and down just beyond the rocks. We could imagine that Chris was not having a very good time either, and hoped

249

that he was not too worried...

The night passed very slowly. For a while we lay down, all three of us across the mat, but the parts of us off the mat were hardly protected from the ice below. Sometimes we sat up with our knees raised, and as if by common assent all assumed the same position. One of the best, which Julia called the 'frozen mantis position', was kneeling on one edge of the mat with our elbows on the far edge, heads down onto our forearms and bottoms in the air. Had anybody come into the tent they would certainly have taken us for praying Muslims, but that way there was less of us in cold contact with the floor.

We were delighted to hear the soft calling of Diving petrels, obviously in burrows in the tussock bank within a few metres of the tent. Some of them hit the tent as they flew in from the sea. Ghostly cries and snorts came from the seals all night long, and once one squeezed itself between the tent and the bank. Heavy breathing close outside made us think that some wanted to come in to join us...

None of us said anything about it at the time, but we were all thinking the same thing: if we had to stay another night on the ice, we would probably die. I said my prayers. My feelings of responsibility for my companions weighed heavily on my mind. Periodically we sat up together and ate another biscuit, and at 0200 hours Julia rationed out our last gulp of tea from the flask, but it was cold.

Wednesday 7 August

It snowed in the early hours and the temperature fell still lower. We all managed to doze for brief spells, but we talked a lot. 'Gerry, are you freezing?' 'Yes. Are you?' 'Yes.' We kept our spirits up by joking and laughing, but were very relieved when the dawn came and we were able to walk about to warm our feet and loosen stiffening muscles. We ran the gauntlet of the seals to go down to the landing place and saw Chris up the mast of *Totorore*, now farther out than when we had last seen her. He saw us and climbed down. The sea had moderated a little, but still looked wickedly dangerous and quite out of the question as far as launching the dinghy was concerned. Once again we patrolled up and down, looking for a better place. There was none. Taking our snowshoes we climbed up onto the hill above to walk along to the next small bay to see if it were better there. Later, Chris told us that he had thought with amazement that we were on our way to do another albatross count...

Back at the beach it did seem that the fury of the waves was lessening and there were short periods when we could probably make it. If we did not time it right then we were in for another wetting, which could be fatal; if caught by a breaker near the outer rocks we would, in our weakened state, be drowned. Our tiredness, and the vivid memory of our being flipped end over end in the dinghy yesterday, made us all afraid. But the white horses outside were becoming more numerous, and it seemed that it could rapidly get worse...

Mark volunteered to stay behind again, as two stood a better chance. Eventually Julia and I were on our way, albeit with some trepidation. It was exciting to be rowing through the turbulent channel with the huge

250

breakers on the rocks heaving and sucking, close on both sides. I rowed hard, watching Julia sitting in the stern, directing me. She was calm and determined. 'Now that way, we are close to the rocks. Good. Now that way! Here comes a big one! Good. We made it. Now that way. We will soon be out. Row hard!' The waves broke astern of us, and we rode high over the big rollers. After what seemed an age: 'We are safe! *Totorore* is that way!' Julia was smiling happily, and so was I.

It was not long before we were back on board, where Chris had the kettle boiling. He put on the float suit and went off in the dinghy to fetch Mark and the tent, which Mark took down and packed up only after he had seen that we were safely past the breakers...

After we had had a hot drink, Julia said to me very seriously, 'May I please ask for a very special treat?' I wondered what was coming. 'Of course', I replied. 'What is it?' 'Can I wash my hair?' I laughed. How like a woman! I was thinking of hot food and warm dry clothes, and then sleep. 'Yes, you can have hot fresh water – as much as you need!' Certainly it was a luxury, but she deserved it...

Chris and Mark arrived safely back, quite wet, but equally happy. Chris had a stew on the stove which we soon devoured. It was Mark's turn. 'Can I ask for something special?' he asked. 'Can I have a bacon sandwich?' We had some tinned bacon from Bird Island and some delicious bread which Cal had baked specially for us, so we all had bacon sandwiches. The wind certainly had come up again, and Chris put on his wet-weather gear. 'Where are we going? he asked. 'Nowhere,' I said, 'until we have had some sleep!'

Altogether, it was a wonderful adventure – to look back on!

To complete our Wanderer count on Annenkov we still had the South-west Point area to cover, for which we moved around to Rustad Bay, a little apprehensively because it is wide open to the west.

Saturday 10 August
For this expedition the crew took no chances, and although we could see that the landing would be quite good, one never knows what the launching may be like in the evening. In addition to the tent they took two sleeping rolls and extra dry clothes, as well as the primus with fuel and food. The walkie-talkie is now dried out and recharged...

Chris called up a few times and each time said they could see only a few metres in front of them because of snow. I suggested that they should come back if they could, as I knew that it was a very dangerous place to be, with sheer cliffs and treacherous snow overhangs. They arrived back at about 1400 hours, very wet, very cold, and somewhat dispirited.

Sunday 11 August
Our hopes were dashed by the heavy snow, and from the big swell rolling in it was obviously very bad weather outside. No chance of getting up the mountain in present conditions. To reach the point it is necessary to go up to a saddle at about 300 metres, and it has to be clear up there. Nothing for it but to sit and wait, and hope that our anchorage remains tenable...

251

The next day the weather was superb, and it was my turn again to go with Julia and Mark. From high up on the mountain the views were exceptionally splendid, and at one point Mark said that he would not want to be anywhere else in the world just then, and we had to agree with him. Our total count for the island was 149 chicks. Having finished Annenkov, we started to make our way 'home' to Bird Island.

Thursday 15 August

...Cape Paryadin itself is forked, open to the south-west; between the prongs of the fork is Greene Inlet, nearly a mile long between sheer walls of almost black rock rising to over 300 metres. I have never passed there without seeing an iceberg trapped inside, and sure enough today we could see a good cluster of them...One which had great towers and steeples was particularly interesting, and as we passed between it and another, no more than twenty metres from it, I had the idea that *Totorore* passing through the gap would make a good photograph if taken from the dinghy. I would drop the crew off in the dinghy, and then motor around behind the berg, to come through again. We were moving into position and still about 70 metres away from the berg when we heard a loud report and saw a big crack appear in its side. Suddenly the whole thing disintegrated and huge blocks of ice flew into the air. It was frightening to see from so close, and we half expected to see the underwater part of it roll up beneath us. At the first sign I gave the engine full throttle to get away from the big splash, which was fortunately damped down by the huge conglomeration of fragmented ice. Enormous pieces heaved up out of the water and rolled about, giving us a rare and impressive spectacle which we shall never forget. A few minutes earlier we had been right there alongside it, and to have been caught would have been to be taken to the bottom under tons of ice...We wondered if, in the enclosed space of the inlet, the vibrations from our engine had set it off. A cheap lesson to be more careful, and not underestimate the dangers...

Icebergs jammed in the entrance channel to the cove in Bird Island almost prevented our getting in, and for several days while we were there would certainly have prevented our going out. As it was, we had plenty to do in preparing for our coming voyage and we took the opportunity to enlist the assistance of our friends to take lice specimens from various large birds, and also wing silhouettes. To draw on paper around the outstretched wing of a Wandering albatross, with a total wingspan of about 3.4 metres, takes many hands!

After a week we were at last ready to go, and said goodbye to our three friends with whom we had shared many adventures and who had looked after us with genuine care. We motored up Bird Sound and watched silently until the snow hid Bird Island from view.

Having counted this year's Wanderers on Annenkov, it seemed right that before we left South Georgia we should also count them on Albatross Island in the Bay of Isles, which has a similarly sized population but is a smaller and lower island and much easier to work on.

Sunday 25 August

Although the barometer was still falling, it was fairly calm early this morning so we moved around to the southern cove of Albatross Island where the landing looked remarkably easy. Julia and Chris were soon on their way ashore to do the count. I watched them climb up to the first ridge, and when they had disappeared from view I busied myself around the deck, coiling up ropes and attending to lashings.

I thought I would take the opportunity to write some letters to have ready to post at King Edward Point when we called in a few days time. The opportunity was shortlived because the wind increased to gale force, blowing right into our cove and giving us a lee shore. With a fetch of less than five miles, and heavy beds of kelp outside, the sea was not too big, but it did have *Totorore* pitching violently and burying her bowsprit into the oncoming waves, with some occasional heavy pounding...

I considered moving anchorage and trying to pick up my crew from the lee side of the island, but the anchor seemed to be holding although I was a little concerned about the large pieces of ice which the wind was bringing into the cove. It is always quite difficult to get away from a close lee shore by oneself so I stayed put, hoping that the anchor chain would help deflect the ice enough to avoid damaging us. I paid out the chain to 35 fathoms and then put on the nylon spring...

Chris and Julia reappeared on the beach at about 1330 hours and I paid out a floating line, 100 metres long with a buoy on the end of it, letting the wind carry it to the shore to assist them in pulling the dinghy back to the boat. They did not wait for it to reach the beach and made a good launching in a corner of the cove. Luckily there was a comparative lull in the wind, but it was still hard work for Chris to row against it and they were pleased to have the security of the floating line. They were cold, wet, and covered with ice. Chris's beard was completely iced up, making it white, and with an ice fringe around the hood on his red heavy-weather suit he looked just like Father Christmas. They were somewhat discouraged. The weather had been so awful, and the visibility so bad, that they could not see where they were and had counted only fifteen albatross chicks. To avoid counting the same ones twice they had built small snowmen next to them, but the wind had knocked the snowmen down and the snow had covered up their own footprints, making it all very confusing...

I set about recovering the floating line and found that while the buoy was being tossed around in the surf it had made an indescribable tangle with the kelp! It took me over an hour to get it back on board...If I had had more sense we would have shifted anchorage then, while we could. I thought the wind was moderating, and as the anchor had a good hold it seemed safe enough. I was very mistaken.

...The wind gradually increased in force and backed to the south-west, swinging us close to huge black rocks on the northern side of the cove, where the sea was breaking with extreme violence. As the seas built up, the motion inside *Totorore* became fearsome. The nylon spring carried away and I replaced it with a short one. An occasional enormous sea broke right over the boat, and it became obvious that we could not stay where we were as the anchor chain could only take so much of that terrible treatment.

I called the others out at about 2130 hours and while they were dressing I tried to ease the strain by motoring against the wind, but I was very scared that the loose end of the parted nylon spring would foul the propeller...I asked Chris and Julia to wind up enough chain to recover the spring. It meant winding strongly as the bow dipped into the trough, and holding on as she lifted to the crest. The driving snow and sleet made it hard to look forward, and I was frightened that I might see that one of my crew was missing after each wave that broke over us. I was out of communication range because of the noise, but Julia crawled aft to receive my instructions...

We cleared away from the rocks on that side of the cove, but lost control when the breakers came over us, throwing the bow away. I was very nearly washed right out of the cockpit when she was lying on her beam ends, and after that crouched low in the cockpit, hanging on for dear life and using all my strength to force the tiller over. We came dangerously close to the rocks off the spit on the other side of the cove when the bow would not come round to the wind. If I eased the throttle she would be swept rapidly beam on to the stony beach at the head, now lined with huge blocks of ice. I prayed aloud constantly. Only God could save us now.

A slight easing of the wind and the bow came round, agonisingly slowly, and we moved away from that fearful white death-trap, already covering us with its foaming spray. First one side, and then the other. It was terrible. We could not make headway against it, and were barely holding our own to prevent our being carried back into the cove. How long it lasted I cannot tell, but it seemed for hours...

In my prayers I asked that the engine would not overheat, as it normally did when hard pushed in rough weather, when the intake for the cooling water in the bottom of the boat came out of the sea. I had never asked so much of the engine before. Julia reported that the needle of the temperature gauge was just on the edge of the red, but holding.

My other worry was the kelp. I could feel the propellor chewing through it, and knew that if it really tangled the prop badly, as it had done before, and stalled the engine, we were lost. I consider it one of the many miracles of the night that it did not.

As our bow was forced towards the wicked northern shore, the wind screamed at us with hurricane force and there was no way that the bow would come round. 'Let go the anchor!' I yelled to Chris, who kept close by me for instructions. He moved as fast as he could in the circumstances, but I knew it was too late. Nothing could save us. We were about to die, and we all knew it. It all seemed so obvious, and we could see everything so clearly.

Totorore was swept beam on to the rocks, huge and black, covered and uncovered by the frenzied sea. We waited, terrified, for the crash, me with pleading prayers on my lips. I thought the engine had died on me as I could hear nothing above the roar of the waves. The nearest visible rock suddenly showed no more than two metres off our starboard beam. Thoughts of my family flashed through my mind, and then I could see again the rocks of Chatham Islands where I had previously faced death in another boat, and a miracle had saved me. Dear God, please save us! In spite of the terrific wind, the backwash of a huge wave off the rocks held us clear, just as the bow snubbed suddenly, incredibly, to the short anchor chain. Our dear old Bruce anchor must have caught a good hold on a rock even though the chain was almost straight up and down. To my great joy I found that the engine was still running; with the tiller hard over we took advantage of the snubbing on the chain and the bow came away from the rocks, heading us out into the cove again.

If only we could clear before the next breaker lifted her up on top of the rocks! 'Try to get the anchor up!' I yelled to Julia to tell Chris. They were having a bad time up there on the foredeck, constantly in danger of being swept off by the green water...

Chris and Julia managed to get the anchor off the bottom, but I could not steer *Totorore* up into the wind so she was being swept back into the cove. 'Let it go again!' I shouted, but nobody could hear. Julia came aft. 'Up or down?' 'Down – down – down! Quickly!' I shouted as loudly as I could. We were in the breakers and it seemed that we were destined to be wrecked on the beach. She snubbed slightly and the bow came round, our stern no more than twenty metres from the shore. Chris came aft. 'How much chain is out?' 'I don't know,' he replied, 'Probably about five fathoms!' 'Not enough, but we can't pay out any more or we'll smash the rudder!' I tried desperately to keep the bow up to wind, but she kept sheering off to one side or the other, and I could not believe that the anchor would hold us off the shore.

Chris took the tiller while I went to the radio and sent out urgent signals on the single sideband radio on 4125 kHz, and Channel 16 on the VHF. 'PAN PAN PAN. This is *Totorore*, *Totorore*, *Totorore*, Zulu Mike Sierra Charlie (ZMSC – *Totorore's* call sign). In difficulties on south side Albatross Island, Bay of Isles, South Georgia. Likely to be wrecked soon!' I repeated it several times, then took over the tiller again from Chris.

'It's looking bad' he said, as we sheered again close to the rocks, 'We'll try to keep her on the beach to survive the wreck' I replied. 'On the rocks there's no chance.' 'Shall I get emergency gear ready?' 'Yes, and quickly! With tents!'

I continued my nightmare struggle to keep her off the shore while he and Julia tore everything out of lockers and off bunks. Our neatly stowed boat was soon a shambles, but afterwards I was full of admiration for their efficiency and speed...Tents, sleeping bags, extra clothing, primus stove and fuel, and food for about a month, were packed up in boat-bags and plastic bags, ready to heave ashore, all under the most appalling conditions with the packers being flung about unmercifully...

When Chris came out into the cockpit I told him I thought we were actually gaining ground and that the beach looked farther away. There was still a chance! We did not dare to try to retrieve our anchors and our only hope was to drag them forcefully away from the shore. As we sheered from one side to the other, definitely gaining, our echo-sounder started to register again when we had moved away from the aerated turbulence of the breakers. Slowly but surely we were winning, and then I was able to ask Chris and Julia to heave the anchor home so we could have another go at getting out of the cove. The wind had eased a little but still came in tremendous gusts which gave us the same problems as we'd had before when she was out of control, heading for the rocks. Chris swore that by the time she came round he lost sight of one rock under the bowsprit! To and fro she went, from one crisis to another, and again there were moments when I doubted *Totorore's* ability to avoid destruction, but each time she made it by a mere whisker...

Monday 26 August

...It was after midnight. After an hour of plugging away into the wind we were finally clear of the cove and its rocks and conscious of disbelieving relief. I cancelled my PAN messages on the radio and VHF and Julia made coffee, stumbling over the heaps of emergency gear in the cabin. We could hardly appreciate that we were still alive, and that *Totorore* herself was still intact. It seemed too impossible. The gale was still blowing and the sea was rough, and it took another hour to work into the anchorage off Salisbury Plain, a mile and a half away. There we were out of the big sea, but still in the wind. It was perfect. We lit the cabin heater and peeled off our sodden clothes, able at last to relax. It could not have been possible to come closer to death than we had come this night and live to tell the tale. I thanked God for our salvation from the bottom of my heart. After another hot drink we all turned in, and I did not rouse my crew with their cup of tea until 0900 hours.

We named the cove from which we had escaped Miracle Cove.

Wandering Albatross

Chapter Fifteen

Ice and Storms

King Edward Point — Larsen Harbour — Return to K.E.P. for repairs —
At sea — South Sandwich Islands — Pack ice — Icing up — Storms
— Bouvetoya — At sea — Cape Town

Julia said it was like watching TV as she sat up in her bunk, sipping her cup of tea, nibbling at a piece of cake and looking out of the port at the long line of King penguins walking along the shoreline against a background of towering icy mountains shining pink in the early morning sunlight.

In the afternoon we returned to Albatross Island, but this time anchored close to a landing place on the east coast from which Julia and I were able to count the Wanderer chicks on the southern half of the island. For safety, we took *Totorore* back to Salisbury Plain for another quiet night, and then went back again to the same place on the following day to complete the job.

The wind stayed from the north-west so the island gave *Totorore* shelter, but a change would have left the anchorage badly exposed. One has always to accept a certain amount of risk or nothing is accomplished.

We found a total of exactly a hundred Wanderer chicks on the island — disappointingly less than the 109 we had found last year. In fog and sleet we left the Bay of Isles, heading east.

Wednesday 28 August
Lovely sunshine gave added beauty to our surroundings this morning, making it almost impossible not to go ashore to explore the valley next to us which leads over to Blue Whale Harbour...Julia and I went ashore to investigate. We searched the wide beach area and the valley with its typical moraine ridges, and a stream which could be seen in a few places under the deep snow. It looked an ideal spot for the penguins and I tried hard to remember where they had been last year.

My report showed that there were 141 chicks, so there should be more than that this year, but we could not see even an adult...I followed some tracks higher up the valley which were probably Gentoo, while Julia went to the northern end of the beach area to look behind a rocky ridge into another cove. I was rewarded by magnificent views of Antarctic Bay and its glaciers...Above the highest ridge I came to a big lake, but I did not walk across it as I could see no more tracks. Instead I went over to the rocky point to the north, and down below I saw Julia with the Kings. Mystery solved! I had made a mistake, and the colony was actually in Windy Cove itself.

There were 387 chicks – another healthy increase...

Today we made an unfortunate discovery. One of the cakes which Julia had baked at Bird Island – our last one – had been hurriedly packed on Sunday night with the emergency gear and had become tainted with kerosene. Julia tried eating it, but the kerosene repeated on her for hours afterwards.

Friday 30 August (At King Edward Point)

Chris and I went to find the sergeant of the Royal Engineers who had just arrived in *Sir Geraint* to maintain the generators and other services for the garrison here. We went to the Engineers' mess – with 'Grytviken Hilton' written above the door – and were invited into their overheated but rather smart quarters and shown into a comfortable lounge where one of the engineers was watching video. That amused but saddened us. He had only just arrived, and in daytime in beautiful weather in these magnificent surroundings he could think of nothing better to do!

The sergeant was friendly enough and we asked him if we could use their workshop facilities to do our repairs, to which he readily agreed.

Saturday 31 August

More snow today made the whole untidy place look clean again. Elephant seal bulls are beginning to arrive, and on the radio Rob told us that Hannibal had arrived back at Bird Island.

In a shed near the jetty we spotted a large old Argentinian propane gas bottle, and on giving it a shake found that it had some in it...I asked Major 'Hotsocks' if we could have some. He said we could have what we could get out of it, as they did not use it. I also gave him a list, at his suggestion, of stores we would like – a ship had just brought them new supplies...Later, we were delighted when a young soldier brought us down a sack of potatoes and half a sack of onions, together with four dozen eggs and a few tins of porridge oats. His comment was 'You must be bloody mad to go to sea in this!'

While Chris finished the work on the lifeline stanchions, and re-rigged the lifelines, I slung the big gas bottle upside down from the roof of the shed, using a handy-billy tackle, and with a borrowed hose and the fittings we had found at the Leith whaling station, filled our own gas bottle. We now have full fuel and full gas, and will try to top up our water on our way down the coast if we can find a stream which is not completely frozen.

Sunday 1 September

Another glorious sunny day. Before sailing we went up to Shackleton House to say goodbye and thank you to Major 'Hotsocks' but could find only a sergeant, who said the major was still in bed. It was after 0900 hours. We left a message, and called in to see the engineers in the Grytviken Hilton, but they were in bed too. It would have been the right time for the Argentinians to attack! All very different from the efficient atmosphere when the Coldstream Guards were here.

...We were soon out in Cumberland Bay motoring against a light headwind across the blue, blue water. We are all lighthearted and happy, pleased to leave King Edward Point...and looking forward to this next phase of our expedition. We saw again herds of reindeer browsing on the steep tussock slopes, and as always, kept a sharp lookout for King penguins. Of Gentoos there were plenty, both on beaches and porpoising in the sea.

Rounding Cape Harcourt outside Royal Bay, the wind freshened to a gale from the south-west with a bitter cold bite, the temperature at $-3\,^{\circ}$C. The seas were short and steep, and very splashy. Chris had a job to keep her heading into the wind when the fierce squalls, laden with freezing spray, swung her off. We plodded on slowly to seek shelter in Moltke Harbour, averaging only one knot. When we anchored close up to the beach we could see two large Elephant seal bulls fighting, and another hauled up farther along. In a couple of weeks from now such a long wide beach as this will be packed with large numbers of bulls, with the cows following, ready to pup...

Monday 2 September

After rounding Cape Charlotte we had a quiet run down the coast with light variable winds...We carried on around Cape Vahsel, and could barely see big Cooper Island in the mank. One of my regrets is that I have never landed on Willis Island in the north, or Cooper Island – a fascinating looking place – here in the south. One must leave something exciting for another voyage, perhaps! The wind freshened up considerably as we came through Cooper Sound, and the sea became rougher, the lumps of floating ice and icebergs more frequent, and the visibility much worse...

I had in mind to make Esbensen Bay on the south coast of South Georgia our place for preparations and departure for South Sandwich Islands, but it seemed that Esbensen Bay did not agree with that idea. It is really a most spectacular narrow fjord with high, steep mountainsides, which we could only vaguely see. As we approached, extremely violent spray-laden squalls of hurricane force came roaring out with only brief intervals between... Laid almost onto her beam ends, *Totorore* struggled in, but it was a losing battle. The fjord was like the mouth of the Devil blowing out smoke...We could not help laughing. It was one of the windiest places we had ever seen...We gave up, and retreated.

Once around Natriss Head the strong and gusty winds hit us again, funnelling down the larger fjord...Again a long slow struggle dodging ice, and it fell dark before we arrived at the entrance to Larsen Harbour. At about 1830 hours with only half a mile to reach Williams Cove, the engine suddenly stopped! What a blow! It was running very hot, but after its admirable behaviour at Miracle Cove eight days ago, I could not believe that overheating was what had stopped it. We put her round so that the wind was on the port side, fore-reaching away from the land, and I told Chris to lash the helm down to hold her beam-to-sea and lessen the drift...I made hot Milo for us all, and then bled the fuel system on the engine, finding much air in it.

In the gale we were drifting faster than the ice, having much more windage, but there was nothing we could do about it, and we hit some large pieces with nasty grating noises. As soon as the engine was cool enough we tried again...In the prevailing weather the only real alternative was to drift away offshore and head for South Sandwich Islands, but I did not like that idea as there were many things to be attended to before we actually set off across the ice-dangerous open ocean. So we tried again to reach Larsen Harbour, from which we had drifted over two miles.

It was a traumatic journey, easiest for me inside, anxiously watching the engine temperature and the radar, and worst for Chris and Julia outside getting soaked. None of our wet-weather gear keeps heavy water out any more. The worst part of it was that we had to motor hard to steer at all in the violent squalls, and in the driving sleet and spray it was impossible to see the ice. Sometimes we passed huge pieces very close, and three times we met such concentrations that we just had to throttle back, losing hard-won ground. Twice we hit very big pieces with a heart-rending crash...At 2135 hours we dropped anchor in Williams Cove in twelve fathoms with a rocky bottom, described on the chart as 'foul ground'. Beggars can't be choosers! The anchor caught immediately, and we were very thankful to be able to relax...

Chris's eyes looked bloodshot and salt-rimmed. 'I have gone off ice,' he said. We all laughed. We seem to go from one crisis to another. What on earth were we doing here? We must be mad!

Tuesday 3 September

In the morning the wind was still strong with violent sleety squalls, but it gradually improved and the sun shone, revealing to us the breathtaking beauty of our immediate surroundings. While the weather was good it seemed sensible to find a stream to top up our water, so we all went ashore in the dinghy to search, and to look at some Weddell seals, two of which had new pups. The pups were just gorgeous, golden brown in colour, obviously only a day old at most, and looking very cuddly. The cows, as gentle and placid as ever, did not mind our having a look at their pups. One of them was making a mooing sound, followed by the trill-like song. There were seven Weddells in the cove, not counting the pups. There was no fresh water – only ice. On the radio, Cal had told us that the only known breeding colony in South Georgia is here in Larsen Harbour, mainly on Bonner Beach, a little farther up the narrow fjord...

Rowing back out to *Totorore* we noticed that the gap under the bowsprit, between the bowsprit and the stem-head, had widened to a full centimetre; to our horror, close examination showed that the bowsprit had broken right across, underneath, for half its thickness, and both forestays were very slack! What a disaster! We could not understand it, but knew that the trouble had already started when I spotted it at Bird Island. That is when we should have done something about it, before it was too late. We had thought it would hold until Cape Town, but obviously the heavy treatment it has had of late, pounding into a head sea and probably magnified by hitting ice with the bobstay and further loosening it, has really finished it off. What on earth to do now, far from any repair facilities, and obviously in an unsafe condition to go to sea at all?

Somehow we must try to repair the bowsprit with what we have, by robbing material from some other part of our ship. No simple solution presented itself. We slackened off the backstays and stripped fittings off the end of the bowsprit, struggling hard to find inspiration. Then we carried on with other jobs – Julia stowing down below, myself stowing the after locker to make room for the dinghy now in use, and Chris repairing the compass light and the wind battery charger...I was feeling very low at this new and unexpected setback but was determined to somehow make it strong enough to see us on our way. We can only hope the weather will be kind to us to give us a chance to do something about it, as even our anchoring arrangements are dependent on a good bowsprit, with the chain leading over a roller on its end. To have to put to sea now would probably cost us the mast.

Wednesday 4 September

...We were able to make temporary repairs so that we could again tension our fore- and backstays, but the ideas I had for a more permanent repair job using lengths of our stainless steel sheet track, both for the bowsprit and fitting for the bobstay, and as strapping to strengthen our broken bowsprit, had to be abandoned. Chris tried drilling the stainless steel with the breast-drill, but just chipped the drill bits. Reluctantly and unhappily we decided that we would have to return to King Edward Point, where we could use the power drill in the engineers' workshop and possibly find some other materials to strengthen our broken bowsprit over at Grytviken.

When the mast was again securely stayed and we felt it was safe to proceed – albeit with caution to avoid heavy head seas or hitting ice – we thought that before we left we should try to record the voice of a Weddell seal. We had been entertained by them all morning, with their singing in the water which we could hear through the hull. It was a strange musical whistle, sometimes sounding like water running out of a bottle. At other times it was percussive; as Chris said, like somebody building a house not far away.

We rowed ashore together and I managed to record the song of the South Georgian pipit while Chris and Julia tried to encourage some seals to sing. They had no luck on that big snow slope, so we rowed across the cove to where there were more. On the way we came across the rounded back of a Weddell seal sticking out of the water, like a rock surrounded by kelp. We approached slowly and it did not move at all. 'It must be asleep,' said Julia, and scratched its back. She told us that through the thick fur the flesh felt almost liquid. Still the seal did not wake up. Then she pulled at some of the kelp draped over it and immediately it awoke and lifted its head high out of the water with such a surprised look on its face that we all burst out laughing. Gradually it sank back into the water and we watched it following us underneath...

The cow Weddell seals are larger than the bulls, about three metres long and weighing half a tonne...A cow with a pup did make some mooing and globbing noises for me to record, but not the musical whistle. As we still wanted to count the Weddells farther up the fjord on Bonner Beach and report their numbers to Cal on the radio before starting on our way north again, we could not wait any longer.

Snow started to fall again as we went round to the beach, but there was no wind, so I drifted while Chris and Julia rowed ashore to make a close inspection in the reduced visibility. On the two beaches, one on each side of the fjord, and in Williams Cove, they counted a total of 95 adults, eighteen pups, and three dead pups, which so early in the season looks like a fast-growing colony from the previously reported 30 pups annually, as there were few males. At least it made us feel that we had done something useful here, in spite of our troubles.

The snow was thick when we left the harbour at dusk, thinking we might go around to Wirik Bay for the night. However there was just so much ice everywhere that I decided that it was not safe to press on in the dark, and instead we followed the coast down and around Natriss Head and slunk up into Esbensen Bay, which we had been physically unable to enter two days ago...

Thursday 5 September

There was no wind in our little resting place, and soft snow was falling as we made our way down the fjord at 0740 hours looking in awe at the magnificence of the fantastic place which we had been unable to see last night. To overcome her radio shyness, Julia has been making the call to Bird Island in the mornings and having amusing conversations with the boys. Mark and Cal had apparently dyed their hair blond. In daytime and fine weather it is very easy both to see and to avoid ice, provided it is not too thick. To the east of Hamilton Bay is an unnamed cove which I was reluctant to enter for the first time the other night in the dark and in bad weather, so I decided that we should have a quick look in passing, just in case we should need it another time. Not too difficult to approach, as the rocks were plainly visible, it is well sheltered except from the south and looked attractive. I called it Parece Buena Cove (Appears Good).

...I called up King Edward Point on the VHF and reported that we were returning because we had suffered storm damage and wished to make our repairs there. The answer was, as usual, brief to the point of rudeness. 'Is that all? Roger. Out.' One would have expected the operator to be a little more conversational.

We sailed into the Cove, past Shackleton House, lowered our sails and motored alongside into the permanent large oil slick on the icy water. It must have started when the RFA ship wrecked the wharf just before we arrived the first time, breaking the fuel pipe. Since then the engineers repaired the pipes, but so inefficiently that one can see diesel leaks all the way along the pipeline right up to the big storage tank; where the hose is for fuelling the tractor the ground is saturated with it, as all the joints are leaking. The wharf damage was three months ago, so it is inexcusable; there are at least six men from the Royal Engineers here all the time, whose job it is to maintain and service the facilities for the base. Nobody came to see us, or so much as gave us a wave as we passed...

Friday 6 September

Not a cloud to be seen this morning, and it is very still. The air is −6 °C and the cove is frozen over. An excellent day for getting jobs done. After breakfast we went to pay our respects to Major 'Hotsocks' and request permission to again ask the engineers if we could use the workshop facilities. He received us unsmilingly, and as usual did not invite us to sit down. During a short conversation he said that he and most of his men were looking forward to leaving this place in the not-too-distant future. He told us that Elephant seals were coming ashore at King Edward Point, but they would much rather they went to the other side of the bay to breed, as they are dirty, smelly things! He also said that some people would question our sanity in doing what we are doing. I replied that we ourselves did sometimes, too!

Back at the wharf one of the soldiers was fishing and we stopped to have a chat with him and then invited him on board for coffee. A friendly and interesting young man, he told us more about snow caves and igloos, and how to build them. He was one of the few who was interested in the wildlife around here, and asked us many questions.

We started work in earnest on our repairs...Chris made a good job of mending the bowsprit, using wood and bolts from Grytviken to fix two strongbacks underneath.

Saturday 7 September
...A very large bull Elephant seal hauled himself out onto the beach near the wharf...I don't suppose the Major will be very pleased. The untidiness around the buildings of the base, and the heavy oil pollution everywhere, is far more offensive than the natural excrement of the seals...

Monday 9 September
...After lunch the wind increased to a fresh and gusty north-wester, making it too bumpy for us alongside, so we moved out to anchor in the centre of the cove to see if we could catch some fish. Chris and Julia tried for several hours, standing out in the cockpit in the rain and using tinned bacon for bait. Chris did catch one crocodile fish – a peculiar-looking fellow, about 40 cm long, and with big sad eyes which made us feel sorry for him. However we ate him for dinner, but as he was nearly half head, and very full of bones, there was not much to share among the three of us. It was delicious, but I hope we catch some Antarctic cod instead.

By the evening of 10 September we had done all that we felt we could and were in good spirits, confident that this time we would reach South Sandwich Islands – if the pack ice allowed it! Having seen how the King penguins were increasing at an amazing rate in South Georgia and were expanding into new colonies, we wanted to see if they were extending their breeding area to the South Sandwich Islands. Earlier reports located them on some of the northern islands, but it was not known if they were breeding.

Unfortunately, our delay made it likely that the pack ice would arrive there before we did. Under the influence of wind and currents, it moves up from the Weddell Sea and in most years surrounds South Sandwich Islands completely during September, October and November. In some years it extends over 100 miles north of the islands, and occasionally even engulfs South Georgia! It was becoming a race, and we were counting on our luck.

South Sandwich Islands are in a north-to-south chain about 200 miles long lying on the Scotia Ridge, a submarine range of mountains connecting the Andes of South America with the mountains of the Antarctic Peninsula. There are eleven main islands, and the northernmost, Zavodovski, is about 300 miles east-south-east of South Georgia, which is on the same ridge. Most of the islands show signs of volcanic activity.

After casting off from the jetty at King Edward Point at 0700 hours on 11 September, we had a fine run down the coast under our twin headsails to Parece Buena Cove, a distance of 50 miles which we covered in nine hours. As the wind had increased to gale force we decided to hole up there and make our final departure preparations.

Wednesday 11 September
...Julia made a pudding with semolina given to us by the army, but it was very old and tasted mouldy. She tried to disguise the taste with cocoa and raisins, and we did manage to eat half of it, but Chris got the giggles and that started Julia and me off too. We laughed until it hurt, and that probably did us good. I think we are all a little uptight about our coming voyage, as we have completely missed the moon now and there is bound to be ice to make our nights dangerous.

Thursday 12 September
...When it was light I could see a very rough sea outside the cove and great clouds of spray being lifted across the entrance, apparently from a westerly direction. I did not call my crew too early because it really did look imprudent to sail out into that lot, but by 1030 hours when we declared ourselves to be ready it did not look quite so fierce. None of us is superstitious, we say, but nobody wanted to sail tomorrow on Friday 13th, so away we went across a rough and boisterous sea, dodging floating ice.

...As soon as it was dark it was too difficult to see the small bergy bits or growlers, because the breaking seas looked white all around us...in these ice-infested seas it is necessary for one of us to be outside keeping a lookout all the time, so we started our watch system of three hours on and six off, continuously, day and night...Watches were very cold and wet, with a lot of sea coming on board at times; those of us not on watch also felt very cold, even in our sleeping bags with our clothes on.

Saturday 14 September (sea temperature −1.2 °C)
...Towards evening we headed over towards one of three large icebergs in sight and were excited to see that it had large numbers of birds on it. As we came closer we could identify them as Chinstrap penguins, in a large group on one side and all along the ridge...Rounding the end we were amused and amazed to see how high the penguins could leap out of the waves to scrabble up the steep slippery sides, often slipping back into the water or being washed off by another wave. On the far side we saw that there were about 2000 penguins, and they must have been there quite a long time as the ice was heavily stained by their guano. We wondered how far they had travelled on that berg, and how long would they stay? Their breeding season starts in November, so would they continue on their free ride until

then, before seeking a breeding place on land? So many unanswered and interesting questions...

Monday 16 September
Soon after I took over the watch from Julia at 0100 hours the visibility cleared a little and I thought I could see Zavodovski...we motored very

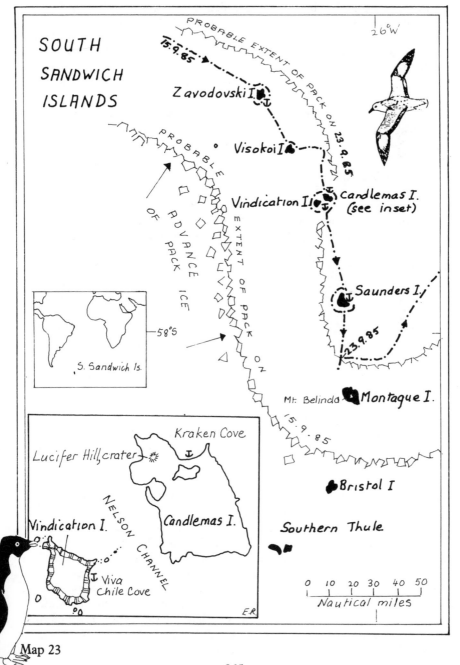

SOUTH SANDWICH ISLANDS

26°W

PROBABLE EXTENT OF PACK ON 23.9.85

15.9.85

Zavodovski I.

Visokoi I.

PROBABLE

EXTENT OF PACK

EXTENT OF ADVANCE PACK ICE

Vindication I.

Candlemas I. (see inset)

58°S

S. Sandwich Is.

Saunders I.

23.9.85

Mt. Belinda

Montague I.

15.9.85

Kraken Cove

Lucifer Hill, crater

Candlemas I.

Bristol I

Vindication I.

NELSON CHANNEL

Viva Chile Cove

Southern Thule

0   10   20   30   40   50
Nautical miles

E.R.

Map 23

slowly along an intricate course among the bergs, passing only a cable's length from some of them without seeing them with the naked eye. Luckily we did not seem to meet small ice between the bergs, and the east coast appeared to be clear. A small indentation looked as though it could offer some slight shelter, so we headed slowly in. When I asked Chris to standby the anchor, he said 'I'll have to believe you that there is an island here!' We could vaguely see a low black cliff on which the sea was breaking noisily, but could make out nothing above it.

. . . The west coast of the island is more precipitous, and some of the high cliffs had a variety of brown, red, and ochre colours and clouds of steam issuing from cracks, right down to sea level. The low clouds cleared enough to let us see almost to the peak at 550 metres, but we plainly saw the huge crater, open on the side of the mountain from half way up and belching out volumes of steam and sulphurous fumes. In parts where it was warm, the mountain was bare rock, but most of it was still covered with deep ice and snow. . .

Tuesday 17 September

. . . With the sea at −1.5 °C and large numbers of Snow petrels and Antarctic petrels flying about, we half expected to meet the pack ice as we sailed the 26 miles south to Visokoi. Snow prevented our seeing the island until we were very close, and then we saw only the lower parts of the great dark cliff and glaciers rising sheer out of the sea. Many offshore rocks with breakers were scattered along the coast and not shown on the chart. . .

There appeared to be a shallow cove sheltered by rocks north and south on the north side of Irving Point, so we started to head into it. The wind changed to ahead, coming along the south coast of the island, and then with frightening suddenness it was blowing a full gale with gusts of Force 10. I asked Chris to furl the jib, and Julia to start the engine. Chris put the furling line on the winch, but could not pull it in. He went forward to see what was wrong, and came back to say that the furling drum was completely broken! He went forward again to try to roll it up by hand, but in that wind it was not possible as there was too much weight in the sail, which started to flog terribly, shaking the mast and the whole boat.

Using the engine we tried to hold her up to the wind, but with the full jib up, she could not do it. Chris was struggling to untangle the furling line from the broken drum. . . then the sheet track broke away from the gunwale, which had been damaged alongside at Punta Arenas, and the flogging of the sheet hammered the heavy lead block and its traveller against the cabin coaming, threatening to stave it in, and the two ports there, too. I kept shouting instructions to Julia at the tiller to try to keep the sail just full, so that I could secure the block, but being on the lee side with too much sail the block was under water. I wrestled with it, leaning out through the lifelines, and green water broke right over my head, tearing back the hood of my heavy-weather suit and completely soaking me right through all my clothes. The shock of the freezing water was painful, especially on my head. Meanwhile we were heading for the rocks, and I yelled to Julia who was very confused as she could not hear me properly in the wind and did not understand. Chris was likewise yelling at me from forward, and making signs to slack off the furling line, but I misunderstood also, and winched it hard instead. We cleared the rocks and ran off downwind, trying to avoid a big iceberg just outside. The wind screamed and the spray flew, and our sail flogged...

All we could do was try to get the sail off, but in that weather it was no small task. While Chris fetched pliers for the halyard shackle and the halyard itself, to take the sail out of its luffspar, I hung over the pulpit to remove the tack lashing on the sail and then unshackle the standing halyard. I hardly noticed the drenching waves, as I was already soaked and was desperate... Julia ran her off downwind and Chris and I somehow managed to get the sail out of its spar and onto the deck... I thought it might be all right if we could get inside, close up to the glacier. At least we could anchor and ride it out.

Chris took the tiller while I kept a lookout for ice and rocks and watched the radar every now and again. Just when we were gaining ground the engine temperature gauge showed overheating, so we had to throttle back and were blown back out to sea. Julia kept a constant eye on the gauge and we tried to keep the engine going at the maximum revolutions it could stand, but several times had to reduce. The wind direction kept changing from one side to the other and for hours we tried hard to make it. It grew dark, and the compass light would not work. One of those days!

...Finally at 1930 hours I decided that we had lost the battle, as we were exhausted and shivering...We ran off downwind to get clear of a couple of icebergs, then set the staysail aback and hove to, with the helm lashed down...'I have gone off the South Sandwich Islands!' said Chris, wringing out his clothes as he peeled them off.

Wednesday 18 September

...At midday we entered Nelson Channel, passing by the warm, snow-free and steaming volcano Lucifer Hill, on the north end of Candlemas Island. The swell still ran high and the sea was rough and wetting as we sailed down the coast. Most of the island is under deep ice and snow, but some cliffs of lava had what looked like recent falls of ash on their snow covers. Landing was obviously not possible on that part of the coast, and as the wind was rising rapidly and becoming very gusty we did not want to repeat yesterday's performance, and headed straight across the channel, past various icebergs, to follow down the lee side of a reef of under- and above water rocks, with small islands, projecting out into the Nelson Channel from Vindication Island...

There were strong gusts of wind, but when we were really in close to the rocky shore, backed by high steep cliffs, we were right out of the rough sea and swell. *Totorore* still rolled, but lay more quietly than we had dared to hope. As today is Chile's most important holiday, celebrating her independence, Julia asked if we could call the cove Viva Chile...

Thursday 19 September

Today was just the day we wanted. We took advantage of the early calm to make a landing before breakfast, and all three of us went in the dinghy to the small rocky spit off the point. It was fantastic! On the steep cliffs above, including a vertical scoria cliff on one side, there was much activity. The lovely Snow petrels appeared to be on nests quite low down, and others were courting together on rocks not far from us, uttering rather harsh grating cries which did not really match their appearance. The air was full of birds, of which the Cape pigeons were the noisiest, flying around and sitting on ledges higher up, whereas the most numerous were the Fulmars, on the highest ledges of all. Above the steep stony beach on which we landed, a small flattish area of ice had eight Weddell seals and two Fur seals. There were no penguins, but the area was pink with the familiar guano of Gentoos. Chris scrambled up as high as he could to take photographs of Snow petrels courting prettily close to him as Julia and I made our way along the outer coast below the cliffs...

Back on board we had a late breakfast and then had a good day to get on with our jobs. Chris put some bolts through the broken furling drum to hold it together at least as far as Cape Town, and I worked on the running rigging while Julia sponged out the bilges. I transferred fuel from the cans on deck to the tanks...Chris had a fishing line over the side, but the bait remained untouched. My knee became swollen and painful during the day and in the evening I fetched out the homeopathic first aid box. Julia read the instructions. 'Arnica,' she said. 'That should do the trick. Take two tablets every three hours.' She handed me a small bottle. By the oil lamp the light was not particularly bright; I took off the cap and tipped the bottle up to shake out two tablets into the cap. Instead of tablets a liquid spilled out, filling the cap and running over my fingers. 'It said Arnica on the bottle,' retorted Julia, so I drank it out of the cap. 'Ugh, it's horrid!' Then I looked at the bottle. 'For external use only!' That started Chris off with the giggles, and soon he and Julia were rolling around unable to stop. Julia found another bottle with tablets in and offered me two, but I said I had had enough. Long after I went to bed I could hear Chris and Julia bursting out again and chortling into their pillows!

Friday 20 September

I had good reason to feel pleased when I woke up this morning. Firstly, my misapplied homeopathic treatment last night seemed to have done a good job and my knee felt much better. Secondly, the sea seemed very calm, which would give us a good chance to land on Candlemas Island.

We motored across Nelson Channel, around the low volcano, Lucifer Hill, and into Kraken Cove, on the north coast of Candlemas, where there is a beach of large rounded stones.

...We made a good landing and secured our dinghy by weighting it with large stones from the beach close up to the bank of ice. Julia and Chris went to have a look at the volcano, after we had stopped to chat with and photograph six Adélie penguins which had just come ashore. They are engaging little penguins, completely unafraid, and very amusing the way they make rapid progress across the ice tobogganing on their tummies, using their feet only and not their flippers...There are thousands of Chinstrap penguins, but they are all out on the icebergs waiting for their cue to come ashore in November to start breeding. How did they know which icebergs to board to come here to this very place?

The next day we sailed down to Saunders Island, with another high steaming volcano in the middle and a remarkable half crater in the south, on the slopes of which were thousands of Adélie penguins. It looked a fascinating island, but the heavy surf on its steep beaches did not allow us to make a landing, although we circumnavigated it and spent two nights there.

Monday 23 September
...We are sailing well, *Totorore* on her ear, in a 25 to 30 knot west-south-west wind, making good speed southwards. There is plenty of ice about, but nothing very big apart from the odd iceberg. Montagu Island is the largest in the group, with Mount Belinda at 1370 metres. I must certainly try to get a photograph of it for my daughter, Belinda!

This is the first island in the southern group of three islands, all of which are normally ice-bound until late November, and are reputed to have a severe Antarctic climate, colder and more harsh than the South Orkneys because of the currents and air streams from the Weddell Sea. We approach with some apprehension!

Up to this point we had been keeping radio contact with Bird Island, but for several days had been able only to hear Rob, while he could not understand what we said and continued to think enviously of us climbing mountains on Montagu Island long after we had retreated.

...At about 1230 hours Chris, who was on ice watch outside, said he could see the pack away to westward. We all had a look, and below the telltale blink observed that the horizon was all lumpy, and the sea and swell were considerably damped down. It was an exciting moment! A large iceberg on the edge of the pack had penguins on it, so we headed over towards it, passing through an increasing amount of small-ice debris. From a quarter mile off, the pack looked absolutely amazing with its clearly defined edge like a long wall of ice stretching north and south out of sight. It was not too solid, we saw when really close, as it was heaving in the swell, and consisted of very dense brash with innumerable large ice shapes from car – size up to icebergs...Ice for thousands of miles, although we could not see across it very far as it disappeared into the whiteness of the blink.

...It is now 1700 hours and we are sailing north-north-east away from the ice. It is rather disappointing, as we reached within twelve miles of Montague Island without seeing it, finding that the approaches were completely blocked by ice and it was impossible for us to go farther south. In the corner, as one might call it, where the pack curved around from north-south to an east-west line, there was a great deal of small loose ice and we had to sail very slowly through it to avoid damage. Now we see only comparatively few pieces, but there are still many icebergs about. We are on our way to Bouvetoya, and saying goodbye to the beautiful, rugged, mysterious and captivating South Sandwich Islands, only sorry that we could not see them all.

While it is still daylight and there is less ice we have unfurled more jib to make good speed while we can...Just over 1000 miles to Bouvetoya, but we will not sail a very direct course as we will go north first to try to clear the pack.

Wednesday 25 September

The gale continues, but we are lucky in that we have a good moon and not having seen any more floating ice for more than a day, other than about two icebergs per watch...

I came off watch at 0400 hours, handing over to Chris, and went to sleep. At about 0510 hours I was awoken by the dreaded 'CRASH!' In the big sea she hit several times, followed by a graunching of the ice down the side of the hull. I could see Chris standing with his head out of the observation hatch in the dodger and called out to him, 'Is it a big bit?' 'No,' he replied. 'About three metres long. I didn't see it until it was right up under the bow!' He was peering around to see if there was any more, then went forward to make an inspection. 'I can't see any damage,' he said...*Totorore* still seemed to be sailing along all right, so I lay down again to try to get some sleep, listening for water coming into the boat.

Soon after 0600 hours Chris looked in at me. 'We have a problem,' he announced. 'The bobstay is broken. I've reduced sail.' I told him to take all the sail off the forestays while I put on my heavy clothes. Using the boathook he fished up the trailing bobstay, still attached securely to the forefoot under water, and we found that the Tufnol sheave I had used to fit in the bend of the U-bolt which was the top fitting on the end of the bowsprit, and which carried the clevis pin for the stay itself, had sheared right through the centre, and the clevis pin had sheered off its split pin. It was not too bad. Without the bobstay we would have been in danger of losing the mast again, but it seemed that we had a good chance of repairing the visible damage. I managed to find a small block with a sheave of a similar size, and Chris was able to enlarge the hole for the centre pin. Using the windlass to haul the bobstay up tight, we fitted it all together again. I kept *Totorore* sailing off downwind while Chris lay down on the bowsprit, and leaning well out and reaching underneath managed to do it without getting more than his hands and gloves wet. What a relief!

...In the afternoon the sea and sky were a beautiful blue and I was just about to say that I was half expecting to see a coral island with palm trees when I spotted another berg...Then Chris caught sight of two more. We are still not out of the ice area! We must be more vigilant! We do not know how many more such collisions *Totorore* could stand.

Saturday 28 September

...The wind turned very suddenly to the south with an immediate drop in temperature to −7 °C. As the wind freshened much spray came on board and froze instantly, so *Totorore* began to ice up. We did not think too much about it – we have had it happen often enough at South Georgia. However by late afternoon we could see that this was more serious, and Ivon, the self-steering gear, turned into a block of ice, with nothing we could do to free it.

She was broaching a great deal and heavy seas were breaking on board. This was proper Antarctic winter weather which we thought we had missed as it is now spring! We were all soon soaked to the skin and freezing. We tried steering by hand at the tiller but the wind, near gale force, was too bitter. In desperation we experimented with lines and shock cord extending from the tiller to the comparative shelter of the dodger over the hatch, but it did not work. We started chopping ice off the decks, the cabin and the rigging, but it was back again so quickly we could not keep up.

Sunday 29 September

The weight of ice all over the boat made her feel sluggish and unnatural. I have never seen it so bad before. The pulpit was almost solid ice which had built up on the upper and lower rails until it met, and then extended downward. The furling gear for the sails was completely invisible, as were all the lines. Fortunately the spray had reached only a third of the way up the mast, so the upper part was clear. At the bottom even the tiny cord we use for a flag halyard had a build-up seven centimetres in diameter, while sheets had fifteen centimetres. The tiller was immovable under a block of hard ice which completely covered the after deck, in places 30 centimetres thick, as it was trapped in between the cockpit coaming, the jerrycans, bucket and legs of the radar tower. The winches were also invisible. It was a dramatic and sobering sight. By 0800 hours it was blowing 35 knots, and with the sea at $-1.3\,^{\circ}C$ and the air at $-7\,^{\circ}C$ the spray, and sometimes heavy water, were freezing immediately. We had to get rid of the ice, or as much of it as we could, to avoid the risk of capsizing; we also had to get her sailing downwind so that she would not take so much water aboard.

It was a desperate situation. The cockpit kept filling with water and the drains were blocked with ice. Luckily the violent movement emptied a lot of the water out again. Using a claw hammer, a very large screwdriver, a small crowbar and a large knife, we chopped and bashed and levered at the ice to dislodge it. The hard work kept us warm, but we were very soon soaked to the skin in the heavy seas. Our boots were full of water, and it poured down our necks and up our sleeves.

The most important job was to free the tiller so we could steer, and then the staysail sheets and some cleats. Finally we managed to let the staysail draw, but one of us had to steer all the time, while the others chopped at the ice...

Twice during the day *Totorore* was laid on her beam ends. The first time, I was in the pulpit with an arm around a cleared rail, so the weight of the sea on me was lessened by the barrier of ice. She seemed to take a while to come up again, but when she did I was relieved to see the heads of Julia and Chris down aft, so I knew that they were still on board. Julia had been steering and suddenly found herself 'swimming' as she called it, without anything to hold on to, and did not know if she was overboard or not, so was happy to find that she was still in the cockpit when *Totorore* came up again. We had not been wearing safety harnesses up until then but thereafter we did. Everything down below was wet, and our wet clothes did not help. Bilge water sloshed over the sole, which became horribly slippery...

We chopped ice all day until after dark. In the afternoon we were able to free one jib, but could not get her to steer herself downwind on it. Realising that we could not possibly steer all night – with the wind chill factor and our wet clothes it was murderous – so we hove to again, this time under the jib, and retired below. We had not seen any icebergs so I said we could all turn in and not keep watches. We were dead beat, and shivery...I thought that at that speed, fore-reaching at about two knots, our chances of hitting an iceberg were slight; in the gale conditions it was almost impossible to see anything in the dark anyway.

There were mutterings between my two crew members about heading north to warmer latitudes and forgetting about Bouvetoya, but I said that it would take a long time to notice the difference anyway, and that these depression systems are very extensive...Having come this far I am not going to give up on Bouvetoya, but I admit that this ice business scares me.

Monday 30 September

I did not sleep very well, I was too cold. I had gone to bed in my wet underclothes and socks, hoping to dry them out a bit, but it was not a good idea. It is becoming more difficult to see the funny side of the situation, but I make an effort as my crew are rather silent...

The gale became worse and the seas were mountainous, and the icing up was just incredible, even worse than yesterday. *Totorore* was wallowing, listing to starboard under the excessive top weight. It is difficult to assess the weight of ice on board, but each piece we chopped off was heavy, so it seemed she must have had about two tonnes. I was out early chopping away at it, clearing the tiller, and that alone took half an hour. The next job was to clear the furling line and sheet for at least one jib. Chris came out to help me and we managed to get one clear after about an hour and a half, so while I steered Chris unrolled a little bit of jib. Suddenly it ran away from him, unrolling half the sail. He could not hold it – none of the winches worked, the cam cleats would not hold, and even the ordinary cleat was iced up.

I struggled to keep her heading downwind as she took off at about nine knots, leaping and rearing, and shipping heavy water. In the cockpit the level of the slurry of ice and water was often over my knees. 'Try to get it off!' I yelled. 'The furling line has come off the drum!' Chris bellowed. He went forward to try to clear it. After a time of struggle, frequently dunked into the icy water, he came back and said, 'It's no good, it's so tangled and tight. I will have to let the sail full out. I'll be as quick as I can! 'O.K.' I said, 'Go ahead. I only hope it doesn't bring the mast down!'

He did a great job up there on his icy platform on the bowsprit, and although it seemed an age to me, he really did get it back under control in a remarkably short time...Truly a magnificent and courageous effort.

I certainly felt happier when all sail was off; we were still doing nearly five knots downwind under a bare pole. The only trouble was that she had to be steered, and that was killing because of the cold. Finally and with much difficulty we set a tiny jib with two sheets well forward, holding the sail hard amidships. We tried lashing the tiller but she would not stay downwind as each particularly large sea threw her, and then she wallowed with the wind on the beam, heeling far over and with seas breaking over the top, adding to the ice. The temperature was −8 °C. In the afternoon we found the right place to lash the helm to let her run off, taking the seas on the quarter. I was not concerned about the course – all I wanted was that we should survive! We chopped and hacked at the ice because we could not let it build up again and become worse than it was this morning.

My crew both retired early to their bunks to try to get warm, but I stayed out until well after dark until I was too exhausted to do any more. When I came into the cabin, Julia asked, 'Are you still alive?' 'Of course,' I replied. 'Are you?' The effort of chopping at the ice had kept me warm, in spite of my sodden clothes and the ice in the end of my mittens. My wet-weather gear was coated with ice which I could not help scattering around when I came in . . .

We were not making much speed, and had not seen any icebergs for the second day running, so again we did not keep watches. I allowed myself the luxury of some dry underwear and socks to wear in my bunk and I did get warm, but had a bad night, as did we all. It was rough and bouncy. I kept getting water on my head and could not puzzle out where it was coming from. My pillow was saturated. In the morning I discovered that the canvas pouch above my bunk, which holds my lifejacket, had filled with water from a sea which came in the hatchway, and every time she heeled a long way to port, water emptied out all over me. My towel was stiff with ice.

Tuesday 1 October

In the early hours Julia woke me up. 'Gerry, I'm frightened. I think we're in the pack ice!'

Totorore had turned and gone off on the other tack, heading south-east instead of north. The port deck was now awash, instead of the starboard, and the noise was the sea on the different and greater accumulation of ice on that side . . . Poor girl! What an introduction to ocean voyaging!

. . . I know that both of them would be happier if we were heading north, hoping to get into warmer weather.

During the next few days the icing became less and less, and we had everything under control again.

Thursday 3 October

During my watch I increased sail, unrolling some more of the jib. Visibility had improved enough for us to see any icebergs before we hit them, and we continued our wild ride, often broaching in the big seas with noisy bumps and splashes. Chris took over at 0100 hours and I went to bed. At about 0230 there was a crash, *Totorore* went over on her beam ends to starboard, and a bucketful of water poured over me accompanied by a bombardment of tins and boxes of foodstuffs from a large case which had been securely wedged into the port quarter berth. I thought for a moment that we were rolling over, but she came upright and continued her wild lurching ride. Pulling myself out of my saturated bunk, I could see Chris through the perspex washboard. The weight of water had pushed the hatch partly open, as Chris had not secured it. 'What happened?' I asked. 'She took a big sea over the stern,' he said.

What a mess. The water had found its way everywhere, soaking everything in the chart table area, including the clothes I had taken off to go to bed and my box full of papers and letters, wedged on the chart table seat. In the evening Julia had helped me to put a roll of paper towels folded between all the pages of the wet log book. Now the whole thing was a sodden mess...

Chris came inside and saw the state of affairs. He could not help laughing...at least he had a dry bunk to go to!

...Conditions became hectic and frighteningly unpleasant. We had a few complete knockdowns, mast into the water, and in spite of careful stowage, down below is somewhat chaotic with a great deal of water everywhere. We hove to at 2200 hours as she would not run downwind and kept broaching...When a big sea hits her it is as though she has run into an iceberg. The noise and the shock make us wonder how she can stand up to such collisions. She is a strong boat, bless her, and she certainly needs to be in this part of the world! Nobody got much sleep, and my bunk was again drenched. A Force 10 storm in the Southern Ocean. It is impossible to describe it adequately, and only those who have experienced anything like it themselves will be able to really appreciate what that means.

Friday 4 October

...My crew spend most of the day in bed, but they are very good about doing the cooking between them and still turn out excellent meals considering the frightful conditions. Our teatowels are rather revolting and wiping the dishes is really just a token gesture, but we do try to keep up the niceties. In the evening the weather moderated somewhat, and the barometer started to rise, so we were full of hope...

We did have one bad knockdown when the stove on its gimbals jammed at an angle of 90°, so that when *Totorore* came upright, the top plate was vertical. The kettle and saucepan were lashed on, and stayed in their places. Chris tried to dislodge it, heaving on it and kicking it, but it would not budge, so he left it until the morning...

Saturday 5 October

...the wind began to increase again, and soon it was once more blowing a near gale...I was surprised to see some ice floating past, some pieces as big as *Totorore*...We took a sea temperature and it was −1.7°C, only 0.3°C above the freezing point of salt water...The wind was coming away from the north-east, which will spoil our anchorage at Bouvetoya...

We were closer to the island than I had thought, and by 1600 hours we were running down its west coast, keeping just under a mile off to clear the rocks. The wind had increased to Force 10 again, and the seas were terrible. Chris stayed manfully out on the tiller, working hard to keep her downwind, racing along under a tiny jib.

We could just see the island through the snow – a huge cliff of ice with vertical black lava streaks and spray flung hundreds of feet into the air from the horrendous breakers beneath. As soon as we were clear of the Horn Reef off the south-west point, Cato Point, and a small island called Larsoya, we tried rounding up with the engine to close the south coast for some shelter. We were back to our old trouble – with the wind on the port side, the cooling water intake came out of the water and the engine overheated. What we endeavoured to do was to run eastwards under a small jib without being blown too far off the land, and then come in on the starboard tack with the engine at maximum revs. It worked, but it was

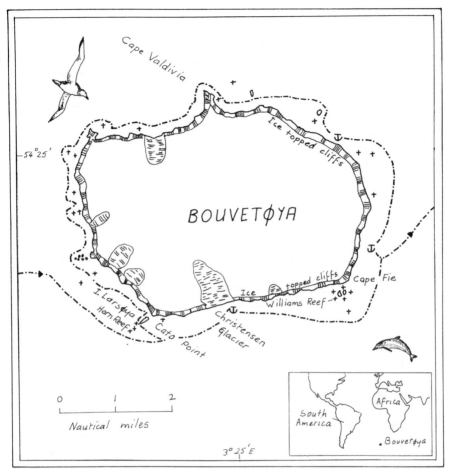

Map 24

another long battle, and it was after 1800 hours when we anchored about one and a half cables off the face of Christensen Glacier.

There was a big swell, but we were out of most of the wind. However we were in only about nine fathoms, and uncomfortably close to us we suddenly saw one of the swells turn into a great rolling breaker – like those amazing photographs one sees of people surfing inside them at Hawaii – and we knew that if we were caught in one of those it would be the end. So we weighed the anchor again and moved farther eastwards and offshore to twelve fathoms, where we tried again...

So here we are! I for one am thrilled: it is the most remote piece of land in the whole world, and one of the most inhospitable places I have ever seen. If we are going to learn anything about its birds at all we are going to need much better weather than this! To celebrate our safe arrival Julia opened a tin of whole chicken, which we had been saving specially, and we had a generous nip of rum each. Chris tried to get the cabin heater going, but it did not like the violent squalls which blew back down the chimney and put it out...

275

Sunday 6 October

...Julia said that when she did sleep for short periods she had nightmares, but waking up to reality was even more of a nightmare! In the early morning the barometer was down to 962 and the wind was coming at us from the west, creating a rough and punishing sea – the worst I have ever anchored in.

Before breakfast we weighed anchor – a difficult job for Julia and Chris at the windlass, with the bow roller smashed and so much chain out...We turned and ran east under bare pole, having to keep well offshore to clear the terrifying display put on for us by Williams Reef, off Fie Point at the south-east corner of the island. I thought we should feel the protection of the reef but it was not to be. In this storm there is no real shelter...

As we closed the coast, which is just an ice wall over 120 metres high with nothing but ice above it disappearing up the invisible mountain, we came out of the worst of the wind and sea. Close to the ice cliff we could see that the swell again turned to rollers in the shallower water, so anchored a quarter of a mile off in eight fathoms, among bergy bits and brash ice...

During some of the knockdowns it is obvious that the mast must have been well down into the water, far below the horizontal, because so many things went upwards to places higher than they originally were. Sometimes I wonder about *Totorore's* ability to handle this sort of thing, but I think that really she is doing very well for her size, considering the seas we have been meeting, and those we have yet to face! From the point of view of distance this is the halfway mark for our expedition. We are back in east longitude for the first time since we left New Zealand; from now on we really will be getting closer to home, instead of farther away..

Monday 7 October

...There is much for which we must be thankful. Considering the continued discomforts of being cold and wet we are all in good health. Julia has many bad bruises from being thrown about, but she is very uncomplaining. Both she and Chris have developed a strong dislike for Bouvetoya, but I say that we cannot blame the island for the weather.

By mid morning the wind freshened and the sea rose, and we had to move again...The anchor chain showed signs of bad strain with a distorted link over the tight nip of the bar on which the roller used to turn, which is hardly surprising when one consider the rough seas in which we are anchoring.

Tuesday 8 October was a rare fine day and a chance to circumnavigate the island to see if we could learn something about its birds. In sunshine we found it to be a beautiful place, with a 780 metre volcanic cone, sloping down to precipitous cliffs and glaciers all around the island. On the west coast the cliffs are of black lava, and in one place we saw steam issuing from a crack. Elsewhere most of the cliffs are of ice, but Cape Valdivia on the north coast is almost vertical rock, free of ice, with caves, arches and pillars at the bottom. A new lava outcrop low down on the north-west coast had three small, box-like huts, which must have been dropped by helicopter. [The island is owned by Norway, but was surveyed recently by South Africa.]

...As we approached our proposed anchorage we heard a roar and a crash, like a jet plane, and through the murk of snow we could see a huge icefall from above the black cliffs to east of the glacier itself. The debris of ice spread fast across the water, urged on by the waves from the splash it made and also by the strong squalls which hurtled at us. We sheered away from it but, remembering the rollers, did not want to go far past that spot, so dropped the anchor and let the ice rapidly surround us...

We are becoming a little concerned about our diminishing supply of fresh water, so Julia picked up a large piece of land ice out of the sea and broke it up to put in our pots to melt. She said that meant we could still have puddings, so tonight we had dried apricots with custard...

Wednesday 9 October

...We ran off down the coast under a bare pole, using the engine only to prevent her rounding up and heading towards the reefs close inshore...The wind was screaming Force 10 in white squalls, and when it was time to come round to seek shelter under the east coast, *Totorore* lay on her ear and we had the usual engine overheating problem and could not use full revolutions...We were making no progress, and were being blown farther away from the island, now quite invisible in the flying spray. Reluctantly I decided that we would have to carry on with our voyage to Cape Town, 1380 miles away.

After leaving Bouvetoya the weather improved rapidly as we sailed northwards. We saw no more ice, the winds and seas became more moderate, and temperatures rose about 1 °C each day. Soon we were able to work without gloves, and even sleep without bed socks! It was like a different world as soon as we left the 'Furious Fifties' and started to cross the 'Roaring Forties'.

My crew came back to life and took a new interest in the wonderful birds which accompanied us; we were seeing Albatrosses, Grey petrels, White-headed petrels, prions, and Soft-plumaged petrels. It was like being on holiday, and by the time we were half way to Cape Town everything was beginning to dry out. On 17 October there was a severe gale from the north, which rather set us back, but with the sea at 9 °C it did not seem so bad. On the 19th we were becalmed all day and had Wanderers, Black-brows, White-chins and Cape pigeons paddling around the boat looking at, or eating, tit-bits with which we enticed them to come close.

Sunday 20 October

...During the morning Chris put out a trolling line hoping to catch a barracuda or something similar, but straightaway it was pounced upon by one of our attendant White-chinned petrels. He hauled the unfortunate bird aboard while it voiced its indignant disapproval. It had the hook caught in its beak and appeared to be quite unharmed, so we took the opportunity to draw a wing silhouette and weigh the bird for Dr Warham, and then Julia searched its feathers for lice, using a pair of tweezers while I held it. It had a very small patch of white on its chin, but we have noticed that many around here have far more white on them than any we had seen farther west. Both Chris and I suffered numerous punctures in our hands and wrists from his sharp claws, and were careful afterwards to put disinfectant on the affected places...

Chris spent the rest of the morning experimenting with a piece of tin, trying to make a paravane shape which would take his lure down deep, as I objected strongly to his catching any more birds. At one stage we were surrounded by the handsome Great shearwaters, with their distinctive white collars, and we saw our first confirmed Yellow-nosed mollymawk. Most of the afternoon we were becalmed again, and we all changed into lighter clothing. Chris actually sunbathed on the deck in swimming togs, with a turban and sun glasses! I had my shirt off for a while, but still found it rather chilly. Julia spent much time learning to play the penny whistle which Callan had given her at Bird Island, and I could tolerate it because whistling is supposed to bring wind. Sure enough, in the evening a light wind came away from the north-east and we were again on the move.

Bird-watching became very exciting, and on 22 October we saw nineteen different species of sea bird, which is a record for the whole of the *Totorore* expedition.

Wednesday 23 October
...Progress is good, considering the big seas, and we are beginning to 'get the Channels' – that strange feeling of excitement mixed with apprehension which seamen used to feel on their close approach to port after a long voyage. When it was very cold we longed to arrive at Cape Town. Now that we will soon be there we are beginning to feel afraid of it. This is something we have discussed, and we all feel the same.

One of the birds which we see quite regularly here is the Shy mollymawk – so named because apparently it shuns ships, but it does not seem to mind us. It is rather nice to think that those we see probably come from our New Zealand Auckland Islands, although some do breed around Tasmania. In any case, a long way from home, like us!

Friday 25 October
Chris was up early today to see if he could see the land. The wind had gradually decreased during the night and gone back to south-west, so he rigged the twin headsails to keep us moving. There are Portuguese men-o-war, the jellyfish-type animals with little sails, and some smaller creatures also with sails which Chris calls By-the-wind sailors – all sure signs that we are in warmer waters. Soon after 1000 hours we could see a vague shape of land ahead, but it was still far away and it was well into the afternoon before we could pick out the great Table Mountain, partly hidden by cloud, and then the Lion's Head, a conical mountain peak which we had to pass to get into Table Bay.

We contacted the Port Control on the VHF to announce our arrival, and to ask for permission to go to the Royal Cape Yacht Club basin. They gave us the go ahead and said they would arrange Customs and Immigration formalities for us...

As we came closer, we could see the extent of the great city of Cape Town stretching for miles on the flatter land of the coast and all around the mountains, and with the almost sheer rock faces above, it was a colourful and pleasing sight.

The wind came up fresh against us as soon as we rounded Green Point and we had to motor to reach the entrance to the dock area behind a long protecting breakwater...At the end of the dock ahead the masts of hundreds of yachts became visible; it certainly looked rather daunting. We poked our bow inside and found a great complex of pontoons and marinas, all appearing full.

The wind was strong and squally, and it was very hard to know what to do. It was difficult to handle *Totorore* in the narrow channels left between the rows and rows of yachts, and I was scared of getting into a corner from which we could not extricate ourselves. I instructed Chris to have the anchor ready just in case we needed it.

The first attempt was abortive and we narrowly avoided collision with several yachts, and ended up by being blown out again, back into Duncan Dock. Chris said he had seen a vacant marina berth in there, so in we went again and wove our unsteady way towards it. On the way we spotted a larger and more suitable-looking place hard up against a sort of promenade running the length of a long low building, obviously the Club itself, which by this time had its lights on and seemed to be full of people having a party. Somehow we managed to reach that berth, and two men came running down the boarding ramp to take our lines. 'Welcome to the Royal Cape Yacht Club,' said Bobby, the dock superintendent.

Great Shearwater

Chapter Sixteen

Capsize

*Cape Town — At sea — Capsize — Lost mast — Jury mast —
Prince Edward Island — Marion Island*

Our legal entry into Cape Town could not have been easier. A friendly Customs officer came aboard, but it seemed that his visit was mainly to offer helpful advice about the port. We were able to call into the Immigration Department on our way uptown, and I expected some slight difficulty there as none of us had visas for South Africa. It came as a very pleasant surprise when we were told that as members of the crew of a visiting yacht we did not need to have visas, or even a stamp in our passports on arrival or departure. 'We hope you will enjoy your stay in Cape Town,' they told us. How nice if it could be like this the world over!

The Royal Cape Yacht Club marina was already full, but they let us squeeze in, and we joined as temporary members. It is a very big club with excellent facilities, lacking only washing machines or any place where one could wash clothes. Social activites play an important role in the Club, but racing is taken very seriously and we were impressed by the keenness and competence of the members. The day after we arrived, a gale was blowing with winds between 40 and 60 knots, and the race which was to end in Hout Bay, with a champagne breakfast the morning after, was still run as scheduled. Thirty-odd boats started, a most intrepid lot! Before a member can sail as skipper he must obtain his skipper's certificate by passing both a written and a practical examination. Amongst other tasks he must bring his yacht into a marina berth under sail, so obviously a high degree of competence is required. Having now seen something of Cape Town's weather, I can see why.

From the sea, spread around the broad sweep of Table Bay and backed by the dominating massif of Table Mountain, Cape Town has few equals as a city of picturesque splendour. In the yacht club basin we were always conscious of the great mountain looking down on us, and constantly watched it for a sign of the 'table cloth', a covering of cloud which spilled over the edge and came pouring down the side like a liquid — a wonderful spectacle and also a warning of what was to come. It was the forerunner of the 'Cape Doctor', a very strong south-easterly wind which often blew for about three days and cleared the city of smog and dust.

In the magnificently laid out city centre, the winds funnelled down the broad avenues between the skyscrapers and pedestrians held tightly onto special railings and chains to prevent their being blown out into the busy traffic. On board we found the strong winds restricting for our repair work, especially after we had been moved to the 'Globe Wall' where it was cheaper than at a marina, and the grit from a sand-blasting yard covered the whole boat.

We were very fortunate in being in Cape Town when the Whitbread Round the World Race fleet arrived, and we were able to see all those amazing racing machines and their crews, and feel very proud of our New Zealand entries. Their way of sea going was in marked contrast to our own!

Our main purpose in going to Cape Town was to effect repairs, and that took considerably longer than we had expected although we received a tremendous amount of very generous help from members of the Club who took an interest in us and our boat, initiated by Stan Gordge, the Port Captain for the international blue water sailors' 'Slocum Society'. After many enquiries we found that to have *Totorore* lifted out of the water anywhere other than at the Club would be prohibitively expensive on our very limited budget, and as the Club racing boats had priority we had to wait for two weeks. Chris and Julia, who had both been in *Totorore* longer than they had originally intended, were under pressure from their families to return home, but kindly stayed with me long enough to get the repair work well under way. Chris saw to our damaged bow and gunwale and we attended to the bobstay and the bowsprit; we checked all fittings and the rudder and self-steering gear, and cleaned and repainted the antifouling on the bottom. To overcome the problem of the engine's overheating we fitted an additional water inlet lower down on the hull, between the keels.

When *Totorore* was again afloat there were still many jobs to be done to make her ready for another long sea voyage, and in all we were at Cape Town for two months. We did manage a day up Table Mountain, and in an afternoon we climbed to the top of the Lion's Head peak. One weekend some friends took us out to the lovely wine-growing area of Franschoek, giving us a needed break.

After Chris and Julia left to go home I was joined by 20-year-old Paul Scofield, a zoology student from Auckland University, and Christine Hänel, 26, a South African girl who was well used to handling penguins in her work at SANCOB (South African National Foundation for the Conservation of Coastal Birds). She took us out to their rehabilitation centre for oiled Jackass penguins and other sick sea birds, and it was a heart-warming experience. Supported by donations and volunteer labour, with some people donating almost full-time work there, it is an extremely efficient unit with a very high success rate. Thousands of oiled penguins have been saved from a slow death by these dedicated people. We saw the various holding pens with their own pools, the washing rooms and the record books. Every single penguin is treated and recorded individually, all details being noted daily so that progress can be monitored. Some of the birds stay there for months and are released only when they are again fit and strong. After a major oil spill, such as from a tanker stranding, they have a mammoth job on their hands, and although they receive many offers to help, each new assistant has to be patiently taught how to handle the birds and how to force-feed them. We came away from there filled with admiration.

In the last few hectic weeks in Cape Town, Christine's three brothers frequently stopped by to lend a hand, and Paul energetically carried on with painting and other jobs while I worked on my bird reports. Finally, by 21 December we were ready to sail, but were delayed by a south-east gale. The American yacht *Appledore 3* which we had met at Punta Arenas arrived in Cape Town, and I had a brief chat with Herb Smith on the VHF. They were on the last leg of their circumnavigation of the globe, with most of their original crew, and would soon be heading home to Boothbay Harbour, Maine.

We sailed out of Cape Town on Sunday 22 December 1985, bound for New Zealand with brief stops planned at Marion Island in the Prince Edward Islands, which belong to South Africa, at Crozet Islands and Kerguelen Islands which are French, and at Heard and Macquarie Islands, which are Australian. All these sub-Antarctic islands are breeding places for enormous numbers of sea birds, but their avifauna has been well studied and documented by ornithologists of various nations so that there was little new work we could do. In actual fact there was scope for much to be done on the lesser known islands in the Crozets and Kerguelens, but we had been forbidden by Paris to carry out any scientific investigations there and could only hope to glean some useful distributional data in passing. Our most important work was behind us, but continuing at-sea observations for different parts of the ocean at different times of the year can provide valuable information, and we would continue to collect sea bird lice. My main intention was to pass reasonably quickly through the Southern Ocean before the winter set in, as I knew it would be dangerous for any vessel, let alone a small one like *Totorore*, to be there then.

Although he had some coastal yachting experience, Paul had never been offshore, and Christine had no sailing experience of any sort, but they were both keen to learn and were enthusiastic bird-watchers. I thought that if we sailed well south before we turned west, we should avoid the notoriously bad seas south of the Cape, and in theory we should enjoy quite good weather conditions at least as far as Marion Island, which should give my crew a chance to get their sea-legs and become useful crew members.

Christmas Day 1985

A beautiful sunny day with gentle breezes promised a nice peaceful Christmas. We have been at sea for three days of fine weather but my crew still do not have their sea-legs and continue to be just passengers. Christine can't stand it inside so sits or lies on deck all day. She is eating a little now. Paul eats everything I offer but just stays in his bunk reading a book or listening to his tape-recorder with earphones, making weird wailing noises in time to the so-called music, his eyes shut, and probably not aware of the fact that he is emitting such unpleasant sounds. I busied myself with maintenance jobs on deck, taking advantage of the fine weather.

Christine prepared a nice fresh salad, working in the cockpit, and I cooked dinner. Christine was sick before we started eating, and Paul after the first few mouthfuls, so I ate my Christmas dinner myself and enjoyed it, washed down with a glass of good red wine given to us for Christmas by Lynnath Beckley, a lady from the university who would also have liked to come with us. She is an experienced yachtswoman and would have been good crew. Realising that it would be too rich for my queasy crew I had not heated our Christmas pudding, so that can wait for another special occasion.

I had intended to take a reasonably big stock of the excellent and inexpensive South African wine, as I always enjoy a glass just before dinner, having become accustomed to that habit most of our time in Chile, but this time finances would not allow so the bottle given to us by Lynnath is very precious.

Thursday 26 December
...In the afternoon Christine put the trolling line out with a lure. Every now and again she squealed when she thought she had a bite, and then finally she did get one and her excitement was hilarious and infectious. Even Paul left his bunk to help us haul in a fine big yellow-fin tuna. Chris will be jealous when he hears about this...I soon dispatched the fish and cut off its head; Christine filleted it, and I fried it for dinner. Paul was sick on his plate at the table before he started, and Christine was sick out in the cockpit, but she did eat a piece of fish and some fresh salad. I enjoyed mine and cooked it all to help it keep for a day or two, as it is still warm at 20°C...

Sunday 29 December
...Christine is adapting extremely well *outside* and was a big help to me as I struggled to make *Totorore* stop broaching, and run off downwind. The wind increased to gale force in the morning, and she behaved beautifully, but in the afternoon it blew a good Force 10 with very big seas and heavy driving spray. Something went wrong with Ivon and *Totorore* constantly broached. We were both soaked to the skin, but Christine was able to laugh and express admiration for the beauty of the wild sea. To be so appreciative pleased me. If only she can get over her seasickness she will be a good crew as she is quick to learn. Poor Paul stays lying down, even when he eats the meals I cook. He says nothing to anybody and looks miserable. Anyway, nothing I could do seemed to help, so I finally took all sail off, lashed the helm amidships, and let her lie ahull, being thumped and occasionally swept by the big seas. She is lying surprisingly well, considering the conditions, and I am glad to see that the barometer is starting to rise again from its low at 978 millibars...

Monday 30 December
The storm became much worse during the night and we suffered a bad knockdown at about 0100 hours. The crash as a huge wave hit *Totorore* sent many things which we had thought well secured flying across the cabin, and the shock cords holding the vegetable baskets came adrift, spilling fruit and vegetables everywhere. The inevitable oil from under the engine slopped out and mixed with the large volume of water which poured in around the washboard and through the ventilators. All my 'office', my box of papers, letters and photographs, as well as a large filing folder, which normally live happily wedged into the chart table seat while I am in my bunk, or in my bunk when I am up and about, went flying and ended up swilling around in the oily water. What a mess! We set to clear it up, my two sea-sick companions struggling bravely but unsuccessfully to overcome their nausea. We pumped and baled and restowed, stuffing everything we could into plastic bags, and while I picked up all the vegetables from forward, Paul and Christine kindly tried to separate my soggy papers and photographs with dry paper towels. We are all very tired, not having been able to sleep at all, and the violent motion did not help us in our efforts.

The wind was really shrieking, I guessed at least Force 11, but by the time we were reasonably squared up it seemed to be decreasing and I thought the worst was over. The barometer had risen to 989. We flopped back into our bunks which were all wet...

It seemed that we had not been in our bunks very long when the ultimate happened. Another truly enormous crash, and *Totorore* went over and did not stop going. It is so hard to know what is happening exactly with the terrible noise and deluges of water pouring over one's head and the sickening feeling that 'This is it!' She must have been almost upside down, and seemed to right herself very slowly. I struggled out of my bunk and put on a light. The mess was incredible, and water was sloshing everywhere. I saw a very dazed Christine extricating herself from a tangle of sodden clothes and bedding from on top of Paul in his bunk on the port side. To my shocked eyes there seemed to be blood everywhere – a trail above Christine's bunk, across the underside of the coach roof, over to above Paul's bunk. What a pity she had not been using her lee cloth! My fault entirely, I should have insisted on it. I grabbed Christine. 'Where are you hurt!' 'It's my head' she said. I looked at the back of her head and it did seem a gory mess, but parting her hair I thought it was probably only a shallow flesh wound. 'I'll get a plaster,' I said. 'No, no, I am all right. Pass me up that sheet.' She made a huge wad of the wet sheet and held it to her head. 'You attend to the boat.' I could tell from the feel of *Totorore*, and the graunching, grinding noises outside, that the mast was gone.

Paul and I put on our wet-weather gear, fished out our harnesses from the locker, took out the washboard and went outside to have a look. It was quite bright in the moonlight and I saw it all. The mast was in the water, with the lower part broken off at the weld where it had been repaired for us at Falkland Islands a year ago. The radar tower was still up but rather bent, and much of the railing and lifelines were down. The seas were bigger than they were last year when it happened before, and many broke right over the boat. It was hard to know what was safe to hang onto because everything seemed to be moving as the mast heaved with the sea, and the stays and shrouds draped over the deck and coach roof slackened and twanged taut dangerously. It was very cold, so we came back inside to collect tools and put on more clothes. I told Paul to put the kettle on to give us a warming cup of coffee to see us through a long task. He had difficulty in getting the stove to light as everything was so wet.

I knew that to try to retrieve the mast this time would be impossible and far too dangerous. Paul was very frightened, and weakened by seasickness, but he valiantly stayed up with me to keep passing tools as I needed them. I wanted to cut the mast and rigging adrift before it damaged *Totorore* any more, but to save the boom and mainsail which had torn off the mast at the gooseneck, and was still hanging from the radar tower at the after end. In the confusion out there it was difficult to think clearly, but I tried hard to plan the operation carefully to cause the minimum of damage. I knew I had to be quick, and started to systematically cut away the rigging; first the cordage, saving as much as I could, and then the stainless steel wires, using the bolt cutters. I hoped the whole mast would fall out away from *Totorore* but it did not, and cutting the port shrouds was the most dangerous part of all, leaning way down on the low side, trying to cut under the water half the time with nothing solid to hang onto, and the foot of the mast still flailing about above me. 'Please help me to see this job through!' I prayed. Finally it all went over, and I watched anxiously as it careered about under water, praying that it would not puncture the hull. Gradually it disappeared completely from my view, and *Totorore* came round to the seas, the mast and all the rigging acting as a drogue, still fast on board from the end of the bowsprit where the forestays were attached. I had planned to leave it that way as a giant sea-anchor, and apart from dipping her bow heavily into each big sea, *Totorore* was riding more comfortably. However, I could see that the jerking on the bowsprit would be too much for it as there was no longer the support of the stays above it. Cutting that adrift while lying down on the wave-swept bowsprit took quite a long time as I could not get the angle I needed for the bolt cutters to cut the wires. At last they went, and sank out of sight. 'Goodbye, my good friends,' I said aloud.

Freed of the weight forward, *Totorore* leaped about and was soon lying beam on to the sea again, rolling mercilessly. 'Go below,' I told Paul, who was still hanging grimly onto the last bit of secure railing on the coach roof. 'Get some rest.' He had done very well, feeling wretched as he did.

It was daylight already. I stayed up on deck trying to tidy up and secure everything that was left. No too bad. The two forward ventilator cowls were gone, and the midship Dorade box on the coach roof was smashed, but the hull and decks were still sound. The radar tower was twisted but still standing, and the Sat Nav antenna mast was bent over at about 50°, presumably by the weight of water. I could not imagine that either the radar or the Sat Nav would still work. The solar panel was bent at right angles and its box of electrics had gone. Two 20-litre cans, one of diesel, one of kerosene, had gone. What else? I was scared to look too hard. This was a tragedy, and I felt bad for my two companions who had been seasick all the time and now had this happen so early in the proposed voyage. I purposely did not try to think of the consequences yet – there was too much to do. I was feeling guilty and ashamed of myself. Lying ahull had been a mistake – I should have stayed outside and steered her downwind, and perhaps towed warps. But self-recriminations are too late, and negative, so...

Down below Christine had done a terrific job, and Paul was helping her, in spite of frequently stopping to vomit. The increased rolling without the mast to slow her down was most unpleasant, but I assured my crew that without it the likelihood of our being rolled over again was very slight. 'Don't worry,' I said. 'We are safe enough, and still have a sound boat, with plenty of food and water.' To their queries about sending out a distress signal I answered that we were certainly not in any danger to our lives, were not in distress, and in any case the radio was no use as the aerial had gone.

The gale continued all day, with the sea still running very high, so we could not do very much except continue tidying up and clearing off some of the oil which seemed to have got everywhere. Paul remained in his bunk, still very sick, but Christine worked courageously on between her spells of nausea. She has a badly bruised back, not showing on her skin but very painful internally, which is a worry. I do hope she has not suffered an injury to her kidneys or any other organ. Characteristically she is very brave about it, but I see her wince frequently as she moves about. I massaged her back with Transvasin, which she said was a help, and I gave her a thermal body belt to put on. We tried to trace her flight path to see what she could have hit, and were all amazed at how she had passed over the table, between the centre pillar and the forward cabin coaming, and over the oil lamp without breaking the glass chimney.

Meanwhile I have been thinking hard about the next move. Africa is only about 300 miles to the north, Marion about 750 miles south-east. The trouble with Africa is that the south-east coast is notorious for its bad seas due to the Agulhas Current and the fearsome rollers. In our disabled state, and having no charts for it, I ruled it out. We are already in the westerlies and should have a good favourable drift towards Marion Island; with a jury rig – fortunately the small spare jockey pole is still intact – we should be able to reach it without difficulty. I do not wish to use the engine more than we have to, as we may need the fuel for coastal work there, and I may not be able to obtain any more from the South African meteorological station on the island for my ongoing voyage. I told my crew that I would put them ashore at Marion Island, to return to Cape Town in the South African research ship *Agulhas* which we know to be calling there in February. I am thinking that I may be able to improve my jury rig while at Marion – they may have an old aerial mast, or whatever – enough to get to Australia by myself, and have another think about it there.

On New Year's Eve the weather moderated enough for me to work on a jury rig using our 4.3 metre jockey pole, and Christine and Paul helped me to erect it up forward, between the windlass and the forehatch. In the afternoon the sun shone, and in spite of the heavy rolling in the swell, Christine fetched out our wet bedding and clothes to dry, or at least lose some of their mouldering smell. The next day I made a square sail out of an orange vinyl tarpaulin which we had used sometimes when camping. Doubled over, it measured three metres high by two metres across, and I lashed a bamboo spreader along the head and the foot and secured a brace line to each corner.

Wednesday 1 January
...At 1300 hours I set the sail, assisted by Paul who was very enthusiastic as he noticed that as soon as he steered *Totorore* back on course the rolling was much less and he began to feel better. It was good fun. The wind was about eight knots, and we seemed to be sailing at over one knot. Given a bit more breeze we could probably average two knots, and with a knot of current we were well on our way. We were all lighthearted. Paul stayed in the cockpit watching the birds after I had re-tightened the cords on Ivon, and made it work again to steer us towards Marion Island. I was pleased with my jury rig which seemed to function well, and feel that it will certainly get us there...for the first time since we left Cape Town we enjoyed our evening meal, sitting together at the table under our only remaining cabin oil lamp.

Friday 3 January

...Christine and I spent much of the day whipping the ends of many ropes which had to be cut to clear away the mast last Monday, and experimenting to work out an easy reefing system for our new sailing rig. That part was not very successful. Our noon-to-noon run was 27 miles but on course of 077° instead of about 130°, so we shortened our remaining distance by only sixteen miles. Paul seemed to find that depressing, but I said that any distance made good was something to be thankful for, because if we meet a gale from an easterly quarter we will be blown back and lose ground, increasing our distance by the hour.

Saturday 4 January

...The wind came up in the evening from the north-east and we were able to resume sailing. I added a bedsheet to the bamboo along the foot of our orange squaresail to give it extra area right down to the deck, and we were making a good two knots. After our evening meal I lit a pressure lamp and hung it outside, and Paul and I stayed in the cockpit with spotlights to attract prions, some of which we wanted to catch to make positive identifications. There were many about, and time and again we attracted them close to the boat and once I even had one in the hand net, but it escaped...

Sunday 5 January

...We all still feel tired, and I cannot bring myself to think too much about what I am going to do. It just seems challenge enough to get my crew safely to Marion Island, but at the back of my mind is an uneasy thought about the extended time it is going to take me to get home. I will be able to let my family know the circumstances by radio from Marion, so that they will not worry about not hearing from me for a long time after that. Perhaps I should try sending my bird records back from Marion just in case? Just in case what? I don't know, but it is a long way to drift, and how else could I possibly get *Totorore* home again? I don't know how I could get home again myself, for that matter. Poor Marjorie had to scrape the bottom of the bucket to send me money to cover expenses at Cape Town. So – that is it. I must endeavour to sail home. Meanwhile, forget it. Better to think of the jobs that still need to be done to get us to Marion. Christine is good about that – she keeps reminding me of things that we should do 'before the next knockdown'!

Thursday 9 January

...The sea was running high and some big white breakers were chasing us from astern. Jolly good! Still on a course and going like a train! I looked at the sails and all seemed well. They, which includes the bedsheet, are standing up to it, so while they are pulling us along at this good speed I will hang on to them as long as possible. I judge the wind strength about Force 6 to 7, but the barometer, after a slight dip downwards, is going up again. I can't help feeling a little apprehensive about bad weather, not knowing how she is going to behave without the mast. In theory I would think that she will be safer but stiffer, with a quick uncomfortable roll; now lighter without the mast and all the rigging, she will hopefully be less

287

likely to roll over. If she does, perhaps she might roll over and over without the rigging to brake the movement in the water? Who knows? I wonder if very big seas might pitchpole her. But why now if not before? I don't know, but somehow without her mast she seems so naked and vulnerable...

Noon to noon we had sailed an incredible 103 miles! Not bad for a small tarpaulin and a bedsheet!

Sunday 12 January

...At 0700 hours the wind suddenly came away from the south-south-west and freshened rapidly with a rising sea. I braced the sails to make the best course we could, but I know that with the wind on the beam she will be making a great deal of leeway, so we are probably not doing much better than east. The course we want is south-east to Prince Edward, which we have better hope of reaching than Marion if this southerly weather continues.

At noon we had made good 36 miles, leaving us 130 miles to go to Prince Edward, which Paul is longing for. I hope the anchorage is fairly calm for his sake. He is not at all happy at sea. Christine on the other hand is full of busy energy today, bubbling over with excitement when she sees anything unusual, like a Grey-headed mollymawk catching and eating a squid on the surface. When she feels nauseous, which is becoming less often, she lies down for a little while, or sits out on deck, and soon comes right again. She is gradually assuming control of the galley.

Out on deck is noticeably colder, and we both put on socks and boots for the first time, and even wore gloves this afternoon. The air was 8 °C, but it was wet and windy, and we could not resist watching, and trying to photograph, the amazing spectacle of about 30 huge Wandering albatrosses, as well as numerous Grey-headed mollymawks, Yellow-nosed mollymawks, and Sooty albatrosses, all flying around *Totorore*, often sitting on the water in large groups and frequently nibbling at our fishing line.

Monday 13 January

...We were becalmed most of the day, which upset Paul. With less wind there were not many birds. At night after dark we put the pressure lantern outside and used our spotlights to attract them. Christine's excited exclamations when we nearly caught one brought Paul from his bunk and he held the hand net ready...after many attempts he finally caught a prion. It had us puzzled at first, but measurements confirmed that it was a Salvin's prion – not easy to identify with conviction when flying, but we were sure that they had been all around us during the day as they breed on the Prince Edward Islands. We caught a nice collection of lice from him and let him go. I did not take a wing silhouette because I thought that really he had had enough handling, and did not want him to come to any harm.

Tuesday 14 January

Rain and rough sea, with a heavy northerly swell which I did not like the look of for anchoring in Cave Bay at Prince Edward Island. We were surfing along making six knots at times and I watched the sails rather anxiously. I decided to take off the lower sail – the bedsheet – but was just too late and it tore right across from side to side, the remnants flying out and flogging in the wind, like household washing on a line. Both Christine and Paul came forward to help me to lower the sail altogether and secure it, after which we motored the last few hours towards Prince Edward Island. Paul stayed outside, desperately wanting to see land...

There was much kelp around, but we managed to get quite close, well out of the swell and in a reasonably calm sea disturbed only by williwaws with belts of rain. We drifted a while, while I gave my crew further instructions in handling the windlass and anchor before going in for the real thing. At 1445 hours we dropped the anchor close to a colony of Rockhopper penguins chattering noisily from the rocky cliff. We could see Sheathbills – Lesser sheathbills, new birds for me – in attendance, and Giant petrels wheeled overhead occasionally uttering their harsh cries. All around us flew literally thousands of prions, and the vegetated land above the cliffs looked riddled with burrows. What a wonderful, magical place! The rain swirling around, and the seas breaking on the rocks at the foot of the cliffs, gave the perfect atmosphere for such a setting.

Paul and Christine were beside themselves in their appreciation and excitement. Paul is a different chap – alive and full of enthusiasm. He is quite amazed at the wonders of navigation – being able to pick up this small island right ahead after wandering across the vastness of the open sea for 23 days. 'The birds, the birds! Just look at all the birds!' he kept saying...We called the place 'Jury Squeal Cove', because of our rig and the way Christine had squealed with excitement at being there.

Strong winds from the west forced us to move to Cave Bay on the east coast and remain there in the shelter for a whole day. Prince Edward Island is one of the few islands in the whole of the sub-Antarctic region which is still in its pristine state. The Department of Nature and Environmental Conservation, in Pretoria, had turned down our application for a permit to land, and we felt glad that its sanctuary is being well protected. It was a pleasure just to look at it, and admire the green rolling hills, red cliffs, lava scree slopes, and an impressive cave behind a beach which was full of King penguins. At night we used lights to attract birds aboard, from which we took lice.

Thursday 16 January
We passed high steep cliffs covered with Yellow-nosed mollymawks on their nests, with hundreds wheeling around above, and saw wide grassy plains with Wandering albatrosses on nests scattered around looking like sheep on a farm. The wind was freshening and the sea building up, so that the big rock stacks offshore were drenched by high-flung spray. The swells became mountainous as we plugged our way around the western end of the island and set off to motor the sixteen or so miles to Transvaal Cove on Marion Island against a west-south-west gale.

...South Africa maintains a meteorological station at Transvaal Cove, and when we rounded the next point we could see it. The size of it amazed us – there seemed to be about twenty buildings, all rather ugly in their aluminium colour and stretching from a black rock promontory on which we could see a crane, well up the grassy slopes towards the hills. There were tanks and aerial masts, and we could distinguish the big meteorological balloon shed and the dome of the tracking radar.

The approaches to the so-called cove were covered with thick kelp, and we looked in vain for a passage through it...

We anchored in three fathoms of water after ploughing our way through thick kelp to a position close to the big rock on which the crane stood. As soon as all was secure, Christine threw her arms around me, saying 'We made it! We made it! Oh thank you!' You would have thought we had been away at sea for months!

Most of the team of nine young men were on the rock, waving to us and calling cheery greetings. We rowed ashore and landed on the boulder beach, but we all had boots full of water and wet trousers before we made it to the higher ground. There they met us with bottles of champagne and corks popping. It was a great welcome! We were led up to the accommodation block which consisted of long shed-like buildings, joined and interconnected at the ends, with comfortable sleeping accommodation for about 60 people... Their leader, Marius, told us that we could make ourselves at home, and that they would do everything they could to help us. Paul and Christine could temporarily join the team and stay until the *Agulhas* came with the changeover team in May – not February as we had thought.

They told us that they had had a very bad storm with mighty seas on the night on which we lost our mast. Wind speeds to 90 knots were recorded, and the sea was breaking right up to the crane on top of the rock. Heavy spray and kelp were flung at the buildings and several kilometres of Rockhopper colony on the cliffy coast were washed right out, and most of the chicks perished.

Christine and Paul moved ashore, and the South African Government generously confirmed by radio that my crew would be accepted as shipwrecked mariners and returned to Cape Town without any charge. Furthermore, they extended my permit to stay at Marion Island from ten days to a month to allow me to improve the jury rig with whatever help the team could offer.

To facilitate landings from *Totorore*, the team lowered an aluminium ladder down to the bottom of the eleven-metre promontory on which the crane stood, so that we could climb from the dinghy onto a ledge and then use a rope which hung down from the top to ascend the rest of the way. We laid out a stern line so that we could keep *Totorore* close to the rock and haul the dinghy across by it as we had done at Bird Island. There were several Orcas patrolling the island's beaches almost daily, and the first time I saw a big male, with his fin sticking up almost two metres, heading to pass between *Totorore* and the rock, I wondered what on earth would happen when his fin hit our stern line! I need not have worried, as the intelligent monster skilfully ducked underneath and came up the other side without having touched it.

I soon learnt that the Orcas played an important part in the lives of the young men on the island, and in ours too while we were there. Two of the nine men, Peter and Anton, were marine biologists and included them in their studies of the other mammals, but the rest, who were meteorologists and support staff, took a keen

interest too. If anybody saw an Orca – and they kept a very good lookout for them
– a great shout went up. As many as could rushed down to the rock to watch, and
Peter in his wetsuit took a flying leap off the rock into the water and then climbed
into the cage which they had suspended from the crane, with its top just awash.
Usually the Orca, or family of Orcas, would pass close to the cage to have a look
at Peter, who was watching them. At that time they did not have an underwater
camera so I lent them mine, but they had some excellent photographs taken from
above the water.

Marion is a beautiful island, teeming with wildlife, and Christine and Paul were
both very happy to be there which made me feel better about having got them into
that unforeseen situation. It is about fourteen miles long east to west, and nine miles
north to south, with rocky cliffs all around its shores, some of which, especially
on the south and west coasts, are very high. Volcanic mountains, still mildly active,
rise to over 1100 metres, and there is a permanent icecap on the central plateau.

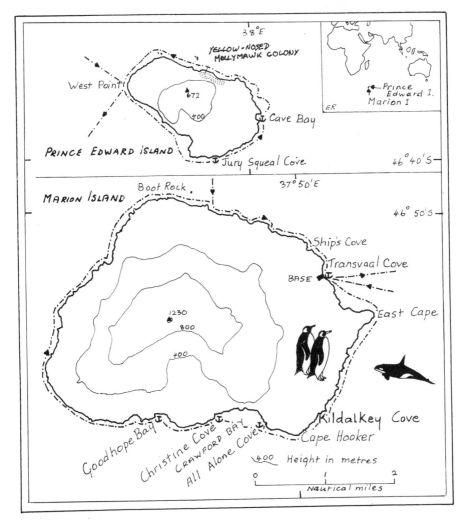

Map 25

Grass-covered coastal plains sport numerous red volcanic cones. Wandering albatrosses were scattered over the plains, incubating eggs while I was there, and King, Gentoo, Macaroni and Rockhopper penguins were all looking after their chicks. Feral cats were everywhere a menace to the smaller petrels, but there were still large numbers of both Sooty albatrosses and Light-mantled sooty albatrosses on the cliffs, and a good colony of Grey-headed mollymawks, as well as White-chinned petrels, Giant petrels, prions and many others. Skuas and Sheathbills were always to be seen near the penguin colonies, and many Skuas lived permanently close to the kitchen at the base where they had to be discouraged from coming inside looking for scraps.

I did manage to go for a few walks on this delightful island, but never dared to go far away from *Totorore* because of the uncertainty of the weather. Gales were frequent and often severe, and whenever the wind came from the north, or anywhere east, I had to move her to a safer place, away from the dangerous lee shore. On my own that was never an easy undertaking, because of the thick kelp which tangled with the anchor chain and both anchors and threatened to foul the propeller at a critical time.

On one occasion I was caught ashore when the wind came in suddenly from the north-east, bringing a nasty sea with it and making launching the dinghy off the rock ledge and returning to *Totorore* a hazardous and nerve-racking operation, which came close to costing me my life. I had asked Munnik, the diesel engineer, to assist me, and I know I could not have managed on my own. As it was, the dinghy with me in it was thrown almost vertically against the cliff wall three times, and I still cannot understand how I stayed in it, but I made it safely to *Totorore*. Munnik cast off the stern line, almost being swept off the rock himself while he did it, and I had the usual traumatic anchor-weighing and departure. Finally we were clear of the kelp, and in a rough sea motored off down the coast, thankful to be safely away.

Tuesday 28 January
... The rain was torrential and very cold as I tried to see ahead to find a way into a tiny cove just inside Crawford Bay. It was very spectacular with high black lava cliffs all around, covered with countless thousands of Rockhoppers, as was the surface of the cove itself, where they looked like kelp. I dropped the tandem anchors in the centre of the cove in twelve fathoms, giving her all 40 fathoms of chain. By the time the anchors grabbed we were half way out of the cove again, but she seemed safe, and in spite of the swell which still rolled in, lay comfortably enough. There is not a lot of swinging room, but I am hoping that the backwash off the rocks will keep her away from them. Squalls tear down over the cliffs but *Totorore* is more demure than she used to be with a full mast and rigging, so it is not too serious. I could not get inside fast enough to shed my cold wet clothes and put on something dry. Writing up the logbook and feeling rather lonely, I called the cove All Alone...

Wednesday 29 January
...I feel like a man returned from the dead. It is now about two o'clock in the morning, and I have just survived a most terrible experience – terrible,

and yet wonderful. I just can't stop thanking God once again for my deliverance...At the moment we are in a gale. We are about half a mile off the coast and I am drifting away in *Totorore*. The anchor is still hanging out with about fifteen fathoms of chain...

Around midnight the sea built up rapidly and came rolling in, starting to break. I knew I had to get out fast. I tried to weigh anchor. I had the engine running, but it was very, very difficult. The weight was terrific. The wind came up with tremendous force – hurricane force – in enormous squalls in very rapid succession. The water was absolutely white spray, flung high, high up into the air in these terrible williwaws which came down from the cliffs up above. But mostly it was blowing right into the cove. I was scared and I prayed loudly. I struggled hard, trying to get the anchor up, running aft, attending to the engine and to the rudder, lashing the tiller...

We were in about ten fathoms, but when I had the main anchor up to five fathoms the small anchor was still catching on something with a terrible jerk and I just could not get it clear. I tried to motor ahead, motoring fast, hard. But I could not, she would not come. And then the wind caught her again and she started to head back fast into the tiny cove. I rushed aft, but just as I got there the engine stalled. It stopped. Oh God! What a time to happen! I didn't know what to do. I went quickly forward again to pay out more cable, hoping the anchor would hold. She started to pull up, and then there was a terrible crash and she hit the first big rock! The sea lifted her right up on top of it, and then I thought she was going to turn over because she went over on her side with another terrible crash on the keels. The next wave lifted her and she was over that rock, and hit on the other side on the shore itself. I really thought it was the end of the expedition, the end of *Totorore*, the end of me. Even had I got ashore, there were big black cliffs up above...

She was washing back again in the waves and I went down below and at last managed to start the engine. The propeller was all tangled in the kelp and there was an awful clatter. I think I might have picked up my chain. I tore the lid off the engine box and the actual shaft coupling had not broken. I grabbed hold of the tiller and I gave her as much throttle as I dared. She hit again when I was running straight back onto the rock offshore. I had no option – there was nothing else I could do! She hit again and then she bounced over the top of it. The rock showed at times three metres out of the water; the seas were terrible, they were breaking right over the top of the rock and right over the boat. And somehow she got over it – she got over it!! She was dragging this great length of chain and anchor – twenty fathoms – I hardly dared pray that I could be saved...

Once outside I kept the engine going and tried to wind up the anchor in case it should foul and snub us around again onto those awful rocks...I don't know how much is still out...we are in deep water and we are drifting off, the wind blowing us along the coast. I just can't imagine what the damage might be underneath. The rudder seems all right. I haven't even had a chance to look at the self-steering. The keels took a terrible hammering...

Two days passed before the sea conditions allowed me to motor *Totorore* back to Transvaal Cove from about 40 miles away.

The nine South Africans at the base were of that special breed of resourceful young people who man those small isolated bases on sub-Antarctic islands and were a happy lot, living in harmony with each other and with nature all around them. The base at Marion Island was extensive and complex; in addition to full meteorological equipment there were numerous large laboratories for use by scientists of a wide range of other disciplines. The spacious accommodation was apparently full for several weeks during the normal team's changeover period. As well as the laboratories there were good workshop facilities, and luckily for me they had welding equipment. Anton Hunt, one of the biologists, made me up a beautiful bipod mast of 50 mm water pipe standing 4.9 metres high at the apex. Plates on its feet fitted around lifeline stanchion sockets, and a wire jackstay down to the windlass bed held it down. It did not need shrouds, and stainless steel forestays and backstays were secured with bulldog grips, tightened by the original rigging screws. Paul and some of the lads helped me to erect it, and we were all proud of it.

Meanwhile Christine had been busy making me a fine big sail from a discarded tent, and painted a female Killer whale on it, while Peter Bartlett, the other biologist, painted a male on our original orange sail which Christine had repaired and strengthened for me. Sometimes they were distracted from their artistic efforts by Rockhopper penguins which lived all around and underneath the shed; these often came inside and walked across the sails they were painting. Brian, the radio technician, cleaned and serviced my electrical and electronic gear and put it all back in working order. We were particularly impressed by the Furuno radar because it still worked even though its whole scanner had been right under water several times. He cleaned and sprayed the contacts, and it was as good as new.

With such good company and hospitality, my stay at Marion Island was a happy one but the many repair jobs all took time and I was rather concerned about the prospect of still being in the Southern Ocean in the more dangerous winter season. To repay the team for their generosity and assistance all I could think of was to take them for a sail. They had all looked across the channel and seen Prince Edward Island looking rugged and mysterious and very much wanted to see it from close up. Of course nobody, even the biologists, had a permit to land, so all we could do was circumnavigate the island and admire its beauty from offshore. Seeing the great colony of Yellow-nosed mollymawks, which do not breed on Marion Island, was the highlight of each of the two trips I had to make to take everybody.

On another day I took Anton and Peter, the biologists, for a circumnavigation of Marion Island itself as they particularly wanted to see the seals on beaches which were inaccessible from the land. With us came Marius Bezuidenhout, the leader, and Marius Marais, known as M2. Both had drawn lots for the privilege. In Kildalkey Cove on the south-east coast, where we had poked in to look at a huge colony of King penguins and an even more vast colony of Macaronis, we were entertained by six Orcas which seemed to play just for our benefit, the two calves 'standing' on their heads with their tails out of the water. The weather deteriorated rapidly as the day wore on, and we sheltered for a while in Goodhope Bay before tackling the west coast, and then back along the north coast.

By the time we arrived at Transvaal Cove the wind was 40 knots, gusting to 60. I tried to bring Totorore close enough to the landing rock to find a lee in which to disembark my passengers, but although the rest of the gang were up there

We thought that John must have had his tongue in his cheek when he asked us to count this lot. King penguins at St Andrews Bay.

We are among the few people to have ever landed on this island. Chris and Julia, Vindication Island, South Sandwich.

We meet the pack ice. The horizon was all lumpy, and the sea and swell were damped down considerably. It was an exciting moment.

'It was a pleasure to watch the snow petrels on their nests from close up.'

Antarctic fulmar. This was the first time we had seen them nesting (Vindication Island). *Jim Watt*

Adélies, engaging little penguins completely unafraid of us.

Conditions became hectic and frighteningly unpleasant.

'It is the most remote piece of land in the whole world.' Bouvetoya.

'We could see the extent of the great city of Cape Town. It was a colourful and pleasing sight.'

Drying out and restoring order after the chaos.
Paul Scofield and Christine Hänel.

Macaroni welcoming party on top of the
landing rock at Transvaal Cove.

'We've made it!' After anchoring in the kelp at Transvaal Cove, we rowed ashore. Paul, Gerry
and Christine. *Anton Hunt*

Proud mother with baby. Grey-headed mollymawk, Marion Island. *Anton Hunt*

The Light-mantled sooty albatross has a loud and haunting cry which echoes around the cliffs.

Anton Hunt gets to know one of his young friends.

Leaving Marion Island. *Anton Hunt*

Anse du Volage. A perfect anchorage.

'My chances of survival are becoming almost negligible.'

Wearing our yellow quarantine flag, we cross Gage Roads as a huge yacht sailed out past us. Later I learnt that she was one of our Kiwi 12 metre yachts.

standing by with spotlights to assist, it was just too dangerous so we moved back outside the kelp and anchored, much to the disappointment of Marius B. who was seasick and longing to get ashore.

Monday 10 February
...Five of us on board was a real squash, as we all had wet gear. After I was sure that the anchor was not dragging I made everybody coffee then helped by Peter cooked a good big dinner, while Marius 1 and 2 and Anton curled up where they could and slept...By about 2300 hours I had all four of them bedded down reasonably comfortably, and said I would keep anchor watch to check on our position and watch the wind for any change...It was steady at 60 knots, but luckily straight offshore.

Tuesday 11 February
Soon after midnight the wind had definitely eased to a mere gale. We seemed safe enough, so I fetched out a sleeping mat and lay down to sleep on the cabin sole, next to the table, having mopped up some of the wetness...At 0600 hours the wind had dropped to 30 knots but the barometer was still low. Thinking I had better get the crew ashore in case it became worse, we weighed anchor and moved in very close...

Peter asked Munnik to lower the cage down on the crane, on the beach side of the cliff where the breakers were less fearsome. Christine, ever attentive and helpful, was right there to direct Munnik who could not see the dinghy. He kept the cage just above the swells; using the engine, I took *Totorore* to the end of the chain, close to the rock, and Anton, watching to avoid the biggest breakers, rowed the crew to the cage one at a time. They clambered up the big mesh on the side and Munnik quickly hoisted them to safety...

Before we left Marion Island, Marjorie urged me by telegram to head direct for Fremantle, where Jim Watt would be able to meet us and help get *Totorore* re-rigged. It was still summer, when easterly winds prevail at Fremantle, and I knew that with a rig which could only take us downwind we would never get there. Our only chance of reaching New Zealand lay in our staying well south in the belt of westerly winds. By way of 'stepping stones' from which I could hope to send messages home, we would still call at Iles Crozet, Iles Kerguelen and Macquarie Island, all close to the Antarctic Convergence and thus of ornithological importance, so that I could continue with the work for which the *Totorore* Expedition had been planned.

We were delayed for another two days by storm-force winds gusting to 90 knots, again fortunately from off the land so that we were able to ride it out just outside the kelp at Transvaal Cove.

The team gave me a good send-off on the night before I left. Marius B had cooked a special trifle, which he knew I liked, and Marius M made a big pizza that I could take with me. I was given many good photographs, and bottles of wine from their personal stores, while Anton presented me with a beautiful wooden plaque, carved by himself in the shape of Marion Island and with a big Killer whale on it. It bore a copper plate engraved 'To Gerry, from Marion 42', which was the designation for that particular team. Christine gave me five films, which was very generous of her as she still had several months left to stay on the island, and I was grateful because I had none left at all. Paul kindly and helpfully gave me almost new wet-weather gear, as my own was worn out.

Sunday 16 February

...I rowed back to *Totorore*, lifted, deflated and stowed the dinghy, stowed away the stern line which Paul cast off, and heard the whole team singing 'For he's a jolly good fellow'. I was moved almost to tears and glad that I was far enough away so that they could not see. There was a break in my voice as I shouted 'Thank you'.

It took me a while to wind up my 40 fathoms of chain, having to keep stopping to hack away the kelp, and when all was ready I was quite a long way offshore. I hoisted the orange sail with its Killer whale on both sides, and then motored back through the kelp to pass very close to the point where all eleven of the team, now including Paul and Christine, were waiting, watching and cheering. Anton fired some Very lights as I turned short round to pass extremely close again, and I blew three blasts on my foghorn. 'Good luck, Gerry!' they all shouted, waving. It was a terrific, heart-warming send-off.

At last I was on my way, headed for Crozet Islands, one month to the day since we arrived. I waved until I could see my friends no more, but was filled with mixed emotions. What a fine bunch of chaps, and what good friends they had been. And yet I was also glad to be on my way home 'Más aventuras!' More adventures!

Yes indeed. New horizons, new islands, new people. I wondered what new adventures lay in store for me.

Rockhopper

Chapter Seventeen

Jury Rig

At sea — Îles Crozet — Îles Kerguelen — Heard Island

Thursday 20 February
Today there is thick fog and few birds to be seen. It is fascinating to watch the big seas suddenly appear, with tumbling crests, rushing at us from out of the fog. Sometimes they hit with a fearful thump and a big splash, but most of the time *Totorore* lifts to them with a sudden lurch, and they go hissing past to disappear back into the fog away to starboard. As there is nothing around here to hit — at least I hope there isn't — I rather like the fog. It shuts us into the tiny world of our immediate surroundings and the sunlight which filters through is of a strange and unreal colour. It all seems rather intimate and cosy.

I expect that is enhanced by the warm temperature today. Both air and sea are nearly 10°, which is exceptional. We are sailing well, with a northerly wind on the beam, and I watch the big Killer whale on the khaki-green sail pulling us steadily onwards into the mysterious fog-veiled beyond.

Friday 21 February
. . . I am trying to maintain the niceties of life, and for my evening meal I sit at the saloon table by the warm and gentle light of the kerosene lamp. Such was our custom previously, whenever the weather was not too violent, or seasickness did not prevent one or both of my crew from sitting up to enjoy the meal. Now I take up my glass of wine from the swinging tray in the centre of the table. 'Salud,' I say, and remember all the various people who have sat opposite and next to me. Often somebody used to add, 'Here's to a fine day tomorrow,' or 'Here's to less ice.'

Now I am all alone, but *Totorore* is still pushing on — still on expedition! This is not what I had planned at all! I can hear Tchaikovsky's Nutcracker Suite, and it transforms this little cabin into a different world, making it hard to believe that outside is cold and wet. . . the music makes me sentimental, and I dwell on thoughts of my loved ones at home. I keep thinking especially of my youngest daughter, Penelope. It is this month that her second baby is due, and I pray that all may go well for her. Is it, or will it be, a boy or a girl? It will still be a long time before I hear. I can only hope that I can send a message from Crozet Islands to let them know how I am progressing. Enough of this, I must do the dishes! Bah! It is funny how it always seems to be my turn to do the dishes these days!

Sunday 23 February
... While working I kept hearing my King penguin friend calling, so I thought I would play a little game with him. I fetched out my tape-recorder, and played the sound of a small colony of Kings at South Georgia. His response was immediate and he and two others appeared close alongside. They were very excited and swam around the boat under water, surfacing briefly... When I tried a tape of a big colony, their response was equally immediate but quite opposite. They all dived down out of sight and far away! Later, I heard them calling again without being able to spot them, so once again I tried the sound of the small colony and sure enough back they came!

Îles Crozet, to which we were heading, are volcanic islands in two groups about 55 miles apart. The western group, which we would come to first, consists of Les Apôtres to the north, Île aux Cochons in the centre, and Île des Pingouins in the south. The eastern group has the two largest islands, Île de la Possession, site of the French base and the only inhabited island, and Île de l'Est. Our expedition had been forbidden to carry out scientific work on French islands, but I thought that merely looking as we passed by could hardly be construed as doing scientific work. Île des Pingouins, which is considered inaccessible, had been one of my original goals, but in the interim had been visited by the French in a helicopter. Les Apôtres, as far as I knew, had never been visited by an ornithologist, so it was there that I directed our course.

I had been seeing ever-increasing numbers of Black-browed mollymawks which rather puzzled me, because their nearest known breeding places were South Georgia and Kerguelen Islands. They were definitely not breeding on the Prince Edward Islands, but it seemed to me highly likely that there might be a colony as yet undiscovered breeding on Îles Crozet. If I could discover that, I felt it would be

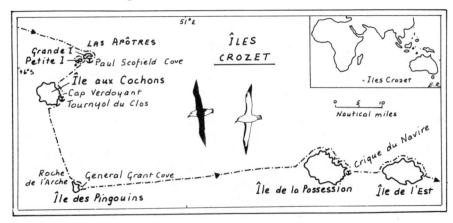

Map 26

298

a real plum for the *Totorore* Expedition, and prove that even in our disabled state we could still do useful work.

For the first five days out of Marion we did very well, averaging about 3.2 knots, but then followed two days of light winds and calms. At noon on Sunday 23 February we had 88 miles to go to Les Apôtres. After three days of easterly winds we had lost ground, and had 153 miles to go! That knocked our average speed back, so by the time we arrived at Les Apôtres on 1 March, our average speed for the 712-mile voyage was only 2.3 knots.

Saturday 1 March

It is evening now and I have just had one of the most fabulous days of the whole expedition. The only thing wrong with it was that there was nobody to share it with me. . .this group of Apostles is perhaps the most exciting, the most incredible, of all the islands that I have ever visited. And my wish to find some Black-brows nesting was fulfilled! I have actually found a colony here on this Grande Île and also a smaller one on Petite Île.

I have spent the whole day wandering around through little narrow gaps between the rocks, surveying the incredible coast, which is mainly steep cliffs with great big caves. There is beautiful tussock up there – tussock such as I never saw on Marion Island. It is absolutely teeming with life! Mostly of course it is covered with Macaroni penguins, but there are cormorants and gulls, and Sheathbills; higher up on the ledges are enormous numbers of Yellow-nosed mollymawks and of course my Blackbrows. . .I have no doubt there are burrows galore! I have never seen such a dense concentration of prions. They are literally black on the water and black in the air above. Millions of them, so closely packed together. A wonderful sight! I think they are probably Salvin's prions. There are lots of Diving petrels flying around too. I have seen a few terns – not very many though, and of course the ubiquitous Giant petrels. High up on top of the island there are obviously lots of Wanderers. . .

I am hoping for a quiet and peaceful night. I need a good sleep after last night. I think I will call this place Paul Scofield Cove, because I'm sure he would have revelled in it just as I am doing. . .

In thick fog in the morning we motored across to Île aux Cochons, which was much more like Marion Island. Near the north-east coast we found ourselves among breakers over submerged rocks and had to cautiously retreat. Farther south the fog thinned and I could see a mile-long black beach densely packed with King penguins which extended up into the hills in the largest colony I had ever seen.

Sunday 2 March

. . .Finally we arrived at Cap Verdoyant, a high but narrow rocky cape with cliffs and caves, protecting a tiny cove named Tournyol du Clos. To the south a spit of black rock projected well out to sea, effectively guarding the cove from the southerly swell, and a large rock half closed the entrance. Ideal! I anchored in the centre of the cove in 2½ fathoms and could hardly believe my luck, it was so still. I pumped up the dinghy and headed for the beach, where I landed among a crowd of freshly moulted and now extremely handsome King penguins, and some Gentoos, which were unconcerned at my approach.

The fog banks came and went, and I had brief views of the red conical hills with lush green plains littered with jagged lava outcrops, complete with incubating Wanderers and Giant petrels. The vegetation was thick in places, but never more than knee height, and easy to walk on if one avoided the yellow grass which is usually the sign of a bog. I found the camp which no doubt had been used by the French biologists about ten years ago. They certainly did not allow themselves much luxury. There were about twelve wooden crates, each about two metres square and 1.5 metres high, in two rows, the space between them forming a passageway. Boards had been taken from the sides facing into the passage, to give access to these 'rooms'; the wood that had been removed was used to cover up the passage. The whole structure had been nailed together, well roped down, and previously had been covered with plastic sheeting.

Inside, many of the occupants had striven for a little more comfort by sticking plastic tape over the cracks between the boards. There was a box full of rusting tins of food, and outside there were still about forty full bottles of wine, both red and white. The labels had nearly disappeared. I must admit that I was tempted to sample one, although I wondered about the effect of their lying exposed to the sun all these years. Anyway, they were not my property and it seemed wrong to help myself; I left them for any possible future French expedition which might occupy the camp.

At about 1400 hours we left the cove and with the wind freshening to Force 5 to 6 we sailed down the coast, heading out towards Île des Pingouins, about twenty miles away.

...It was late afternoon when we arrived off the island and had a quick look at its rugged west coast and then rounded the massive fortress-like Roche de l'Arche, off its northern end. This had huge vertical columns and caves, an arch right through, and a weirdly sculptured top. A narrow waterfilled chasm separated it from the main island. Around about, the sea and swell were confused and toppling, and where I thought I could find a bit of lee behind it, there were fierce williwaws and the sea was just as bad.

The sun set and I was losing the light, but I soon found the colony of Yellow-nosed mollymawks, and of course hordes of penguins. I was most impressed by the island which had an extremely rugged dignity and consisted mainly of a long narrow ridge well over 350 metres high, barren and rocky on the top, but falling away to dense green vegetation covering almost vertical deeply gorged faces, right down to bare rock cliffs at the bottom. I could see scattered small colonies of Black-brows up in the tussock, and the air was full of Mollymawks of all sorts, White-chinned petrels, Kerguelen petrels, and prions, all ready to go ashore. I fell in love with the place at sight.

Already I had seen a good landing place where penguins went ashore...the supposed inaccessibility of the island was just not true at all...

Outside, the wind was a fresh northerly and the barometer was falling. We could be in for another easterly blow. Discretion being the better part of valour, I decided we would be safer at sea! Reluctantly I headed out into the night, motoring for three miles to clear the offshore rocks, then hoisting the little tri-sail. It was all very frustrating! If only I had had Chris and Julia with me – what a plum we could have made of these wonderful islands, and wouldn't Alan Cowan and Peter Harrison have loved them! It would have been well worth spending several days on each! To have read about them for years and then to just pass them by with such a brief look from offshore seemed very painful!

A day of calms, then a day of south-west gale took us to mountainous Île de la Possession, where I skirted close along the north coast, probing into the bays and marvelling at the glorious scenery.

Tuesday 4 March

...As we rounded the easternmost point of the island I suddenly saw the ugly collection of buildings, larger than I had expected, right on the top of the ridge to the south of the cove. The cove itself is in a valley between steepish green hills, and on the beach and in that valley is a very large colony of King penguins. Right in the middle of the colony stand several large and environmentally disgusting sheds, together with some tanks. So this was Crique du Navire! It looked very different from when Bill Tilman visited in *Mischief* in 1960 before the French had established a scientific station here. I could see a number of men on the beach, so I anchored, pumped up the dinghy and hastily stuffed a towel and washing things into a pack.

Many willing hands helped me haul the dinghy up through the small surf and secure it to a large post. Then the doctor, who spoke reasonable English, introduced himself, and also the khaki-clothed, black-bearded 'Chef de District', who was wearing a Russian-looking hat. The Chef did not speak English. The doctor said 'Welcome to Crozet Islands!' but I was soon to learn that he did not really mean it.

I was conducted to one of the sheds, which had inside a few spartan comforts in the way of chairs and a table. There I was given a paper cup of black coffee while the Chef looked at my papers. Then the doctor told me that they had received a radio message from Marion that I was coming, so had advised Paris, which was the normal procedure. They did not know that I would be alone. Paris sent back a message saying that 'we' were not to be allowed to land on the Crozet Islands! The doctor and the Chef were very apologetic, and indeed embarassed. They said, 'This is politics, this is not French hospitality! We are very sorry!' Then they asked if there was anything I needed, and I said, 'Yes, a hot shower!' Again they were sorry. I was allowed no farther than the beach! I could not even go up to the base! However they did say they could send a telegram home for me, provided that it was short, and would advise Marion Island, through Kerguelen, that I had arrived safely.

...I returned aboard to a lonely dinner of my own cooking, washed down with good South African wine, and really couldn't help laughing...I was not upset, but I did wonder about my reception. It could have been that Paris remembered that two years before they had refused to give *Totorore* permission to work in the islands, although now being on my own I hardly posed a threat to their scientists! On the other hand, it could have been our New Zealand flag, and the strained relationship between our governments following the Greenpeace and *Rainbow Warrior* incidents.

In the morning when the weather eased I went to the beach again to meet the friendly doctor and fill in various health forms, plus one to say we had no rats on board. He very kindly gave me three small loaves of good French bread. On my return a call came over the VHF. Would I please go to the beach again as there was another paper to sign? It was a note to say that I owed the Government of France the sum of ninety francs for the telegram I had asked to be sent.

All the time we were at Crique du Navire the King penguins were swimming splashily around *Totorore*, beating a tattoo on the hull with their beaks. I had never known them to do that before. Could it be because they were French? Perhaps it was just that they could see their reflections on the wet hull.

As we left Île de la Possession, the radio operator, whom of course I had not met, called me on the V.H.F. to wish me 'Bon voyage. Good luck and have courage!' which I thought was very friendly of him, and made me feel better about the place. There is no doubt about it, ordinary people – with the possible exception of some politicians – are nice the world over. C'est la vie!

Thursday 6 March
...I waved goodbye to the Crozets and set course for Kerguelen. I have enjoyed my brief look at these remarkably attractive islands, even if it is a rather windy place. Records show that the wind reaches a speed of 70 knots on about a quarter of all the days in the year. Marion was like that, and at Kerguelen the winds reach gale force on average every day! As Julia would say, 'Hmmm!'

It blew a Force 9 gale that very night and broke the batten in the sail, which I had to take down in a hurry. Normally I take it off for safety in winds of that strength, but that one came up very quickly. I found that in ordinary gale conditions I could reef the orange sail down to half size, which kept us moving, although not very fast.

Kerguelen is the largest island in the South Indian Ocean, irregularly shaped and with major peninsulas joined to the main part of the island by extremely narrow isthmuses. Mountains, valleys and lakes cover most of the island, and several peaks rise to over 1000 metres with one reaching 1960 metres. There are some extensive ice sheets with glaciers flowing from them, mainly in the west of the island, and the whole island is deeply indented by fjords and bays. Clustered around it are about 300 smaller islands and islets, which although not large in area are of considerable botanical and zoological importance because they are mostly free of introduced rabbits, cats and rats, which infest the main island. To give an idea of the size of the whole group, to sail right around the outside would involve a distance of about 250 miles. The base at Port aux Français, where the French maintain a large scientific station, is in Baie du Morbihan, on the eastern side. Because of the almost constant heavy swell and strong winds, the waves around the outer coasts often

302

build up to horrendous proportions, but calm water can usually be found in the many deep inlets where, however, severe williwaws can often be expected.

On arrival at Kerguelen on 16 March, exactly four weeks after leaving Marion, I was extraordinarily lucky in that the weather allowed me to have a good look at the normally wild west coast. To my untrained eye, the rock formations and general topography all looked remarkably like Southern Chile, and I felt quite at home exploring the bays and going close up to glaciers. On the first night I stopped in a well sheltered anchorage tucked in behind Île de l'Ouest and named Port Curieuse.

Sunday 16 March

...It is so quiet here than I can hear my chronometer ticking – I can't remember when I last noticed that! It's like an old grandfather clock in an empty house. It has been a surprisingly good passage from Ile de l'Est in Crozet: nine days and twenty hours – much better than I had expected. An average speed of 3 knots.

I have no idea what lies ahead of me when I arrive at Port aux Français. It is probable that I will be told I cannot land or go anywhere in

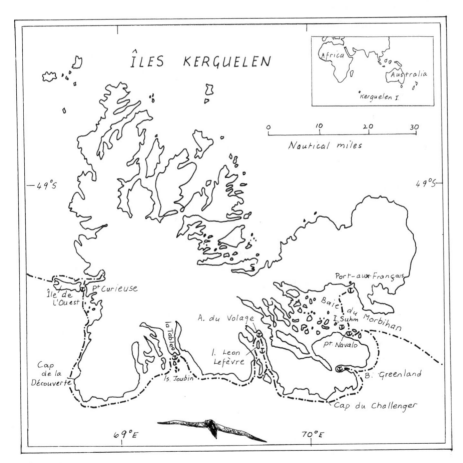

Map 27

303

Kerguelen, so that is why I am having a good look now before I make myself known...

Monday 17 March

...I had no idea that Kerguelen was such a superlatively beautiful place. I could not take my eyes off the everchanging scene of majestic beauty as we made our way south, close to the coast. Sheer cliffs, mighty columns, gaping caves, green valleys speckled with albatrosses, yellow sandy beaches dotted with penguins, and high above, mighty peaks poking up out of the icy slopes from which melt streams sent great waterfalls cascading towards the sea. In one place, just south of Cap de la Découverte, I was surprised to see enormous gouts of steam issuing from a mountain slope. I had not known there was still any visible subterranean activity on the island...

The rain cleared enough for me to see the gap north of the Joubin Islands that I had been looking for. The only trouble was that it was not the gap that it appeared to be on the chart, but after many frights somehow we found our way into the cove, seemingly out of the weather. It was like a millpond, but with a deal of kelp in it and very shallow at only two fathoms, but the anchor took a good hold, and I feel safe...

I was both amazed and amused, when I filled my sink with salt water to wash the dishes, to see dozens of little creatures swimming wildly round and round. They were like sea lice about a centimetre long, and they kept doubling up heads to tails. I hadn't the heart to put detergent in the water, so kept pumping it out until I could get a sink full of water without any in it!

Tuesday 18 March

...Five of the dear little Commersons dolphins, the first I had seen since Chile, followed us along the coast and right up into the bay. They looked brown and white, rather than black and white, and even the white parts looked dirtily marked with brown, unlike the clear-cut black-and-white markings of the Chilean variety. I enjoyed their company as they played around the bow, dived underneath us, and dashed around us for the eleven miles it took to reach the head of Anse du Volage, a delightful sheltered place with rich green slopes on either side, looking more like a river. We anchored at about 1530 hours and as I desperately needed some exercise, I pumped up the dinghy and headed for the shore. I could see curious rabbits everywhere, watching my approach. There were hundreds of them. I climbed up the bank and tried to count how many I could see at once, and it was well over fifty. The ground, covered by the green mat of acaena, was riddled with their burrows. I found a way to get above the great jagged cliffs which overlooked the fjord, and then walked along a gentle slope of soft loose stones with round clumps of azorella moss. Near to a big rocky bluff I saw a cave which I felt drawn to explore. It led downwards, and I clambered over big boulders until I came to a hole with light showing through. Looking down I was startled to see a flattish plain about 150 metres vertically below me. I had not realised that I was still so close to the cliffs, and this particular rocky bluff that I was in was actually an overhang! To avoid slipping out of that hole I chose my foot and hand holds very carefully indeed as I climbed out of the cave. From higher up, the views across the fjords and the islands in the bays were breathtakingly spectacular. There was white water almost everywhere except where *Totorore* was lying, so we were anchored in a good spot.

I did some good island exploration, and could see where there were no rabbits by the healthy growth of Kerguelen cabbage. I found burrows of Blue petrels and Great-winged petrels and had a thoroughly good time.

Wednesday 19 March

...We entered a small but well sheltered cove at the end of an island called Léon Lefèvre, which also had plenty of Kerguelen cabbage...Grey petrels were pouring in while it was still light enough to see them diving into burrows in the acaena. I was thrilled to bits! I had only ever seen a very few at a time, usually only singly and out at sea. There were also some Wilson's storm petrels flitting about, but I knew I would need lights after dark to see the Blue petrels. That meant staying there for the night, so with the rising wind I thought I had better test the anchors and motored full astern. I almost wished I had not tried them when we dragged rapidly astern...in the dark I decided it was better to stick to an anchorage I knew to be good, so moved back to where we were last night.

During the night another gale blew up, but in the good sticky mud in Anse du Volage the anchors held well. We stayed where we were until midday and sailed twelve miles through multidirectional squalls to the open sea. In the bay it was awful but outside it was worse. The ten metre seas were short and steep, and steering was difficult because *Totorore* kept wanting to broach and lie beam to sea. I had to keep the hatch closed because in the gale a lot of water was coming aboard, so I could not look at the temperature gauge as often as I should.

Just as we were coming up to the dark cliffs of Cap du Challenger, the engine stopped. I closed the throttle and opened the hatch, to be greeted by the tell-tale smell of the overheated engine! *Totorore* lay beam to sea again, and seemed to be drifting straight towards the murderous breakers battering at the foot of the Cape.

She would not answer the helm, so I ran forward and hoisted the tri-sail to try to gybe her round. The only effect of the sail was to speed us towards our impending destruction. There was no time to do anything else but pray. Finally there seemed to be a longer trough and *Totorore* came around, a breaker filling the cockpit.

I was very disappointed about the engine because I thought that I had finished with overheating problems after fitting the new water intake at Cape Town. When it was cool, I changed the water pump impeller, and while doing so noticed that hot oil had squirted out all over the inside of the engine case. I knew that I was in real trouble. Luckily, I was able to get it going again and nursed it gently along against strong headwinds to reach an anchorage in Baie Greenland at 2200 hours.

All next day a gale discouraged me from trying to move around to Port aux Français, the French base in Baie du Morbihan, only 27 miles away. On the following day, I went to start the engine and found it full of water! The realisation of what this meant made it one of the more unhappy moments of the whole expedition. I had come to rely very much on the engine, and had been of the happy opinion that it was in good shape and would see me safely to New Zealand. I am not a good mechanic and normally tackle engine repair jobs only when there is no alternative solution, because without much experience I cannot judge the correct tension when tightening bolts and am scared of breaking them or stripping the threads. With excessive movement in the boat, such jobs are doubly difficult. Anyway, there was nothing else for it but to strip the engine down.

Apart from the obviously blown gasket, I found that the head block of the after cylinder was deeply scored, and I wondered how the engine had kept going so long. There was not much I could do except try to fill the score up with gasket cement, which I knew could be only a temporary measure, and fit a new gasket. To give it the best chance I did not open the sea water inlet for a whole day, to let the cement set in the cold temperatures.

Monday 24 March

...I would certainly have felt a lot more confident about things if I had had Jim or Malcolm or Chris on board to look after the engine for me! Every now and again I burst out laughing when I think back to some of our former crew members. Andreas, for example. One of our catchphrases when he was here was 'Many a slip twixt cup and lip.' And then Chris – 'It could be worse!' with the inevitable rejoinder, 'And it probably will be!' I am not really downhearted. I still have my comfortable home and plenty to eat and drink, so whatever the outcome I can survive a long time yet!

After breakfast I finished off all I could think of to do on the engine and then with trembling hands, weak knees and a prayer on my lips, I tried to start it. It coughed, spluttered, fired a few revolutions and died. I tried again with the same result. Woe upon woe! I tried bleeding the fuel line yet again. I turned the switch to put all the batteries on to starting the engine, instead of just the one. I tried again. It was reluctant, but then it ran!

Ever since we had left Marion Island I had enjoyed an easy, comparatively carefree voyage. I had every confidence in *Totorore*, which seemed to be able to handle heavy weather very well, and without her high mast and rigging seemed less likely to capsize. I knew that with land about, the engine would always get us out of trouble. Now, suddenly, it was all different, and the engine weighed heavily on my mind.

By using it as little as possible and keeping the revolutions low when I did, I managed to keep it going, when required, for a few more weeks. To start with, we moved around to Baie du Morbihan and anchored for a night near Port Navalo, rather than negotiate too many of the dense kelp beds in the dark to reach Port aux Français. In daylight it was no trouble, and we entered the small cove next to the base at 1400 hours.

Tuesday 25 March

...On arrival I saw two white craft in the cove, one a reasonable-sized fishing boat type and the other a small landing craft sort of vessel. Another was up on the shore. There is a wharf with a big shed on it, and lots of buildings of various shapes and colours spread out along the low and uninteresting shoreline. Reaching up from over a ridge there are literally dozens of masts, I suppose for radio or for lights, and a very big one about 60 metres high. Farther away on the other bank I could see isolated buildings which may have been the upper-air observations sheds from

306

which they release and track meteorological balloons. I noticed some roads and a couple of vans and a truck.

In the rain, the whole scene was depressingly dreary. The water was shallow close in and I was preparing to anchor when a shout from the wharf attracted my attention. There was quite a crowd there, and one of the men waved me to come over. We had no sooner touched the big tyre fenders than the same man, whom I found later was the Chef de District, waved me away. Then a Zodiac came past and indicated that I should go to a buoy, where its crew helped me to make fast. They returned to collect the Chef, a dumpy man with grey hair, a kind face and wearing a black cap, and the lean young doctor.

Paper formalities completed, the chef said that they could send a telegram home for me and post my letters, but that I must remain on board. After Crozets that did not surprise me. I did not really mind because it looked a bit of a dump ashore, although I would have liked a hot shower. The inflatable came back and the three seamen fished up a very heavy mooring wire from the bottom, and placed it over the forward bollard. They said we would need it, as it could be very rough in the cove. How right they were! One of them handed me up a carton, 'Pour moi?' I asked. 'Oui – c'est le vin!' It contained six bottles of red wine. He put his fingers over his eyes, then to his lips. I understood – it was to be in secret. At least they made me feel welcome, and outside of politics

The next day the Chef must have relented, or spoken to Paris on the radio, because I was allowed ashore but told that I was not allowed to do any scientific work in the islands. The postmaster told me that he had sent my telegram home, but being unable to reverse charges or accept an IOU had paid for it himself, for which I was very grateful. Here, I was treated to real French hospitality, and was able to shower and use a washing machine for my clothes in the seamen's and engineers' comfortable accommodation block, which also had its own bar. Nobody offered to show me around the base, but I was given every other consideration, and for two days had lunch with them in the huge dining hall where all 80 of the base personnel sit down together. The meals were sumptuous in the best French tradition. As I walked into the hall there were many calls of 'Bonjour' from different tables, to which I replied, feeling rather self-conscious. Regrettably, few of them spoke more than a smattering of English, and my schoolboy French was rather rusty, so communication was limited. My overall impression was that they were genuinely friendly.

The cove, which is open to the south-west with a fetch of nine miles across the bay, seemed to have been sadly ill-chosen for a harbour for vessels. When the big seas came in it felt as though the heavy mooring wire would tear *Totorore's* bow right off. While the weather was like that I could not think of leaving, so had to wait for an opportunity.

When we finally got away, *Totorore* was laden down with more diesel than she had ever carried before, ten bottles of wine and extra stores including fresh meat and six huge loaves of delicious bread. In addition they gave to me six cartons of Vittel natural mineral water, even though I protested that I had nowhere to stow them. I jammed it all as tightly as I could on the unoccupied port bunk. Not many weeks later I was to be very glad that I had accepted.

It was well into the afternoon on Friday 28 March when I finally dropped the mooring in Port aux Français and we motored out against a Force 6 south-wester ly wind with a short choppy sea. By the time we were half way across the bay the wind had increased to gale force, and as I wanted to make final preparations for the voyage to Heard Island, we sought shelter under the lee of lovely Île Suhm, where hundreds of Great-winged petrels and Blue petrels were wheeling about before diving into their burrows on the island. With the musical calls of the birds it was a very pleasant anchorage; although I am not superstitious, it did seem better than sailing on a Friday!

In the morning I had to exercise much self-discipline to resist the temptaton of going ashore and exploring when I could actually see petrel burrows in some earthy banks. In such fine weather I thought we should press on while we had the chance to make good distance, so I weighed anchor and we were soon bowling across the bay towards the open sea.

The Great Circle route to Macquarie Island from outside the Baie du Morbihan is a distance of 3064 miles, starts with a course of 131° and reaches its vertex, or highest latitude, in 60°S. In March there was little possibility of meeting pack ice in that latitude, and even icebergs would not be very common, but there was a strong chance that we would run out of westerly winds so far south. For that reason I decided to go down to about 56° to see how we were getting on, and then follow that parallel until we picked up the continuation of the Great Circle. Not only would it give us the shortest possible distance, but we should also avoid the very worst weather, according to the Pilot.

During out first night at sea a gale blew up from the north and Ivon broke. It had me quite mystified at first because I could hear and feel a different thump from under the boat and it took me a while to trace it to the rudder. The servo blade had broken out of the bottom bearing and was flogging about, still held by the broken and twisted top bearing. It had no doubt been weakened on the rocks in All Alone Cove at Marion but whatever the cause, it was a disaster! Not only did it mean that *Totorore* could not self-steer, but even steering by hand at the tiller was very difficult because the flailing blade threw the rudder about alarmingly. In those weather conditions I was unable to remove the offending part, which was under water, and it took me quite a long time to just get a line onto it so that if it came right off, it would not be lost altogether.

I steered by hand for a while, but could not stand it for long because of the cold. After that I tried to lash the tiller in different positions with line and shock-cord to see if I could persuade her to sail downwind, with the sail braced truly athwartships. It was no good – she just would not hold it, and always rounded to beam-on to the wind and sea, whatever I did. I was very soon cold, wet and dispirited, so I adjusted the sail for 'on the beam' sailing, heading slowly in the wrong direction, and went to bed.

Saturday 29 March

... This really is very serious, and a definite threat to my chances of survival. It is still nearly 4000 miles to go to New Zealand, and I can hand steer for only a few hours each day in these conditions. It was going to take a long time anyway, but this will more than double it. What to do?

Somehow I have got to find a way of making her self-steer, even if only downwind...

Sunday 30 March

With the huge seas in the gale which lasted all day, work on deck was difficult, and although I bent the tri-sail on, I did not hoist it, as I did not want to over-canvas our frail mast and rigging. I also spent considerable time experimenting with tiller lashings, but in the wild conditions I accomplished nothing...Every now and then she insists on turning herself right around after a big sea has hit her, and I have to lean hard on the tiller to bring her round again...The only warm place on board is in my sleeping bag, and it takes a lot of effort to crawl out and get dressed to go outside, where the wind seems determined to reach the marrow in my bones. There is a limit to how many clothes I can put on and still fit into my wet-weather gear.

Last night I looked in vain for Halley's comet. I know it should be somewhere around the Scorpion now, and April should be the best month in which to see it...a bit of sunshine this afternoon helped to cheer me up, and of course I always have the birds!

Most numerous were the Blue petrels and White-chins, with the dear little Wilson's storm petrels next. There were plenty of Light-mantled sooty albatrosses, and Black-bellied storm petrels, but I stopped seeing Soft-plumaged petrels by the third day.

Monday 31 March

The big tent sail blew out early in the morning. The clew at the port foot came adrift, and much of that corner is shredded. The PVC pipe batten for the foot is broken in the middle. Another serious blow. Anybody would think we *had* sailed on a Friday! The barometer is high, but it was still blowing Force 9, so I just left the tri-sail up for most of the day. With that alone, wind abeam, she hardly moves. It is just too small, even in a strong wind.

I decided that we must try to call at Heard Island to do something about the self-steering gear, as it was not far off course and I had always wanted to go there anyway. Being south of the Antarctic Convergence it is, like South Georgia, considered to be an Antarctic island, and consists mainly of a large mildly active volcano of 2745 metres named Big Ben. The whole island measures about twenty miles by ten and is mostly covered by permanent ice, so that the coasts are mainly glacier cliffs or outcrops of black lava. It is owned by Australia which used to maintain a meteorological station and scientific base there, but this was closed down in 1955 and apart from occasional scientific expeditions the island has remained uninhabited ever since.

Tuesday 1 April

April Fool's Day! Nobody played any tricks, but I still feel well and truly fooled! I just cannot get *Totorore* to steer herself, however hard I try. Whatever I do she always turns beam to sea and lies athwart the wind on one side or the other...The only thing I actually accomplished today was that I took the adjusting lines off Ivon, worked from a small drum with a handle close outside the companionway, and with a shock-cord on each side, attached the lines to the tiller. That does mean that I can alter course by reaching out of the hatch, above the washboard, and turning the drum, now like my steering wheel. But she still will not hold a course.

Wednesday 2 April

This has now become a survival exercise. Although I am more frightened in storms when I am by myself – I cannot quite understand the psychology of that, unless it is just because there is nobody to give me a hand in an emergency – I like to think my survival chances are pretty good. I really do have a good deal of food on board, and the six cartons of mineral water which the chaps at Kerguelen gave me are a supplement to my water supply. In fact I am using them just as ordinary water, for tea and coffee and for cooking. Each carton contains twelve plastic bottles of 1.5 litres, so they alone will keep me going for a long time, and then I should still have over 300 litres in the tanks. As long as *Totorore* holds together, and nothing else breaks, we must eventually drift somewhere close to New Zealand...

To the west of Heard Island and about 23 miles away lies McDonald Island, three-quarters of a mile long and rising to 230 metres. It is steep and surrounded by cliffs, and had never been landed on until 1971; since then it has been explored only once, in 1980, when it was discovered that Black-browed mollymawks nest on it, in addition to the hordes of Macaroni penguins and other sea birds. Both visits were by helicopter. Immediately north of the main island is Flat Island, a plateau about 55 metres high.

Friday 4 April

I had hoped for nice weather conditions to arrive at McDonald Island, but instead it blew Force 9 with heavy rain and a very rough sea, which made any kind of steering really hard work...I began to doubt the chances of anchoring near McDonald Island as we passed the offlying stack of Meyer Rock, 170 metres high, because the swell followed us round and down the eastern side of the island. The chart shows nothing at all, so I had to see for myself...

Mightly breakers were exploding well offshore from the next point south and I thought there could be some shelter from the sea on the other side of that reef...I dropped the anchor in ten fathoms with all our 40 fathoms of chain. Luckily it held first time. When the blinding rain stopped there were some periods of sunshine, and I was able to look around. Another absolutely fabulous island! How I love a place like this! Just to see it, and be here, makes the discomfort of the journey to it so worthwhile. The northern part was densely covered with Macaroni penguins, and they were even plastered over steep slopes of the southern end, right to the very summit. In greenery on the cliff faces, on the very edge of the penguin colony, I could see Black-brow nests, the chicks stretching out and exercising their wings in preparation for their first flight. The air and sea were full of birds, and in the squalls it rained feathers from moulting penguins, which covered the decks for a few moments, then collected in the cockpit and cabin.

I had wanted to remove the upper part of the remains of Ivon from the rudder, but the wind was far too strong for me to do anything and I could only hope for better weather at Heard Island. Although it seemed rather precarious, and I was scared of a wind change from the east, I decided to stay in the cove as I wanted to arrive at Heard Island in daylight. I called it Ivon and Barbara Cove.

Because of the steering problems we had taken nearly six days to cover the 245 miles from Kerguelen, so it was obvious that some form of self-steering was top priority. I had in mind to try to erect an additional bowsprit high up, out of the sea, like a flying jib-boom, on which to set the tiny tri-sail well forward and sheeted hard. That, I hoped, would give her directional stability to keep the wind dead astern, which would be something. For the purpose I could use the jockey pole which had formerly served us as a jury mast. I also wanted to find a spar which could be used like a boom on the foot of the tri-sail, and take the sheets through blocks direct to the tiller, which might work to steer *Totorore* with the wind on the quarter. I was determined that we would not leave Heard Island until I had rigged up something satisfactory.

Saturday 5 April
...The frequent violent snow squalls were the worst, but in between them the sun shone cheerily, beautifying the blue sea and the tumbling white crests. Heard Island was all white except for the Laurens Peninsula sticking out towards us, which had lovely green slopes at the foot of its snowy mountains. It was a breathtaking scene, but as we neared the island and shallower water, the seas steepened dramatically and towered high over us!

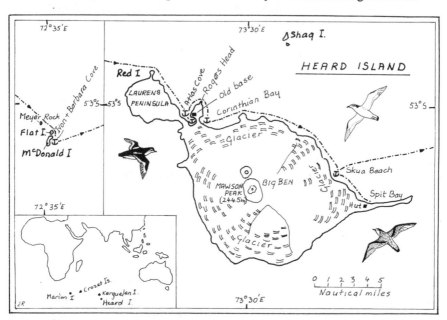

Map 28

311

I was really frightened, and I think I must have said a prayer as every great wave came roaring up, threatening to pitchpole *Totorore*, or when she was out of control, to roll her over and over.

It did not seem possible that any boat could survive that violence. Many times *Totorore* was carried along on the crests, completely out of control and on her beam ends, heavy volumes of water pouring over the top. I had early felt it was too dangerous to remain in the cockpit even with my safety harness on, so I steered with my arm outside the washboard, my hand on my little steering wheel, but most of me safely inside where I could not be washed overboard. My body filled much of the hatchway, but a lot of water passed me and went below, wetting me pretty thoroughly on the way.

On the chart, Atlas Cove – where the base used to be – looked a trap open to the north-west, but as we came close to it I could see a low stony spit protecting an ideal boat harbour. Above the beach was a ramshackle collection of derelict buildings, bigger than I had expected, with the usual untidiness left by human occupation. There were various posts and masts, and old tanks, and to one side a cross, no doubt on a grave. Unfortunately the water behind the spit was shallow and we could not go very close to the beach. If we had had more time, I would have deliberately beached *Totorore*, but I could not risk having difficulty in getting her off again.

Sunday 6 April
...I rowed ashore and landed on the beach near the spit, where large numbers of young Fur seals and Elephant seals were playing in the shallows. I had to almost push a way between them, and even the Gentoo penguins, so timid on Marion Island, here were reluctant to move out of the way to let me drag the dinghy up the beach to secure the painter to a wooden post. A single King penguin walked along the water's edge with characteristic dignity.

The old Australian base looked completely derelict. Elephant seals lay in heaps between the mostly roofless buildings, among the debris. I knew that several expeditions had spent summer months here since it was abandoned, so I expected some huts to be in better condition for temporary occupation. I soon found that three French-built prefabricated galvanised steel huts were still habitable, but I did not examine them until after I had gone for a walk and found a suitable spar for what I wanted. It had been used as a small aerial mast and was round and made of hardwood; about six centimetres in diameter and 3.5 metres long. I also found three wooden oars which will probably come in useful for poling out sails. An old waterproof cape, hanging in a shed, I thought could provide material to patch the torn sail. There were also quite a lot of big gas cylinders and I found one with some gas in it. If I get a chance to come back I will top up our own gas bottle.

A low sandy isthmus, less than a mile across, separates Atlas Cove from Corinthian Bay. Backed by a glacier, the Bay certainly looked calm enough, tucked into the corner formed by Rogers Head, a 100-metre hill, green with azorella. The slopes leading up to it from the sand flat were of lava stones in black sand with azorella clumps scattered all about. The whole area was absolutely honeycombed with burrows, only a few of which were still occupied. Three Skuas sitting around told me that not all the petrels had departed, and remains in the middens indicated that the smallest burrows were of South Georgian Diving petrels, and the larger ones were of Antarctic prions, or 'Totorores'. As I neared Rogers Head itself I could hear the unmistakeable chatter of Marcaroni penguins, and then I saw them on the eastern side of the Head, from the sea right up the very steep side of the hill. Like those on McDonald Island the adults had gone to sea to fatten up after breeding and were now back on the breeding site to fast while they moulted for about four weeks. They will probably go back to sea in about two weeks or so from now.

It was snowing, and I noticed that the wind had turned north-east which could mean trouble and made me feel glad that we were not in Corinthian Bay after all. I made my way as quickly as I could back to the old base and had a look in the best huts. They had good wooden floors, but no windows. Light came in through translucent sheets of heavy plastic in the roof. One had beds in it, with useable dry mattresses. Another had a sign outside – 'Heard I. Hilton, Reception. Vacancy.' Inside was clean and dry. There was a table with some stationery, and a zip-closed folder marked 'For Visitors'. Inside were some maps, and sheets of paper with details of all the various expeditions which had visited the base since it was closed. I would have liked to have studied them all but I could hear the wind rising and was anxious to return aboard.

One note did catch my eye and that was *Damien*, signed by Jerome Poncet in 1972. That would have been his first *Damien* and not the larger one we met at Falklands, and which later arrived at South Georgia soon after we left. Several other papers showed that there had been a sizeable expedition here in October last year. I wrote a hurried note to put in the file and then carried my various spars down to the beach.

The snow had turned to a nasty wet sleet and the wind was freshening by the minute. I towed my laden dinghy along the beach in the shallows, among the seals, and started rowing from directly upwind of *Totorore*. The dinghy came down to her at surprising speed and I was glad I was not rowing against the wind. The barometer was falling fast, as I had rather guessed.

While the dinghy was still in the water I tackled the job of removing the broken self-steering gear from the rudder. The choppy sea splashed water constantly into the dinghy, and careful as I was, I soon had a boot full of water, a wet bottom, and arms wet to above my elbows. I felt pleased when I finally got it off, only just in time as the wind started to shriek in fierce squalls. It took a long time for my hands and wet foot to thaw out.

Meanwhile the barometer continued to fall. I did not like the look of it at all. Here in the cove we seemed sheltered but there was so little water under us! Should I move out now, while I could?...I tidied up and secured everything, inside and out, then ran the engine, to warm it up...The wind started to howl, and *Totorore* became lively. I made the decision – we must go! Was it too late already?

...Eventually we made it safely out into the middle of the channel, and by 2200 hours we were anchored in seven fathoms just over a cable outside the spit. As predicted, conditions were horrible. The heaving, reeling, jolting, and thumping were extremely disconcerting, and the barometer had fallen to 969 millibars. The wind screamed with demonic fury, trying and succeeding to strike terror into my heart, but I did not give it the satisfaction of telling it so. Instead I apologetically declared to all who would listen that we would keep anchor watches. I would keep the first watch, Gerry the second, and the skipper the third. In other words, I would not be able to lie down to relax all night. Innumerable cups of coffee. Golly, I am going to need that gas!

Monday 7 April

Four times during the night I had to go forward on my hands and knees to attend to something. Once the nylon spring on the anchor chain parted and had to be renewed. Once the chain jumped off the bow roller and jammed down the side. I could tell something was wrong by the feel of the boat and the different sounds. Another time my tri-sail had burst from its lashings on the lifeline and was flogging badly. Each time I went was a traumatic experience and also a wetting one. The wind was so strong that I could not stand up, and during the frequent hurricane-force squalls I could not move, but just closed my eyes and hung tightly on to anything in reach. Out on the bowsprit was the worst, and several times I was lifted clear of the deck by the wind and suspended in the air with my arms wrapped around the rails. Seas broke right over the bowsprit and threatened to wash me out under the lower lifeline...

Back in the cabin I let my wet clothes warm up on me, as I had not enough gear to keep changing. Around 0200 hours the barometer bottomed out at 967 millibars and after an hour began to rise rapidly. When daylight came, accompanied by heavy dark snow clouds, the wind eased to a mere gale, and the barometer had risen to 976 millibars. As we had neither dragged anchor nor carried away the chain during the night I considered that we were not likely to now, so at 0600 hours I risked lying down on my bunk to have a sleep...

I took *Totorore* around to Corinthian Bay, about an hour's run, and found that it was much better anchorage, close up to the lava cliffs in a corner near the beach of black sand at the head. The weather was almost constantly bad, and in the eight days that we were there I had only one more opportunity to go ashore. We returned to Atlas Cove just long enough for me to take a gas bottle ashore to fill up from the big one I had seen in a shed.

Back in Corinthian Bay my deck work was hindered by the strong winds and blizzards. Eventually I finished rigging my 'flying jib-boom', which stuck up like a unicorn's horn, and tried the tri-sail on it. It all looked rather peculiar, but it was strong and I was pleased with it. My idea of a boom on the foot of the sail with sheets to the tiller was more difficult, so I shelved it after wasting considerable time. As a compromise, I led cords from the top part of Ivon with the windvane, which was still intact, direct to the tiller. I knew it could not work efficiently as there was not enough total movement for the tiller, but it should help.

Apart from the weather, and the fine sand which blew over *Totorore*, stinging my face and finding its way right through the boat, I quite enjoyed my stay at Heard Island. On one side we had a mighty glacier, on the other the lava cliffs with swarms of Fulmar prions flying up and down and round in circles, accompanied by some Cape pigeons. The prions would stop off on a rock ledge or pop into a small hole in the cliff for a little rest, most 'unprion-like' behaviour which I had never seen before. There were large numbers of Diving petrels, Wilson's storm petrels, and some Giant petrels in the bay.

On Tuesday 15 April I felt that I had done all that I could except for changing the engine oil, necessary after the troubles I had had with the engine, and tightening down the cylinder bolts again to prevent leakage past the damaged head. To warm the engine for these jobs I motored about fifteen miles around the coast to Spit Bay.

Some of the larger glaciers had receded a long way even since the chart was made in 1949, when they were depicted as bulging out into the sea. Now they form bays, with a line of dangerous moraine rocks across the mouth of each one, showing the original extent. Many of the ice cliffs were very dirty with volcanic ash, and from a distance could be taken as lava.

I cannot describe the feeling of awe which overcomes me when I am the only human being here, observing the wild birds and animals apparently undisturbed for countless centuries. It is true that the sealers disrupted the general flow of life here for a time, but the only signs of their occupation are the old cast-iron try-pots still on some of the beaches, as they are on most sub-Antarctic islands.

We sought out the best place to anchor off Skua Beach, and then, to my horror, I found that the engine had squirted black oil over everything! It seemed that I was too late in tightening the bolts. It was a very exposed position that we were in, and I did not like to remain there too long with the engine out of action. There did not seem to be any water in the sump, so I just tightened the bolts, changed the engine oil, and adjusted the tappets. It seemed to be successful and the engine ran well without any apparent leakage. At 1700 hours I weighed anchor and sailed thankfully away, bound for Macquarie Island.

Skua

Chapter Eighteen

Survival

At sea — Storms and capsizes — Survival voyage — Fremantle — Return home

Wednesday, 16 April
...I put the tri-sail on the flying jib-boom to try it out, with the orange square sail on the mast. It was fiddly work without light, and with gloves on, but it was worthwhile in that I found that she would run downwind, which was what the whole idea was all about. I was delighted! I also set up the self-steering arrangement I had worked out from the wind vane direct to the tiller, and that too seemed to give a measure of control – at least in these conditions! We progress!

Thursday 17 April
...It is strange to be allowing 60° of westerly variation which makes the compass course most peculiar! The trouble is that we are right off the ordinary charts and onto the South Polar Chart with a polar projection on which plotting is difficult and on which no variation is shown at all! Macquarie has a variation of 30°E so in the course of this voyage I must change the variation I allow through 90°! I have tried to extrapolate from other charts farther north, but as the lines of equal magnetic variation, called isogonic lines, are curved, that method is not easy either!

Saturday 19 April
...A night of terror has shattered my confidence and has left me in serious doubt as to my chances of survival...

It is not possible to describe the violent shock to the whole boat as each enormous wave hit her and I could not believe that even my dear strong *Totorore* could stand such treatment without being crushed. I tried lying down on my bunk, with the lee-cloth secured, but I had not been there long when the mightiest impact yet rolled *Totorore* upside down and right over, filling me with panic. The cartons of plastic bottles of mineral water, which I had thought well wedged into the port bunk so that they could not move, hurled themselves onto me with crushing force, together with a plastic 25-litre can of diesel which had been wedged and lashed on the other side of the table. Fortunately the two steel drums of similar size stayed put. Icy water seemed to come from everywhere and I was soaked.

When she came upright again I put on the light, quite surprised that it still worked, and surveyed the shambles. There was so much water everywhere that I thought we must be sinking. More crashes followed and the horror continued. I tried hard to stuff things away into places from which they could not move, but I was scared to stay long away from the supporting doorway in the bulkhead in case I was violently thrown. The end of my bunk, where my feet tuck underneath in a sort of tunnel, was a good place to stow loose gear, as I did not dare to lie down again. Much of the water had come over the top of the washboard and a great deal had come down the ventilators, all of which I had closed. . .

Once again she was rolled during the night, but the effect was not quite so disastrous as I had got most things under control. The catches on some locker doors had burst open and the contents were strewn in the water, which took much sorting out. I felt really sick with cold and fear as the night passed. . . I knew the jury mast had gone, and the grinding, graunching noises on deck were terrible, but I also knew that I could not survive on deck against the force of the waves which were breaking over her, especially as the lifelines would be down. What other damage there might be I did not even like to think. . .

The seas remained big all day, but lost their fury; I was able to crawl around the deck securing the wreckage – a nerve-racking business with so little left that seemed strong enough to hold onto. The bipod mast was still on board but completely collapsed and bent nearly double, with its feet over the side. The pulpit was smashed beyond repair and my lovely flying jib-boom I had been so pleased with yesterday had gone, but aft seemed in a better state.

I had not locked the propeller shaft, and with the violent movement in the storm a rope had tangled around the propeller. It took me several hours trying to clear it, and eventually I succeeded by tying my carving knife onto the end of two sticks joined together and hanging myself out over the side on my safety harness so that I could reach far enough out to cut it.

Sunday 20 April
. . .It all looked so hopeless on deck that I just could not think what to do about the mast. One stay had stranded, but all were still fast top and bottom, and one rigging screw was bent. If I could erect it again, misshapen as it was, and possibly strain it into a reasonable shape with ropes, I could shorten the stays and use it as a short mast, probably only about three metres high but better than nothing. It was a slow job, using blocks and purchases and the windlass, but I managed to get the feet, bent as they were, back to where they had been before. On board I had no chance of straightening the mast, and the bends I put in were fighting me all the way. Although I finally got it up, so that its top is over the same place as before, it is all under tension, and I don't know if it will work. Each leg is bent at right angles, but over a long curve, and I can't seem to make anything feel rigid, which is rather distressing, as nothing else is rigid enough to hang onto either. The handrail from the top of the dodger over

the hatch is still firm although it is buckled and one of its strut pads is torn up...

The worst part of the job today was working on the end of the bowsprit to shorten the stays. With nothing to hang onto I was lying down, and was frequently dunked in the water. I laughed to think of what Chris would have said: 'That's not very nice!' I wish he were here to help me! The barometer has started to fall again. I am in such a funk that the thought of another storm terrifies me.

Tuesday 22 April

The weather continues to be reasonable, but the heavy rolling makes most work on deck a hands-and-knees job...I carried on with preparations and then tried the tri-sail on the forestay. Just hopeless, as it is far too big for the small stay that is left. I might try folding it and securing it, but the way I had it tied up, *Totorore* barely moved at all. Then the wind freshened and the whole mast shook so much as the sail flapped that I took it off. It blew a moderate gale in the afternoon so I worked inside, trying to be better prepared for the next capsize!

...I ran the engine for an hour, making myself very cold and wet steering out in the cockpit. When I came inside I noticed a smell of hot oil! I hardly dared to look. What I feared, had happened. It had blown the gasket again, squirted oil all over everything, and was full of water!

I felt very weak. My chances of survival are becoming almost negligible. I still have one gasket left, but if that goes I have really had it. Feeling exhausted, beaten, finished, I could not face the job. All I did was drain out the water and oil while it was still hot.

The Pilot says 'The maximum wave height to be expected over most of the west-wind region is about 25m, but this rises to 35m near Kerguelen in winter. The Southern Ocean is a stormy region and the possibility of an abnormally high wave developing among the general run of high waves is very real.' I could believe it!

Having repaired the orange square-sail, I tried it on the strange-shaped mast, which I called 'Jury No. 3', but I just could not get *Totorore* to sail with it. The mast was not high enough, and I could not manage to improve on it. Making a sudden decision, I started to dismantle it, but had to be very careful. Big and cumbersome, it was not easy to heave over the side without damaging the lifelines, which I had taken much trouble to rig up again to give me some form of protection on the unstable deck. I had to plan the operation and carry it out methodically. Just before dark I said goodbye and thank you to it for all the good work it had done, and then cast off its last retaining lashing and watched it sink rapidly out of sight. The deck looked terribly empty.

Thursday 24 April

The worst day yet – hurricane-force wind and incredibly huge and murderous seas. We were rolled right over three times – I cannot describe the terror. I cut my head – blood everywhere – and sprained my thumb. My neck hurts and I am scared that I have damaged something. Water poured in – locker doors burst open – everywhere a complete chaos – the only good thing was that at least it was daylight this time. The radar has

318

gone. The tiller was smashed, and I fear for the rudder which is thrashing madly about. The railings were torn off the coachroof with the weight of water on the main boom and other spars. Port lifelines bent right over (inside was one-inch steel bar stiffening). My hopes of survival are almost extinguished. There is very little left on board that is dry. I was dazed with shock, and cannot say how much time elapsed between the capsizes – probably an hour or so...

Each time she was rolled over she came up heading in the opposite direction. I said aloud after the second time – 'At least that has headed her back near her course!' I think I was suffering from hypothermia as I began to feel very calm and resigned to my fate. I was soaked to the skin with sea water only 1° above freezing and I stayed that way all day, thinking that as I was already numb with cold I would die more quickly...I kept pumping out the water and trying to get some order back in the cabin, but all the while I kept praying. In the evening, quite surprised to be still alive, I thanked God, and promised to do all I could to stay that way. Only then did I change into less wet clothes. I had a little laugh when I thought of what Jim Watt would have said: 'Everything in our favour is against us!'

Friday 25 April

The storm moderated during the night. In the morning I fitted the spare tiller – a difficult job in the conditions – and then had to jettison the fuel cans on deck as there is nothing left to secure them to. The tattered remains of the big whale sail also went, along with the main boom and mainsail which I had thought of as a last-resort spare. I lashed the few remaining bits of wood – old oars, the small spar from Heard Island etc., down near the scupper on the coachroof, hoping they will offer less resistance but stay there, in case I get the chance to rig some sort of sail. To give the seas a clean sweep across the deck I even jettisoned the liferaft...it was a four-man Avon, and I had had it since 1970, so it was quite a friend, but I had never seen it out of its case before, and it was fun to see it bobbing about in all its red and black glory.

As far as messages are concerned I have launched a few in bottles – asking the finder to pass them on to Majorie, and giving the date and position as far as I could estimate. I have taken a couple of sights, but they were not very good in these impossible conditions, and in any case exactly where we were at the moment is one of the least of my worries!

The words of a popular song of a few years ago keep going through my head, and I find myself frequently singing, rather grimly, 'Hang down your head, Tom Dooley, hang down your head and cry! Hang down your head, Tom Dooley, tomorrow you're gonna die!'

Saturday 26 April

Life is pretty grim as I have no lights except for two hurricane lamps now, both of which got broken but still work after a fashion. It is very cold. I worked all day on deck, as the weather was quite good, and rigged the spar from Heard Island as my jury mast No. 4. I don't know what chance it has of lasting... Keeping busy helps to keep my mind off things, but the nights are the worst.

When I say my prayers, which is often, I do not like to be forever just asking for something, so I make a point of listing all the things for which I can say 'Thank you, God,' first. It is a useful discipline, and even at the very worst times I am always surprised at how much I can think of that is good. That helps to cheer me up, and gives me strength to continue...

Noon position today was 54° 59′S, 82° 18′E.

Sunday 27 April

Good weather again, so I tackled the engine job. The cylinder head is very bad, but I am hoping that with plenty of gasket goo it might work enough to keep the batteries charged, if I do not put the engine into gear. I was not able to complete the job as it is nearly dark, when it is overcast, at about 1600 hours. It will be worse in the winter, but I shall probably not live to see it.

It is so easy to be wise afterwards, and of course I am feeling very stupid for being here at all. I had thought it would be no worse than when Mike and I crossed the Pacific and I was rather misled by the Pilot which shows only between five and ten percent gales for the area. I had not reckoned to lose the mast again, and I had expected to have the engine. What a waste of my life when it still had so much to offer, with my lovely family. I will never even know if my second grandchild is boy or girl! I feel so very sad at the incomplete nature of everything and feel that it is a most unsatisfactory way to leave the world with so much undone. I pray constantly, but it would need a mighty miracle to get me out of this mess now...I always include special thanks that my gas stove still works, and I am able to have hot food. Without that, life would be pretty miserable. All in all, I suppose that really I am a very lucky fellow, and I have a wonderful little boat which has stood up to incredible punishment! Long live *Totorore!*

Monday 28 April

My sights showed very little progress in the westerly current. The north-west winds are pushing us farther south towards the ice, unless I can get some sort of sail to keep up to the north. Early morning (which I long for, as the nights are so long, and I cannot sleep – I wish I had sleeping pills) I rigged up the orange sail on the new mast, but it did not set well and we are hardly moving.

I carried on fixing the engine, but I cannot get it to work. I have not the strength to start it by hand but there is still something very wrong with it. My batteries are nearly flat. I will try once more tomorrow, but after that there will be nothing more I can do. It would have been so nice to have the occasional warmth to dry out some clothes.

I am tempted to step over the side and call it a day, but where there is life there is hope, and it would seem wrong not to keep on battling. Besides which, I am a coward, and at this stage I can't face the thought of that icy water! My guess is that soon I will have no option. I try to keep my spirits up by carrying on as normal, keeping the boat a bit clean and tidy...I have endeavoured to block up the ventilators, a job not finished yet. I think there is only one vent cowl left...I used some rubber sealing on the wash board but it does not stick very well. It is too cold for most of the glue. I crack a few jokes to myself and sing little songs, but the one that seems to come up most often is 'I'm tired and I want to go home!'

Tuesday 29 April
At about 0100 hours the big thumps and splashes told me that trouble was on the way. Sure enough the barometer was falling, and the wind had gone north-west, which is always the bad one. I struggled into my wet-weather gear in the dark – oh, how I miss the lights! I was thankful to the invisible moon which cast some light to help me with my work outside. I took off the sail then lowered my precious little mast to the deck, took it down into the cabin and lashed it securely. This is just about my last hope, this tiny mast, so I must care for it as best I can. The whole job took me nearly two hours, fumbling in the dark with numb fingers, and getting wet again.

I was glad the blow did not come to much – those storms terrify me. Early in the morning I re-rigged the mast, hoisted the sail again and worked on the self-steering. I never did have a chance to get back to the engine today. The wind gradually backed to the south-west – usually the best weather even though cold with snow – and by 1500 hours I actually had her running downwind, steering herself. If a big sea knocks her off course she cannot rectify it but if I put her back she holds it. The speed came up to about three knots – fantastic! We have no electric power, so have no log, and can only guess.

I was thrilled to bits. The nearest to progress since the Marion Island mast came down ten days ago! A ray of sunshine, with a glimmer of hope! Everything up forward there is rather frail, and probably cannot last the distance but it is doing the job at the moment, and that is definitely cheering. If only the good God can spare me from those terrible storms, there is a chance I might escape yet. I am feeling very tired and weak, and my various cuts and bruises are a hindrance to my work, especially those on my hands, including my painfully sprained thumb.

...Terrified though I am, my mind is clear and I am definitely not hallucinating, but since the first capsize I have had an uncanny feeling that I am not alone in the boat. It is quite weird...

Wednesday 30 April
As the wind increased, my 'half Ivon', as I can now call the makeshift self-steering gear, could not cope too well, so I was up and out often during the night to put her back on course. A nuisance, but I was not complaining as long as were were making progress.

By mid morning the wind increased to gale from nearly south...I found that as long as she ran true downwind, the sail stayed nicely asleep and there seemed to be no risk to it or the mast.

Good miles are very precious, so I steered all day, but as the seas became larger, it was arduous to concentrate so hard. If I relaxed for a moment she was thrown off course and the sail shook the mast fearfully, in addition to which the sea filled the cockpit. Eventually I was so cold that I rigged a line to the tiller by which I could control it from the hatchway, with me inside, reaching over the washboard. My former small wheel steering from the position is of course now converted back to adjusting 'half-Ivon'.

The seas were huge, but nothing – absolutely nothing – compared with those of the north-wester, so did not frighten me at all. This kind of gale is what we expected in the Pacific and the South Atlantic, and this I can cope with, but I now live in mortal fear of the north-westers. Squalls of snow and sleet brought the fiercest winds, but as we were making about five knots to just east of north, I was well pleased, in spite of the odd nasty sea which came over and into the cabin. A few times I had to go forward to tighten up the backstays, and then of course she broached, but all in all she behaved pretty well. I was hard put to get anything to eat or drink, but I grabbed a block of dates and a bar of chocolate, and they kept me going...

Just before dark the lower batten broke on the sail...How I can make it last for another 2000 miles or more I can't imagine, but I will have to try somehow as it is all I have, except for the tri-sail which at the moment is too big for Jury No. 4. Anyway, I took it off and bundled it down into the cabin, which is the safest place on board – although that is not saying much! and let her lie ahull. This evening I finished the last of the French bread from Kerguelen, after cutting away the mouldy crusts. Pretty good considering it was five weeks old today! I dare not waste anything because if I survive, it might take a very long time!

My regular bird observations had been rather disrupted, but I still noted them down when ever I could, even though I doubted if anybody would ever see them. I worked for another whole day on the engine, knowing it was my last chance. Using plenty of starting ether, and having changed the after injector, I actually got it working again! I knew I dared not propel *Totorore* with it, but at least I could charge the batteries, which meant lights, and a little warmth. My elation was shortlived. When I stopped the engine, it was full of water!

Even my mung beans had stopped growing. The whole boat inside was dripping with water, except up in the head and the forepeak where it was ice.

Without an engine I realised that we could never make it around to the lee side of Macquarie, and if we missed, it was wide open ocean. For a while I was tempted to try, because the engineers there would, I was sure, get our engine going again, but it was too risky, and I had to think purely in terms of survival. Our best chance seemed to be to try to reach Australia, but the frequent northerly and north-westerly winds made it appear almost impossible.

The pages of my logbook had been headed 'Heard Is. Towards Macquarie.' In sailing vessel logbooks one does not write 'To' somewhere, but only 'Towards' – just in case! At that stage all I could write on my logbook pages was 'Heard Is. Towards???'

Thursday 1 May

...We are still plodding slowly northwards under sail, the wind now very light and the barometer high. I can't even see the sail, because although I have two torches, I have very few spare batteries for them, so keep them for an occasional look at the compass. Likewise I have few spare batteries for my little shortwave radio, so am keeping it just to try to get time signals for navigation, but am not having much luck so far. We must be in a bit of a blind spot. I can always pick up Radio Moscow, but have not heard them give a time signal. I can't help laughing sometimes when I think of what a silly situation I am in...

I continued to do everything possible to make *Totorore* safer and more water tight for the next capsize. During the rollovers, which obviously involved complex movements of *Totorore* when underwater, I had been amazed by the displacement of different articles inside the boat. Nails and screws from small lockers up forward appeared everywhere, even abaft the engine under the cockpit, where I also found potatoes and onions which had come from the same compartment. Tins of food and spare bedding, stowed in boxes jammed into the quarterberths, had turned up swilling around in water up in the head. The cooking stove had jammed upside down, and the catches on the oven door had burst open, releasing five dozen eggs which had been stowed in cartons. For literally months afterwards I kept finding broken eggshells in every conceivable corner of the boat.

To avoid a repeat of things flying dangerously around inside the boat I made sure that nothing could move, boarding up the quarterberths and the port bunk tunnel, and nailing or lashing everything else. In the violence, many of the catches on the boards of the cabin sole had slipped and the boards had come flying, so I screwed them all down tight. For the hatch I made a board with a rubber lining, which fitted inside held by a tower bolt when the hatch was closed, making it even more watertight. I screwed boards up underneath the ventilators, and fitted plugs sealed with silicon rubber on the outside, and screwed a large block of wood onto the windlass bed to keep the navel pipe shut tight. I worked ceaselessly at these tasks, or to improve the sailing or self-steering, from first light in the morning until dark, and as the days passed I began to kid myself that I was an expert at being rolled over, and that *Totorore* and I 'could handle it'. But whenever the wind backed to north-west, and the barometer was falling, I was terrified.

Sunday 4 May
Around 0400 hours the barometer had fallen to 973 millibars and the north-wester had started. Again I left the comparative comfort of my sleeping bag and struggled outside to lower and secure the mast. Wearing wet woollen mittens with fingertips free, I thought I could more easily undo the lanyards securing the backstays and thus get the job done more quickly. It did not work. One of them gave me a lot of trouble because my fingertips lost their feel...

Finally I got the mast down. I have arranged it now so that all I have to do is let go the backstays, ease the lashing on the foot, and lower the mast forward on its after halyard. As soon as it is down I cast off the foot lashing altogether, then pull the whole mast and rigging aft, so that it can be lashed along the deck, leaving its forestay and shrouds still attached. In daylight it is not too bad...

My sleeping bag is like a haven. Even its smell is a sort of comfort to me, like an animal in its lair. I try to shut myself off from the cold and inhospitable world of reality, and even though it is damp and my clothes are wet, after a while I do warm up. I do not take any clothes off at all, even my woolly hat and my seaboots come into the bag.

The gale, though severe, was not a storm and although the seas were big

323

and horrifying to behold, *Totorore* coped well, as she has always done. The barometer stopped dropping at 970 millibars and started to rise.

Monday 5 May

...When I am cold and wet and thoroughly frightened, I can hear Marjorie saying, 'Well you are doing what you want to do!' That's true, but only up to a point. I would like to be anywhere but here just now. Like in front of our nice open fire at home, eating hot buttered scones!

...I try to write up my diary each evening by the flickering light of my little hurricane lamp as I cannot spare any daylight hours which are fully occupied in this survival operation...I tend to do things like licking my spoon clean and putting it back in the drawer because water in the sink slops out with the violent rolling. If ever I have the chance, I will try to get back to more civilised ways.

Wednesday 7 May

...I am beginning to feel a proper old crock, full of aches and pains and always tired and lacking in energy. I think the constant violent motion is very tiring, and then there is the psychological factor. It is like being in prison, in the condemned cell. When the barometer rises and the wind goes south-west there is a slight reprieve – a stay of execution. When it goes down fast, then I feel I have little hope. Generally, I have more of a chance than I had two weeks ago, but that is not saying much. The trouble is, I have so little control over where we go.

Friday 9 May

My birthday today. I am 59. Two weeks ago I hardly expected to be still alive. But God is good and has seen fit to save me so far, so I continue to hope and to pray that I might eventually come to safety.

It is not so easy to be hopeful on a day like this. In the morning the barometer was down to 970 (it might have already been on the way up when I saw it) and it has been blowing a severe gale all day from the west-south-west...There was not a lot I could do. I wanted to work on the mast while it is down, and in the afternoon I plucked up enough courage to go onto the foredeck, but I did not stay long. It was just too dangerous, too cold and too wet. However I did manage to stick some patches on the torn sail, and also on my wet-weather gear, and pump several buckets of water out of the bilges. I have to do this daily, and I do not know where it all comes from, but suspect that it is at the feet of the badly strained radar tower, which although twisted and topless, is still standing.

I am feeling more and more tired, and have to exercise great self-discipline to get even the smallest tasks done...

Every time it blows a gale I am very frightened. One would think that by now I would be used to it, but I am not, and after the terrible experience of those storms, I probably never will be. If I can make it back home I will find enough excitement playing Snakes and Ladders with my grandchildren. Up forward I have a tiny Christmas Pudding which I have been saving for a birthday treat, but in this weather I do not feel very hungry. I might still try it, for the principle of the thing – who knows, I might not live to have another chance.

Saturday 10 May

...I tried the tri-sail abaft the mast, with the clew tacked down on deck on the weather side, the tack hoisted on the halyard from the mast, and the head being used as the clew, with the sheet well aft. This way I got a better angle of sail for a beam wind, and with the two sails together we are making nearly two knots. This is progress. I am learning all the time, and in all honesty, I must say that this is the first time I have really enjoyed sailing since we left Heard Island. I have been thinking I would like to try to get to Fremantle which should be possible in wintertime.

Sunday 11 May

...At about 0230 hours all hell let loose on deck...I discovered that the new lower batten on the sail, made of heavy Australian hardwood, had somehow come adrift from its centre tack line and its braces, and was flying high on the end of the sail, flogging unmercifully. To get it under control looked a dangerous business, as I had no wish to be crowned by that thrashing pole. Luckily I managed it without injury and sadly took the sail down into the cabin, leaving just the tri-sail and making only about one knot.

Monday 12 May

Happiness is a fair wind! Early morning, as dawn broke, I made sail and we went romping away to the north-east at two knots. The sky was clear, and later we had lovely sunshine. This is the life! My great joy was shortlived. The wind almost died, and during the day it gradually veered, pushing us south again. And now, in the evening, it is back to north-east which is no good at all. At the moment we are still sailing, wind abeam, making about one knot to the south-east. Maybe the wind will be back in the night and improve our course?

Our noon position was very disappointing: it showed that we were ten miles astern of where we were yesterday. That means that for four days we have made good only 29 miles, and now we are not making anything towards Fremantle at all. It is hard not to be despondent. I may have to drop the idea of going to Fremantle, as we just can't get north at all. But where else? To keep going east makes everywhere else so much farther away...

I also started work on the smashed tiller, so that I will have a spare again. I could do nothing to repair it so all I could do was shorten it, but making it fit the jaws on the rudder stock fitting is no easy task at sea! I wished I could use a router, or better still, I wished Chris were here with me to do the job! It is the short jerky roll which makes everthing so difficult. I timed only three seconds to complete a 20° roll back to the same side, i.e. from 20° to port, over to 20° to starb'd, then back to 20° to port. Anybody who has experienced this will know just how trying it is, and how seemingly impossible carpentry is in these conditions!

Thursday 15 May

...I worked out today that since we lost our Marion jury mast, nearly a month ago, we have averaged only twenty miles per day which certainly does not get us far. It is still well over 1500 miles to Fremantle, but we never seem to be able to make the course in that direction...

The birds are a never ending source of pleasure, just to watch. We usually have one or two of the lovely Light-mantled sooty albatrosses wheeling around us, and once yesterday there were four. They seem to be curious, coming time and again to have a look at us, and they really do appear to show off, putting on a specially graceful flying display. White-headed petrels and Grey petrels are common visitors, and I often have one or more King penguins paying a courtesy call. I can bring them closer by imitating their call. Much as I would like to, I do not use the tape-recorder for that purpose any more, because I cannot spare the batteries which I must keep for radio time signals and my navigation calculator. Pelagic sightings of King penguins are not often recorded, probably because they are hard to see or hear from a fast-moving vessel...Surprisingly, the Kings I have seen have had bright orange-yellow ear patches, making them adults and not the first year immatures which usually wander farther. We are now nearly 700 miles from Heard Island, their nearest breeding place.

Friday 16 May
...Towards evening the barometer started to rise rapidly, bringing wind from the south-south-east. She makes her best speeds with the wind right aft, but will not steer; although it took us a bit west, this gave us valuable northing which I could not miss, so I stayed up to steer all night...

Saturday 17 May
I was a bit zombie-like by morning, and had to force myself to go forward to tighten up the backstays and re-arrange the jib. Good progress continued until about 1000 hours when the wind eased, but we still held course all day. I managed to wrest one sight from the overcast sky, but did not get another so could only guess that we had made over 50 miles of northing...

Last night I treated myself to a cup of Horlicks as an extra, but otherwise I have cut myself down to four cups of tea or coffee each day to conserve water, and for me that is a terrible hardship...

Monday 19 May
We have made 138 miles in the last four days, mostly north, which was what I wanted. We are back on the Indian ocean chart again and off the South Polar chart. Fremantle is on it, too!

Tuesday 20 May
...Five or six times each day I do my ten-minute bird observations and record them all in a book. After dark I keep pottering away as long as I can without lighting the lamps, to save kerosene. At 1700 hours I have my 'Happy Half Hour', which I have been looking forward to all day. I put the kettle on, make myself a cup of coffee, lace it with a small measure of whisky – nearly all gone, unfortunately, like the rum – and then sit down at the table with some nuts, pickled onions and salty cheese biscuits, and relax. It is always such a pleasure just to sit down, as I feel very tired, especially in my legs. To spin it out, I cover my coffee cup to keep it warm. Then I fetch out my other lamp which is kept in a locker for safety, with its chimney in a different locker wrapped up in clothes, and set it in a

special wooden bracket I have made on the swinging centre portion of the table. When that too is alight I write up the logbook, plot the day's fix (if I have one) on the chart, and then write this diary.

Wednesday 21 May
The present torture is steadily driving me mad! I refer to the inane jolting and jerking motion when becalmed in a confused sea with a heavy swell, especially in a boat without a mast. One cannot stand, sit or lie down without hanging firmly onto a strong point to avoid being catapulted into the air. It is exasperating to the nth degree, and infuriating in that it is all to no purpose. I am consuming precious food, water and kerosene for my lamp, without any useful gain apart from staying alive...

Thursday 22 May
...I do talk to *Totorore* and to the mast and sails, which are good friends, and I have also made friends with the hurricane lamp. To get around to the port side of the table, I have to squeeze past the lamp which is now lashed to the central pillar. I never do that without remembering to say 'Excuse me', and when I put it out at night I always bid it goodnight, and say thank you to it for having brightened my last few hours. I just call it 'dear little lamp' as I have not thought of a suitable name. I considered Florence, but somehow it does not suit.

Saturday 24 May
Another good day's progress – in fact the best yet. We made 86 miles from noon to noon, and now we are dashing along again at 4 knots, unfortunately heading due east with a fresh northerly wind. Not the best, but better than nothing at all. The winds are becoming less predictable, but I am hoping that during the night it will back to north-west which will help our courses...I am beginning to rate my chances of survival as better than 50/50 which puts a new light on things. Just now life itself seems very precious, and I want to hang on to it.

One of my disappointments at having to abandon my original southerly route to Macquarie was of course the birds. I particularly wanted to record all I saw on that route as it has been little covered in the past...I would be in a bit of a quandary if I meet up with a trawler or other ship which could rescue me, as the sensible thing would be to accept it and save my life for sure, but things are going well at the moment and I am feeling inclined to be independent and try to save *Totorore* as well. Nice as it would be to be saved, I think I would have to take the risk, possibly asking for some more water, and maybe a spar if they had one – perhaps a lifeboat mast, to improve my jury rig...

Tuesday 27 May
...We are probably now slightly less than 1000 miles from Fremantle, but I will not eat that pudding until I have confirmed it by my sights...We are still being accompanied by one, and sometimes two, of the little Grey-backed storm petrels, but I have not seen any Diving petrels for a few days.

Wednesday 28 May
...I cannot help feeling dejected. The wind is still northerly. For three

days it has been strong or gale force always from the north, with a nasty rough sea and heavy swell. I think it has now definitely put paid to any chance whatever of making Fremantle, so where the heck we will end up I have no idea...

I am fed up. This constant violent jolting and being thrown about is wearing me down. I want off. I want a walk on dry land! I want a hot bath! I want to be loved and cuddled! I would jolly well mutiny if I knew how, or if it would help. Help! I would scream if I could, but I can't pitch my voice high enough. Better still, I would get drunk if I had some liquor! I finished my bottle of whisky and now I am having a wee tot of liqueur in my coffee for my Happy Half Hour...

Friday 30 May
Last night the wind became light, about fifteen knots, and actually went back to west! We did not make much speed, wind abeam, but it was wonderful to sail north at last. By morning it had changed to north-west – not so good, but still not too bad. For a few hours it was lovely with sunshine and a moderate sea, and I was able to get sun sights, which put her in 42° 44'S, 107° 04'E at noon. Not too disappointing, but Fremantle is definitely out. Although I have no charts I am now thinking with a bit of luck we might be able to make Albany on the south coast, and only about 700 miles away. It all depends on the winds, of course.

Monday 2 June
...I was not sure if I could see the horizon, but I took sights which put us only 500 miles from Albany. That is really exciting, and so over the next few days, weather permitting, I will start making my preparations. One thing I want to do is put all my records and films into a watertight container which might have a chance of being saved if we get wrecked on a lee shore – a strong possibility – or if for some reason I have to abandon ship. I would not want too much to have to worry about, but I might prepare a 'panic bag' with some dried fruit and a couple of bottles of water in case of my surviving a wrecking on a desolate coast. I will have my float suit handy, with my lifejacket.

Thursday 5 June
What a glorious night sky I had last night! It did my soul good to see so many of my starry friends and I spent a long time outside, just looking...

It is a strange thing, our contrary human nature. Here am I, having been longing for the safety of a sheltered anchorage for the last seven weeks, and now that we are coming into a belt of better weather I start to have mixed feelings about arriving in Australia. I know that I must try, as it is the obvious thing to do under the circumstances, but now that it seems to be a distinct possibility, I rather dread the human contact.

However, I do look forward to speaking to Marjorie on the telephone...

Friday 6 June
One nasty thought which keeps gnawing at me is that I have failed. Under the circumstances I did not have much option, but the fact remains that I did not fulfil my originally declared programme, which included a visit to Macquarie...

The truth is that I have had enough. I just want to go home, and that will be by the shortest possible route, around the north end of New Zealand.

Sunday 8 June
...This evening I saw a big container ship, east bound, passing about six miles astern. We are still over 200 miles from Cape Leeuwin, so I was surprised to see her. I hope there will not be many ships nearer the Cape, because we have no navigation lights, and I certainly do not wish to stay up all night keeping a lookout. She is the first ship I have seen since Cape Town. Had I seen her a few weeks ago I would probably have attracted her attention. Six weeks ago, I would have sent up a distress rocket! Life is pretty good now that I can just casually watch a ship go past.

Thursday 12 June
I am both astounded and confounded by this continuing easterly weather. In the afternoon it rained and the wind freshened Force 5 – but still from the east! Had I known we were going to have five days of easterlies I would have gone up the coast to Fremantle...

A week ago we were doing well and I was filled with confidence, almost sure that we would reach Albany. Now it comes home to me how helpless we really are – entirely dependent on the way the wind blows, with little we can do to control our drift. I was beginning to relax my rationing but I think I had better re-impose strict control, because if we do not make Albany, I can't imagine how long it might take to reach somewhere else!

Friday 13 June
...Now six days of easterlies, and we are being set farther away from Albany. It just isn't fair! Bah! Life is becoming grimly serious – all the French wine is gone, and I am down to the last few dregs of liqueur. Also my various 'nibbles' – peanuts, cheese straws, pickled onions etc. – are practically exhausted, so my Happy Half Hour is becoming less happy, and soon will be just a memory, alas! If we keep going as we are at present, we will end up back in Kerguelen where at least they would probably give me some more wine!

Saturday 14 June
During the night I had developed a stiff neck, in the area which I had injured when we were rolled. It became so bad that I wondered if I had twisted an artery, or had a blood clot, or something else really serious. I was completely incapacitated and could hardly move, but what made it particularly bad was the jerky movement of the boat. Frequently I yelled aloud with the sudden pain. It had me really worried, but I must admit that for the first time I was thankful that the wind was still easterly and I did not have to do any sail work. The thought of something like that happening to me close to the coast is truly frightening, and I can't think how I could have managed in gale conditions.

Monday 16 June
The decision has been made! We are on our way to Fremantle. It continued to blow easterly all night, and freshened to a gale this morning. I have just

heard a forecast on the radio from Perth and it will still be blowing a gale tomorrow, and possibly even the next day! So now we are making north at about four knots. No chance of sights as it has been heavy overcast with showers, but I think we are about 100 miles off the coast...

Thursday 19 June
Hate is a word I do not like. It is ugly. But I am beginning to have very strong feelings about this easterly wind with its beastly persistence. The constant succession of big foaming seas which bombard us in bone-jarring sequence – 'Whoomp, splash, CRASH!' In my present state of infirmity it is absolute torture. 'YES, YES! I will confess! Anything you want! Just STOP! For the love of Mike!' But they are deaf, or will not listen, 'Whoomp, splash, CRASH!' and so on, ad nauseam...

Friday 20 June
...In this wretched place I hardly even see birds. For about three weeks I have seen almost entirely Soft-plumaged petrels, Great-winged petrels, and Yellow-nosed mollymawks. Now even those have become very scarce...

My big problem is what to do? How long do I wait for a westerly, while the wind pushes us farther and farther away? Sights today showed that we are again 200 miles away from Australia, no better off than we were two weeks ago!

Monday 23 June
...Light north-west winds continue, so we plod slowly onward. I wonder if we will be able to make it this time? We are heading for Fremantle, distant at noon 110 miles. The weather has been splendid today; the wind was gentle and there was no splashing. I fetched out my sleeping bag and pillow for a much-needed airing, and then soon I had the decks covered with clothing.

I did not want to get too carried away in my enthusiasm, but I did drag out a good long towline which I coiled down, stopped, and secured on the foredeck, ready to accept any kind offer which might come our way. I started sorting out mooring lines, but all our ropes are now in a mess. Given good weather tomorrow, I will do some more whipping and splicing.

My most difficult task is to try to find something clean and respectable to wear on arrival! I look like a gollywog, my hair is so long, but I have never been able to cut my own hair, so I contented myself with cutting my eyebrows and a fringe across my forehead just to keep the stuff out of my eyes! The last haircut I had was in December, in Cape Town...

Thursday 26 June
I could see Rottnest Island in the morning, and hoped to sail north of it to go racing down to Fremantle with the forecast north-west wind. Unfortunately the wind stayed north-east, and we were pushed south of the island, too far to be able to make the pass.
...During the afternoon I saw a large launch or fishing boat, but before I could do anything to attract her attention, she disappeared into the rain. Then I saw a fairly large warship which must have been surveying or carrying out some sort of exercise, as she kept going round in circles. She was quite a long way off, and I saw her only occasionally because of the

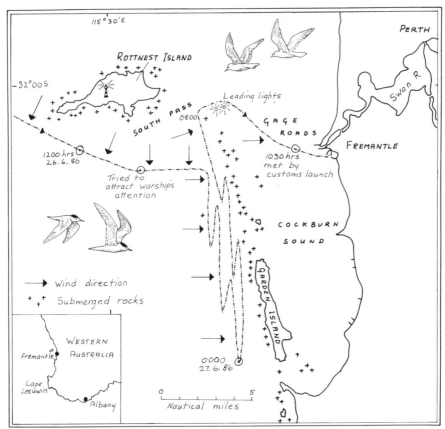

Map 29

rain showers, and the swells getting in the way. I thought if I could contact her, she could radio for a port authority launch or something similar to come out and give us a tow. I fetched out the parachute flares, but stopped just before letting one off. In the rain, in daylight, she probably would not see it. I had better save them for a real emergency. Instead, I let off an orange smoke-float, but although it worked quite impressively and was a nice colour, the wind was too strong for it, and the smoke streamed away very close to the water. When it did rise it was so diffused that it looked merely like a tint of sun's colour on a raincloud. What a waste!

Now, as I write, we are becalmed, but the swell is pushing us ever towards the long line of rocks offshore. Sometimes by moonlight I can see white foam and spray – not a pleasant sight just now, but otherwise rather beautiful. When the moon shines through I can see great towering clouds of spectacular design in silver...

About 2100 hours the wind came again, but due west, the worst. It varied in strength, strong and gusty in the rain squalls, but sometimes dropping to less than Force 3. What a worrying time I had, on the tiller the whole night long, and the next day as well. I had concentrated so hard to take advantage of every slight slant away from west – a point to the north, or a point to the south. I kept turning *Totorore* round to make best use of even the smallest change...

Friday 27 June
I was too anxious, knowing my life probably depended on my vigilance, to feel tired. In the early morning I started to feel that we were winning. For several minutes at a time we were able to steer 30° away from that lee shore, and I decided to gamble on it and try to make the South Passage into Fremantle. I had the Rottnest light to watch, although anything right ahead is hard to see because of our sail. For hours it seemed touch and go, but finally and with much relief, we turned in towards the leading lights marking the channel between the rocks. Wonderful. At last we could use the westerly wind the way it deserved to be used!

A big swell lifted us in over the shallows, but more worrying was losing sight of the leading lights in the frequent heavy rain. Once inside, the sea flattened out a lot, and we had a nice run of five miles across Gage Roads to the port.

I could see some beautiful big yachts, all obviously of the same class, sailing around in the Roads, and several passed close by to see what strange craft was coming into the harbour with its little orange square sail. Then an attendant high-speed inflatable, with a flag with a tiki on it, came roaring over to see us. 'We are the New Zealand Challenge,' said a cheery young man. 'When you get in, come and have a drink with us.'

The very first person to speak to me was a Kiwi! 'What Challenge?' I thought. The wind was very light as we crossed the Roads towards the port. Frequent heavy showers spoilt the view, so I took the opportunity to have a quick shave. In my hurry I cut myself and bled profusely. What a nuisance! Then I laughed aloud. What did it matter? What did anything matter? We had made it! We had arrived in a safe place.

Our entry into Australia was very different from our entry into South Africa. On arrival off the port of Fremantle a very large and powerful Customs launch escorted us to the new 'Challenger Harbour', and then gave us a line to tow us inside. The formalities including Customs, Immigration, and Department of Agriculture and Fisheries involved about a dozen people, a veritable mountain of paper work, and a 'sniffer' dog, and took from 1115 hours to after 1800 hours! By the time I could take down the yellow quarantine flag, *Totorore* was in the worst disorder since the big storm, with most of the contents of the lockers scattered about, and spilt rice, sago and dried fruit scrunching underfoot. All nice, friendly chaps, doing their job. I suppose we could easily have had a load of drugs on board, and gone south and chucked the mast overboard as a blind!

The Customs officers told me that we were in the new annex harbour belonging to the Royal Perth Yacht Club, that we were not allowed to stay, and that as soon as we were cleared, I would have to take *Totorore* somewhere else. When I asked where, they said they did not know, as everywhere else was full up. One of them suggested Two Rocks, a place about twenty miles up the coast. I began to wonder why I had bothered to come to Fremantle!

Fortunately I met Rod Tweddle, the Harbour Master, and after he had heard my story, everything changed. We could stay in the harbour where we were, and

I could use the bathroom at the new clubhouse. He did everything he could to help me and was a real friend. Tony Barnet from Channel 7 came to interview me with his cameraman; I felt so ashamed that they, and all the viewers, should see *Totorore* in such an untidy state! In spite of my being so tired, I did not sleep well that first night in port – *Totorore* felt too unnaturally still.

Tony Barnet looked after me all the next day, attending to my needs, and he took me to meet Alan Robinson, the co-ordinator for the NZ Challenge for the America's Cup, and other members of the team. At the dock in the Challenger Harbour I was introduced to Michael Fay, a most charming and approachable man, who was interested to hear about the *Totorore* expedition and my more recent adventures. He gave me a tremendously exciting boost when he said that the syndicate would be pleased to put *Totorore* back into a fit state to sail to New Zealand! 'We want to see you leave here looking like the Queen Mary!' I could hardly believe my good fortune, and freely acknowledged the providential guidance which had brought us to Fremantle.

The syndicate staff put me through to Marjorie on the telephone; we had a wonderful talk together and I learned for the first time about the arrival of another grandson the previous February.

It had been my intention on arrival at Fremantle to borrow some money, have the engine repaired, obtain a larger pole for a better jury mast, buy a new piece of orange tarpaulin, and then continue on our way back to New Zealand, after an estimated two-week stop. Because of continuing trouble with my neck, injured during one of the rollovers, I asked Marjorie to find me a crew who could accompany me on the last leg of the voyage home. Now, with the offer of help from the NZ Challenge team and from friends at home, we could repair the bottom damage from All Alone Cove, fix the self-steering gear, and re-rig *Totorore* with a proper mast and sails, so that she would be very much more seaworthy to undertake the voyage home across the Great Australian Bight and the Tasman Sea.

For several weeks following my interview on televison there was a steady stream of sightseers and wellwishers to the wharf where *Totorore* lay, and we had many genuine offers of help. I soon had a strong liking for West Australians generally, whom I found to be very natural and open, and during my stay I made many good and lasting friends. In the two months that I was there, only twice did I have dinner on board by myself!

My good friend from home, Ted Leeds, who had helped me when building *Totorore*, came over to assist with repairs and with designing the new rig, and he was followed by another friend, Ross Ewens. It was hard work, but thanks to the NZ Challenge and the other help received, by early September *Totorore* was almost as good as new.

The voyage home was easy and relaxing, in good weather. We called at Albany, where the Port Royal Sailing Club looked after us very well, and where Ross had to leave to return by air. His place was taken by Lola Broadhust, a good friend and supporter of the *Totorore* expedition since its conception, who came with me to Hobart. David Trow, also from Kerikeri, made the Tasman crossing with me.

On 6 November, we sailed into the Bay of Islands where we were cleared by Customs with the minimum of formalities, and then by prior arrangement I was met by all the family for a joyful private reunion. The next day, with my family aboard, we motored up the Kerikeri Inlet.

On 21 February 1983, our vicar standing on the landing steps in Kerikeri had asked God to grant His blessing on *Totorore* and her crew, and as we moved off downriver at the very start of the *Totorore* expedition, a number of craft led by the ketch *Janthina* escorted us out into the Bay. Now, after three years and 8½ months, as *Totorore* motored up the river, *Janthina* was again there to escort her, and Rev. Bill Law was standing on the same landing steps to lead a prayer of thanksgiving for the safe return of myself and my craft. A large crowd had gathered, and a group of girls from the Kerikeri High School gave us a beautiful traditional Maori welcome. In the picturesque riverside garden of the Stone Store Tea Room I was met by Barton Evans, the chairman of the *Totorore* expedition committee, other committee members, many former crew members, and hundreds of supporters and friends of the expedition. I could not keep the tears from my eyes, or the catch from my voice, as I was welcomed with handshakes and kisses. I was overflowing with love and happiness.

The *Totorore* expedition was over.

White-Faced Storm Petrel

Appendices

S.R.V. (Sailing Research Vessel) *Totorore* and her equipment

Totorore is a wooden cutter-rigged vessel with a bowsprit and twin ballast keels.

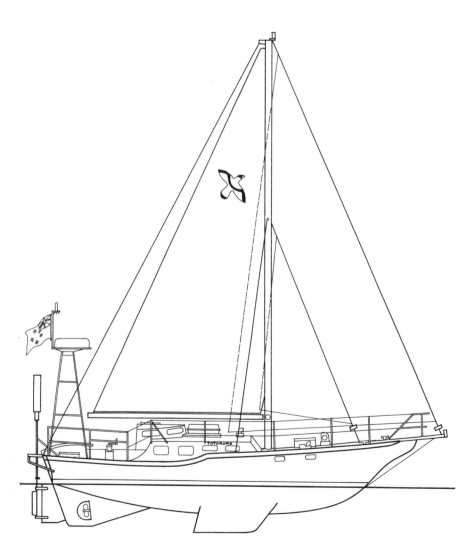

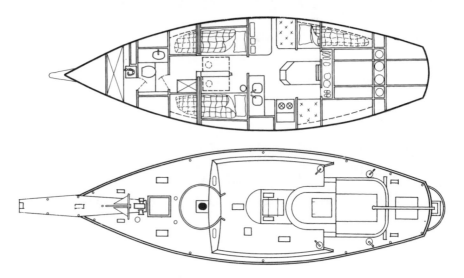

Length over all including bowsprit: 11.1 m
Length of boat excluding bowsprit and extension to clipper bow: 9.8 m
Length of boat on normal working water line: 8.5 m
Beam: 2.9 m
Draft: 1.3 m
Ballast (in twin keels): 1815 kg
Light displacement: about 5½ tonnes
Designed by Gerry Clark, based on lines by Alan Wright.
Built by Gerry Clark at Kerikeri, New Zealand. Completed 1982.

ANCHORS   One Bruce 20 kg. By far and away the best holding anchor in
all conditions. Originally kept as a storm anchor, we soon started to use it as
our working anchor, and never had trouble in retrieving it except in very
heavy kelp. Awkward to stow on deck, we normally carried it hove up snug
against the bow roller where it fitted neatly.
One C.Q.R. 35 lb (16 kg). A good holding anchor, but the shank bent badly
at Juan Fernandez Islands rendering it unuseable until we had it repaired.
One C.Q.R. 24 lb (11 kg). A very useful kedge, and usually used as first down
in tandem with the Bruce for the violent conditions in southern waters.
One Danforth 27 lb (12 kg). This was not the high tensile model and bent
easily until we had it reinforced. An excellent kedge, and a good spare anchor
in sand or mud.

AUTO PILOT   Autohelm 2000. Excellent while it lasted, but wore out very quickly.

BILGE PUMPS   One Whale Gusher 10 operable from the cockpit. Very reliable. One Meteor Pump operable from inside the cabin. This doubled as a sink pump via a two-way valve. It suffered badly from internal corrosion, and several makeshift repairs were required to keep it going. One Gem electric submersible pump 1400 gals per hour. Very good. One Rule 700 submersible pump in a sump below the engine. This was very good while it lasted, but after about 18 months oil penetrated the seals and put it out of action. The hull shape of *Totorore* does not lend itself to the provision of a satisfactory well, or sump, for the collection of bilge water for pumping out, so that in a seaway any water in the bilge tends to be somewhere other than where the suctions are. We usually had to resort to a bucket and sponge method.

CHAIN (anchor)   40 fathoms $5/16$ chain, galvanised. Under stressful conditions I often wished that we had a larger chain, but it never failed. We always used a 16 mm nylon spring to give elasticity, and we gave the chain a generous scope whenever space permitted. This had the added advantage of keeping the crew warm when heaving it up. Used so often on rocky bottoms, the galvanising wore completely off the chain and had to be re-done at Cape Town. There were two lengths each of 15 fathoms $5/16$ inch chain, small link, as spare.

CHAIN LOCKER   This is only 240 mm square in section, and is full depth from foredeck to keel, so that when weighing anchor the chain is completely self stowing, and never tangles or fouls up in use. Only when *Totorore* capsized did the chain fall upon itself and prevent free running up the pipe. Fortunately this was discovered a few days before it was needed, and the chain was cleared manually from below.

CLOTHING   Among us we used a variety of outer clothing and wet-weather gear, but most of us used 'Damart' Thermolactyl underwear which was extremely good and had the advantage over wool of being able to drip-dry. Gloves or mittens were frequently a problem as we never found a way to keep them dry. Waterproof 'outers' never stayed waterproof for long, and could not stand working wear and tear.

COMPASSES   The steering compass is a binnacle mounted 'Sestrel Major' on the bridge deck. Extremely easy to read, and completely reliable. The internal gimballing sometimes allowed the lubber line to roll right around when *Totorore* went upside-down, so that it pointed astern instead of ahead, but I would not blame the compass for that! Frequent dunkings under salt water corroded the light fitting so that we eventually fitted an independent external light. The hand bearing compass is a Sestrel with Beta-cell lighting. Excellent. This one is now sixteen years old and is still easy to read at night.

COOKING STOVE   Eastham Maxoll BG for Butane or Propane gas. Very satisfactory, but the burners rusted away frequently and had to be replaced. Luckily I had taken six spares. The grill also rusted away.

DINGHIES   2 Avon 'Redcrest' 2.743 m (9'0"). We had a Johnson 4 outboard, but used it only in very sheltered waters in the Chilean Archipelago, as the dinghies were too liable to be 'flipped' in the more exposed places. Apart from in-port use, we landed in about 266 different places, and managed very well with just oars, but did have many oar breakages. The dinghies were superb, and stood up extremely well to constant rough usage. Having two enabled us to always have one in a good state of repair, even with 'Hannibal' and 'Gertie' around, but we sometimes had trouble with getting the glue to set in cold temperatures.

ECHO-SOUNDERS   Seafarer 3. The transducer was mounted inside the hull, where a small circle of wood planking had been cut away and the hole filled with fibre-glass. The display unit was mounted under the dodger in view of the helmsman, whenever it was needed. This had already served me in a yacht sailed from the United Kingdom to New Zealand, and continued to give reliable and excellent performance throughout the *Totorore* expedition. One of my best friends. Particularly useful in critically shallow waters.

Furuno FE 300 Mark II. Also very good and reliable, but lacked the fine resolution for very shallow water. The transducer was mounted externally, and we wiped it off on the ice in Antarctica. Otherwise trouble free.

ENGINE   Volvo Penta MD2B. 2 cylinder diesel. 25 H.P. This model was out of production even before the building of *Totorore* was completed. Sea-water cooled, it started to have over-heating problems after about 18 months due, as we discovered much later, to internal corrosion and the blocking of waterways. However its overall performance was very good, and we used it extensively in Chile and South Georgia. By the time it blew a gasket at Kerguelen Island it had done 3,400 hours.

FRESHWATER   363 litres (80 gals). In built-in tanks under bunks.

FUEL   243 litres (53 gals). Stainless steel tanks, one in mast compartment, three under quarter berths. We usually carried extra in jerry cans on deck.

GAS (COOKING)   27 kg. Two 9 kg bottles in aft cockpit locker, two reserve 4.5 kg bottles. Five months was the longest time we went without being able to refill the bottles, and we still had a 4.5 kg bottle full.

HEAD   Wilcox-Crittendon, 'Head-mate'. Excellent, trouble-free use throughout the expedition.

INSULATION   To reduce condensation, maintain some warmth in the cabin, and to add buoyancy to slow the rate of sinking in the event of the hull's being holed, the inside of *Totorore* is lined with closed-cell polyurethane foam. Inside the hull 25 mm, underdecks aft 25 mm, forward 12.5 mm and in coachroof 18 mm. All side ports in the cabin coamings are double glazed with 9.5 mm Lexan outside, and 5 mm Perspex inside.

From my own observations *Totorore* was much drier inside than most boats which we met in Chile, but in the Southern Ocean when the humidity was for long periods over 95% with very low temperatures, heavy condensation was a problem, and nothing would dry.

INTERNAL LAYOUT   The internal layout was designed so that there would be no large open spaces in which one could be thrown, and one could never be out of reach of a strong hand-hold.

KEROSENE (PARAFFIN)   For lamps and camping primus. 16 litres in stainless steel tank under starboard quarter berth.

LIFERAFT   Avon 4 man.

LOCKERS   To facilitate finding anything in a hurry, lockers were generally small and numbered 1 to 110. A record of locker contents was kept in a book and (in theory) up-dated regularly. Because of the tremendous amount of gear and equipment which had to be carried, every possible space in the boat was fully utilised.

PORT HOLES   The two port holes in the bottom of the hull for viewing submarine life, sea beds for anchoring purposes, and anchors, are of 18 mm plate glass outside, with an air space and 9.5 mm Perspex inside.

RADAR   Furuno 1600. 16 mile. Excellent. By having the scanner mounted on a structure at the stern we still had the use of it after we lost the mast on both occasions, and it continued to work even after the scanner had been totally submerged at some depth in a capsize. Worked until the scanner was completely smashed in storm off Heard Island.

RADIO   V.H.F. Radio. Belcom. MC 5500. Excellent performance. Invaluable use in inhabited places and for 'ship to shore' use with our walkie-talkie.

S.S.B. Radio. Codan Type 6924-S Mk2. Excellent performance in New Zealand area, up to 1000 nautical miles. We found it of limited use elsewhere, and for some strange reason always had difficulty in communicating with the Armada stations in Chile.

RIG   Furling spars on twin fore stays and on inner fore stay for staysail. The only disadvantage was the extra windage on the furled sails. With only one headsail, the lee sail was used, and to go about that was rolled up, and the other side unrolled as she came round. Each sail had only one sheet, and the sail set outside the pulpit and lifelines, and was not subjected to chafe. They were big sails and were reefed to suit, from genoas down to storm jibs. Seldom did the system give trouble except when iced-up. About 50% of the time we sailed with the mainsail furled.

Poling-out spars for both headsails had their inboard ends on a long track on the mast up to the spreaders, so that their effective length could be varied. They were housed with their ends all ready in the mast fitting, so that the downwind twin headsails were exceedingly easy to set. Mainsail, roller reefed and furled on boom by direct through-the mast reefing handle.

RIGGING   Standing rigging S.S. 1 × 19, 8 mm. Twin backstays and diamond shrouds 6 mm. Running rigging Terylene.

SATELLITE NAVIGATOR   Furuno FSN 80. Excellent performance. It did not work well when the antenna housing was covered with ice, but after Fremantle we found that it worked satisfactorily with the antenna inside the boat near the chart table.

SELF-STEERING GEAR   ('Ivon'). Home-made servo-tab on bracket about 210 cm abaft rudder, actuated by horizontally pivoted 'flip-flop' wind vane. Not as effective as servo-pendulum type.

SEXTANT   'Husun'. My trusty sextant, the only one I have ever owned, and which I won as a prize as a cadet in the training ship H.M.S. Worcester just before I went to sea in 1944. To conserve electric power I navigated by sextant rather than the Satellite Navigator when possible, and entirely after leaving Heard Island.

SINK (and WASHBASIN)PUMPS   'Fynspray' rocker pumps. Trouble free service throughout.

TENTS   Macpac Wilderness 'New Horizon'. Excellent. Used in a variety of conditions, e.g. a gale on the peak of Cape Horn, and on ice in Antarctica. Difficult to erect in a gale, but very secure when up. We added large pockets around the fly for snow or stones to weight it down. The zip slides corroded in the salt air conditions and had to be replaced.

Hallmark 'Chrysalis'. An excellent tent for one man with negligible weight for carrying. We used ours in the rain forests of Chile, and also in the mountains of the Cape Horn islands.

WINDLASS   Nilsson H 700M. This was ideal for our work, and gave excellent performance throughout. The only trouble we had was with the top bearings which had to be renewed. It is understood that the simple copper sleeves used have been replaced by 'Oilite' bearings on newer models.

Glossary of nautical terms used in this book

ABACK   A sail is aback when it is held out to the side from which the wind is blowing (weather side).

ABAFT...   Closer to the stern than...

ABEAM   In a direction 90° from ahead, on either side.

ABOUT   To put a vessel about, or to 'go about' is to turn the vessel through the wind to bring the wind from one side to the other.

AFT   Towards the stern.

AHULL   Drifting with no sail set. In this condition vessels always lie across the wind, parallel to the seas.

AMIDSHIPS   On the centre line of a vessel; in the middle part between forward and aft.

ASTERN   Away from the vessel in an aft direction.

ATHWART   Across; sideways.

AWEIGH   The anchor is aweigh when it has been lifted off the bottom.

BACK   (a) To back a sail is to haul it to windward, i.e. to bring it aback q.v. (b) The wind backs when it changes direction anticlockwise.

BEAM   Extreme breadth of vessel. Structurally, an athwartship member tying frames together, and supporting the deck. 'On the beam' is the same as abeam.

BEAM ENDS   A vessel is on her beam ends when wind or sea have heeled her to put the mast horizontal.

BEAT   To sail to windward by tacking, q.v.

BLOCK   Called a pulley by landsmen.

BOBSTAY   The wire stay which holds the end of the bowsprit down against the upward pull of the forestay from the mast head. It is usually secured to the stem of the vessel on or below the water-line.

BOOM   The spar to which the foot of the mainsail is secured. It is hinged to the mast by a gooseneck q.v.

BOTTOM   Bed of sea or other waterway. Also, the underwater part of a vessel's hull.

BOW   The fore part of a vessel.

BROACH   A vessel broaches when she is forcibly turned by wind or sea to lie parallel to the seas (waves).

BRUCE ANCHOR   A modern design of anchor with extraordinarily good holding ability in the widest range of bottoms.

BULKHEAD   Vertical partition in a vessel, corresponding to wall in a house. Athwartship bulkheads are structural strength members.

BUNK BOARD (or LEE BOARD)   A board, often hinged, raised along the edge of a bunk to prevent the occupant's falling out. See also 'LEE CLOTH'.

CABLE   Unit of distance measurement of one tenth of a nautical mile. The anchor chain is also often called cable.

CAPSIZE   When a vessel is forcibly turned upside down.

CHAIN PLATE   Metal strap bolted to the side of a vessel to which the lower end of a shroud is fastened. In *Totorore* they are internal with top brackets to which the shrouds are secured by 'U' bolts passing through the deck.

CLEVIS   A 'Pin', or unthreaded bolt held in place by a split-pin, used in rigging and passing through holes in two plates to secure an eye or other end fitting between them.

CLEW   The after lower corner of a triangular fore-and-aft sail, to which the sheets are attached.

CLIPPER BOW   A rather old fashioned shape of bow with a pleasing concave curve, as seen in the fast clipper ships of last century.

COMPANIONWAY   The access from the cockpit to the cabin, usually closed by a sliding hatch above, and vertical washboards in the bulkhead.

C.Q.R. ANCHOR   A patent anchor with a single fluke shaped like a plough share. There have been many copies, but few can compare with it for holding power. From the author's experience, second only to the Bruce for use in all conditions.

CUTTER   A yacht with a single mast, mainsail, jib and staysail. This was *Totorore's* rig, although she often sailed 'sloop rigged', with a large jib and no staysail.

DANFORTH ANCHOR   A patent stockless anchor with two hinged flukes. This type has the advantage of stowing flat on deck, and has exceptionally good holding power in sand or mud bottoms. *Totorore* used a 12.3 kg model mainly as a kedge, q.v.

DORADE VENTILATOR   A water-trap type ventilator with the cowl mounted at one end of a box inside the other end of which is the upstand air pipe from down below. Drain holes in the box allow any water which enters the cowl to escape onto the deck.

DOWN   Used with reference to the helm (tiller) when it is pushed to the lee side of the boat (when sailing and the boat heels, the lee side is literally down). This has the effect of turning the boat towards the direction of the wind.

ECHO SOUNDER   An electronic machine which records the depth of water (the sounding) by sending an impulse down to the seabed from a transducer in the bottom of the boat, and recording the time to receive the echo. The information can be given in fathoms, metres, or feet. In *Totorore* we found feet to be the most convenient unit to use in very shallow water.

EYE   A formed loop in the end of a rope.

FALL OFF   A vessel is said to fall off when she tends to turn away from the wind.

FAST   Secure. To make a rope fast is to tie it to something or secure it on a cleat.

FATHOM   Unit of depth measurement of 6 feet (1.83 metres) now being replaced by metres. It was used in *Totorore* for depths and for lengths of anchor chain in use because most of the charts on board still showed depths in fathoms, and the anchor chain was marked accordingly.

FIDDLE   A raised edge on tables, shelves or benches to prevent articles from falling off when a vessel is moving.

342

FLOG　A sail or rope is said to flog in the wind when it is loose and shakes violently.

FORE, FORWARD　Towards the bow. Forward is usually spoken as for'd.

FOREFOOT　The rounded part of the bow below the water.

FORE-REACH　A vessel is fore-reaching when she moves slowly ahead.

FURIOUS FIFTIES　The stormy region of the Southern Ocean between 50 °S and 60 °S.

FURL　To gather up and secure a sail while it is still on its spar, e.g. the mainsail furled on its boom. *Totorore* used self-furling spars on the twin forestays for the jibs and the inner forestay for the staysail.

FURLING GEAR　At the bottom of the furling spars fitted on the stays for the jibs and staysail of *Totorore* there were drums with furling lines wound onto them. When a furling line was pulled, it turned the drum and the spar and thus wound up the sail tightly around the stay, furling it very neatly.

GALLEY　Boat's kitchen.

GIMBALS　Two concentric rings which allow a compass or lamp to remain horizontal. 'Gimballed' is often loosely used for a stove or a table which can swing only in an athwartship arc.

GUNWALE　A plank or other strong member fitted along the top edge of the side of a boat.

GOOSENECK　A fitting securing the boom to the mast but giving it universal movement.

GYBE　To turn the boat to bring the wind around the stern from one quarter to the other. An accidental gybe is when running before the wind and the wind catches the wrong side of the mainsail and swings the boom across, sometimes violently.

HALYARD　A rope used for hoisting a sail or a flag.

HEAD　The top corner of a triangular sail to which the halyard is attached. The word head is also used for the toilet in a boat, and in a loose sense, the compartment where the toilet is situated. In sailing ships this was called the heads.

HELM　The means of turning the rudder, i.e. tiller or wheel.

HELMSMAN (or HELMSWOMAN)　The person who is steering.

HULL　The main body of a vessel.

JAM CLEAT　A type of cleat for making a rope fast instantly, and with the ability to release it just as quickly when required.

JIB　The forward headsail.

KEDGE　An anchor lighter than the main anchor, used for carrying out in the dinghy to a distance from a vessel to haul her off when aground (kedging).

KEEL　The main backbone of a vessel. In a yacht it is extended deeper to give 'bite' in the water to enable her to sail to windward, and to carry the bulk of her ballast weight to give her stability. *Totorore* had a centre structural keel inside the hull and twin ballast keels on which she could stand when aground.

KNOCKDOWN　When a vessel is thrown onto her beam ends, q.v., by wind or sea.

KNOT　Unit of speed of 1 nautical mile per hour.

LEAD BLOCK　A block used to lead a rope in the right direction, as clear of an obstruction or to a winch.

LEE Away from the direction of the wind. In the lee of... means, in the shelter of...

LEE BOARD See BUNK BOARD.

LEE CLOTH A canvas secured from the outside edge of a bunk to points above used additionally and for the same purpose as a bunkboard in more severe conditions.

LEE SHORE A shore to leeward (pronounced loo'ard) or downwind of a vessel, to which she would be in danger of being blown in heavy weather.

LEECH The after edge of a fore and aft sail.

LINE Sailors' term for small ropes.

LUFF The forward or leading edge of a sail.

MAINSAIL The sail set on the aft side of the main mast.

MILE The miles quoted in this book are nautical miles of 1852 metres, and are longer than land or 'statute' miles (1690.3m). Nautical miles are used by navigators rather than kilometres because 1 nautical mile = 1 minute of arc of latitude.

PILOT A book of navigational information and instructions for mariners. Many volumes are published by the British Admiralty to cover all parts of the world.

PORT The left hand side when looking forward. Loosely used for port light, or port hole, or 'window' in a vessel.

PULPIT The safety rail in the bows of a yacht, its shape suggesting its name.

PUSHPIT A name sometimes used for the safety railing around a yacht's stern.

QUARTER The part of the hull on each side between amidships and astern. As a direction, 'on the quarter' means approximately 45° from astern or either side.

QUARTER BERTH A bunk fitted inside the quarter. In a yacht, such as *Totorore*, these are somewhat tunnel shaped which have the advantage that it is difficult to fall out of them.

REACH To sail with the wind on or near the beam. Usually an excellent point of sailing in reasonable weather conditions.

REEF To reduce the area of a sail by rolling up or otherwise securing part of it.

ROARING FORTIES The region of consistent westerly winds between 40°S and 50°S latitude.

ROUND UP To turn bow into the wind.

RUN To sail with the wind coming from astern.

RUN HER EASTING DOWN An old term used by ships making good distance to eastward in the Roaring Forties.

RUBBING STRAKE A heavy strip of wood fitted around the outside of the hull to take the rubbing or chafing when she is moored alongside another vessel, wharf, or other object.

SCOPE The length of chain out to the anchor.

SEA Sailors' term for a wave.

SELF-STEERING GEAR In *Totorore*, a home-made device (named 'Ivon') actuated by a wind vane and linked to the rudder to enable her to steer herself without a helmsman.

SEXTANT   An optical instrument used for measuring angles, particularly between celestial bodies and the horizon, for navigation purposes.

SHEAVE   The wheel in a block, over which the rope runs.

SHEER   To swerve to one side or the other, either purposely or inadvertently.

SHEET   The rope secured to the clew of a sail, used to trim it. On the mainsail the sheet is secured to the end of the boom.

SHROUDS   The rigging wires which support the mast athwartships, or sideways.

SKEG   A projection from the bottom of the hull to support the heel of the rudder in boats where it is remote from the after end of the keel. In form it is like a small keel itself.

STARBOARD   (Pronounced starb'd.) The right hand side of the boat when looking forward.

STAYS   The rigging wires which support the mast fore and aft, i.e. forestays and backstays.

STAYSAIL   The sail set on the inner forestay, abaft the jib.

STERN GLAND   A packing gland to prevent the entry of water into the boat past the propeller shaft.

TACK   The forward lower corner of a triangular sail; the point from which it is 'tacked down'. To tack is to sail a zig-zag course to windward by sailing close-hauled on alternate sides or alternate 'tacks'. The tack is named according to which side the wind is on, e.g. wind on the port side, the vessel is on the port tack.

TANDEM ANCHORS   Two anchors pulling in line on the same chain, one backing up the other with a short length of chain from the anchor farthest ahead shackled to the crown of the after anchor. This method of anchoring gives extremely strong holding, but produces some handling difficulties.

TRIM   To adjust the sheet of a sail so that the sail sets correctly.

TWIN JIBS   A pair of jibs set side by side on twin forestays, or sometimes hanked to the same stay, usually held out by poles from the mast, one on each side of the vessel, for running downwind. An extremely useful rig for long voyages in Trade Winds or the Roaring Forties.

VEER   The wind is said to veer when it changes direction clockwise.

WASHBOARDS   Portable boards fitted into a companionway to close it, to take the place of a door. In *Totorore* these were in one piece made of two thicknesses of 9.5mm Perspex with a similar air space between them for insulation.

WAY   A vessel is 'under way' when she is not at anchor, or made fast to the shore, or aground. She is 'making way', or has 'way upon her', when she is moving through the water.

WEIGH   To weigh anchor is to raise the anchor from the bottom.

WINDLASS   A winch for hauling in the anchor chain or rope.

WINDWARD   The direction from which the wind is blowing.

Beaufort Wind Scale

Beaufort Number	Descriptive Term	Mean wind speed in knots
0	Calm	1
1	Light air	1 – 3
2	Light breeze	4 – 6
3	Gentle breeze	7 – 10
4	Moderate breeze	11 – 16
5	Fresh breeze	17 – 21
6	Strong breeze	22 – 27
7	Near gale	28 – 33
8	Gale	34 – 40
9	Strong gale	41 – 47
10	Storm	48 – 55
11	Violent storm	56 – 63
12	Hurricane	64 and over

Voyage Statistics

Time away, Kerikeri to Kerikeri; 3 years, 8 months, 16 days
Distance on ocean passages; 24, 531 nautical miles
Distance, coastal; 13,882 nautical miles
Distance logged on whole expedition; 38,413 nautical miles
Anchored 630 times in 372 different places

Acknowledgements

I wish to give foremost thanks to all members of my crew for their fortitude, support, and companionship; for the considerable assistance of their very helpful financial contributions. I was most fortunate indeed to have had them as co-participants in the venture.

The *Totorore* voyage was carried out not only by the ship and her crew, but by all who generously gave a tremendous amount of time, energy, or financial donations in support of the underlying conservationist principles on which the Expedition was based. On behalf of myself and all my crew members, I sincerely thank every single one of you who made it all possible for us to enjoy and experience the more exciting part of the whole enterprise. When the going was tough we knew that you were with us in spirit, and with your support and God's help, we did what we could, and we all survived.

Special mention must be made of the following major contributors: The Ornithological Society of New Zealand; Jim and Enid Watt; Alison Atkinson; A. Highet, Minister of Internal Affairs New Zealand (1982); Tudor and Jenny Atkinson; Colin Little; Roy McKenzie; Alan Cowan; Ray Richards; Anthea Goodwin; Australasian Seabird Group; Royal Forest and Bird Protection Society of New Zealand; World Wildlife Fund N.Z.; Ivon and Barbara Coates; Silverfish Publishing Co.; Sir Charles Fleming; Maud Bates; Kim Admore; Bay of Islands Auto and Marine Electrics; Kura Beale; Chris and Annette Booth; Alex Black; Bill Bourne; Lola Broadhurst; Duarte Camara; Phil Campbell; Crawford Hardware; David and Ruth Crockett; Damart Thermolactyl; Ann Dodson; Barton and Howard Evans; Electronic Navigation; W. Gregg and Co.; Rosemary Hemming; Anne Herron; Geoff Holdridge; Ted and Molly Leeds; Kerikeri Marine Installation and Maintenance; Horace and Joyce Mason; Richard and Joyce Mason; Howard and Helena Mulholland; Brian and Leslie Newby; Norah Newton and Cicely Hoddenot; Basil (Snow) O'Connor; Paul Martin; Nancy Pickmere; Reidrubber; Chris, June and Vern Sale; Alex and Isobel Smailes; David Stretton Pow; John and Nancy Wood; Squirrel Wright; Michel; Jane de Ridder; Ovlov Services; Palmer Canvas and Synthetics Ltd.

Chile   Armada de Chile; A.J. Broom y Cía, Valparaiso and Santiago; Peter Smith; Rodney McIntosh; Gonzalo Cordero; Dr J. Rosenstock; Agencias Maritimas Unidas, Puerto Montt; Andreas and Julia von Meyer; Agencias Maritimas Broom, Punta Arenas; Guillermo Gallardo; Sergio Barria; Carlos; Peggy Fell; Helen and Pedro Gomez; Ernesto and Marcia Dietert; Dr Raul Baya; Dr Reinaldo Hernandez; Victor Hernandez; Capitan Vasquez; Dr Claudio Venegas; Pesquera Magallanes; CONAF.

Falkland Islands   British Royal Navy, in particular Chief Petty Officer Tony Atkins; Jorge and Monica Alonso; Mario Zuvic.

South Georgia   Mark O'Connell, Callan Duck, Simon Pickering, Rob Lidstone-Scott. The O.C.s of the British military garrisons at King Edward Point.

Cape Town   Royal Cape Yacht Club; the Inflatable Boat Centre; Brian Bradfield; Stan Gordge, port captain of the Slocum Society; Eric Herzberg; Peter, Stephan and Reinhardt Seickmann; Christine Hanel; Lynnath Beckley; Svend and Fay Schmitt; Bill Crook.

Fremantle   Lorna and Paul Comely; Bruce Beaton; Brian Ewens, Don White; Stephen Brown; The New Zealand America's Cup Challenge Syndicate and its team members at Fremantle who made it possible for *Totorore* to return home.

In the preparation of this book; for transcribing numerous tapes made during the voyage, June and Vern Sale; my wife Marjorie for months of typing and forbearance; my daughter Annalie for drafting maps; Elizabeth Rippey for her painstaking work in producing the finished maps and most of the black and white drawings in the book; Peter Harrison for his drawings of birds (pages 20, 231, 256, 296, 314, 334); Martyn Evans for the drawings of *Totorore* (pages 335 and 336).

For supplying of photographs I thank John Atkinson; Alan Cowan; Anthea Goodwin; Peter Harrison; Anton Hunt; Mike Hurst; Jay Nelson; Andreas von Meyer; Julia von Meyer; Chris Sale; Jim Watt.

We can all share in some satisfaction in the degree of success achieved by the *Totorore* voyage, but we must reflect that it was but a small step in the right direction. If we are to save Antarctica and its marine environment from the ravages of exploitation, we must all continue in our efforts to persuade the Antarctic Treaty Powers and the United Nations General Assembly to declare Antarctica a World Park, so that its wildlife may be preserved for the benefit of future generations. People *can* play an effective role in influencing political decisions made by governments, and it is up to us to make the World Park a reality.

For further information on what can be done to help, write to World Wildlife Fund; Greenpeace; or the Antarctic and Southern Ocean Coalition, P.O. Box 371, Manly, 2095, N.S.W., Australia, or the Antarctic and Southern Ocean Coalition, 1751 N Street N.W. Washington D.C. 20036, U.S.A.

Index

Spanish words used in names: *Bahía*, Bay; *Cabo*, Cape; *Caleta*, Cove; *Canal*, Channel; *Ensenada*, Bay; *Estero*, Inlet, Fjord; *Estrecho*, Strait; *Golfo*, Gulf; *Isla*, Island; *Islote*, Islet; *Paso*, Pass; *Puerto*, Port, Haven; *Río*, River; *Roca*, Rock; *Seno*, Gulf, Sound; *Ventisquero*, Glacier; *Vulcan*, Volcano.

Map No. with page is shown in brackets, e.g. Baily Point (M22, 222) 223 means that Baily Point is shown on Map 22 on page 222, and a reference is made to it on page 223.

353

354

356

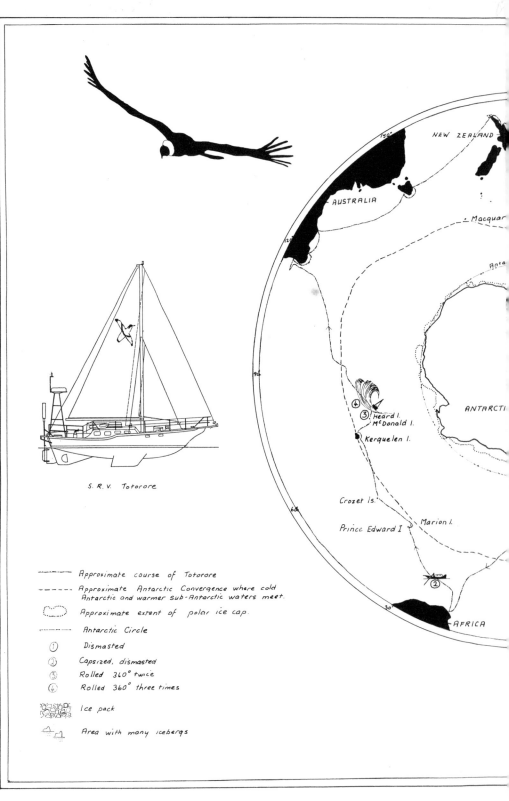

S. R. V. Totorore

------- Approximate course of Totorore
-------- Approximate Antarctic Convergence where cold
 Antarctic and warmer sub-Antarctic waters meet.
 Approximate extent of polar ice cap.
-------- Antarctic Circle
① Dismasted
② Capsized, dismasted
③ Rolled 360° twice
④ Rolled 360° three times
 Ice pack
 Area with many icebergs

NEW ZEALAND
AUSTRALIA
Macquar
Anta
ANTARCTI
④
③ Heard I.
 McDonald I.
 Kerguelen I.
Crozet Is.
 Marion I.
Prince Edward I
②
AFRICA